UNEMPLOYMENT
IN
EUROPE

UNEMPLOYMENT
IN
EUROPE

Edited by

Jonathan Michie
*Judge Institute of Management Studies
and Fellow of Robinson College,
University of Cambridge*

and

John Grieve Smith
*Fellow and Senior Bursar
Robinson College, University of Cambridge*

ACADEMIC PRESS
Harcourt Brace & Co., Publishers
London – San Diego – New York – Boston
Sydney – Tokyo – Toronto

ACADEMIC PRESS LTD
Harcourt Brace & Co., Publishers
24–28 Oval Road,
London NW1 7DX

United States Edition published by
ACADEMIC PRESS, INC.
San Diego, CA 92101

This book is printed on acid-free paper

A catalogue record for this book is available from the British Library

ISBN 0–12–494065–X

Typeset by Phoenix Photosetting, Chatham, Kent
Printed and bound in Great Britain by Mackays of Chatham PLC, Chatham, Kent

Contents

List of Figures

List of Tables

List of Contributors

Edward Balls	Economics leader and feature writer, *Financial Times*
Ray Barrell	National Institute of Economic and Social Research
Guglielmo Maria Caporale	National Institute of Economic and Social Research
Jane Collier	Judge Institute of Management Studies and Fellow of Lucy Cavendish College, Cambridge
Francis Cripps	Director of Alphametrics Ltd and member of ARCA (Association for Applied Research in the Community)
Guillermo Davila Muro	Commission of the European Communities
John Eatwell	Fellow of Trinity College, Cambridge
Andrew Glyn	Fellow of Corpus Christi College, Oxford
Wynne Godley	Professor of Economics and Fellow of Kings College, Cambridge, and member of Treasury Advisory Panel
John Grieve Smith	Fellow and Senior Bursar, Robinson College, Cambridge
Serge Halimi	Journalist, *Le Monde Diplomatique*
Ruth Kelly	Economics Writer, *The Guardian*
Michael Kitson	Fellow, St Catharine's College and Lecturer in Economics, Newnham College, Cambridge
Stefan Lehner	Commission of the European Communities
Jonathan Michie	Judge Institute of Management Studies and Fellow of Robinson College, Cambridge
Seumas Milne	Labour Correspondent, *The Guardian*

Peter Nolan	Montague Burton Professor of Industrial Relations, University of Leeds
Paul Ormerod	Visiting Professor, University of Manchester
Brian Reddaway	Professor of Economics Emeritus, University of Cambridge
Horst Reichenbach	Commission of the European Communities
Bob Rowthorn	Professor of Economics and Fellow of Kings College, Cambridge
Malcolm Sawyer	Professor of Economics, University of Leeds
James Sefton	National Institute of Economic and Social Research
John Tomaney	Research Associate, Centre for Urban and Regional Development Studies, University of Newcastle upon Tyne
Terry Ward	Director of Alphametrics Ltd and member of ARCA (Association for Applied Research in the Community)
Frank Wilkinson	Senior Research Officer, Department of Applied Economics and Fellow of Girton College, Cambridge

Preface and Acknowledgements

The background to this book is discussed in more detail in the foreword and introduction, but in brief it sets out to consider what sort of policies are needed to combat unemployment in Europe. One of the key developments – politically, socially and economically – of the late 1980s and early 1990s was the formulation of proposals and policies for the further integration of the European Community, first with the Single European Act and the '1992' process, and then with the Maastricht Treaty's proposals for moving to a single currency by the end of the century. Alongside this, Britain has experienced the longest recession since the 1930s and Europe generally seems set for economic stagnation and mass unemployment through the 1990s. These economic developments have made the Maastricht Treaty inadequate at best, and as Jacques Delors and others have publicly acknowledged, the need for the rest of the 1990s will be for policies to tackle unemployment. These cannot be limited to 'labour market' policies – there is a requirement also for positive fiscal and industrial policies. It is these policies for growth and for tackling unemployment which the book analyses. If there is a common conclusion, it is that there is no excuse for fatalism: unemployment has been defeated in the past and can be defeated again.

All the chapters were commissioned specifically for this book and draft versions were discussed at a working conference in May 1993 at Robinson College, Cambridge. We are very grateful to Robinson College for hosting and funding this event. We are also grateful to William Brown, Dan Corry, Patricia Hewitt, William Keegan, Mića Panić and John Philpott for their participation.

Our thanks as editors go to all the authors for the speedy incorporation of points made in May 1993 on their draft chapters; Bryan Hopkin, Alan Hughes, Jane Humphries and Robert Neild for chairing the sessions at the May conference; Sutapas Bhattacharya, Nick Grant and Jennifer Pegg of Academic Press for the speedy turnround of the manuscript; Lesley Haird and Kath Wilson for typing and other help; and Brian Reddaway for his wide-ranging and very detailed comments on several of the chapters as well as for contributing the Foreword. Our personal thanks for putting up with weekend editing go respectively to Carolyn and three-year old Alex, and to Jean.

JONATHAN MICHIE
JOHN GRIEVE SMITH

Foreword

Brian Reddaway

It is traditional for writers of forewords to start by saying that 'this books fills an obvious need', and in the present case I follow that tradition with an absolutely clear conscience. Policies to combat unemployment have slipped out of the priority role in economic discussions which the obvious importance of the issue seems to me to demand, especially when one considers also the additional miseries which come on top of the direct sufferings of the unemployed. Much more important, however, is the very small scale of the *action* which most governments are taking to combat unemployment, despite the fact that the percentage of recorded unemployment in the European Community in 1992 was more than three times as high as it was 20 years earlier, and that this position (or worse) has prevailed consistently for a dozen years. (See OECD, *Economic Outlook* for December 1992, Table R19.)

The various chapters in the book consider a series of different aspects of the problem, in terms both of actions relevant to a single country's policies and to those which call for some form of international cooperation. Inevitably, these chapters cover a very wide field, because in the real world (as opposed to some theorists' models) there is no single factor which determines the level of unemployment; a whole host of different factors mutually influence each other in complex ways, and each separate chapter cannot possibly deal in detail with all of them. The main object of this Foreword is therefore to emphasise this complexity, and to give a simplified outline of how the picture as a whole looks.

On the *policy* side, it is important to recognise that one cannot hope for perfection, whether on unemployment or on other desirable objectives: 'half a loaf is better than no bread at all' – a policy is to be welcomed if it will produce (say) a reduction in unemployment with more of the side-effects being favourable than unfavourable.

Multiple Objectives and Policy Instruments

The first point which needs emphasising is the fact that every government has a host of different objectives, besides combating unemployment. The object of this book is not to deny the desirability of a low rate of inflation, or a sound balance of payments, or reduced environmental pollution: it is simply to stress that quite inadequate importance has been attached to policies for combating unemployment in comparison with (for example) the objective of lowering inflation. This applies both to individual governments and to international bodies.

At the same time governments have a range of different instruments which they can bring to bear in seeking to achieve these objectives – e.g. taxation policy (both in its make-up and in its total yield), expenditure policies (with the composition again being very important, as well as the aggregate), interest rate policies, exchange rate policies, industrial policies, privatisation (or nationalisation), environmental controls. One important feature of these is the government's ability to enter into 'commitments' about its future behaviour: this raises the important matter of credibility and political acceptability.

While governments have many powers – and should not be allowed to deny their ability to influence the level of unemployment – their powers are *not* unlimited; moreover there are other power centres, which may be induced to help, but which may also seek to counter government policies. And the government of any individual country has to pay heed to the possible actions of other countries: sometimes these will be helpful (e.g. over the introduction of policies to raise the level of real demand in a slump), but sometimes independent actions by separate governments may be of a 'beggar-my-neighbour' kind. (With exchange-rates, one must of course always remember that there are two ends to each rate.)

Economic Uncertainties

One very real difficulty about policies to combat unemployment is that economists are not in complete agreement about the effects which the use of various measures can be expected to produce. In a number of important cases this reflects different assumptions about how *governments* will behave in terms of their other policies, which are often not specified, or which are hidden by an ambiguous assumption of *ceteris paribus*. Does the assumption of 'an unchanged budgetary policy' mean, for example, 'an unchanged budget surplus' or 'unchanged tax rates, etc.', when some policy is likely to raise employment?[1]

There may also be an ambiguity about the *time period* to be considered: devaluation in the face of a balance of payments deficit is sometimes rejected, 'because experience shows that the gain in competitiveness is all lost within *x* years'. But those who support devaluation point to the benefits obtained during those years (including greater freedom to manage the internal economy); they may add that 'so they lived happily ever after' is a conclusion found only in fairyland.[2]

Besides the possibility of disputes about 'how the economy works', there are also likely to be different assessments of the current position, or of what is likely to happen in future if no action is taken (since most policies have to be based on a forward look, if only to take account of things already 'in the pipeline' – e.g. planned capital expenditure).

This (inevitable) problem over the choice of optimum policies being rendered difficult by the absence of relevant information is likely to be more serious where international cooperation is involved. In particular, countries are especially interested in what is likely to happen within their own borders, and their assessments are likely to differ – even if an impartial report might make similar assessments about all countries.

International Cooperation

It seems to me obvious that governments can do something to combat unemployment, even if they act independently. It has been done in the past in many different countries, and it is being done now in the USA. Nevertheless, successful cooperation between countries could secure better results, and it is a tricky problem to decide on the best procedure.

To my mind the really crucial piont is to secure a general agreement that under present circumstances combating unemployment is a high priority objective, whether the measures which different countries should adopt were to be largely independent or would involve a lot of rather formal cooperation. With all types of cooperation there is a serious problem of deciding how far there can be concrete agreements – e.g. on tariff rates – and how far decisions have to be in more general terms. This problem is particularly acute on exchange rates, where many people would argue that it is necessary to preserve the scope for future changes, at least 'by agreement'; others, however, say that general provisions about 'fundamental disequilibrium' and the like leave competitor countries with too much scope to go in for 'competitive devaluations', which would prejudice the objector's own country. Especially when rival experts take different views about how economies work – or about the current economic position and prospects – it may be very difficult to get international agreement on anything more than platitudinous generalisations.

A particularly serious point arises out of the Maastricht provisions about the 'convergence conditions' which any country would have to meet in order to become a full participant in the new exchange-rate regime. These conditions are all concerned with indicators of a country being possibly 'too inflationary'; there are no provisions to ensure that the country has an adequate level of activity (e.g. a specified acceptable maximum percentage of unemployment). If this set of rules becomes effective, the danger of the present levels of unemployment persisting would be increased.

Some Overall Conclusions

This brings me back to the crucial question to be faced by successful policies to combat unemployment. The great problem is to secure general agreement that government action can and should be taken to reduce unemployment, at least when it is above a certain level. In view of the relatively low levels of inflation which now prevail in most European countries, the doctrinal battle about the relationship between inflation and unemployment may not be too acute, at least so far as the next few years are concerned; it might not be too difficult under one of the procedures followed by the European Community to get a provision about unemployment effectively incorporated in the Maastricht rules.

If success can be achieved on this point, then most of the 'action' will need to be taken by individual governments, possibly working within targets fixed by the Community. There will doubtless be scope for joint action on international projects, which should mostly be justifiable for their own sake, quite apart from their effect on employment. 'Cohesion' funds to help the poorer countries and regions should also help to reduce unemployment, as well as improving life in the backward areas. Financial help to countries with balance of payments difficulties – coupled with assistance over *curbing* the deficit, as well as covering what remains – could also combat unemployment throughout Europe. As emphasised above, many objectives can be pursued simultaneously – without too much debate about priorities, unless there is a genuine conflict (e.g. 'growth' versus 'reduced pollution'); there are many possible instruments to use, some of which need international cooperation, but many of which can be operated effectively (and with less delay for discussions) by countries on their own.

Introduction

Jonathan Michie

According to the May 1993 UN *Human Development Report*, the world-wide growth of unemployment is 'the issue of the 1990s' and represents a 'dangerous potential for human strife'. The first year of the European Community's single market, 1993, saw a third year of slow growth in the EC and the worst recession for two decades, with 17 million people unemployed. Employment in the EC fell by about three-quarters of a percentage point in 1992 – the first time since 1983 that the number of people in employment actually decreased – and a similar reduction was expected to take place again in 1993 (Commission of the European Communities 'Annual Economic Report for 1993', *European Economy* no. 54, May, p. 7). In absolute figures this means that in 1993 almost 2 million fewer people than in 1991 would be employed in the twelve member states. At 11%, unemployment has returned to the peak of 1985 – the gains made during the second half of the 1980s were lost in the first three years of the 1990s. This has left less than 60% of the EC's population of working age actually in work in 1993, compared with more than 70% in the US and Japan; there is therefore a pool of hidden unemployment which has to be absorbed before numbers on the dole will fall substantially.

The German economy stopped growing in summer 1992 and by March 1993 industrial output was 10% below the March 1992 figure. Britain saw negative growth rates for 1991 and 1992, from which it was recovering only in mid-1993. This made Britain the only major EC country not in recession in 1993; ironically, the weak recovery experienced by Britain is less thanks to the completion of the single market than to the interest rate cuts and devaluation which followed sterling's departure from the Exchange Rate Mechanism in September 1992.

Community Policies for Jobs

A jobs initiative was debated at the Community's Copenhagen summit in June 1993, involving radical changes in the EC's tax and social security systems. The Commission wants member states to reduce employers' national insurance contributions, shifting the tax burden onto others. The rationale for such policies is that non-wage costs such as employers' social security payments add far more in the EC states on average than they do in Japan or the US. Yet such non-wage costs are already down to Japanese and US levels in Britain, so there is clearly no automatic link between this and low unemployment. Indeed, employment in manufacturing – which should be particuarlly sensitive to factors affecting competitiveness – is lower in Britain as a percentage of the population in work than it is in Germany or France, despite the far higher indirect employment costs in those countries.

An additional policy idea from the Commission has been to introduce such reductions in employer taxes on unskilled labour in particular. The more general idea of an employment subsidy is discussed by Glyn and Rowthorn (Chapter 12) who argue that expanded public employment is a more effective method of tackling unemployment, particularly if there are either inflation or balance of payments constraints. The specific idea of a differential subsidy for unskilled work – generally defined in these contexts as low-paid work, which raises a rather separate issue of why skills such as cooking or cleaning tend not to be recognised as skills – is considered in Chapter 1, where the danger is discussed of such subsidies reducing the incentives for firms to improve productivity and upgrade production techniques. Investment in research and development is already lower in the EC than in Japan or America. In 1987 the EC went into a deficit on international trade of high-tech goods – a deficit which has been deepening since. Yet while both Japan and the US announced public measures in 1993 to boost spending on R&D, the EC remained preoccupied with Maastricht.

As for Maastricht itself, apart from France, the only other member state which in 1992 satisfied the convergence criteria was Luxembourg. In 1993 Luxembourg looks likely to be on its own. It is vital, as several of the chapters stress, that these convergence criteria give way to policies for recovery. Quite apart from the short-term damage which adherence to the convergence criteria would cause, the longer-term aim of monetary union is ill-conceived without major political and economic changes not envisaged in the Delors Report or Maastricht Treaty. Thus, for example, the MacDougall Report suggested that a Community budget equivalent to 7% of GDP would be necessary just to tackle 40% of existing inequalities, yet the budget at present is set at 1.27%; the more ambitious proposal rejected at the 1992 Edinburgh summit was for this to have risen to only 1.38%. And the Treaty's specific provisions, such as the requirement for an independent central bank, with an overriding objective of achieving price stability, would risk locking the Community into recession.

Plan of the Book

The 26 authors share a common concern at the economic waste as well as the human misery which mass unemployment represents. Together, the chapters in this book analyse the causes of the emergence of large-scale unemployment and evaluate practical policy proposals for combating it. As Brian Reddaway argues in his foreword, quite inadequate importance has been attached to policies for combating unemployment – governments have many powers, and should not be allowed to deny their ability to influence the level of unemployment, even if they have to act independently.

Unemployment and government policy

The rise in unemployment in Europe is due, according to Jonathan Michie and Frank Wilkinson in Chapter 1, to the interrelation between macro-economic policy, balance of payments constraints and deindustrialisation. The idea of pursuing active macroeconomic and industrial policies has given way to an adherence to monetarism, privatisation and labour market deregulation. Yet the resulting growth in low pay, poverty and unemployment have, ironically, placed an increasing burden on the public purse. At the same time, productive efficiency is harmed by the resulting instability in the labour market – particularly within the increasingly low-paid sectors – and the loss of incentives for producers to upgrade their productive systems. A vicious circle of low-wage, low-productivity, low-investment activity is generated, leading to loss of competitiveness and growing unemployment, with the increasing burdens on the exchequer provoking yet further moves down the recessionary spiral.

The effects of expansionary policy measures on output and employment are simulated by Ray Barrell, Guglielmo Maria Caporale and James Sefton in Chapter 2 using the National Institute model. Like most such models, this assumes that in the long run the variables return to their equilibrium paths, so that any effect from, say, fiscal policy is only temporary. But as is made clear, such 'temporary' effects may be quite long-lasting – thus, for example, abandoning Maastricht and reflating the European economy would be predicted to reduce unemployment for several years, at least. This then begs the question of whether output, employment and the other variables would still revert to the same equilibrium paths. Higher demand and output in the short and medium term would mean that the economy would have higher industrial capacity, a more qualified workforce and a wider variety of products. If the world is changing, the very notion of an 'equilibrium' loses its relevance.

The BBC Panorama Programme 'Pandora's Box' included a description from Paul Ormerod of the economy as a living organism – if you poke it, one time it may jump one way yet the next time it may jump the other. And as he documents in Chapter 3, the reaction of economies to adverse or beneficial shocks may be very different between countries and over time; hence the worthlessness of the concept of the Non-Accelerating Inflation Rate of Unemployment (NAIRU) – the idea that at any point in time there is a unique level of unemployment at which inflation will neither accelerate nor decelerate – which plays such a central role in contemporary macro-economics. A shock to the system will not just knock the system off the path for a while, but may shift the system onto a quite new path.

Another implication of NAIRU-type analyses is that the removal of 'rigidities' in the economy becomes the key to reducing NAIRU. Yet as Peter Nolan demonstrates in Chapter 4, so-called rigidities in Germany have forced employers to respond by upgrading through investment, thus shifting the economy onto a higher growth path than if employers had had an easy life free of all such 'imperfections'.

Lessons and prospects

With talk today of the possibility of a 'two-speed Europe' – with Germany and the Benelux countries (with or without France) moving more rapidly to monetary union – Michael Kitson and Jonathan Michie in Chapter 5 recall that the ill-fated gold standard did not collapse in one go in the 1930s: some countries attempted to maintain the fixed exchange rate system, thus heralding a two- (or multi-) tier system. The ones which stuck with the system grew more slowly, those which left first grew fastest. Hence the 'speed' with which countries move towards fixed exchange rate systems should not be confused with the speed at which their economies will grow. In a two-speed Europe the 'slow' lane may be preferable.

Several of the chapters refer to the expansionary policies of the Mitterrand Government in 1981, and its subsequent U-turn of 1983. The orthodox interpretation of this experience is that the Keynesian policies were discovered to be unsustainable because of balance of payments and exchange rate constraints and hence had to be abandoned. Serge Halimi, Jonathan Michie and Seumas Milne demonstrate in Chapter 6 that this is simply false: these difficulties were not learned from the 1981–3 experience in France but were perfectly well understood and stated quite explicitly by, among others, the French Socialist Party before taking office. The problems which any government pursuing such expansionary policies would encounter were documented in advance, as were the additional policies which would be necessary to see through the expansion – including the use of trade policies to ensure that imports grew only in line with exports. The point is that no attempt was, in fact, made to actually introduce these additional, necessary policies; the government instead chose the beggar-my-neighbour route of 'competitive disinflation'.

In Chapter 7, Edward Balls argues that account needs to be taken of the 'non-employed': those who do not have jobs but are not registered as unemployed. Thus the OECD prescription for unemployment, of cuts in the level and duration of unemployment benefits, risks simply pushing the unemployed off the official jobless count and into economic inactivity. The alternative of subsidising their employment, in either the private or public sectors, makes more sense than leaving the long-term unemployed to decay.

In Chapter 8, Horst Reichenbach, Guillermo Davila Muro and Stefan Lehner suggest that the peripheral member states of the EC have benefited more than proportionately from integration. They see growth and integration as self-reinforcing, and consider these to have had a positive impact with regard to the objective of cohesion, with further potential from the internal market and from economic and monetary union.

Regional and industrial policies

The single European market has tended to increase industrial concentration and exacerbate regional disparities, as documented in Chapter 9. Jane Collier argues that the 12 member states hardly constitute an 'optimum currency area', and that active regional and fiscal policies are needed if the very process of integration itself is not to be threatened.

The tendencies in industrial restructuring that are working to disadvantage the weaker regions are identified by John Tomaney who presents various case-study evidence, including from his own research on the railway equipment sector. He details in Chapter 10 the impact which the completion of the internal market and the transition to economic and monetary union is likely to have on the less favoured regions of the Community, warning that Maastricht's convergence criteria will have to be abandoned to allow the necessary latitude to be able to deal with the resulting regional problems, and that an active industrial policy is needed to ensure the development of industrial activity outside the European core.

The nature which such an interventionist strategy to bolster industrial performance might take is discussed by Malcolm Sawyer in Chapter 11, who draws a distinction between the notion of a developmental state, organised and concerned to promote economic and industrial development, on the one hand, and a regulatory state on the other, concentrating instead on competition policy. A broadly conceived industrial strategy (as opposed to just a 'policy') is needed to offset the forces of cumulative causation which otherwise will increase disparities and exacerbate the under-utilisation of resources in backward regions in particular.

Andrew Glyn and Bob Rowthorn in Chapter 12 evaluate the relative merits of two policy packages for job creation: first, wage subsidies, whereby the cost to government of having someone unemployed (unemployment benefit and tax lost) is paid instead as a temporary and declining subsidy to employers taking on the unemployed worker; and second, a programme of greater government expenditure on public services and infrastructure. The public services route has balance of payments advantages as well as a more predictable effect on employment. While coordination is preferable (as pointed out by Kalecki in 1932), there is nevertheless a viable programme for raising employment in a single country; indeed, the only way of building support for an EC-level expansion may be through the contagious impact of a successful expansion of employment in one country first.

In a technical appendix to Chapter 12, Wynne Godley and Bob Rowthorn illustrate how it is that public expenditure can be self-financing. This is an edited version of a paper submitted to the Treasury Advisory Panel, of which Wynne Godley is one of the seven members, appointed after having been the only modeller to forecast the 1990–93 recession.

Combating unemployment in Europe

John Eatwell in Chapter 13 sets out the various exchange rate regimes which might allow output and employment growth to be pursued, concluding that the theoretically preferred option would be to tackle the competitive imbalances within the EC by discriminatory 'trade' policies between the regions of the EC; this would then allow a single currency to be adopted, while avoiding the damage which these structural differences would otherwise cause within a monetary union.

A range of exchange rate issues are analysed by Ruth Kelly in Chapter 14, including the problems associated with the 'theoretically flawed and practically unworkable' Exchange Rate Mechanism. She also deals with the problems caused by currency speculation; these could be tackled by taxing foreign exchange market transactions, simply reducing the profitability of such activity. Speculators might move 'offshore', but in that case their transactions could be exempted from legal status, so that unpaid debts would not be backed by the force of law.

In a comprehensive discussion of the state of the EC's economy, and what could be done about it, Francis Cripps and Terry Ward argue in Chapter 15 that in the short term, changes in the conduct of monetary and fiscal policies are needed so that they support rather than impede growth, and that structural policies should be strengthened to boost development and job creation in those regions which are most in need. Longer-term policies are then also needed for boosting investment – and developing mechanisms for funding public investment – as well as for developing specific job creation measures.

In the concluding chapter, John Grieve Smith argues that current levels of unemployment are a reflection of the political priorities attached to different objectives of economic policy. The low demand created by monetarist and restrictive economic policies has eroded the capacity to produce: plant capacity, management structures, sales organisation, skilled and experienced labour, and the number of firms have all settled down at a level consisted with 9 to 10% unemployment. Higher demand is therefore needed, but it would have to be sustained if capacity is to be rebuilt. This is unlikely with an independent European central bank dedicated to the achievement of price stability. The emphasis has to be shifted towards restoring full employment. If this involves a short-term increase in government debt then this would be – in the words of ex-Chancellor Lamont – a price well worth paying.

PART I

Unemployment and Government Policy

1

The Growth of Unemployment in the 1980s[1]

Jonathan Michie and Frank Wilkinson

A man grows rich by employing a multitude of manufacturers: he grows poor, by maintaining a multitude of menial servants. (Adam Smith)

The second half of the 1980s saw relatively fast world economic growth, with some fall in unemployment, although this remained high, especially in Europe; the revival came to an end, however, with global recession and a return to mass unemployment in the early 1990s. Figures for growth and unemployment are given in the Appendix to this chapter, but briefly, the early 1990s have witnessed recession and unemployment comparable to the 1930s. Indeed talk of the need for a 'New Deal' has re-entered the economic policy vocabulary. In April 1993 Japan's government introduced an £82 billion set of economy-boosting measures, including a £53 billion public works programme, while in the US President Clinton was elected in 1992 on an explicitly interventionist economic platform. In the EC12, on the other hand, policy is still stuck on the Maastricht Treaty – drawn up in the late 1980s era of economic growth, falling unemployment and concerns about rising inflation. Yet the suggestion that Maastricht should give way to policies for combating unemployment immediately raises the spectre of high inflation in the minds of policy-makers.

This threat receives its support in the economic literature from the concept of NAIRU: the assertion that there is some level of equilibrium unemployment at which inflation stabilises. Indeed, Chapter 2 in this volume, by Ray Barrell, Guglielmo Maria Caporale and James Sefton 'is based on the theoretical framework developed by Richard Layard and Stephen Nickell', aiming to forecast 'at what level *consistent with stable inflation* unemployment is expected to settle down'. We do not find this NAIRU framework helpful, since it rests on the implicit assumption of unchanged and unspecified policies and practices; we have plotted elsewhere the relationship between unemployment and changes in earnings variously measured for Britain in the 1980s, and the results could not be more at variance with the notion of a predictable relationship between the two variables.[2] Paul Ormerod, in Chapter 3 of this volume, convincingly demonstrates econometrically how fragile the historical evidence is for any credible relationship between the level of joblessness and the rate of inflation. The basic Layard and Nickell model is taken from Rowthorn (1977),[3] where it was argued that in the event of the combined claims of labour and capital summing to more than the total resources available for distribution, the consequent inflation could be contained by an increase in the reserve army of labour and/or of capital. By contrast, the Layard and Nickell results depend on a downward-sloping aggregate demand curve derived by aggregating from individual firms,[4] and is based on the idea that as unemployment falls, the bargaining wage increases but the feasible wage does not. Dropping the latter assumption, and allowing that productivity and hence the 'feasible wage' may increase with output, destroys the immutability of the NAIRU law. If increased capacity utilisation and, over the longer term, an increased and more technologically advanced capacity itself, allows a growth of the feasible wage then there may be no unique 'equilibrium' point (NAIRU) with only that one level of unemployment associated with non-accelerating inflation. Thus even if the bargaining and feasible wages happened to coincide at a given level of unemployment, if unemployment falls with the feasible wage increasing (due to increased productivity) more than the increase in the bargaining wage, then such a model would actually predict that the reduction in unemployment would result in inflation falling rather than rising.

Deindustrialisation in Europe

The rise in unemployment in Europe can be more usefully analysed with reference to the interrelation between macroeconomic policy, balance of payments constraints and deindustrialisation. European unemployment has been accompanied by a relatively rapid decline in manufacturing employment in the EC12, and in this process Britain has shown the lead. The share of employment in manufacturing fell in the decade 1976–86 from 22.8% to 19.1% in the US, from 25.5% to 24.7% in Japan, and from 28.9% to 24.4% for the EC12. This relative decline represented an absolute fall for Europe of almost 5.5 million jobs. Of the EC12, only Portugal and Greece avoided a fall in manufacturing employment, with the UK experiencing the most extreme cut (of 16%, representing more than 2 million jobs). The decline in UK manufacturing employment as a percentage of total employment is illustrated in Figure 1.1, and manufacturing investment as a proportion of total investment is illustrated in Figure 1.2. The UK was responsible for more than 40% of the EC12's loss of manufacturing employment.[5]

There has been considerable debate over the determinants of 'deindustrialisation'.[6] A shift in employment from manufacturing to other sectors could simply be the result of a shift in consumption patterns and/or

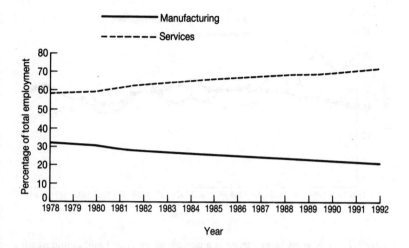

Figure 1.1. UK manufacturing and service sector employment as a percentage of total employment, 1978–92.
Source: Department of Employment, *Employment Gazette, Historical Supplement 3*, June 1992.

differential productivity growth. However, two important points are clear: first, the decline in manufacturing employment in the EC12 – and in particular, in the UK – has not been caused by shifts in consumption patterns, nor by other sectors' requirement for labour. The loss of manufacturing jobs has been accompanied by an increasingly adverse balance of trade in manufactures and by a rise in unemployment. And in the UK most dramatically, manufacturing has not experienced rapidly rising output as a result of fast productivity growth, but on the contrary, a stagnant trend in output, with the productivity growth hence translating directly into falling employment.

And second, as stressed by Ajit Singh in his original development of the concept of deindustrialisation, an economy's distribution of output (and employment) between sectors can lead to balance of payments constraints, and hence can impact not just on relative shares of output and employment but also on absolute levels. It is this danger of a balance of payments constraint of economic recovery and the achievement of full employment which should be of concern for the EC12 in the 1990s. As usual, the UK shows this danger earlier and most dramatically. (The current balance is shown in Figure 1.3 and the contribution of manufacturing is shown in Figure 1.4, having moved into deficit for the first time in 1983 and remaining there since.)[7]

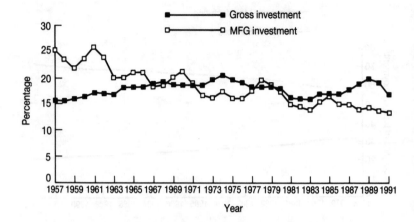

Figure 1.2. UK gross investment (as a percentage of GDP) and manufacturing investment (as a percentage of total investment), 1957–91.
Source: Central Statistical Office, *United Kingdom National Accounts*, London: HMSO.

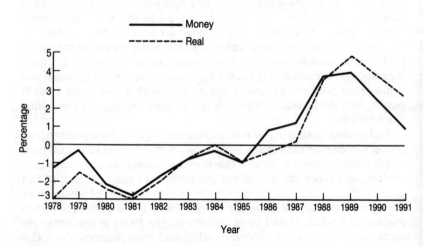

Figure 1.3. UK current balance deficits, 1978–91.
Source: Central Statistical Office, *United Kingdom National Accounts*, London: HMSO.

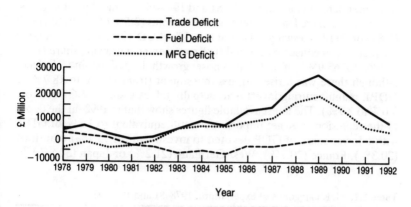

Figure 1.4. UK trade, fuel and total manufactures deficits, 1978–92.
Source: Central Statistical Office, *Monthly Digest of Statistics*, London: HMSO.

Balance of Payments and Exchange Rate Constraints

Exchange rate mechanisms and balance of payments balances have had two major implications for unemployment in Europe. The Exchange Rate Mechanism imposes requirements for monetary and interest rate policy, and domestic fiscal policy. These requirements are biased towards requiring deflationary interest rate rises on countries whose currency is under pressure, rather than reflationary policies on economies with strong currencies. Given the level of domestic demand so determined, the balance of trade indicates the degree to which this is translated into domestic production and employment.

It might be thought that trade imbalances between the EC12 themselves could not have deflationary implications in aggregate, since for any deficit countries there would be corresponding surplus countries, with any deflationary implications thereby balanced by expansionary implications for the surplus economies. The effects are not, however, quite so symmetrical. The key surplus economy has been Germany. The German productive system has, since the Second World War, generated growth, and hence the ability to export. The tight monetary policy pursued by the Bundesbank has sterilised the potentially reflationary impact of the resulting trade surplus by restricting domestic demand, translating this growth into export surpluses.[8] Traditionally this combination of economic competitiveness and tight monetary policy has delivered an export surplus plus full employment; now, however, they are combining to deliver an export surplus and growing unemployment.

As for the deficit countries such as the UK, for any level of domestic demand, the more that is met by net imports, the lower is domestic output and employment. Thus Table 1.1 illustrates that (at 1985 prices) the rise in consumer demand between 1978–81 and 1989–92 was met by net imports, resulting in a move from current account surplus (2.5% of GDP) to deficit (3.8% of GDP) – a swing eqivalent to 6.3% of GDP in real terms – so that the increase in consumer expenditure represented a growing share (from 59.9% to 65.9%) of a GDP whose growth lagged behind. Indeed, although there was a rise in gross investment (from 16.5% to 18.7% of GDP), manufacturing investment actually fell as a share of GDP (from 3.0% to 2.7%). The latest available figures show that in 1992, at the depth of the recession, UK net imports were still equivalent to 1.7% of GDP, with a lower share of GDP devoted to investment (at 15.1%) than Italy (20.3%), France (20.7%), West Germany (21.2%) or Japan (30.9%).[9]

Table 1.1.   UK categories of expenditure, 1978–81 and 1989–92.

as % of GDP	Current prices		1985 prices	
	1978–81	1989–92	1978–81	1981–92
Consumer expenditure	60.4	64.2	59.9	65.9
Government expenditure	20.1	20.6	21.6	19.5
Gross investment	17.8	17.8	16.5	18.7
of which				
Manufacturing	3.1	2.5	3.0	2.7
Current surplus	+1.7	−2.3	+2.5	−3.8

Source: Central Statistical Office, *United Kingdom National Accounts*, London: HMSO.

Government policy and low pay in Britain

The switch in macroeconomic policy towards the belief that direct government intervention is counter-productive and that the economy can only be effectively regulated by monetary means has as its microeconomic corollary the assertion that joblessness results from impediments to the working of the 'invisible hand' in the labour market. As a result, the policy response to the growth of unemployment resulting from restrictive monetary policy and balance of payments constraints has been labour market deregulation. A consequence of such liberalisation is that inequality has increased in most EC countries over the 1980s (see Chapter 6 by Halimi, Michie and Milne for a discussion of growing inequality under Mitterrand); but it was in the UK that inequality was most deliberately pursued through the government's labour market policies.

British governments since 1979 have attributed much of the blame for unemployment to 'market rigidities'. In particular, ministers have argued that 'artificial' constraints on the labour market have prevented wages falling to adjust to changed conditions, and that for many groups wages are being held above their true market level, thereby 'pricing' workers from jobs. To cure these supposed rigidities a large number of measures have been implemented designed to reduce wages and to 'enable the market to work more freely'. Employment rights such as unfair dismissal protection and maternity provisions have been weakened and their coverage reduced; public services have been contracted out to private firms, often at wages and conditions much poorer than in the public sector itself; other government services have been privatised, which has removed the low-paid from the coverage of collectively negotiated agreements; wage protecting conventions such as the fair wage resolution and Schedule 11 have been abolished; and the wages councils, introduced to set legally binding minimum wages in low-wage sectors, their scope and powers drastically reduced in 1986, were abolished in 1993. Concurrently, the rolling programme of trade union legislation has seriously impeded trade union organisation and the ability to gain bargaining rights – to the particular disadvantage of low pay sectors.

The effects of government policy on relative pay is demonstrated in Table 1.2: the tendency has been for the earnings of females to grow more rapidly than for males, and for the pay of the higher-paid males and females to grow more rapidly than that of the lower paid. This is reflected in the more rapid increase in non-manual earnings and for the increase in pay to be higher at successively higher points of the earnings distribution. Thus at the lowest decile for manual males the increase in real pay from 1979 to 1992 was 4%, while at the highest decile for non-manual it was 53%; for females these increases were 10% and 60% respectively. However, when considering the relative performance of female earnings, account should be taken of the increase in part-time from 40% to 46% of female workers, and the fact that hourly pay for part-time work is on average less – and has increased at a slower pace – than hourly pay for full-time work.

Table 1.2. Percentage increase in UK earnings at different points in the distribution, 1979–92 (1979 retail prices).

| | Males | | Females | |
	manual	non-manual	manual	non-manual
Lowest decile	4.0	21.8	9.6	28.6
Lower quartile	8.1	30.7	12.5	36.7
Median	11.4	38.1	15.5	46.1
Upper quartile	15.2	45.1	21.4	60.5
Highest decile	18.3	53.2	31.1	60.3
Mean	13.3	44.1	19.9	51.6

Source: Department of Employment, *New Earnings Survey*, London: HMSO.

This change in the structure of earnings can be explained by three main factors. First, the decline in employment in manufacturing and in other non-service sectors was mainly concentrated in the middle range of the earnings distribution. Second, the increase in employment was concentrated in sectors such as banking, insurance, finance and business, where earnings are relatively high, and in hotel, catering and other such services, where earnings tend to be low. The disappearance of jobs from the middle of the earnings distribution and the increase at each end would explain at least part of the widening of the earnings distribution shown in Table 1.2. The third factor explaining the changed distribution of earnings is the tendency for the earnings of the relatively higher paid to grow rapidly and those of the low paid to increase relatively slowly since 1979. This is indicated by Table 1.3, which gives the rates of increase in earnings for selected industrial sectors. Thus earnings in manufacturing grew by 5 percentage points more than in services. But the main differences were within the service sector, with earnings in the highly paid banking, insurance and finance sector growing 2.5 times more than those in the low-paid distribution and hotels and catering sectors. Moreover, it is in the low-paid service sectors where the growth in part-time female employment has been located.

Table 1.3. Percentage increase in UK average earnings, 1979–92 (1979 prices).

Whole economy	31.7
Manufacturing	35.8
Services	30.3
Distribution	19.8
Hotels and catering	20.1
Banking, insurance	
and finance	49.9

Source: Department of Employment, *Employment Gazette*, London: HMSO.

UK governments have added to the regressive effects of their labour market policies on the distribution of income by their tax and social welfare policies. The elimination of higher-rate tax brackets, the change towards indirect taxation, and increases in national insurance contributions have favoured the rich. Meanwhile, the least well off have been hit by the elimination of the earnings-related elements, and dependants' benefits, from unemployment and sickness pay; by the break in the link between social welfare and earnings, and in some cases from inflation (Rowthorn, 1992); and by the restrictions on eligibility for out-of-work benefits, and the coercion of the unemployed into accepting poorly paid jobs by the redefinition and the more rigorous enforcement of availability-for-work rules.[10] As a consequence, in 1989 social benefits were a smaller proportion of GDP than in 1979, despite an increase in the number of pensioners of around 1 million, a similar increase in those without work and claiming benefits and an increase in the recipients of family credit of some 250,000. Redistribution has therefore been from the poor to the rich, and within the different categories of the poor.

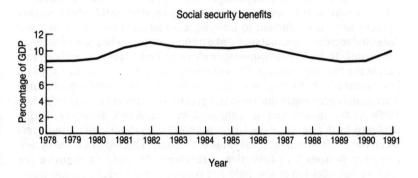

Figure 1.5. UK social security benefits as a percentage of GDP, 1978–91.
Source: Central Statistical Office, *United Kingdom National Accounts*, London: HMSO.

The overall effect of the increase in unemployment, differential rates of pay increase, the growth of part-time work and the government's tax and welfare policy is that between 1979 and 1989 the share of household income of the bottom two-fifths fell from 24% to 19%, while that of the top two-fifths increased from 58% to 64%.

The objective of labour market deregulation – rooted as it is in the notion that social welfare and labour standards, imposed by trade unions and government, seriously impede the effective working of the labour market – is to generate a higher level of employment by securing equilibrium between supply and demand. However, the evidence is that the labour market is in unstable equilibrium, only held in balance by high levels of unemployment, and that low pay is a major cause of labour market instability. For example, almost 40% of the vacancies notified to the Department of Employment Job Centres[11] are in the distribution, hotels and catering and repairs sector, although this accounts for only 20% of total employment. As a percentage of employment, notified vacancies in distribution, hotels, catering and repairs were 23% in 1988, the peak of the boom, declining to 14% in the first half of 1991. Comparable figures for all other industries and services are 10% and 7% respectively. This suggests that except, possibly, in periods of exceptionally high unemployment, in the low pay segments of the labour market there is a substantially greater degree of unsatisfied demand for labour, meaning that compared with other sectors, wages are too low. Recession brings supply more into line with demand by destroying alternative job opportunities. Thus, rather than low pay being an answer to unemployment, high levels of joblessness are a precondition for many people accepting low-paid jobs, which they soon quit when job prospects improve.

Low pay and the resulting labour force instability also prove to be major obstacles to effective training and personnel policy. When unemployment is high the pressure on management is relaxed and when the labour market tightens firms are reluctant to train because labour turnover is high and potential recruits are reluctant to take training seriously because of the poor job prospects. Entry to low-paying trades is often a last resort, and entrants quit at the first opportunity. Consequently, investment in training shows a poor return to both employer and employees. These problems became increasingly pressing in the low-paying sectors of British industry in the late 1980s as the labour market tightened with economic recovery, as the declining birth rate threatened the supply of cheap labour, and as employers faced the implications of equal value legislation. This led to a spate of new company policies and collective agreements designed to improve the relative pay position of low-paid and part-time workers, to extend fringe benefits to part-timers, to introduce job evaluation and to more effectively train, motivate and involve workers at the lower end of the job hierarchy.[12] But these necessary reforms were confined to the leading firms and sectors where unions are well-organised. The vast majority of undervalued workers were not included. Moreover, with the growth of unemployment, the threat of the 'demographic time bomb' has receded, and with it any pressure on firms to improve their personnel policies so as to increase pay and to improve productivity and quality of service. In fact, quite the opposite has happened. Major employers, such as the Burton Group of retailers, have taken advantage of high levels of unemployment to casualise jobs, cut pay and worsen conditions of work (IDS Report, April 1993). Elsewhere there has been widespread use of new legal powers and other more legally dubious devises to intensify the exploitation and intimidation of an increasingly vulnerable workforce. Reporting on the increasing levels of enquiries about employment problems, the National Association of Citizens Advice Bureaux concluded that:

> Numbers of employees are faced with impossible choices – accepting a
> severe deterioration in their working conditions; or losing their jobs. With
> unemployment standing at over 3 million, the implications of this dilemma
> are obvious. (March 1993, p 49.)

Thus the aim of social security legislation has increasingly been to sharpen 'work incentives', on the assumption that the unemployed are made reluctant to take up available paid work by the receipt of benefits and by the poverty and unemployment traps. Simultaneously, paid work at the lower end of the labour market has been made more and more unattractive, both to the unemployed and those in employment, by the dilution of social and employment protection and the consequent decline in job quality. It is a matter of fine judgement whether the net effect of this policy of making the receipt of out-of-work income increasingly unattractive, while at the same time reducing the range of decent jobs available within employment, has been to induce greater labour market participation amongst the unemployed. But there can be little doubt of the degenerative effect on economic efficiency of employment practices and intensified exploitation.

Labour Undervaluation and Worker Efficiency

Orthodox economists argue that low pay reflects low levels of productivity. When, as is the more usual case, low pay and poor working conditions result from the undervaluation of labour due to the imbalance of power in the labour market, the direction of causation runs in precisely the opposite direction. Such circumstances are not conducive to worker cooperation, and workers might use the power they derive from their ability to withhold labour and from the additional skill and information they acquire from work experience by, for example, keeping effort within prescribed limits, working closely to the 'rules' so as to resist any flexible use of their time, failing to keep managers informed of improvements to technology and working methods learned on-the-job, and pilfering or even sabotage. The consequence of all these is a reduction in work effort (the avoidance of which might require more ingenuity and effort than the work itself) to match the pay. But in these cases the direction of causation runs from low pay to low effort, rather than the reverse.

Another way by which the undervaluation of labour leads to its dissipation can be accounted for by the relationship between low pay and poor working conditions on the one hand, and skill and training on the other. The orthodox explanation is that low pay is the result of a lack of training and skill, and that an increase in pay will further discourage employers from providing training. But a closer examination reveals again a quite different direction of causation. First, low-paying employers are the least likely to train. Inefficient low payers require undervalued labour to subsidise poor management or keep obsolete equipment in production, and cannot afford to train except in the narrowest sense. The interests of predatory low payers are in exploiting human capital rather than creating it. Second, skill is to an important degree a social category, and jobs with poor terms and conditions of employment are unlikely to be afforded high status, whatever their skill level. Moreover, status as well as the content of jobs will determine the willingness of individuals to acquire the necessary entry qualifications by undertaking education and training. The identification of particular jobs with socially deprived groups lowers their skill status and the training routes by which they are acquired. One of the effects of the process of deindustrialisation in the UK, France and elsewhere has been a decline in levels of pay and conditions of work in industries directly affected and those into which the redundant workers have been crowded.

Deindustrialisation creates conditions for social deskilling in four closely related ways which add to the spiral of decline. Rapid increases in unemployment weaken workers' resistance to employers' offensives against the terms and conditions of employment and traditional forms of control of skilled work. A second common response by firms to their declining fortunes is to cut back on training. This may take the form of a reduction of in-house training and/or a decline in support for external provision by training agencies, so that the local infrastructure for skill generation is weakened. This, and the migration from the trade of workers in a position to do so, creates a skill shortage. The response to this, in the face of the decline in formal training, is the substitution of on-the-job instruction with a focus on a narrow range of specific skills to meet firms' immediate needs. Consequently the skill content of jobs is diluted, and this interacts with the deterioration of the terms and conditions of employment and the increasing pessimism about future prospects of the industry to discourage new entrants from traditional areas of recruitment (Wilkinson, 1992). Any subsequent relaxation of hiring standards to meet the labour shortage serves to futher reinforce the social downgrading of the job, the dissipation of skills, the loss of competitiveness and industrial decline.

The response by governments to the twin problems of increasing unemployment and a growing skill shortage has been to institute new training schemes. Whatever the original intention, or indeed the quality of much of the training, these schemes acquire a reputation for disguising unemployment, creating new forms of cheap labour and for failing to provide adequate training. The general effect is therefore a downgrading in labour market terms of the participants and the job areas at which the schemes are targeted. Individuals then become less and less willing to take part in training programmes, because of the knowledge that the time and effort spent is wasted and individuals who have so trained tend to quit the resulting job at the earliest opportunity. A related problem is that targeting training at the unemployed to get them into jobs with low-paying firms in need of undervalued labour, to keep obsolete equipment in operation and outdated product lines profitable, is a waste of training resources. Such firms need skills which are specific to outdated technology and are therefore effectively obsolete. The cumulative effect of low pay and poor working conditions and the policy responses by employers and the state is therefore to weaken the skill base (in both technical and social terms), discouraging individuals from undertaking training and misallocating training resources. In these circumstances, lack of demand for training, rather than paucity of supply, explains skill shortages and reinforces deindustrialising processes.

Costs of Inequality

Inequality and poverty also have detrimental effects on both the balance of payments constraint, with a transfer of resources to those with a higher marginal propensity to import (Borooah, 1988), and on the PSBR, as the costs of welfare, benefits and income support grow. A growing share of the income of the working poor is met not by their employers but by government. This not only increases both the spread and the grip of the poverty trap (whereby any increase in pay by employers is matched by an equivalent loss of benefits from government), it also increases the burden on public expenditure. And if total government spending is constrained – for example by the Maastricht 3% formula – then this burden has to be met by public spending cuts imposed elsewhere, cuts which may well exacerbate unemployment. An alternative response is to cut per-capita income to the poor, as was done in Britain in the 1980s[13] and as is being considered by the EC.[14] A further possibility which is increasingly being touted is a direct subsidy to employers to provide jobs for the out-of-work.[15]

This increasing use by private capital of low-paid workers, requiring public funds to subsidise their income, is in essence a return to the Speenhamland system of Poor Law used in Britain in the eighteenth and nineteenth centuries.[16] The Poor Law was thus no longer something to fall back on, but became the general framework of the rural labourer's life. 'The distinction between worker and pauper vanished.'[17] There are also parallels with the currently fashionable 'basic income' schemes; indeed, the following description sounds uncannily like an advocacy of the present 'basic income' ideas:

> No measure was ever more universally popular. Parents were free of the care of their children, and children were no more dependent on their parents; employers could reduce wages at will and labourers were safe from hunger whether they were busy or slack; humanitarians applauded the measure as an act of mercy even though not of justice and the selfish gladly consoled themselves with the thought that though it was merciful at least it was not liberal; and even the ratepayers were slow to realise what would happen to the rates under a system which proclaimed the 'right to live' whether a man earned a living wage or not.[18]

It is therefore perhaps particularly important to remember that 'It was at bottom an attempt to maintain the ancient ideal of a stable though unequal society',[19] 'setting its face against the only thing which could have at least provided some defence against the fall in wages, the combination of the workers'.[20] However, some (such as Blaug, 1963) have defended the old Poor Law as a rational device for maintaining surplus labourers who could not have been employed at a living wage. Given the danger of the EC following Britain down a low-wage, low-productivity trajectory, it is worth quoting at length on the implications for the productive system of the Speenhamland system – and, we would argue, of the present move towards inequality in Europe:[21]

> The traditional social order degenerated into a universal pauperism of demoralised men who could not fall below the relief scale whatever they did, who could not rise above it, who had not even the nominal guarantee of a living income since the 'scale' could be – and with increasing expense of rates was – reduced to as little as the village rich thought fit for a labourer. Agrarian capitalism degenerated into a general lunacy, in which farmers were encouraged to pay as little as they could (since wages would be supplemented by the parish) and used the mass of pauper labour as an excuse for not raising their productivity; while their most rational calculations would be, how to get the maximum subsidy for their wage-bill from the rest of the ratepayers. Labourers, conversely, were encouraged to do as little work as they possibly could, since nothing would get them more than the official minimum of subsistence.
>
> Nobody can measure the dehumanisation or, in economic terms, the fall in productivity which resulted.[22]

Conclusion

Even the IMF believes that labour market policies 'have been unsuccessful in addressing persistently high unemployment, especially in Europe'. Much of the criticism from the IMF's spring 1993 *World Economic Outlook* is reserved for the European Community countries; despite cuts in short-term German interest rates, monetary conditions are held to be tight, exacerbated by 'substantial interest rate differentials relative to Germany, associated with recent exchange rate turbulence'; the weakness of the German economy is said to justify further cuts in interest rates; and economic recovery is predicted for Britain only because of the lower interest rates coming from sterling's departure from the Exchange Rate Mechanism.

Unemployment in the European Community can in large part be attributed to restrictive macroeconomic policies, and its distribution between member states to a failure to develop balance of payment adjustment mechanisms which do not throw the burden of adjustment on the deficit countries. Persistent unemployment is creating increasing pressure for the abandonment of minimum social welfare and labour market standards, orchestrated by free marketeer theorists who mystify real world processes by reference to immutable economic laws which load the responsibility for economic stagnation onto its principal victims. But the fatal flaw in the argument that the way to economic and social progress is by immiserising an increasing proportion of the population is to be found in the UK and USA, where the experiments in competitive economic and social degradation have been taken furthest. There the Speenhamland trap has already been sprung, with its downward spiral of social welfare and labour market standards and economic performance and its upward spiral of exchequer costs: processes which interrelate to produce social, political and competitive degeneration.[23]

With its escalating internal problems there is every danger that the EC will follow Britain in a drift towards poverty, low wage and poor employment conditions for a large and growing section of its workforce. The dangers in this cannot be overemphasised and their avoidance depends on the ability of the countries of Europe to come together to produce expansionary policies which have at their core full-employment and high and equitable social welfare and labour standards. In economic terms a strong welfare state is essential for a healthy, well educated and well trained workforce; high wage and employment standards are essential for inducing the most effective use of such a workforce; and full employment is the guarantee that no part of the workforce is diverted into non-productivity. To achieve this collectively the European states require two essential safeguards regulating their relationships: first, measures are needed to deal with countries with persistent balance of payments surpluses so as to prevent deficit countries adopting persistently deflationary policies, thereby beggaring themselves and their neighbours; second, free trade and free capital movements require complementing with centrally enforced common labour and social standards to prevent companies and nation states competitively devaluing their workers.

Statistical Appendix: Main Economic Indicators, 1990–94, EC, USA and Japan

(a) GDP at constant prices (annual percentage change)

	1990	1991	1992	1993[a]	1994[a]
B	3.4	1.9	1.0	0.5	1.75
DK	1.7	1.2	1.0	1.75	2.25
D	5.1	3.7	1.5	−0.5	1
D+	—	—	1.7	0	1.5
GR	−0.2	1.8	1.5	1.75	2
E	3.6	2.4	1.2	1	1.75
F	2.2	1.1	1.9	1	2
IRL	8.3	2.5	2.9	2.25	2.5
I	2.2	1.4	1.1	0.75	1.5
L	3.2	3.1	2.2	2	2.5
NL	3.9	2.2	1.3	0.75	1.25
P	4.4	1.9	1.7	1.25	2.5
UK	0.5	−2.2	−0.9	1.5	2.75
EC	2.8	1.4	1.1	0.75	1.75
EC+	—	—	1.1	0.75	1.75
USA	0.7	−1.3	2.0	2.5	2.75
JAP	5.2	4.4	1.5	1.5	2.5

(b) Domestic demand at constant prices (annual percentage change)

	1990	1991	1992	1993[a]	1994[a]
B	3.5	1.6	1.9	0.5	1.5
DK	−0.8	0.1	−0.4	2	2.25
D	4.9	3.1	1.3	−0.5	0.5
D+	—	—	2.2	0	1.25
GR	0.8	2.3	1.1	1.5	2.5
E	4.7	2.9	1.8	0.5	1.75
F	2.6	0.8	1.0	1	1.75
IRL	6.3	−0.7	−0.9	2.25	2.25
I	2.7	2.2	1.3	−0.25	1
L	5.1	8.4	3.3	2.25	2.75
NL	3.5	1.7	0.6	0.25	1
P	5.4	4.1	3.6	3.25	4
UK	−0.5	−3.2	0	0.5	2.5
EC	2.8	1.2	1.1	0.25	1.5
EC+	—	—	1.3	0.5	1.5
USA	0.1	−2.1	2.1	2.25	2.75
JAP	5.4	3.0	1.1	1.5	2

(c) Deflator of private consumption (annual percentage change)

	1990	1991	1992	1993[a]	1994[a]
B	3.1	2.9	2.4	2.75	2.75
DK	2.1	2.4	2.1	1.5	2
D	2.7	3.9	4.0	3.5	3
D+	—	—	4.8	4.25	3.5
GR	20.1	18.4	16.0	13.5	9
E	6.4	6.3	6.0	5.5	5
F	3.2	3.2	2.6	2.75	2.5
IRL	1.7	3.2	2.9	2.25	2.25
I	5.9	6.8	5.3	5.75	4.75
L	3.6	2.9	3.4	4.75	3.25
NL	2.3	3.3	3.1	2.75	2.5
P	12.6	11.9	9.1	6.75	5.75
UK	5.3	7.2	5.1	5	3
EC	4.5	5.3	4.5	4.25	3.5
EC+	—	—	4.6	4.5	3.5
USA	5.0	4.2	3.1	2.75	2.75
JAP	2.6	2.6	2.4	2.5	2.5

(d) Balance on current transactions (as a percentage of GDP)

	1990	1991	1992	1993[a]	1994[a]
B	0.9	1.7	1.8	1.75	2
DK	0.5	1.3	3.0	3	2.75
D	3.5	1.2	0.4	0	0
D+	—	-0.7	-0.8	-1.25	-1
GR	-6.2	-5.1	-3.3	-3	-2.25
E	-3.7	-3.5	-3.7	-3.5	-3
F	-0.8	-0.5	0.1	0.25	0.25
IRL	1.3	6.0	6.7	6.5	7
I	-1.4	-1.9	-1.9	-1.75	-1.5
L	34.2	27.9	19.9	18.75	17.5
NL	4.0	3.9	3.9	3.75	3.75
P[b]	-2.5	-3.5	-0.2	-2.25	-3.25
UK	-4.2	-1.8	-2.1	-2.75	-3
EC	-0.3	-0.5	-0.5	-0.75	-0.5
EC+	—	-1.0	-0.8	-1	-0.75
USA	-1.4	0.2	-1.0	-1	-1.25
JAP	1.3	2.5	3.2	3.25	3.5

(e) Number of unemployed as a percentage of the civilian labour force

	1990	1991	1992	1993[a]	1994[a]
B	7.6	7.5	8.2	9.25	9.75
DK	8.1	8.9	9.5	9.5	9.25
D	4.8	4.2	4.5	6	6.5
D+	—	—	7.5	8.5	8.75
GR	7.2	7.7	7.7	8.5	9
E	16.1	16.3	18.0	19.5	20
F	9.0	9.5	10.1	10.75	11.25
IRL	14.5	16.2	17.8	19.25	20.5
I	9.9	10.2	10.2	10.5	10.75
L	1.7	1.6	1.9	2	2
NL	7.5	7.0	6.7	7.5	8
P	4.6	4.1	4.8	5.5	5.75
UK	7.0	9.1	10.8	12.25	12.75
EC	8.3	8.8	9.5	10.5	11
EC+	—	—	10.1	11	11.5
USA	5.5	6.7	7.3	7.25	7
JAP	2.1	2.1	2.1	2.25	2.25

(f) General government lending and borrowing (as a percentage of GDP)

	1990	1991	1992	1993[a]	1994[a]
B	−5.7	−6.6	−6.7	−6	−5.25
DK	−1.4	−2.0	−2.3	−2.75	−1.75
D	−2.0	−3.6	−3.4	−3.75	−3.75
D+	—	−3.2	−3.2	−3.5	−3.75
GR	−18.8	−15.4	−13.4	−9.75	−7.75
E	−4.0	−4.9	−4.6	−4.25	−3.75
F	−1.4	−1.9	−2.8	−3.25	−3.5
IRL	−2.5	−2.1	−2.7	−3	−3.75
I	−10.9	−10.2	−10.5	−10.25	−9.25
L	5.0	−0.8	−0.4	−1	−0.75
NL	−4.9	−2.5	−3.5	−3.5	−3.25
P	−5.5	−6.4	−5.6	−4.75	−3.75
UK	−1.3	−2.8	−6.1	−8.25	−8
EC	−4.1	−4.7	−5.4	−5.75	−5.5
EC+	—	−4.6	−5.3	−5.75	−5.5
USA	−2.5	−3.4	−4.8	−4.75	−4.5
JAP	3.0	2.4	2.2	0.5	0.5

(g) Total employment (annual percentage change)

	1990	1991	1992	1993[a]	1994[a]
B	1.1	−0.3	−0.7	−0.75	0.25
DK	−0.5	−0.9	−0.7	0	0.25
D	3.0	2.6	0.8	−1	−0.25
D+	—	—	−0.5	−1	−0.25
GR	0.2	−2.0	−0.5	0	0.25
E	2.8	0.2	−1.6	−1.5	0
F	1.0	0.4	−0.2	−0.25	0
IRL	3.3	−0.1	0.1	0	0.25
I	1.1	0.8	0.1	0	0.25
L	4.3	3.6	1.5	1.5	1.75
NL	2.3	1.3	0.4	−0.5	0
P	0.9	0.9	−0.2	−0.5	0
UK	0.7	−3.1	−2.3	−1.75	−0.5
EC	1.6	0.1	−0.5	−0.75	0
EC+	—	—	−0.7	−0.75	0
USA	1.2	−1.6	0.7	1	1.25
JAP	2.1	1.9	0.5	0.25	0.75

(h) Compensation of employees per head (annual percentage change)

	1990	1991	1992	1993[a]	1994[a]
B	7.7	6.8	5.4	4.75	4.5
DK	3.4	3.7	3.2	2.5	2.75
D	4.7	5.8	5.3	3.5	5.5
D+	—	—	—	—	—
GR	19.7	15.0	12.3	11.25	10.75
E	7.9	8.7	9.0	7.25	5.75
F	5.0	4.2	4.1	4	4
IRL	4.4	4.4	6.3	6	3.25
I	10.5	8.7	5.1	4	4.75
L	6.9	5.4	5.1	6	4.25
NL	4.1	4.3	4.8	3.25	3.25
P	18.7	19.0	14.9	9.75	8.75
UK	9.5	8.9	6.0	3.75	4.75
EC	7.5	7.2	5.8	4.25	4.5
EC+	—	—	—	—	—
USA	4.9	5.1	2.4	2	2.25
JAP	5.3	4.4	3.2	2	2.75

(i) Investment in construction at constant prices (annual percentage change)

	1990	1991	1992	1993[a]	1994[a]
B	7.1	2.0	3.8	−2.75	1.25
DK	−4.6	−8.1	−4.5	4.5	3.5
D	5.3	4.1	4.5	0.5	2
D+	—	—	5.6	1.75	3
GR	2.2	−6.4	−3.0	3	5
E	10.8	4.3	−3.4	−3.25	0.5
F	2.7	0.6	2.3	0.25	1.75
IRL	11.7	−1.4	2.5	3	2
I	2.5	1.2	0.4	−0.75	0.5
L	8.0	7.1	6.0	3.25	4
NL	0.6	−2.1	0.0	−0.5	0.5
P	5.3	4.5	2.5	2.75	5.75
UK	−0.6	−8.4	−1.4	−1.5	5.5
EC	3.8	0.5	1.0	−0.5	2
EC+	—	—	1.5	−0.25	2.25

(j) Investment in equipment at constant prices (annual percentage change)

	1990	1991	1992	1993[a]	1994[a]
B	10.9	−1.9	0.7	−4	1.25
DK	3.7	2.8	−12.0	−0.75	4.75
D	13.3	9.1	−2.0	−4	1.75
D+	—	—	1.3	−1.5	3.25
GR	7.9	3.3	4.5	6	7.5
E	1.4	−2.5	0.2	0.25	2.25
F	4.1	−2.5	−4.3	−1.25	1.5
IRL	7.2	−11.6	0.5	1.25	1.5
I	3.5	0.7	−0.7	−1.5	1.25
L	10.9	11.4	3.5	1.75	3
NL	7.6	2.6	−0.8	−0.75	1.5
P	5.8	1.0	4.8	3.75	6
UK	−3.6	−11.9	0.6	0	3.75
EC	4.8	−0.2	−1.5	−1.5	2.25
EC+	—	—	−0.7	−1	2.5

(k) Gross fixed capital formation at constant prices (annual percentage change)

	1990	1991	1992	1993[a]	1994[a]
B	8.4	0.3	2.5	−3.25	1.25
DK	−0.5	−2.8	−8.3	2	4.25
D	8.7	6.5	1.3	−1.75	1.75
D+	—	—	3.6	0.25	3
GR	4.8	−1.9	0.6	4.5	6.25
E	6.9	1.6	−2.0	−2	1.25
F	3.1	−1.3	−1.5	−0.75	1.75
IRL	10.2	−7.2	1.6	2.25	1.75
I	3.3	0.9	−0.2	−1.25	1
L	2.5	9.8	4.5	2.25	3.25
NL	3.6	0.1	−0.4	−0.75	1
P	5.9	2.8	3.6	3.25	5.75
UK	−3.1	−9.9	−0.4	−0.75	4.75
EC	3.9	0.0	−0.3	−1	2
EC+	—	—	0.4	−0.5	2.5
USA	−2.8	−8.5	5.2	4.5	5
JAP	9.5	3.4	−0.7	1	2

(l) GDP per head (EC = 100) at current prices and current PPS

	1990	1991	1992	1993[a]	1994[a]
B	97.5	103.5	103.1	106.7	107.1
DK	115.2	110.1	114.2	107.5	108.4
D	124.3	116.7	119.2	116.3	114.7
D+	—	—	—	—	—
GR	34.4	50.6	50.1	46.8	46.9
E	58.3	76.4	70.6	77.2	77.6
F	107.7	112.7	112.2	113.3	113.5
IRL	57.2	55.5	60.1	72.3	72.8
I	86.6	93.4	102.6	103.8	103.9
L	155.4	138.9	124.9	130.6	130.8
NL	116.8	111.4	104.5	104.0	103.3
P	37.2	54.1	50.7	58.1	58.8
UK	122.6	103.5	101.3	95.2	96.3
EC	100.0	100.0	100.0	100.0	100.0
EC+	—	—	—	—	—
USA	182.6	155.6	146.4	136.8	137.7
JAP	54.1	92.8	105.2	118.1	119.3

Source: Commission of the European Communities 'Annual Economic Report for 1993', *European Economy* no. 54, May, pp. 28–30.

Notes: D+ and EC+ : these aggregates include values for unified Germany.

[a] Based on the forecasts of January 1993 (final). Unusually high uncertainties surround the winter 1992/93 economic forecasts which are based on the standard assumption of 'no change in economic policy', implying that projections for 1994 are essentially extrapolations of expected 1993 trends. Actual outcomes for 1993 and, particularly, for 1994 might differ substantially from present forecasts if, *inter alia*, economic policies were to be significantly modified.

[b] Break in series in 1991–92: until 1991: national accounts data; from 1992 onwards: balance of payments data.

2

Prospects for European Unemployment

Ray Barrell, Guglielmo Maria Caporale and
James Sefton

Unemployment, like inflation, is a very persistent phenomenon. Once it has risen it is difficult to persuade people to change expectations and behaviour, and this may be necessary to reduce unemployment. The unemployed become gradually deskilled, and there is a lot of contagion in the process generating unemployment. Increases in unemployment in the early 1980s followed from a tightening of fiscal and monetary policy throughout continental Europe. These policies are discussed in the first section of this chapter. Over the same period the UK authorities used a high real exchange rate as an anti-inflationary tool, and this caused a rise in unemployment and a collapse in manufacturing. The recession of the early 1980s was followed by a boom driven by financial liberalisation and high consumer expenditure; new jobs were created in different locations and for different types of employee than those who had lost their jobs early in the 1980s. As a result, UK unemployment has been persistently high. We believe that a sustained overvaluation within the ERM would have kept unemployment above three million for some years.

The second section of this chapter discusses the system of wage determination in Europe and the role of collective bargaining. The National Institute of Economic and Social Research has developed a model of the world economy, the National Institute Global Econometric Model (NIGEM), and in its construction we have undertaken extensive analyses of European labour markets. Our approach has been based on the bargaining approach advocated by Stephen Nickell and Richard Layard. Our work has helped us understand differences between the European economies. In particular the combination of bargaining-based wage behaviour and the pricing behaviour of firms seems to impart a lot of inertia into the evolution of output and employment. In common with much 'new Keynesian' analysis, we find that a given structure of bargaining will in the long run produce a constant level of unemployment at a stable rate of inflation. However, sticky wages and prices determined by the bargaining process imply that departures from the long-run level of unemployment can be sustained for a long while, and that although the forces of the market will ensure that a return to equilibrium is eventually achieved, economic policy makers may be able to aid the process of adjustment by using traditional demand management policies.

We use our world model, NIGEM, both for forecasting and for policy analysis. It can be a useful tool for gauging the scale of effects of various policies that may be adopted, and for analysing the time period over which policies are of use. The third section of the chapter analyses three scenarios. The first is a permanent, but sustainable change in the budget deficit in each of the European economies. In order to understand the options that may be available for Europe we assume that exchange rates can be fixed while the Maastricht Treaty targets for government budget deficits are relaxed by 1% of GDP. This policy appears to have sustained, but not permanent, effects on unemployment. If this change took place there would still have to be a significant fiscal tightening in, say, Italy. We would, however, argue that high unemployment in the UK can, in the medium term, only be dealt with by removing the effects on manufacturing of the overvaluation of the early 1980s. Hence we analyse a low exchange rate policy for the UK and the resulting employment gains. Finally we assess the effects on unemployment in the long run of policies to moderate the growth of real wages. We show that a permanent reduction in the unemployment rate can be achieved by changing the structure of bargaining without cutting the real wage.

The Rise of Unemployment in Europe in the 1980s

It is often suggested that contractionary fiscal policy was a major factor driving the rise of European unemployment in the 1980s. This 'Keynesian' hypothesis ascribes low employment in that decade in part to fiscal austerity and in part to the effects of high real interest rates. After the emergence of sustained budgetary disequilibrium in the 1970s, a reduction in borrowing became the main objective of fiscal policy, and there was a widespread process of budgetary stabilisation. Figure 2.1 and 2.2 plot the unemployment rate and the deficit-to-GDP ratio respectively in Germany, France, Italy and the UK over the 1980s and over the Institute's forecast period. It appears that there was some degree of variation in the budgetary experience of the individual countries in the 1980s. The UK, for instance, saw a marked improvement in the net position of the public sector, which swung into surplus, with the borrowing requirement being renamed public sector debt repayment (PSDR). In France, fiscal policy was initially expansionary, but following the failure of the Mitterrand experiment a much tighter stance was taken. The Italian budgetary position hardly changed, and no significant reduction in the deficit-to-GDP ratio was achieved. In Germany, government current expenditure and also capital transfers were cut, but owing to cyclical factors the budget deficit exhibited little or no change. Although the timing and extent of changes in the fiscal stance differed across countries, there was considerable uniformity in the rise of unemployment, as can be seen from Figure 2.1. In all four countries there was a sharp increase in the early 1980s. This was only partially reversed in the second half of the decade in Germany and the UK, before the number of unemployed shot up again as the new recession started. In France and Italy, unemployment exhibited a higher degree of persistence, and stabilised at a higher level.

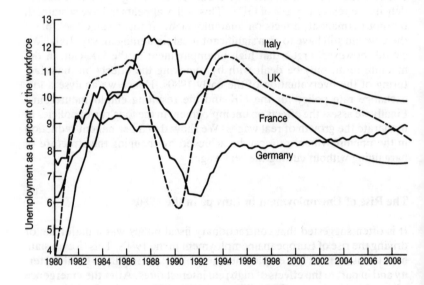

1980–92 figures are data, the remainder are NIESR forecast

Figure 2.1. Past and prospective unemployment in Europe.
Source: Department of Employment Gazette and OECD 'Labour Force Statistics'.

The mirror image of the rise in unemployment was the deceleration of inflation (see Figure 2.3). By the end of the 1980s the rate of increase of prices had slowed down considerably everywhere, and inflation differentials relative to Germany had become much narrower. The better inflation performance of the ERM countries is often attributed to the workings of the ERM. A system of stable exchange rates requires convergence of

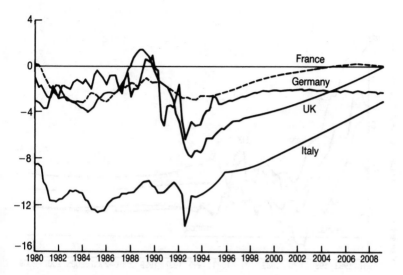

Figure 2.2. Government deficit as a percentage of GDP, 1980–2008.
Source: OECD *Economic Outlook* and NIESR data base and forecast 1980–2008.

prices and inflation, and as the effective anchor of the system is a low-inflation country, Germany, convergence meant reducing inflation in the other ERM countries, which partly involved cutting fiscal deficits. (It must be stressed, though, that much of the convergence achieved can be attributed to the recent increase in the rate of inflation in Germany.)

The deflationary monetary policies adopted in many of the European countries in the 1980s were the results of the constraints of ERM membership, and they could help to provide an explanation for the rise of unemployment throughout Europe. Monetary policy was very tight in France, Italy and the UK in the early and mid-1980s. Real interest rates were at historically high levels, and real exchange rates, especially in France and Italy, were continually held at a high level as part of an ERM-related anti-inflationary stance. In the first few years of the operation of the ERM there were a number of realignments. After 1983 a stable structure of exchange rates in the ERM became an objective for its members, and realignments became less common. However, inflation in France and Italy, for instance, remained above that in Germany, and as a result the initial overvaluations of these currencies worsened. Each realignment was designed to remove part (in fact half) of the worsening in competitiveness

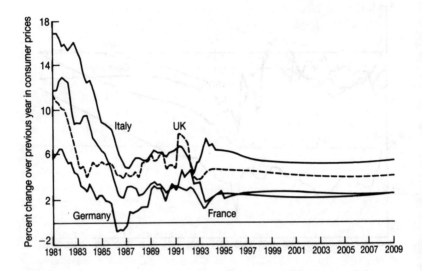

Figure 2.3. Inflation in Europe, 1981–2009, Consumer Expenditure Deflators, OECD Quarterly.

National Accounts and NIESR data base and forecast.

since the previous change in exchange rates. This strategy put continual downward pressure on wage and price inflation, and was a major factor behind the sustained level of high unemployment. The policy was designed to give the authorities 'credibility'. Wage and price-setters were supposed to recognise the reputation and the resolve of the central banks had changed. However, reputation is won only slowly, and the costs of this intentional policy were clearly high.

Realignments ceased for a period after 1987, and overvaluations gradually emerged in both France and Italy. We argued in 1991 that the French franc was 5 to 10% overvalued, and that the Italian situation was marginally worse (see Barrell and in't Veld, 1991). The recessionary impact of these misalignments was offset in part by the upswing in world activity in the late 1980s. The Continental countries also benefited from the boom generated by German unification. The UK benefited from a strong upswing in the late 1980s, but the subsequent recession was exacerbated by the impact of an overvalued exchange rate. Our calculations in 1991 suggested that sterling was overvalued by 5 to 10% when it entered the ERM, and work by Keith Church (1992) suggests that this estimate may have been conservative. Although misalignments of this magnitude were not uncommon under floating exchange rates, the implications were different in a fixed exchange rate regime. The deflationary impact was inevitable. The evidence of the 1980s was that the costs could be considerable.

The unemployment costs of the deflationary policies pursued to achieve nominal convergence with Germany obviously depended upon the perceptions of bargainers in labour markets. A recognition that the exchange rate commitment was permanent could change expectations of inflation, and hence wage settlements. As in most cases anti-inflation reputation was only established, if at all, in the late 1980s (see Weber, 1991), high rates of unemployment prevailed for some time. Furthermore, although markets for a while seemed to have taken the view that exchange rates had become fixed, the fact that the step to a system of fully fixed exchange rates had not been taken meant that interest rates were still reflecting the possibility of further realignments. Sustained overvaluations put considerable political pressure on the ERM. The convergence of inflation did not systematically result in lower interest rate differentials, and hence realised real interest rates were high in France, Italy and the UK. In countries with a weak fiscal position like Italy, where the commitment to a stable exchange rate was not entirely credible, the high real interest rates made the debt burden even heavier. ERM membership and the low inflation policy also implied a shift in deficit finance from money to debt creation. Increasing ratios of debt to GDP resulted in larger risk premia and higher real interest rates, which affected real aggregate demand and employment. In order to reduce the exchange-risk premia in real interest rates, a reduction in budget deficits was sought, with further adverse effects on employment.

The Determination of Unemployment in Europe

The different aims of wage and price setters must be reconciled in the labour market when prices are set as a mark-up on wages by imperfectly competitive firms, and wages as a mark-up on prices in the wage bargain.[1] In equilibrium, the level of unemployment will have to be consistent with a non-accelerating level of inflation, and consequently the 'target' real wage implied by the wage setting behaviour of wage bargainers will have to be consistent with the 'feasible' real wage implied by the pricing behaviour of firms. For instance, let us assume that the 'target' real wage is above its equilibrium level. Then nominal wages must be rising relative to prices. In order to be able to keep their mark-up on prices constant, firms will have to increase prices proportionally, thereby bringing real wages back to their starting level. This spiralling process can only come to an end if the desired mark-up on prices and wages falls as a result of an increase in unemployment.

The bargain will determine the mark-up of the union over the non-union wage, and it will depend upon factors such as the level of unemployment, the relative power of trade unions, and the degree of product market competition.[2] The aggregate wage in the economy will depend, *inter alia*, on these factors, on the proportion of the population covered by bargaining and by the wage in the non-unionised sector. This in turn will depend upon the level of benefits paid to the unemployed and on the other factors affecting the supply of and demand for labour in the secondary sector. There has been considerable debate about the factors affecting the bargained wage and we must be careful to include them in our analysis. In a perfectly competitive market with a fixed labour supply the wage producers' pay would be invariant with respect to changes in direct or indirect taxes in the long run, all of which would have to be paid out of the consumption wage.

Although the establishment of the ERM should not have changed the long-run structure of wage bargaining, it may have affected the dynamic response of wages to prices by changing the structure of the labour market. If the anti-inflationary credibility of the authorities increases, agents have less need to insure themselves against inflation surprises, and it is likely that contracts will be renegotiated less frequently. The abolition of wage indexation mechanisms in Italy, where the *scala mobile* was gradually dismantled, is a good example of this process. The ERM could have affected the dynamic response of wages to prices through many channels, in particular by prompting legislation and institutional developments which changed the environment in which bargains are struck. This took the form of dismantling backward wage indexation systems (e.g. Italy) or reducing the degree of centralisation (e.g. France).

We have argued that fiscal policy was a major factor behind the rise in unemployment in Europe in the 1980s. The speed of response of the economy to a fiscal contraction depends on the dynamics of the wage and price system, and this will depend upon the structure of bargaining. As Lucas (1976) stresses, even the rules of behaviour of the economy may in some sense be endogenous. The frequency with which bargains are struck will depend upon the bargainers' perceptions of the environment within which they find themselves. Re-contracting is an expensive business, and the costs of frequent negotiation have to be offset against the benefits. These will depend in part on the likelihood of expectations being wrong. If bargainers live in a world where inflation is variable and uncertain, then they will prefer shorter contract periods than they would if they lived in a world of constant (or no) inflation. The perception of the world that bargainers hold may depend in part on the actions of the authorities and the credibility of their commitments.

We have undertaken extensive work on wage determination in Europe, and we have concentrated on investigating the differences between the economies as well as looking at the effects on the ERM on wage bargaining. Our research, reported in Anderton, Barrell, in't Veld and Pittis (1992), suggests that there has been very little structural change in

European labour markets in the 1980s. German, French and UK labour markets operate in essentially the same way now as they did in the 1970s and early 1980s. The successful pursuit of low inflation may have raised the standing of European central banks but it does not appear to have affected the nature of bargaining in much of Europe. Credibility has to be won by hard work – it does not descend like manna from heaven. Changes have taken place in the Italian labour market, but their implementation has not been costless. The dismantling of the *scala mobile* has been a slow and painful process.

Our analysis demonstrates that there are significant differences between the European economies. The dynamics of the wage-setting process are very slow, especially in Germany, and this implies that it can take some years for real wages to adjust after a shock. This is particularly important in a world where price adjustment is also slow. A fiscal contraction can push the labour market away from its long-run equilibrium, and this will feed into other markets. In particular we have to take account of the effects of slow adjustment elsewhere. Individuals accumulate assets, and if prices change they will find themselves out of equilibrium. Barrell and in't Veld (1992) stress the extended reactions to asset disequilibrium. A fiscal shock could, we believe, mean that unemployment is away from equilibrium for a decade or more.

All of our empirical work is embedded in our world model. We used NIGEM to look at the level of unemployment which is consistent with a stable rate of inflation in the individual countries in the long run (see Figures 2.1 and 2.3). The unemployment rate settles down at around 9.5% to 10% in Italy, where inflation remains at above 5%. Although the inflation rate is the same in France and Germany in the long run (2.5%), unemployment stays higher in the latter, at around 8.5% to 9%, compared to 7.5% to 8% in the former. The long-run inflation rate of 4% in the UK is lower than in Italy, but higher than in France and Germany, and unemployment converges towards 8% to 8.5%. Our estimates for sustainable unemployment in Germany and France are not very different from the value of 8% for both of them reported in Coe (1985). However, they are much higher in the case of Italy and the UK, where sustainable unemployment is estimated by Coe (1985) to be 6.5% and 6% respectively. These rates of unemployment can be considered as unacceptably high, but they are still well below those we currently observe in Europe. There are policies that we could implement to reduce unemployment in the long run, and some of these are discussed in Britton (1993). They would involve changes in the structure of bargaining and in the distribution of income in society.

Policies to Reduce Unemployment

Most European countries are currently entering a recession, yet they have signed up to the Maastricht Treaty which requires a degree of fiscal contraction. None of the major European economies are expected to achieve the Maastricht target deficit of 3% of GDP in 1993, with overshoots varying between 2% to 3% for the UK, Germany and even France to 8% for Italy. Our forecast, published in our February *Review*, is based on the premise that all these countries will make a valiant effort to achieve the criteria, and that this will keep unemployment high for the rest of the decade. This section investigates the effects of different policies to reduce the unemployment rate, and considers in turn fiscal relaxation, a realignment and slower growth in real wages. In this section we use our model, NIGEM, to analyse the policy options available to Europe.

A permanent rise in the deficit of 1% of GDP

In order to investigate the effects on unemployment of a looser fiscal stance than that implied by the Maastricht convergence criterion concerning budget deficits, we looked at a permanent fiscal expansion by relaxing the government budget deficit ratio target by 1%. It was necessary to make various assumptions on European monetary policy. It was assumed that the ERM was in place, and that the Bundesbank set its domestic interest rates to target a weighted average of German inflation and real GDP growth. The other European countries set their interest rates to stabilize their exchange rate with Germany, assuming arbitrage behaviour of the exchange rates.

Our analysis suggests that output would be higher than in the base case throughout Europe for up to ten years, although some crowding out would take place. The fiscal multipliers on our model are small, in part because import propensities are very high in Europe (see Whitley, 1992). Output gains cannot be expected to be large in response to the fiscal stimulus. In all countries the benefits in terms of reduced unemployment are sustained, as can be seen from Figure 2.4 of unemployment in France. The results are similar for other countries. A similar effect is achieved in other countries with a 1% of GDP fiscal expansion reducing unemployment by 0.5% (compared to what it would otherwise have been) for up to ten years and the increase in the level of inflation is transitory. However, in the long run unemployment converges onto its sustainable rate. This is because demand shocks do not affect the supply-side fundamentals of the labour market. Permanent changes in the level of employment require structural changes in the labour market, such as increased training, greater flexibility or more coordinated bargaining.[3]

Our analysis does not take into account the possible benefits from closer monetary union that might offset to a degree the cost of the fiscal contraction. The reduction in volatility of the exchange rate may have positive effects on output. However, the effect is ambiguous, as the reduction in volatility also reduces the probability of making large profits. Recent empirical studies by Hooper and Kohlhagen (1978) and Cushman (1983) have in fact found little or no correlation between exchange rate volatility and international trade.

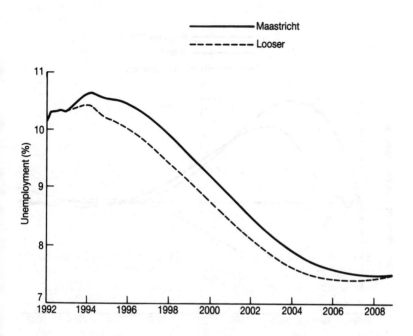

Figure 2.4. The effects of a looser fiscal policy on French unemployment.
Source: As for Figure 2.1.

The effects of a realignment

We argued above that the rise in unemployment in the UK in the early 1980s could be attributed to a large extent to the overvaluation of sterling. Therefore our second simulation aims to show the implications of a lower exchange rate for the economy. A nominal realignment should not change the long-run equilibrium of the economy, because the price level has to change there can be a sustained boost to output. Our results are similar to those described in Pain (1992a) and discussed in the Institute forecast in November 1992 (Pain, 1992b). Figure 2.5 plots the effects of a 10% realignment for the UK with the ERM still in place. Both output and wage inflation rise temporarily and unemployment falls by a point at most, remaining below base for several years. However, this is not a policy option that is really available for Europe as a whole. Increases in output in the UK are offset by declines in output elsewhere. The recent upward realignment of the Mark may be one factor behind the worsening outlook for the German economy.

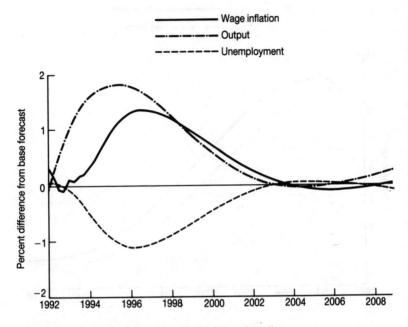

Figure 2.5. The effects of a 10% realignment of sterling.
Source: As for Figure 2.1.

Our empirical work suggests that nominal wages are more rigid in the UK than other EC member countries. Therefore the exchange rate is a more effective instrument than it would be in the other large European economies. In this simulation we have assumed that there is no significant increase in the risk premium after the devaluation, or equivalently the UK authorities are believed when they say that this devaluation is not to be repeated. This implies that there is no reduction in investment to offset the other gains in output.

Moderating the growth in real wages

Expanding demand and devaluation have sustained but ultimately transitory effects. Other policies have then to be pursued to reduce unemployment permanently. There are at least three possible routes. We could change technology in order to substitute labour for capital, we could raise the marginal product of labour by increasing training, allowing more people to be employed at a given real wage. Finally we could subdue the rate of growth of real wages by changing the structure of bargaining. The recent experience of the UK, where in spite of dramatic legislative changes to curtail union power during the 1980s, there were no observable changes to the natural rate of unemployment, suggests that the effects of such a policy are more uncertain. We experimented with reducing the growth of real wages using our model, NIGEM. In our experiment, real wages are 1% lower than they otherwise would have been after 16 years. The effects on unemployment of lower growth in real wages are analysed in Figure 2.6. Unemployment can be reduced by 1% in the long run, and output increases permanently. Inflation drops. In the short run, the deceleration in inflation and the gains in employment are even higher. The positive effect on unemployment comes in part from the effects of lower wages on the demand for labour and in part from the rise in investment that would follow from the increased share of profits in national income. These long-term benefits can be gained by only a short-term (three years) moderation in the growth of real wages, as can be seen from Table 2.1.

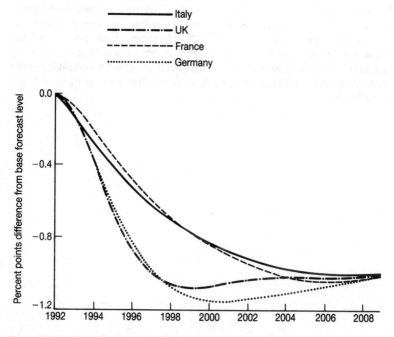

Figure 2.6. The effects of lower real wage growth on European unemployment. Source: As for Figure 2.1.

Table 2.1.   Projected growth in real wages (per cent per year).

	1993 Base	Sim.	1994 Base	Sim.	1995 Base	Sim.
Germany	2.6	0.9	1.2	0.5	−0.8	−0.9
France	0.4	0.0	0.8	0.5	1.3	1.1
Italy	1.7	1.0	0.4	0.2	0.6	0.1
UK	1.2	0.3	0.4	0.0	1.4	1.3

Notes: Values denoted 'Base' are our projections for the relevant years whilst those denoted 'Sim' are our revised projections with more moderate wage growth.

Conclusions

The purpose of this chapter has been to contribute to the policy debate on how to reduce unemployment in Europe by evaluating the effects of alternative policies in the context of a large-scale macroeconomic model. The simulations we carried out using NIGEM suggest that both a looser fiscal stance and a lower exchange rate would have prolonged, but not permanent effects on unemployment. However, permanent gains could be achieved by subduing earnings growth. There does appear to be a role for active demand management policies in combating unemployment, but we cannot expect much to be gained. However, fiscal policy and the reduction of the growth of real wages can both contribute to reducing unemployment. It is clear from our analysis that even if we could leave the problem to market forces, they work so slowly that the transition costs are considerable.

3

On Inflation and Unemployment[1]

Paul Ormerod

The concept of the non-accelerating inflation rate of unemployment (NAIRU) plays a central role in contemporary macroeconomics. The idea is that at any point in time there is a unique level of unemployment at which inflation will neither accelerate nor decelerate. The idea of the NAIRU has been very influential, not just in academic circles, but also with financial journalists and policy-makers. It is used frequently as an argument against policies designed to reduce unemployment.

Despite its dominant intellectual and ideological position within economics, the concept does not lack its critics. In particular, estimates of the NAIRU in any given country seem to correspond fairly closely with the actual levels of unemployment experienced in the recent past.

In the past few years, the problems created for the concept of the NAIRU by the empirical evidence have been such that a number of economists have moved away from the idea of a unique equilibrium rate of unemployment, to one which admits the possibility of multiple equilibria (see, for example, Blanchard and Summers, 1988). Attempts to find evidence of the existence of such equilibria have had mixed results, although the latest attempt by Manning (1992), using British data for 1951–87, supports the view that there are two equilibria for unemployment. In fact, the evidence suggests that, in terms of the relationship between inflation and unemployment, any constant rate of inflation is consistent with *any* constant rate of unemployment (within the range of post-war experience). The concept of the NAIRU is fundamentally flawed.

In most Western economies, the relationship is not in fact between the rate of inflation and the level of unemployment, but between the rate of change of inflation and the rate of change of unemployment. A relationship does exist between the rate of inflation and the level of unemployment, but one which is modified by an arbitrary constant. This is the mathematical implication, obtained by simple integration, of the true, underlying relationship. The arbitrary constant, and hence the precise position of the relationship between inflation and unemployment which holds at any point in time in an individual country is determined by the specific historical behaviour in that country in the recent past.

Economies for much of the time are on solution paths which appear as if the true underlying relationship were between inflation and the level of unemployment. Once settled on such a path, there is no tendency for inflation to accelerate or decelerate over time. But shocks to the system of sufficient size do not merely move the economy up and down a particular path. The whole solution path is shifted in (inflation, unemployment) space. Such impacts, when they occur, take effect very rapidly.

In the post-war period, a weak but stable relationship has existed between the rate of change of inflation and the rate of change of unemployment in a wide range of developed countries. The precise position of this relationship, when placed in (inflation, unemployment) space by integration, is given by reactions to specific events. The oil price shock of 1973–74 and reactions to it can be singled out as by far the most significant post-war event in terms of the relative positions of economies in (inflation, unemployment) space which emerged from it.

An important implication of this analytical approach is that policies which reduce unemployment do not necessarily create inflation. If the economy remains in the same position in (inflation, unemployment) space, there will be an increase in inflation. But if the economy moves to a different path as a result of the policies, it need not. The necessary combination of policies might be hard to get right, but it is not ruled out theoretically.

Inflation and Unemployment in the West, 1952–91: An Overview

An examination of the data in a number of Western countries shows the difficulty of obtaining a stable relationship between the rate of inflation and the level of unemployment over time. This finding is well-documented in the econometric literature, but a more detailed examination of the data is worthwhile. The countries examined are the two major economies, Japan and the United States; the leading European economy, Germany; a range of other European economies which have been in the Exchange Rate Mechanism (France, Italy, the UK, Belgium and the Netherlands); and, for contrast, a Scandinavian country outside the ERM, Sweden. Over the 1952–91 period, a simple correlation of inflation and unemployment in each of these countries reveals the problem at once.[2] Of the nine countries concerned, in only three (Germany, Japan and the Netherlands) does the correlation have the postulated negative sign, and only in the first two of those is the correlation significant at the 5% level. In the other six countries, the point estimate of the correlation is actually positive, and in Sweden and the US this positive correlation is in fact significant at the 5% level. The results are very similar regardless of whether the unemployment rate itself or its log is used. In contrast, the simple correlation between the change in inflation and the change in the log of the unemployment rate gives a negative sign in all nine countries, five of which are significant at the 5% level.

A more detailed examination of the average rates of inflation and average rates of unemployment in the various periods reveals considerably more problems with the potential relationship. The period is divided into six sub-periods, the rationale for which is as follows. The 1968–73 period saw the gradual breakdown of the fixed exchange rate regime of the post-war period, and was the period during which serious problems were first experienced for the orthodox inflation/unemployment relationships. The rest of the 1970s was taken up by the absorption of and reaction to the first oil shock, so we consider 1974–79. The next period saw for the first time unequivocal priority being given to the control of inflation in almost every country, with inflation reaching a low point in most countries in 1986. And the 1952–67 period is split in two, to bring the lengths of the sub-periods onto a similar footing.

Comparing the average rates in the 1952–60 period with those of the 1961–67 period, in every case except France the rate of inflation was higher and the rate of unemployment lower in the latter period. This is consistent with the view of a negative relationship between the rate of inflation and the level of unemployment. The French experience in the 1950s is distorted by the very high rate of inflation (14%) of 1958, a year of very considerable political turmoil and uncertainty in that country. However, the 1968–73 period compared to the 1961–67 period shows serious problems for the orthodox view. In six of the countries, both unemployment and inflation were clearly higher on average in the 1968–73 period. In Germany as well this was the case, although the rise in unemployment was very small. In both Japan and the US, inflation was higher and unemployment lower, but the fall in the latter variable was very small. The experience of the 1968–73 period was repeated in the 1974–79 period, when again both inflation and unemployment in eight countries were higher in the latter period compared to the former. Only in Sweden was inflation higher and unemployment lower.

The average experience of the 1980–86 period compared to 1974–79 appears to restore a negative relationship between inflation and unemployment. Policy responses to the oil price shock in the mid-1970s were mixed. By the early 1980s, though, most governments were giving priority to the control of inflation, which they succeeded in bringing down by depressing their economies and having higher unemployment. In the 1987–91 period, however, problems for the relationship emerge once more. In seven countries, both inflation and unemployment were lower than in the 1980–86 period; only in France and Italy was there a negative relationship.

This overview of the data is sufficient of itself to raise serious doubts not only about the stability of any negative relationship between inflation and

Table 3.1. Average rates of inflation and unemployment (%).

		1952–60	1961–67	1968–73	1974–79	1980–86	1987–91
Germany:	Inflation	1.2	2.7	4.2	5.5	3.5	2.1
	Unemployment	3.9	0.8	0.9	3.6	5.9	5.7
France:	Inflation	4.4	3.4	5.7	10.1	8.7	3.1
	Unemployment	2.0	1.4	2.5	4.5	8.6	9.6
Italy:	Inflation	2.4	4.2	4.9	15.1	12.7	5.6
	Unemployment	7.6	4.5	5.8	6.6	8.9	10.6
Belgium:	Inflation	1.2	2.8	4.4	8.1	5.9	2.5
	Unemployment	4.8	2.3	2.6	6.3	11.3	8.7
The Netherlands:	Inflation	2.4	3.6	6.1	7.0	4.1	1.4
	Unemployment	2.3	1.2	2.1	4.9	10.0	8.3
UK:	Inflation	2.8	3.2	6.4	14.4	7.6	5.4
	Unemployment	1.4	1.7	2.6	4.4	10.6	8.8
Sweden:	Inflation	3.5	4.0	5.1	9.3	8.6	7.0
	Unemployment	1.8	1.6	2.2	1.9	2.8	1.8
US:	Inflation	1.4	1.7	4.8	7.8	5.9	4.3
	Unemployment	4.5	4.9	4.7	6.7	7.8	5.7
Japan:	Inflation	2.7	5.6	6.5	9.5	3.1	1.9
	Unemployment	2.0	1.3	1.2	1.9	2.5	2.4

unemployment, but also about the very existence itself of any such relationship over time.

Inflation and Unemployment, 1952–91: Regression Analysis

In order for a unique NAIRU to exist at any point in time, there must be a relationship between the rate of inflation and the level of unemployment. Examination of the data in Table 3.1 is sufficient to show that even if such a relationship has existed in Western countries, it has been highly unstable. Its very instability leads to serious doubts about the use of the concept in policy analysis. This instability is confirmed by more formal regression analysis. It is not possible to obtain in any of the nine countries a relationship between inflation and the level of unemployment which is stable over the 1952–91 period. Further, the coefficient on unemployment is usually insignificant and of the wrong sign, and in every equation there is very clear misspecification indicated by DW statistics of les than 1. By experimentation, sub-periods can be found for which an apparently well-specified relationship exists between inflation and unemployment, such as for the United States in 1956–64, a period over which a number of initial studies appeared to confirm the existence of a Phillips relationship. But these sub-periods are typically very short, and the equations are unstable outside the sample period.

But the problem with the relationship extends further. The approach which is the current standard in time-series regression work involves a screening of each of the data series in a regression for stationarity. If the series are not stationary, serious doubts are raised about the whole validity of the regression, unless a cointegrating vector exists between a set of variables which individually might not be stationary.

In fact, over the 1952–91 period, in no single country are both inflation and unemployment stationary series.[3] Further, in no single country except the United States is there a cointegrating vector between the two variables.[4] In other words, in almost every country it is not really valid at all to regress inflation on the level of unemployment (or its log) over the 1952–91 period. The sole exception is America, but if the regression is performed for this country, the coefficient on unemployment is positive. For certain sub-periods, cointegrating vectors can be obtained for some but not all countries between inflation and unemployment, but again the resulting regressions are clearly unstable.

In order to obtain a valid regression between inflation and unemployment over the 1952–91 period, lagged inflation must be added to the set of explanatory variables. A cointegrating vector then exists for all countries, although this is still not quite the case for Belgium. But even this is by no means sufficient to produce a satisfactory relationship between the rate of inflation and the level of unemployment. For example, all the regressions indicate clear structural breaks in the relationships around the time of the first oil price shock. Further, in five of these regressions, the coefficient on lagged inflation is not significantly different from one, indicating that the dependent variable should clearly be in difference form. Only in Germany, France, the Netherlands and Japan is this not the case, and in these regressions only in the case of Japan is the coefficient on unemployment correctly signed and significantly different from zero at the 5% level. Moreover, even the apparently well-specified Japanese equation is structurally unstable.

Dividing the sample into two at the time of the first oil shock does not rescue the orthodox inflation/unemployment relationship. In fact, in none of the nine countries is inflation a stationary series over the 1974–91 period, and no cointegrating vector exists between inflation and the rate of unemployment, whether specified as current or lagged, or in levels or log of levels. The same result holds for this sub-period even when lagged inflation is added to the set of explanatory factors. Even if the regression is carried out, in six out of the nine countries there is strong instability in the relationship in 1980/81.

In contrast, it is valid to carry out regressions of the change in inflation on the change in the rate of unemployment, in levels or logs, over the 1952–91 period. Both the change in inflation and the change in unemployment are for the most part stationary, both over the entire sample period and in the two sub-periods divided at 1974, and where this is not the case a cointegrating vector exists between the two. A summary of these regressions is set out in the appendix to this chapter. These equations do not have a great deal of explanatory power. This is to be expected. The model which we have in mind is one of a rather weak, general background law of behaviour, but which can be and is dominated at particular periods by the specific conjuncture of events.

Underlying the relationship is a view of the labour market in which the employed do not really perceive the unemployed as competing for their jobs, regardless of the absolute rate of unemployment. A far more important signal to them in terms of wage bargaining is the rate of change of unemployment, which conveys a great deal of information to the employed about the likely prospects of their own company, its ability to finance pay increases, and the probability of their own job continuing to exist.

Most of the variation in inflation arises from the reaction in each country to specific shocks, and in particular to the oil price shock of 1973/74. For example, the years 1974–83 account for a quarter of the total number of observations over the period 1952–91, yet these years account for more than three-quarters of the total variance in inflation in Italy and the UK, two-thirds in Belgium and the United States, and around a half in Germany, France, Sweden and Japan. The difference in the reaction of different countries to the oil price shock of 1973/74 is extremely important, and the consequences of this are still with us today.

The German economic domination of Europe which has been a feature of the past fifteen years or so owes a great deal to the particular response of the Germans to the oil price shock. In the post-war years to 1974, Germany built a reputation as a low inflation economy, which was recognised in revaluations of the mark as the fixed exchange rate system came to an end. But as Table 3.1 shows quite clearly, the gap in percentage point terms between German inflation and inflation elsewhere in Europe during the twenty-odd years prior to 1974 was not large. After the oil shock, however, the position changed rapidly and dramatically. In 1973, inflation was very similar in a number of European countries: in Germany it was 6.7%, in France 7.1%, in Belgium 6.7% and in the Netherlands 7.7%. The initial reaction in these countries to the oil price shock was very similar, with inflation moving to around 12% in 1974 in each of them, except the Netherlands where it was contained at just under 10%. But by as early as 1975, it is clear that the shock had moved the economies onto different inflation/unemployment paths. In that year, inflation in Germany fell back to only 4.3%, but stayed at 11–12% in France and Belgium, and at just under 10% in the Netherlands.

Looking back at the evidence of Table 3.1, even more diverse shifts are apparent. Over the 1968–73 period, inflation in Italy was barely higher than in Germany, the averages being 4.9% and 4.2% respectively. Even in the UK, inflation only averaged 6.4%. But over the 1974–79 period, whilst inflation in Germany averaged 5.5%, in Britain and Italy the averages were 14.4% and 15.1% respectively. And over this period, compared to the 1968–73 period, unemployment in Germany rose by a very similar amount in percentage points to the European average increase. Thus differing reactions to specific events can be of crucial importance in determining the solution path on which an economy is placed.[5] In summary, the regression evidence across the world is consistent with the view that the true relationship is between the rate of change of inflation and the rate of change of unemployment.

Longer-run Evidence from the United Kingdom

Figures 3.1 and 3.2 plot, respectively, inflation and the rate of unemployment, and the change in inflation and the change in the log of the unemployment rate over the 1872–1992 period (using data from Feinstein, 1972, for the pre-Second World War period). There appears to be a negative relationship in both charts. The reality is more complex. Over the entire period, all four variables are stationary series; excluding the pre-First World War data and the years during and around each war, however, results in no cointegrating vector between inflation and unemployment existing, although the change variables continue to be stationary series. As we saw above, in the post-Second World War period, the same result holds. This initial data screening therefore suggests an instability in the relationship over the long-run.

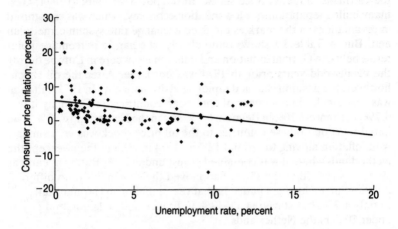

Figure 3.1. Inflation and unemployment in the UK, 1872–1992.

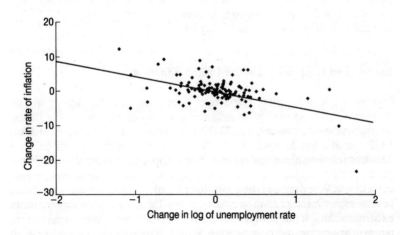

Figure 3.2. Change in inflation and unemployment, UK, 1872–1992.

It is not in fact possible to find a regression linking inflation and unemployment over any length of time after the First World War which is at all satisfactory. Experiments with non-linear terms in unemployment generally yielded even worse results. Using the full data sample, and data before the 1960s, it is possible to obtain a negative sign on unemployment. The equations, however, are very clearly misspecified.[6] The pre-First World War period is an exception, where there is a well-specified relationship between inflation and unemployment:

$$\text{rate of inflation} = 0.018 - 0.00414 * (\text{rate of unemployment}) \tag{3.1}$$
$$(0.005)\ (0.00110)$$
sample:[7] 1872–1913; $\bar{R}^2 = 0.241$; DW = 1.77; Q(3) = 0.67; N(2) = 1.65; RESET(1) = 0.79

A well-specified equation can be found for the change in inflation and the change in unemployment, but it is by no means as powerful. Terms in lagged unemployment and lagged inflation added to equation (3.1) have completely insignificant coefficients. This result confirms the famous finding of Phillips (1958) of a negative relationship between changes in money wages and unemployment, using data from 1861 to 1913. Phillips argued that the relationship was between money wage changes and both the level and rate of change of unemployment. Using the inverse of the level, an equation can be obtained for inflation in which both these terms are significant, and which satisfies most tests of specification. However, there is definite instability in the equation when the sample is divided from around 1890 onwards. This is not the case with equation (3.1).

Phillips did in fact argue that over his data period there was a reduction in the dependence of the rate of change of wages on the rate of change of unemployment, a conclusion which he obtained by a careful analysis of the data, rather than by regression. Present-day techniques enable this finding to be confirmed, since it is the coefficient on the change in unemployment in a Phillips-type specification which is the source of the instability.

Estimating equation (3.1) over the 1923–38 period gives a completely misspecified equation; however, introducing lagged inflation and the change in unemployment gives a well-specified one:

$$\text{rate of inflation} = c + 0.462 * (\text{previous year inflation}) - 0.0049 * (\text{change in unemployment})$$
$$(0.091) \qquad\qquad\qquad (0.00199) \tag{3.2}$$
$$\bar{R}^2 = 0.672;\ DW = 1.971;\ Q(3) = 0.26;\ N(2) = 0.19;\ RESET(1) = 0.02$$

The restriction that unemployment should appear in difference form is not rejected by the data. Further, the inclusion of separate terms for the current rate of unemployment and the rate of unemployment lagged one year worsens the specification of the model. This model is stable according to formal Chow tests for breaks in 1930 and 1931. The model suggests that behaviour was changing in the inter-war period, and the experience of falling nominal prices built inertia into the system. The monetarist critique of Keynesianism which arose from the breakdown of the post-war Phillips curve, argued that 'rational' economic man learned from the experience of inflation and built expectations into his behaviour. In fact, it appears that a fundamental shift in the inflation/unemployment relationship during the inter-war years was based upon 'irrational' opposition to falls in nominal prices and wages.

In Phillips's classic article, he used the relationship he had obtained from 1861–1913 data as a basis for a detailed discussion of the 1913–48 and 1948–57 periods. For certain periods, the model was able to give good predictions. For example, the period 1925–29, for which evidence was used by Phillips to argue that the policy of forcing the price level down failed because of increased resistance to downward movements of wage rates. In fact, a Phillips relationship for inflation gives very accurate forecasts on average for the 1925–29 period, although equation (3.1) is almost as accurate. But both relationships give very poor predictions for years beyond 1929. In general, the original Phillips relationship forecasts poorly outside the 1861–1913 sample period. The evidence in fact points very clearly to different relationships obtaining on average between inflation and unemployment in the pre-First World War, inter-war, and post-Second World War periods. The characteristics of the relationship between inflation and unemployment are summarised in Table 3.2.

Table 3.2. Significant variables in inflation model: evidence from regression.

Variable	Period		
	Pre-First World War	Inter-war	Post-Second World War
Lagged inflation	no	yes	no
Lagged inflation, coefficent = 1	no	no	yes
Unemployment	yes	no	no
Change in unemployment	no	yes	yes

In the post-Second World War period, at any given level of unemployment, the rate of inflation is indeterminate. This pattern of behaviour explains why Kalecki's (1943) conjecture about the inflationary consequences of full employment did not come about. Kalecki believed that it was inevitable under full employment that the 'self-confidence of the working class' would grow and be translated into higher money wage demands, leading in turn to a wage-price spiral. As a result, he argued that the 'assumption that a government will maintain full employment if it only knows how to do it is fallacious', and that industrial leaders would oppose a policy of continuous full employment. Of course, it is possible to argue that Kalecki was ultimately proved right, but the time lag between his prediction and its actual event is one of at least 30 years.

The inflation rate experienced in the 1950s and 1960s was higher than that predicted by equation (3.2), the relationship which characterises the inflationary process in the inter-war period. The constant term in this latter model is effectively zero, so in the absence of large changes in unemployment, inflation over time moves towards zero. From the late 1940s to the late 1960s, inflation averaged just under 3%, but showed no tendency to explode despite continuous full employment.

The inflation rate which obtained over this period was partly a matter of accident. This happened to be the rate at which the economy emerged from the aftermath of the war, being 2.3% in 1949 and 2.7% in 1950. For almost 20 years, these were essentially the rates around which inflation fluctuated. This period is usually thought of as being one from which major shocks were absent. In general this is true, but there was one shock very early in the period which could easily have set the economy on an alto-gether less favourable inflation/unemployment solution path. The response of the labour force to the commodity price shock at the time of the Korean War was very important in preserving this low inflation path. Inflation rose to 9% in 1951, as a result of increases in import prices of 26% and 23% in 1950 and 1951 respectively. However, inflation fell to 5.8% in 1952 and then went back to 'normal' levels in 1953, assisted by a 12% fall in import prices in 1952. Total income from employment and self-employment rose by only 0.7% and 0.6% in real terms in 1951 and 1952 respectively, in other words by hardly more than the rate of inflation. If the workforce had attempted to enforce real increases of 3% a year, a wage-price spiral would have been generated, and the economy would have become locked into a higher inflation path, which could only have been shifted by an abandonment of full employment in the mid-1950s.

The contrast with the response of the workforce to the commodity price shocks of the 1970s is clear. External inflationary pressure was much greater in this period than at the time of the Korean War, but real earnings rose by 4% over the two-year period 1974–5. A large part of this is due to the unusual and highly damaging policy of wage indexation which was in force at the time. The result was a further escalation of costs, and the placing of the economy onto a higher inflation path.

The specific reaction of inflation at different points in time to distinct movements in unemployment is interesting. Table 3.3 sets out the change in inflation in percentage points, and the percentage change in unem-ployment for various periods in which there was a sustained change in unemployment.

Table 3.3 shows that in general, inflation is not particularly sticky either upwards or downwards with respect to changes in unemployment. The evidence suggests symmetrical behaviour with a reasonable degree of flexibility. Although the particular circumstances at any point in time can

Table 3.3. Percentage point change in inflation and percentage change in unemployment, UK.

Period	Change in inflation (% points)	Change in unemployment (%)	col(2)/col(1) (in absolute terms)
1929–31	−3.5	+116	33
1931–37	+7.8	−48	6
1951–53	−7.0	+35	5
1957–59	−2.7	+43	16
1959–61	+2.2	−22	10
1963–65	+3.1	−37	12
1967–71	+5.3	+38	n.a.
1972–75	+15.4	0	n.a.
1975–78	−12.7	+59	5
1980–83	−10.4	+94	9
1987–90/91	+2.2	−29	13

be very important, there is in general a broad stability to the results. A one percentage point change in inflation is brought about on average by around a 10% change in unemployment.

The experience of the 1929–31 period stands out as very different from the rest, inflation falling by only 3.5 percentage points rather than by the 10 or 11 points which would have happened if behaviour had been similar to the average of subsequent experience. Given that inflation was actually negative in 1929–31, the evidence suggests that this is the distinguishing characteristic of the period which explains the exceptionally unfavourable trade-off between inflation and unemployment. Indeed, this resistance to reducing nominal wages and prices explains Keynes's obsession with the downward stickiness of money wage rates, and hence of inflation.

The favourable response of the workforce to the commodity price shock of the early 1950s has been commented on above. Inflation was controlled easily, and brought back down with relatively little change in unemployment. A similar trade-off was achieved in the 1975–78 period, but this time largely through fear. Unemployment rose rapidly to unprecedented post-war levels. But the damage had already been done, by the shock to the solution path which took place during 1974 and early 1975, placing the economy on a much higher inflation path.

The period in the late 1960s and early 1970s does exhibit unusual behaviour, as was noted above in the discussion of post-war experience of inflation in a range of countries. In fact, even over the 1968–74 period, regressing the change in inflation on the change in the log of unemployment gives a coefficient with a negative sign, but one which is very poorly determined, so that factors other than the change in unemployment dominated changes in inflation over this period.

The whole thrust of labour market policy of the British government since 1979 has been to make labour markets 'more flexible'. An important dimension of this has been successive pieces of trade union legislation. If this whole approach had been successful, the inflation/unemployment relationship ought to have improved during the 1980s. But in fact it did not.

Longer-run Evidence from the United States

The pattern of the inflation/unemployment model noted above for the UK in Table 3.2 applies in exactly the same way to the United States. Before the First World War, the rate of inflation was related to the rate of unemployment. In the inter-war period, inertia in the form of lagged inflation becomes important, and unemployment appears as the change in rate, lagged one year. Finally, in the post-Second World War period, the best specification is of the change in inflation on the change in the unemployment rate lagged one year. We simply note here the regression models for the United States, rather than discuss specific historical periods in more detail as was done for Britain (with 'inf' refering to the rate of inflation):

1901–1913:

$$\text{inf} = 0.021 - 2.14\text{E-}05*(\text{rate of unemployment})$$
$$(0.006)\ (6.99\text{E-}06)$$
$$\bar{R}^2 = 0.411;\ DW = 2.112;\ Q(3) = 1.32;\ N(2) = 1.67 \tag{3.3}$$

1921–1938:

$$\text{inf}_t = -0.0072 + 0.414*(\text{inflation})_{t-1} - 0.01*(\text{change in rate of unemployment})_{t-1}$$
$$(0.0065)\ (0.129)\qquad\qquad\qquad (0.0015)$$
$$\bar{R}^2 = 0.739;\ DW = 1.992;\ Q(3) = 1.04;\ N(2) = 1.31;\ RESET(1) = 2.15 \tag{3.4}$$

1953–1991:

$$(\text{change in inf})_t = c - 0.0097*(\text{change in rate of unemployment})_{t-1}$$
$$(0.0022)$$
$$\bar{R}^2 = 0.315;\ DW = 1.760;\ Q(3) = 3.39;\ N(2) = 1.37;\ RESET(1) = 0.61 \tag{3.5}$$

For other countries in the inter-war period, the results are varied. In Germany, once the hyperinflation period is excluded, the effective sample is very short, from 1926 to 1938. Inflation is best represented as a function of lagged inflation and the change in the unemployment rate, just as in Britain and the United States. In contrast, in Belgium over the 1922–38 period, a well-specified relationship exists between inflation and the log of unemployment. In the Netherlands, the data offer no evidence of the existence of inertia, but inflation depends upon the change in the log of unemployment and not its level.

Conclusions

This chapter has analysed the relationship between inflation and unemployment in nine OECD countries over the 1950–91 period, and the longer-run evidence for the UK from 1870 to 1991, for the US from 1900 to 1991, and for Germany, Belgium and the Netherlands for the inter-war period. A variety of analytical techniques was used, from simple screening of the data to cointegration tests between variables. The relationship between inflation and unemployment has altered over time. Before the First World War, a classic Phillips relationship between inflation and unemployment obtained in the UK and the US. In the inter-war period, inertia entered the process, as the labour force resisted cuts in nominal wages. Inflation is represented as a function of lagged inflation and the change in unemployment. A similar relationship holds for Germany, excluding for obvious reasons the hyperinflation period. The evidence suggests very clearly that in the post-Second World War period there are very serious problems with the traditional relationship between the rate of inflation and the level of unemployment, which is the relationship required to hold in order for the concept of the NAIRU to be valid.

In contrast, there has been a stable relationship in each of the countries examined between the rate of change of inflation and the rate of change of unemployment. There are two main implications of this finding. First, for any given level of unemployment, the rate of inflation is indeterminate. There is not a unique rate of unemployment which is compatible with stable inflation. In other words, the NAIRU does not exist. The fact that the underlying, background relationship is between the rates of change of inflation and unemployment implies that there is a relationship between inflation and the level of unemployment, but one which contains an arbitrary constant term. Second, once a particular solution path for the economy is specified – once the arbitrary constant is chosen – changes in the rate of unemployment will impact on the rate of inflation in a similar fashion, regardless of the initial rate of unemployment which obtains. But there is no tendency for inflation to accelerate or decelerate over time on such paths in the way in which many monetarist economists allege.

A large part of the variability of inflation is accounted for by shocks such as the commodity price boom of the early 1970s, culminating in the oil price rise of 1973/74, which jolted the OECD countries very rapidly onto a wide variety of solution paths. The specific reactions in each country to events such as the oil price rise have been very important in determining the subsequent inflationary experience of a country. Once a country becomes set on a high inflation path compared to other countries, its relative position, for that given path, can only be altered by an increase in unemployment. The prime aim of anti-inflation policy should be to shift the economy from one inflation/unemployment path to another. In other words, to administer a favourable shock to the underlying relationship between the rate of change of inflation and the rate of change of unemployment. The conventional view that the underlying relationship is between the rate of inflation and the level of unemployment, in which a unique value of the NAIRU exists, is one which seriously misleads policy-makers.

One possibility is to shock the system from one path to another by draconian measures. In recent British experience, this could have been one potential outcome of joining the ERM, although it was clear rather rapidly that the experiment had failed. An alternative is to try to create a set of values in which a system of social consensus and cohesion prevails. This is a task which ranges far beyond the narrow confines of conventional economic policy; economic policy is far too important to be left to economists. Given the experience of the 1980s, the creation of such a framework of behaviour is a challenging task. But the incentive to succeed is high. Once the true relationship between inflation and unemployment is understood, it can be seen that with luck and skill, a free lunch *is* possible.

Appendix: Regressions of the Change in Inflation on the Change in Unemployment, 1953–91

All the regressions include a constant term. In each of them, the constant is a very long way from being statistically significantly different from zero, and hence is not reported. The dependent variable in each of the regressions is the second difference of the log of the consumer price index. The explanatory variable is the first difference of the unemployment rate lagged one period in Germany, the Netherlands and the United States; the first difference of the log of the unemployment rate in Italy and Japan; and this latter variable lagged one period in Belgium, France, Sweden and the UK.

Country	Coefficient and standard error on unemployment variable	$\bar{R}^2$	Q(3)
Germany	−0.009 (0.004)	0.093	5.32
France	−0.071 (0.040)	0.055	0.96
Italy	−0.061 (0.029)	0.081	0.91
Belgium	−0.025 (0.013)	0.065	4.54
The Netherlands	−0.005 (0.003)	0.037	13.60
UK	−0.076 (0.017)	0.324	2.33
Sweden	−0.061 (0.020)	0.184	2.62
United States	−0.010 (0.002)	0.315	3.39
Japan	−0.158 (0.041)	0.268	1.17

All these equations except that for Italy satisfy a formal F-test for a structural break in each year from 1960 through 1982. There is a general tendency for the absolute value of the coefficient on the unemployment variable to be higher in the 1974–91 period than in the 1953–73 period, but not significantly so. In the unrestricted form of these equations – in which inflation is regressed on lagged inflation and on current and lagged unemployment (levels or logs of levels) – the hypothesis of no structural break in 1974 is decisively rejected for all countries. The sole exception is the United States, where the equation specified in this form is almost identical to the restricted equation reported above.

4

Labour Market Institutions, Industrial Restructuring and Unemployment in Europe

Peter Nolan

Labour market institutions have featured prominently in recent theoretical and empirical studies of comparative economic performance (e.g., Calmfors and Driffill, 1989). Assessments of Europe's recent record and future prospects commonly stress the formidable obstacles inhibiting the 'spontaneous' dynamics of output and employment growth. Among the barriers frequently cited are the allegedly rigid labour market institutions which are said to characterise the central European and Nordic economies. The corollary of this line of argument is that wherever attempts have been made to root out sources of (labour) market rigidity (e.g., in the United States and Britain) employment and productivity gains have followed.

Drawing upon recent developments in Britain and Germany, this chapter advances a different interpretation of the connections between labour market and industrial relations institutions, industrial performance and employment outcomes. The comparative focus is intended to highlight the elements and effects of two competing developmental strategies: the neo-liberal (British) route on the one hand, and the neo-corporatist (German) model on the other. While the main focus of the analysis which follows is on supply-side relationships, it is acknowledged that the current deflationary demand policy bias which dominates the economies of Europe remains a major fetter on employment growth.

Eurosclerosis: Dimensions and Reference Points

The sharp rise in unemployment and the generalised slowdown in output and productivity growth in Europe in the 1980s, rekindled interest in comparative labour market institutions. Many economists in this context

drew adverse comparisons between the allegedly 'rigid' structures perva-
sive in Europe and the more 'flexible' unregulated markets of the United
States (e.g., Minford, 1990). Rapid union membership decline, the
absence of statutory employment regulations and weak welfare programmes, the argument ran, aided the job creation process in the United
States, whereas in Europe the enduring, and in some cases increasingly
strident presence of unionism and other sources of rigidity in the labour
market have inhibited industrial restructuring and the emergence of new
sources of employment.

Such broad-brush comparisons tend to be misleading in two critical
respects. First, the employment and performance gains associated with
union membership decline under the Reagan and Bush administrations
tend to be overstated; and second, the considerable diversity of labour
market institutions, and their associated employment impacts within and
between the countries of Europe, are often understated. The variation in
unemployment rates is described in Table 4.1.

Table 4.1. Unemployment in Europe as a percentage of total
labour force.

	1960	1974	1980	1985	1990
UK	1.3	2.1	5.6	11.5	5.5
Germany	1.0	2.1	3.2	8.0	6.2
France	1.4	2.8	6.3	10.2	9.0
Italy	5.5	5.3	7.5	10.1	10.8
Sweden	1.7	2.0	2.0	2.8	1.5
Total OECD Europe	2.9	3.7	6.3	10.3	7.8

Source: OECD *Historical Statistics 1960–1990*, Table 2.15.

A closer examination of the evidence for the United States suggests that
the conventional wisdom is misleading on at least three counts. First,
unregulated labour markets and weak unionism do not necessarily correlate with low unemployment. The union membership decline pre-dated
Reagan, as did the retreat from social welfarism, yet throughout the 1970s
unemployment in the United States exceeded the European average (see
Table 4.2). More crucially, the employment gains after 1986 were secured
primarily through the proliferation of low-wage, low-productivity, part-
time service sector jobs in personal and recreation services (Appelbaum
and Schettkat, 1991). Since such sectors have never been associated with a
strong union presence it is clearly implausible to attribute recent employment gains to the unions' declining fortunes.

Second, Freeman (1988) has exposed major weaknesses in the research

Table 4.2.   Unemployment as a percentage of total labour force.

	1960	1974	1980	1985	1990
EC	2.4	2.9	6.2	11.0	8.5
USA	5.4	5.5	7.0	7.1	5.4
Japan	1.7	1.4	2.0	2.6	2.1

Source: OECD *Historical Statistics 1960–1990*, Table 2.15.

evidence purporting to show that unemployment is higher and economic growth lower in highly unionised states. After controlling for previously omitted variables, Freeman found 'no consistent relation between union density and the proportion of the working-age population that is employed'. Indeed, 'the economics of several unionised states such as New York or Massachussetts performed better than those of weakly unionised states such as Texas or the Carolinas' (Freeman, 1988: 707).

Third, and more broadly, evidence of the increasing salience of low-wage, low-productivity employment throughout the economy, including manufacturing, and the stagnation of per capita incomes since the mid-1980s, strongly suggests that employment growth in the United States has been secured at the expense of technological dynamism and greater industrial efficiency (Harrison and Bluestone, 1990). The comparative data on trends in manufacturing trade certainly support this interpretation. Between 1984 and 1987 the United States' share of total OECD exports of high technology, high value added manufactured goods fell from 25% to 21%. By contrast, the four largest industrial countries of Europe (France, Germany, Italy and the UK) increased their share from 32% to 35% (Hughes, 1993).

A more disturbing picture of Europe's comparative record emerges when Japan, rather than the United States, is chosen as the relevant reference point. Industrial productivity in Japan has increased by leaps and bounds since the 1960s, averaging 5.1% over the past three decades, and more than 7% annually in manufacturing. Nevertheless, as Table 4.2 indicates, the rate of unemployment has remained very low, averaging around 2.5% throughout the 1980s. With manufacturing output growing more or less in line with productivity, there has been no immediate pressure for a massive labour 'shake-out', similar to that experienced in the United States and the leading European countries in the 1980s.

Rapid growth of exports to other OECD countries helped sustain the expansion of industrial output and employment. In 1970 Japan and Britain each held approximately 11% shares of total world trade in manufactures, but by 1990 Japan's share was twice that of Britain's. Moreover, in contrast to the United States, which has experienced a declining share of exports in high technology products, Japan's share of these expanding markets has grown rapidly. The result is that Japan enjoys a substantial trade surplus in high and medium technology products. Tables 4.2 and 4.3 trace out the employment consequences. What emerges is a record of rapid manufacturing employment decline in Europe, with 15% of the workforce displaced between 1979 and 1990, while in Japan the corresponding figure was a mere 2%.

Table 4.3. Employment in manufacturing as a percentage of civilian employment.

	1960	1974	1980	1985	Percentage change 1980–90
USA	26.4	24.2	22.1	18.0	−19
Japan	21.3	27.2	24.7	24.1	−2
UK	38.4	34.6	30.2	22.5	−25
Germany	34.3	35.8	33.9	31.5	−7
France	27.3	28.3	25.8	21.3	−17
Italy	24.2	28.0	26.8	22.5	−16
Sweden	31.5	28.3	24.2	21.1	−9
Total OECD Europe	27.3	28.0	25.9	22.1	−15

Source: OECD *Historical Statistics 1960–1990*, Table 2.11.

Commentators on the Japanese production system, for example Cowling (1989), have ascribed its success to the existence of strong quasi-state institutions, such as the Ministry of International Trade and Industry (MITI). According to Cowling (1989), MITI has played a crucial part in promoting supply-side improvements, essentially by planning and coordinating restructuring and guiding 'the longer term evolution of the economy'. The lesson for Europe is clear: it 'needs an institution, or institutions, dedicated to thinking strategically about the economy . . . The supranational position of the EC can provide the institutional arrangements whereby competitive and self-defeating national strategies can begin to be avoided' (Cowling, 1989: 29–30).

By contrast, Boyer (1988) warned that the prospects for cooperative coordination and 'consensus growth' strategies would inevitably dwindle in the event of a deepening international recession: and so it has proved. Pressures for fragmentation and rivalry have dominated the forces for cooperative coodination. The Exchange Rate Mechanism débâcle, and the growing (and legitimate) fear of 'social dumping' – exacerbated by the British government's entrenched opposition to the Social Chapter – are but two recent expressions of this tendency.

An important aspect of Cowling's case for collective action at European level is the pre-eminent position of transnational corporations, which he rightly argues threatens to subvert democratic processes and erode the material interests of local, regional and national communities (Cowling, 1989). Recent examples of 'competitive bidding' for foreign investment and the outbreak of national chauvinism – for example, following the Hoover company's threatened withdrawal from France and proposed relocation to Scotland – illustrate the extent of the problem. Yet it is hard to see how, in the presence of enduring variations in skill, technology, and standards of labour protection across Europe, destructive 'self-interest' politics and related pressures to 'level down' worker rights and conditions might be averted. A central issue thus is whether or not such pressures can best be checked at national or European level.

Labour Markets and Industrial Performance

Whatever the prospects for a coordinated European industrial and employment growth strategy, it is clear that the approach of the single market gave employers a renewed impetus to achieve cost-cutting changes in production. The past decade in consequence has been characterised by major shifts and transformations in work organisation, in the nature, scope and boundaries of internal labour markets, and in the substantive content and character of industrial relations. Union membership and influence have declined in most countries – Sweden and Finland are the notable exceptions – thus providing opportunities for employers and governments to redefine the character of the employment relationship and the scope and agenda of collective bargaining.

Within the context of these broader changes, however, the pattern of labour market restructuring at national level has exhibited considerable diversity. Fragmentation and de-collectivisation processes have for example been most pronounced in Britain. The latest survey evidence, as interpreted by Brown (1993), points to 'a substantial contraction in the coverage of collective agreements, the narrowing in the scope of collective bargaining, the decline in the depth of union involvement and the erosion of unions' organisational security' (Brown, 1993: 189). The coverage of collective agreements, which encompassed three-quarters of all employees in 1973, has fallen drastically and in 1990 influenced the wages and conditions of less than half the workforce.

By contrast, in Germany, Italy and Sweden, the drive for enhanced workforce flexibility and productivity has been pursued while maintaining broadly intact the framework of collective labour market and industrial relations institutions elaborated in the previous expansionary phase. What have been the employment consequences of these differing patterns of labour market restructuring?

Figure 4.1 describes for the major OECD countries the relationship

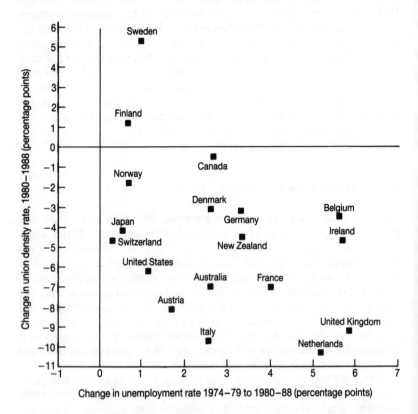

Figure 4.1. Changes in unemployment and union density, 1980–88.
Source: OECD *Employment Outlook*, July 1992, Chart 4.2.

between changes in unemployment and union density between 1980 and
1988. It reveals that heavily unionised countries, like Sweden and Finland,
have outperformed Britain, the Netherlands and France, where unionism
has shown a marked decline. At the very least, such evidence challenges
the argument that unionism *per se* necessarily inhibits employment
growth. More importantly, it calls for a more subtle analysis of the
complex connections between labour market institutions, industrial
restructuring and employment outcomes. The diverse experiences of
Britain and Germany are cited below in an attempt to unravel the relevant
relationships.

Britain

The Thatcher government's strategy for industrial renewal in Britain placed the reform of the labour market and industrial relations system centre stage. The erosion of trade union 'power and privileges' was seen as an essential precondition for employment growth.

Accordingly, a complex set of legislative reforms was introduced, roughly on a two-year cycle, with the clear intention of eroding the social power of unions and increasing managerial control of industrial relations. Among other things, the legislation served to undermine the closed shop, outlaw secondary picketing and sympathetic strikes, introduce compulsory pre-strike ballots and narrow the purposes for which 'legitimate' industrial action could be taken. These tough anti-union laws were accompanied by further measures to deregulate the labour market, and to free employers from the 'rigid' collective structures of employment regulation which had prevailed prior to 1979. What were their employment consequences, and did they succeed in spurring industrial renewal?

The evolution of Britain's employment structure under Mrs Thatcher parallels in important respects developments in the United States under Presidents Reagan and Bush. Key elements include the rapid growth of low-paid, part-time service sector jobs, particularly after 1985, and the accelerating decline of manufacturing and industrial employment. In 1979, more than 7 million employees worked in manufacturing – approximately a third of the labour force – yet in 1993 the figure is close to 4 million.

Encouraged by evidence of surging productivity gains in manufacturing, some analysts took the view that the Thatcher years marked a critical turning point in Britain's post war economic history. The massive shakeout of labour from industry was interpreted as the inevitable consequence of years of managerial neglect and the consequent proliferation of output restrictions by labour. A period of labour 'dishoarding' thus was judged long overdue.

Against this view stands the compelling evidence of the wholesale destruction of large sections of manufacturing industry – much of which was toppled by the sharp intensification of liquidity constraints in the early 1980s, rather than by underlying structural deficiencies (Oulton, 1987) – which in turn led to a deteriorating trade balance. It is clear that the scrapping of apparently unviable productive capital and labout in the early 1980s did little to stimulate a new positive phase of output, investment and capacity growth. Indeed, throughout the 1980s investment in new plant, techniques and labour force skills increased relatively slowly, and failed to reinstate pre-1979 trends.

The much-vaunted productivity 'miracle' of the 1980s – which in any case never extended to private services, where growth has averaged little more than 1% per annum – seemed to derive primarily from the application of more intensive work regimes, which may or may not prove sustainable, and piecemeal changes in work organisation and production technique (Nolan, 1989b). Within the broader international context, moreover, Britain's role as a relatively low-wage, low productivity economy appears to have been consolidated (see Table 4.4).

Table 4.4.   Labour costs and unit labour costs in 1987, whole economy.

	Lab. cost/ employee- (% of EC average)	Unit labour cost	Employees (000)	GDP (Bn Ecu)
Belgium	114.9	105.9	3,044	120.4
Denmark	114.7	109.6	2,302	87.9
Germany	122.1	104.0	22,643	969.5
Greece	44.0	75.4	1,932	41.1
Spain	73.7	88.8	8,303	251.3
France	118.5	102.8	18,166	764.1
Ireland	89.2	104.4	818	25.5
Italy	101.5	87.0	15,499	659.2
Luxembourg	115.7	122.5	151	5.2
Netherlands	127.6	104.0	4,130	184.9
Portugal	26.6	86.7	2,851	31.9
UK	77.0	107.3	22,174	580.1
EUR	100.0	100.0	102,013	3,721.2

Source: Marsden and Silvestre (1992).
Note: Labour cost (compensation) includes gross wages and salaries, employers' actual social contributions, and imputed social contributions; unit labour costs are calculated as labour costs per 1,000 Ecu GDP.

The restructuring of labour market institutions, particularly the weakening of the collective institutions of labour, has helped consolidate these adverse trends (Nolan, 1989a). The availability of a relatively cheap, easily disposable and segmented workforce in Britain has entrenched a particular pattern of foreign direct investment, skewed towards low-skill and low-productivity activities, which has served to reproduce and amplify long-standing structural weaknesses.

Germany

The form and consequences of restructuring in Germany offer a striking contrast. Flexibility and sustainable productivity gains have been sought without a major employers' offensive against collective institutions. In contrast to Britain, bargaining between unions and employers in Germany is still concentrated at industry level and generally serves the purpose of setting a 'floor' to wages and conditions. The agreements which emerge from these multi-employer bargaining arrangements tend to be set with a view to the performance and productivity of the average enterprise in each sector, but in more profitable companies negotiations at works council level may lift pay above the average. Flexibility is thus possible within a system in which collective agreements and regulations remain dominant.

Industrial performance in Germany, prior to unification, was arguably the strongest of all the European economies. Employment in manufacturing industry remains relatively high, certainly by British standards, at around 32% of the total employed workforce, which is only slightly down from a mid-1970s peak of 35%. Productivity levels exceed Britain's by an average of 22%, which is only slightly lower than the comparable figure for 1968 (25%), and the most recent authoritative research (O'Mahony, 1992) attributes the differential to variations in levels of human and physical capital. The differential was found to be most pronounced in the engineering sector, and least apparent in relatively low-technology, low-skill industries such as food and drink and textiles, in which Britain retains a strong international presence and remains attractive as a site of low-wage production for transnationals.

The competitive advantage which Germany derives from its relatively high productivity levels is largely eclipsed, however, by its relatively high labour costs and social charges. Table 4.4 indicates that while the total cost (wages and social charges) of labour in Germany is about 22% above the European average, unit labour costs are only marginally above the average. The contrast with Britain could scarcely be more striking. Britain's labour costs are less than 80% of the European average, yet unit labour costs exceed those of Germany. The difference in cost structures is accounted for by the fact that Germany has sought to compete on the basis of high wages and high productivity, rather than emulate Britain's low-wage, low-productivity route. What combination of labour market and industrial relations institutions accounts for this record of relative industrial success?

Streeck's compelling account of the connections between the labour market, the pattern of industrial restructuring and the performance consequences represents a powerful challenge to the conventional account of the sources of Eurosclerosis. In particular, he argues that the high-quality, high value added production system – what he terms 'diversified quality production' – emerged in Germany precisely because of the existence of powerful and binding 'institutional constraints'.

Especially significant, according to Streeck, was the presence of strong workplace-based trade unions with the organisational capacities to force companies to pursue a strategy of continuous modernisation and improvement. Other vital ingredients which he lists include: a system of 'rigid' wage determination, which forced employers to 'adapt their product range to non price competitive product markets capable of sustaining a high wage level'; a legally enforceable system of employment protection that promotes internal flexibilities and a commitment to invest in training and retraining; and 'a set of binding rules' compelling employers to consult with their employees 'and seek their consent above and beyond what many or most would on their own find expedient' (1986: 22–3; 1991: 52–3).

Proponents of the conventional wisdom would automatically condemn the above system of rules and constraints as a fetter on economic efficiency. Streeck, by contrast, argues that their net effect has been to induce 'a virtuous circle of upmarket industrial restructuring' (1991: 54). By blocking 'quick-fix' solutions, and by blocking low-wage routes to profitability, this framework of rules and institutions has 'forced, induced and enabled' managements to embark on more demanding design, production and marketing strategies.

Streeck's account is buttressed by Appelbaum and Schettkat's comparative study of employment dynamics and labour force restructuring in Germany and the United States. 'The picture that emerges, of a very rapid and dynamic restructuring of the West German labour market economy, is quite different from the usual view and raises serious questions about the hypothesis that labour market structures in West Germany are too rigid' (Appelbaum and Schettkat, 1991: 156).

The relatively dynamic German production system has not only proved compatible with high levels of employment in manufacturing – a feature which marks it off from the experience of all other European economies, although not Japan – it has also helped facilitate the growth of service sector employment. Moreover, the growth in service sector employment in Germany, which as a proportion of the total workforce is not far out of line with the United States, has not been achieved at the expense of the growth of marginal, insecure part-time employment. 'Just 6.6% of wage and salary earners were on schedules of less than 21 hours in 1987' – the other 93.4% qualifying for full entitlement to the German social insurance system (Appelbaum & Schettkat, 1991: 153).

The key point to emerge from this brief discussion is not that Germany bucked the European trend towards higher unemployment, but rather that it is less severely constrained by trade and supply-side weaknesses, and hence more able to expand (output and employment) in the event of the resumption of growth in Europe and the world economy.

Conclusions

Economists have responded to the accumulating evidence of the symptoms of Eurosclerosis (low productivity growth and rising unemployment) by calling for measures to increase the flexibility of labour markets and bring them more in line with the conditions prevailing in the United States. Policies aimed at removing so-called labour market rigidities have been vigorously pursued in Britain by four successive Conservative governments since 1979, yet with no evident benefit for the unemployed. At the beginning of the 1980s there was a threefold increase in unemployment, prompted by a spectacular collapse in output, particularly in manufacturing. Since then employment in manufacturing industry has continued to decline, while service sector, particularly part-time employment has grown rapidly. Yet this structural shift has been achieved without major improvements in industrial competitiveness and efficiency and as a result Britain has continued to lose ground in international markets. The resulting deterioration in the trade balance has become a major constraint on the government's economic policy and a formidable obstacle to employment-generating policies.

Evidence from Germany highlights the fact that employment and industrial restructuring can be successfully achieved within a labour market context supportive of job security and high wages. The high-productivity, high-wage regime in German manufacturing has not resulted in a deteriorating trade payments situation – as Britain's deindustrialisation has – and has actually helped facilitate the growth of service sector employment. Moreover, as noted above, only a relatively small proportion of these service jobs are part-time and fall outside of the scope of the social insurance system.

The contrast between the German and British employment experiences cannot be understood without reference to industrial performance and the broader policy regimes which have conditioned the pattern and processes of employment restructuring in the two countries. This chapter has argued that the relatively dynamic, high-productivity and high-wage German production system has been sustained despite the existence of numerous 'rigidities' and regulations in the labour market. The neo-liberal policy regime which, among other things, has sought to promote employment growth in Britain by waging an offensive against collective and individual employment rights, trade unions, wages councils and other apparent obstacles has failed to produce the renewal of Britain's industries and stem the tide of rising unemployment.

PART II

Lessons and Prospects

5

Depression and Recovery: Lessons from the Interwar Period[1]

Michael Kitson and Jonathan Michie

> The gold standard, with its dependence on pure chance, its faith in 'automatic adjustments', and its general regardlessness of social detail, is an essential emblem and idol of those who sit in the top tier of the machine. I think that they are immensely rash in their regardlessness, in their vague optimism and comfortable belief that nothing really serious ever happens. (Keynes, *The Economic Consequences of Mr Churchill*, 1925.)

This chapter considers the development of high and persistent unemployment during the interwar period, focusing, as in other studies (Temin, 1989; Eichengreen, 1992), on the effects of different policy regimes. From the mid-1920s the world economy embraced the gold standard as a framework for exchange rate policy. We argue that this system slowed world growth during the late 1920s and exacerbated the Great Depression of 1929–32. The subsequent demise of the gold standard enabled many individual countries to implement independent policies which stimulated economic expansion. Despite a cyclical upswing, however, the legacy of the Great Depression remained in the form of persistent unemployment.

As with recent experience in the Exchange Rate Mechanism (ERM) the experience of the gold standard indicates that there are serious dangers, as well as potential benefits, in entering 'cooperative' systems with fixed exchange rates. Such systems may limit the ability to deal with domestic problems, encourage strong countries to grow relatively stronger and weak countries to grow relatively weaker and ultimately become non-sustainable. Similarly, destructive cooperation risks being accelerated by the provisions of the Maastricht Treaty which not only removes discretion over national monetary and fiscal policy but removes any possibility of currency realignment.

This chapter is in four sections: first we consider the extent of the unemployment problem in the interwar world economy; we then evaluate the operation of the gold standard and its deflationary bias; next we consider the benefits of leaving the gold standard, including the freedom to adopt expansionary policies; and finally we highlight some lessons for current policy formulation.

The Unemployment Problem

That mass unemployment was a major problem in the interwar world economy is not a matter of great debate. Measuring the extent of the problem is more. Figure 5.1 shows contemporary (ILO, 1940) estimates of world unemployment which, under the impact of recession, increased to nearly 25% in 1932 before falling during the 1930s, although the level remained high; unemployment averaged 17.5% during 1930–32, and 15% during 1932–37. An alternative measure of labour market performance is employment change, which is subject to less of the problems associated with estimating unemployment. Figure 5.1 therefore also shows world

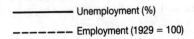

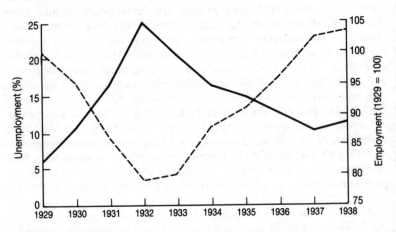

Figure 5.1. World employment and unemployment, 1929–38.
Source: ILO (1940) Table 3.
Notes: 1. Employment index excludes the USSR.
2. Unemployment series is the average of two series (A and B) presented in ILO (1940).

employment which, from the peak in 1929 to the trough in 1932, declined at an annual rate of 7.6%. Employment growth was rapid from 1932: the annual increase was 5.2%, although it was not until 1937 that employment surpassed its 1929 level.

Comparisons of national levels of unemployment are complicated by definitional problems and the paucity of consistent data. Table 5.1 provides a summary of the data from two of the main sources: Galenson and Zellner's (1957) estimates of industrial unemployment and Maddison's (1991) estimates of industry-wide unemployment.[2] The data are averaged over three periods: the period of moderate growth in the late 1920s, the period of peak unemployment during 1930–32, and the recovery period 1933–37. As shown in Table 5.1, Galenson and Zellners's estimates tend to be twice those of Maddison for the European economies and 50% greater for the other countries. The different definitional basis of the data are discussed in Eichengreen and Hatton (1988), who conclude that actual economy-wide estimates of unemployment lie somewhere between the two sets of estimates.[3]

There are further problems in comparing unemployment performance over time as methods of data collection change. This is illustrated in

Table 5.1. Average unemployment rates, 1924–37 (%).

	Maddison's estimates			Galenson and Zellner's estimates		
	1924–29	1930–32	1933–37	1924–29	1930–32	1933–37
Europe						
Austria	6.0	10.1	15.3	—	—	—
Belgium	6.4	8.6	8.2	1.3	11.2	15.7
Denmark	8.6	10.7	11.2	17.1	21.1	22.4
France	—	—	—	4.2	8.0	12.0
Finland	1.8	4.8	3.9	—	—	—
Germany	5.1	13.5	7.4	11.4	33.6	18.4
Italy	—	4.2	5.5	—	—	—
Netherlands	2.1	5.0	10.6	6.7	16.0	29.2
Norway	6.4	8.6	8.2	17.7	23.2	25.6
Sweden	2.6	5.0	6.1	11.0	17.0	15.9
UK	7.5	13.7	10.7	10.8	19.8	15.2
Rest of World						
Australia	5.9	16.7	12.6	8.1	24.3	15.8
Canada	3.1	12.8	14.0	4.8	18.8	19.1
USA	3.7	16.0	19.5	5.7	25.2	29.4

Sources: Maddison (1991) and Galenson and Zellner (1957) and Lebergott (1964), as reproduced in Eichengreen and Hatton (1988).

Figure 5.2, which presents two series of unemployment data for the UK
for the period 1921–92, one based on standard data and the other based on
more recent methods of counting (see Crafts, 1991). The adjusted figures
suggest that contrary to accepted opinion the extent of unemployment was
greater in the 1980s than during the Great Depression; on this basis, UK
unemployment reached 11.1% in 1986, compared with 10.6% in 1932.

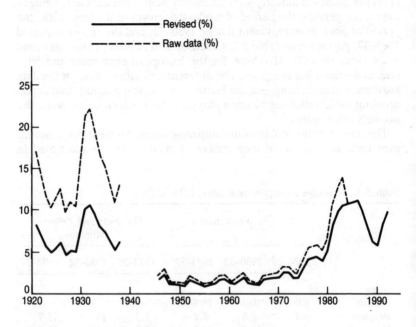

Figure 5.2.   Unemployment rates in the UK, 1921–92.
Sources: Crafts (1991) Table 41.3, p. 818 and Department of Employment, *Employment Gazette* (various editions), London: HMSO.

The limitations of the data cannot disguise the fact that unemployment
was a major economic and social problem during the inter-war period.
Unemployment was a major cause of poverty, driving families below the
most basic of subsistence levels and leading to deteriorating health (Harris, 1988).[4]

Whichever series is used, it is also evident that the major surge in
unemployment came during the Great Depression, reaching a peak in
1932. The behaviour of unemployment in the 1930s depended on the
strength of economic revival; however, what is apparent is that despite
economic recovery and rising employment, unemployment was a problem
that persisted in many of the major economies.

Coordination and Deflation: The Gold Standard

From the mid-1920s, the cornerstone of international economic management was the gold standard. Founded on the questionable success of the classical gold standard (see Panić, 1992), in operation during the quarter century before the First World War, the 1920s variant was intended to bring stability into international trading relations and increase world prosperity.[5] It failed to achieve these objectives. The system depended on nominal convergence; its actual effect was to depress real variables such as output and employment and undermine the capacity of individual governments to deal with domestic economic problems.

As shown in Figure 5.3, the restoration of the gold standard progressed throughout the 1920s. Austria stabilised in 1922, Germany and Sweden in 1924, Britain, Switzerland and the Netherlands in 1925, France and Belgium in 1926, and Italy and Poland in 1927. By 1927 the vast majority of trading nations had joined the system, and the reconstruction of the fixed exchange rate system was in effect complete.[6]

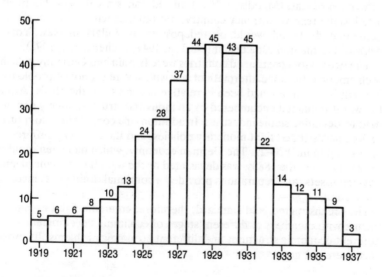

Figure 5.3. Number of countries on gold, 1919–37.
Source: Eichengreen (1992) Table 7.1, pp. 188–91.
Note: The three countries on gold in 1937 were on the 'qualified gold standard' (see note 5).

The initial conditions

The adjustment process integral to the gold standard created a severe deflationary bias for the world economy. To capture this bias the main trading countries can be broadly classified (after Cripps, 1978) into those constrained and those unconstrained by their trade performance. Those countries that could maintain a sufficient level of exports, relative to imports, at a high level of economic activity were not balance of payments constrained. Such countries could pursue easier monetary policies or could accumulate increased reserves. Conversely, a country that could not maintain balance of payments equilibrium at a high level of economic activity had to reduce domestic demand in order to import only those goods and services which it could afford to finance.

The two key unconstrained countries were France and the United States. France recovered successfully from the First World War, helped by immigration compensating for the massive wartime loss of manpower, and prior to stabilisation of the franc (as well as after) exploiting an undervalued exchange rate to generate export growth (Lewis, 1949). The United States had become the world's leading economy during the late nineteenth century; its strength was based on huge natural resources of land and minerals, sustained investment which had significantly raised its capital stock, a large internal market and the development of an industrial structure that encouraged research and development and the exploitation of economies of scale (Maddison, 1991). In addition, since the US effectively acted as the reserve currency country, if it ran a deficit then the reserves accumulated abroad would be redeposited as dollars in New York, neutralising the domestic deficit (Nurkse, 1944; Eichengreen, 1992).

The two major constrained countries were Britain and Germany, which both emerged from the aftermath of war with severe economic problems. The British economy had been in relative decline since the 1870s. After the war it remained encumbered by an industrial structure highly dependent on declining staple industries. In addition, the commitment to return to gold necessitated tight monetary policies, and the economy suffered a severe slump in 1920–21. The German economy, which had been rapidly expanding from the 1880s, was devastated by the war. It lost financial and physical assets, and reparations provided a continual drain on its income and wealth.

The reconstructed gold standard, therefore, created a fixed exchange regime with members at different stages of economic development with different economic structures and different economic problems. Its prospects were not good.

The adjustment process in theory

To be effective, the gold standard depended on a process of automatic adjustment, the classical price-specie-flow mechanism, to correct payments imbalances. Under this system the price level would adjust in response to deficits and surpluses on the balance of payments. A deficit would lead to a loss of gold and a contraction in the money supply, leading to a fall in prices and the eradication of the deficit. Similarly, a surplus would lead to an accumulation of gold, a rise in the money supply and prices, and hence balance of payments equilibrium. But the real world did not work like this. Such a process assumes that all the burden of adjustment is borne by prices rather than quantities, that the law of one price holds, that the demand for money is stable and that monetary authorities do not interfere by preventing changes in gold reserves adjusting their money supplies. Without these assumptions the idea of the adjustment process is seriously undermined. Of course, these realities had been recognised to varying degrees. Indeed, De Cecco (1992: 266) argues that:

> We cannot accept J.M. Keynes's postwar strictures about the prewar perception of the Gold Standard. It was *not* seen as immutable, frictionless, and automatic by its contemporaries. The seeds of postwar criticism and disenchantment were firmly sown before the war. In fact, we might go as far as to say that prewar learned opinion was much less apologetic of the pure metallic standard than would be the postwar economists and politicians.

The adjustment process in practice

As the main trading nations entered the exchange rate system with different initial conditions, it was apparent that the efficacy of the adjustment process would be central to the regime's impact. The option of adjusting the nominal exchange rate was effectively precluded. The adjustment of the real exchange rate was slow and erratic. For the UK, most studies indicate a significant average overvaluation of the sterling effective exchange rate in the period 1925–31, with only a slow movement towards purchasing power parity (Redmond, 1984). Keynes's (1925) contemporary estimate of a 10% overvaluation has proved to be a reasonable approximation of recent empirical estimates. Others have emphasised the high degree of overvaluation in the early 1920s following the appreciation of the nominal rate after the UK implemented policies to facilitate the return to gold (Broadberry, 1984). As the downward pressure on wages and prices was protracted due to established price and wage-setting behaviour, the result was lower growth and higher unemployment. Conventionally, it had been assumed that the unravelling of the price-quantity adjustment process would eventually return the economy to its previous position, with only a temporary loss of output and jobs. However, the legacy of slow growth lowered the long-run capacity of the economy, due to its impact on physical and human capital accumulation.

The sluggishness of real exchange rate changes left two adjustment alternatives. First, changes in the level of demand: deflation in constrained countries and reflation in surplus countries. Second, the financing of the deficits of constrained countries by capital flows from the unconstrained countries. In fact the *ultimate* burden of adjustment was borne by domestic deflation. The surplus countries were reluctant to reflate. The classical adjustment mechanism assumes that gold flows will provide the means of changing the level of demand via prices. But price adjustment was slow, and the reflationary impact of gold flows into France and the United States were negated by domestic monetary policy. Both countries, which by the late 1920s had between themselves accumulated 60% of total gold reserves, prevented these reserves from boosting their domestic money supplies. American policy-makers were increasingly concerned with curbing stock market speculation, whereas the French were wary of inflation. Deflation was transmitted abroad. Low import demand, particularly in America, led to widening balance of payments deficits in many of the key European economies.

The trade performance of the unconstrained countries is illustrated in Table 5.2. Their export growth was reasonable and close to the 5.7% growth of world trade. Additionally, due to their reluctance to reflate, they were able to maintain large balance of payments surpluses throughout the 1920s. During 1925–9, France maintained a surplus that averaged over 2% of GNP, while the US surplus averaged just under 1% of national income. The US surplus was particularly significant, given the size of its economy. Table 5.3 shows that the US surplus averaged 2.5% of world trade, compared to 1% for the French surplus.

Table 5.2.   Asymmetries in trade performance, 1924–29.

	Annual average export growth (1924–29)	Current account as a share of national income (average, 1924–29)
Constrained countries		
United Kingdom	1.6	+1.5
Germany	11.3	−1.2
Unconstrained countries		
France	4.3	+2.1
USA	5.5	+0.8
World	5.7	—

Sources: Mitchell (1975, 1983); Carre, Dubois and Malinvaud (1976) and League of Nations (1939).
Note: Estimates for Germany refer to 1925–29.

The growth of world trade was therefore limited by the domestic policies of the unconstrained countries. Whereas these nations could choose whether or not to reflate, the constrained countries had no such options. The entire burden of adjustment fell on them – they could either deflate to eradicate balance of payments deficits, or they could borrow to fund them. The effective approach of the UK economy was the former and of Germany the latter.

Table 5.3. Current account surpluses as a percentage share of world exports, 1924–29.

	France	USA
1924	1.7	3.5
1925	0.9	2.2
1926	1.2	1.5
1927	1.0	2.2
1928	0.7	3.1
1929	0.5	2.3
Annual average	1.0	2.5

Sources: Mitchell (1975, 1983); League of Nations (1939) and Kitson and Solomou (1990b).

Deflation could be achieved either through allowing reserves to flow out, depressing the money supply and domestic expenditure – the classical mechanism – or by policies that directly affected the components of demand. In Britain it was interest rates that acted as the key deflationary tool. From 1923 there was a trend rise in the Bank of England's discount rate as the authorities adopted policies consistent with the return and maintenance of the exchange rate at the pre-war parity. At the same time the general trend of other central banks' discount rates was downward (Eichengreen, 1991). The deflationary impact of such policies helped to keep the balance of payments in surplus and prevented the loss of gold.[7] The Bank of England also deployed gold market and foreign exchange operations to maintain its stock of international reserves (Moggridge, 1972). The impact on the real economy was slow growth, with the economy failing to reap its growth potential (Kitson and Solomou, 1990a). Despite the level of GDP in 1924 being below that of 1913, the growth rate of the British economy was significantly below the world average.[8] Unemployment remained persistently high, averaging 7.5% for the period 1924–29 (see Table 5.1).

Unlike Britain, Germany maintained a persistent balance of payments deficit throughout the 1920s. Along with reparations this deficit had to be financed, and Germany became heavily reliant on foreign loans, particularly from the United States. Although initially able to attract sizeable capital inflows, the rising debt burden undermined creditworthiness. Germany became increasingly reliant on short-term funds and by 1931 had accumulated net foreign debts equivalent to 25% of national income (Kitson, 1992). The subsequent concern about the German economy and the collapse of American lending abroad from 1928 led to capital flight, the loss of reserves, a credit squeeze and the raising of interest rates. Germany had been able to cope with its balance of payments constraint in the short-term by borrowing; ultimately, however, this only postponed the requirement to deflate.

The asymmetry in the adjustment processes showed in the relative trade performance of the two groups of countries during the 'successful' operation of the gold standard, as illustrated in Table 5.2.[9] The trading position of the constrained countries, the United Kingdom and Germany, differed significantly to that of the unconstrained countries. Although the UK managed to maintain a balance of payments surplus, its export performance was poor, exhibiting slow growth and a declining share of world markets. As Table 5.4 (from Lewis, 1949) shows, the UK share of world markets in 1929 was 3.2 percentage points below its 1913 level, an average annual decline of 1.6%. The German trading position was also precarious, the deficit on the balance of payments averaging 1.2% of national income between 1925 and 1929. Germany's export growth was rapid during this period, but this was catching-up from a very low post-war base and was boosted by enforced exports through reparations in kind. Despite this rapid growth, Germany's share of world exports in 1929 was more than 25% below its 1913 level.

Table 5.4. UK and Germany's percentage shares of world exports, 1913 and 1929.

	UK	Germany
1913	13.9	13.1
1929	10.7	9.7
Average annual % change	−1.6	−1.9

Source: Lewis (1949: 90).

Thus the deflationary bias of the gold standard not only failed to deal with the structural problems of constrained countries, it accentuated them. Countries which had entered the system with major structural problems, left the system weakened as they had to accommodate the burden of adjustment by deflating their domestic economies. This not only lowered growth and raised unemployment but hampered long-run competitiveness. The dampening of domestic demand reduced the benefits of mass production and the exploitation of scale economies. Deflation to maintain external equilibrium raised unit costs and generated a further loss of competitiveness and declining shares of world markets. Such a process of cumulative causation led the constrained countries to suffer a vicious cycle of stagnation. Locked into a fixed exchange rate system, there were few policy options to reverse the process.

The response to shocks

If the gold standard failed to maximise world growth in the 1920s, its shortcomings were also evident with the onset of the Great Depression. The causes of the Great Depression are subject to continual debate. Many studies focus on domestic developments in the American economy which were transmitted to the world economy. Friedman and Schwartz (1963) emphasise tight monetary policy;[10] Kindleberger (1973) stresses the fall in consumption due to a redistribution of income from the agricultural sector, where prices were falling; Romer (1990) points to the decline in the consumption of durables, due to increased uncertainty created by the Wall Street Crash; and Lewis (1949) blames the collapse of American capital exports. Other policy factors include the alleged failure of fiscal policy to provide automatic stabilisers and the argument that the Smoot-Hawley tariff of 1930 initiated a mutually destructive trade war (Friedman, 1978; Capie, 1992). Others studies (such as Fearon, 1979) have focused on the Great Depression as being caused by structural problems in the international economy. An explanation which embraces the cumulative impact of structural problems, adverse demand shocks and policy mistakes would seem to be a more realistic approach than a monocausal view. One such policy mistake was the adherence to gold.

The extent of the Great Depression can be attributed to the operation of the gold standard: the impact of adverse shocks, such as the recession in the US and the collapse in capital exports, were transmitted to the rest of the world through the exchange rate regime. As foreign loans were called in due to developments in the domestic economy, the gold flows to the United States increased. The draining of reserves in the debtor countries accelerated and monetary policy was tightened to ensure gold convertibility. Thus the deflationary bias of the gold standard system resulted in a perverse reaction to adverse demand shocks. Rather than facilitating an expansion of demand to ameliorate the depression, the system magnified the problem, leading to a collapse in world trade.[11]

As countries moved into recession they needed the capacity to initiate domestic policies in order to insulate themselves from the collapse in the world economy. The structure, characteristics and paths of development of the major economies were different and thus the timing and the composition of the policy mix required was also different. The different phasing of the depression of the major countries is illustrated in Table 5.5. There was approximately a three-year gap between the onset of decline in Germany and that in Denmark.[12] Yet during this period economic policy

Table 5.5. The onset of the Great Depression.

	1928				1929				1930				1931
	Q1	Q2	Q3	Q4	Q1	Q2	Q3	Q4	Q1	Q2	Q3	Q4	Q1
Europe	Germany		Finland		Poland		Italy Belgium	Switzerland Czechoslovakia Austria Netherlands	UK Greece Romania	France Sweden Ireland Yugoslavia	Latvia Norway	Denmark	Spain
Rest of the world			Brazil			Canada Argentina	USA	Chile India Malaya	Peru Japan New Zealand				

Source: League of Nations (1932).
Notes: Estimates based on a combination of statistical series indicating a downturn in economic activity.

was constrained by the gold standard, leaving little flexibility to deal quickly with domestic problems.[13]

The impact of the Great Depression also varied across countries: national income in the United States collapsed by an annual rate in excess of 10% between 1929 and 1932, whereas other countries such as Denmark and Norway witnessed little or no decline. In part these variations reflected the speed with which countries left gold, although another major factor was the difference in economic structures and institutions. Britain's relatively moderate depression, an annual decline of less than 2% compared to a world average of over 6%, in part reflected the low dependence on agriculture and the stability of its financial institutions. Thus shocks had different national and sectoral impacts. Binding nations together in a fixed exchange rate regime made no allowance for this.

The Great Depression was caused by a number of self-reinforcing mechanisms. It would most probably have occurred in the absence of the gold standard regime. Its severity, however, was almost certainly exacerbated by that regime.

The gold standard: an evaluation

In his critical evaluation of the interwar gold standard, Eichengreen (1992) argues that lack of credibility and lack of cooperation were the main weaknesses of the system. Credibility required acceptance of the (temporary) adverse impacts on output and employment; cooperation was required to ensure that adjustment was symmetric, rather than solely dependent on deflation by the constrained countries. We would argue, however, that the system was structurally flawed. First, although cooperation would have limited the deflationary bias, it might have only extended the life of the system, rather than preventing its ultimate demise. Even if the stronger countries had been encouraged to reflate, this would not have completely eradicated the deflationary burden on constrained countries, a burden which might have had persistent effects on productive capacity. Indeed, had the system lasted longer, it might have resulted in more divergent growth paths. Reflation in the stronger countries could have led to faster growth of output and productivity, leading to a virtuous cycle of growth, with deflation limiting the growth potential of the relatively weaker countries. Second, the system combined together countries with different economic conditions and problems. These problems were not eradicated by the regime; rather they were accentuated. Discretion over the use of monetary, fiscal and exchange rate policy was removed. Third, the regime was not able to accommodate adverse shocks; on the contrary, the operation of the international monetary system magnified the impact of recessionary forces. The regime was inappropriate for members with different economic structures and a recession phased differently among the international community.[14]

Policy Independence and Economic Recovery: the 1930s

The extent and magnitude of the Great Depression put the gold standard regime under severe strain. A series of financial and balance of payments crises ultimately undermined the system, culminating in Britain's decision to abandon the gold standard and devalue in September 1931. This marked the collapse of the regime. Other countries quickly followed sterling off the gold standard, including most of the Dominions and Empire, the Scandinavian countries, Canada and Japan. It was not until March 1933 that the USA devalued, while a core of countries including France, Belgium and the Netherlands remained on gold until later in the decade. Devaluation was not the only uncoordinated trade policy implemented; tariffs and quotas were increased, while many of the Central European countries, including Germany and Italy, resorted to extensive exchange controls.

The experience of different policy regimes

Devaluation can have beneficial impacts through a number of mechanisms. First, it can directly alleviate the balance of payments constraint on growth. Shifts in relative prices and improved competitiveness can raise exports and depress imports. The conventional account of this process is that it is a 'beggar-my-neighbour' policy, as the improvement in trade performance is reflected in an improving trade balance for the initiating country and a deteriorating trade balance for trading partners. This account, however, ignores the effects of an independently pursued trade policy on the level of economic activity. Increasing exports and reducing the propensity to import will raise the level of demand in the domestic economy. With unemployment and excess capacity, such a policy initiative will raise output and employment and lead to an income-induced increase in imports, so that there need be no change in the actual trade balance.[15] Thus although Britain devalued and adopted widespread protectionism in 1931 allowing output and employment growth, current account deficits still persisted throughout the 1930s. If countries get locked into a pattern of trade which constrains domestic expansion, active and independent trade policy provides one means of overcoming the problem without necessarily affecting adversely other trading partners.

The second benefit of devaluation is that it removes the exchange rate constraint on domestic policy, encouraging expansionary policies. In particular, monetary policy can be relaxed and therefore interest rates can be determined by domestic economic conditions rather than by the need to maintain the exchange rate or to prevent excessive loss of reserves. For instance Britain's suspension of the gold standard allowed the government to pursue a more expansionary policy after 1932. This 'cheap money' policy has been identified as a permissive policy for economic revival (Richardson, 1967), especially important in stimulating a housing boom

(Worswick, 1984).[16] Conversely, the reason that the UK Government's claims on 16 September 1992 – that it would remain in the ERM by raising interest rates as far as was necessary – lacked credibility was that raising interest rates by five percentage points in one day in the midst of the longest economic recession for 60 years was not believed to be a feasible policy option domestically.

Although a wide range of uncoordinated policies were implemented in the 1930s, including devaluation, it is possible to classify the major trading nations into different trade policy regimes (Kitson and Solomou, 1990a, Eichengreen, 1990). First, the sterling bloc that devalued with or soon after Britain and linked their currencies to sterling. Second, other countries which also devalued either early (before 1932) or later (1932 and after). Third, the exchange control group, which were reluctant to devalue for fear of inflation. And fourth, the gold bloc countries that remained, at least in the short-term, committed to the system. Table 5.6 shows the average annual growth rate of output for the four policy regimes for various

Table 5.6. Performance of different policy regimes: annual growth rate of output.

	Depression	Recovery	Inter-period
Sterling bloc	−1.7	4.7	−1.6
– (excluding Canada)	−0.5	4.7	−0.7
Other devaluers	−6.0	6.8	−2.5
– early devaluers	−5.0	7.7	0
– late devaluers	−7.1	5.9	−5.0
Exchange control	−3.5	4.5	−3.3
Gold bloc	−3.3	2.3	−3.7
World	−6.1	5.2	−2.8

Sources: Maddison (1991) and Mitchell (1975, 1983).
Notes:
1. *Phases*
   Depression: 1929–32
   Recovery: 1932–7
   Inter-period: Change in growth performance between two peak-to-peak periods, 1929–37 minus 1924–9.
2. *Countries in sample*
   Sterling bloc: Australia, Denmark, Finland, Norway, Sweden, United Kingdom and Canada.
   Other devaluers: Early devaluers are Brazil, Japan, and Mexico. Late devaluers are Colombia, Chile and the United States.
   Exchange control: Austria, Bulgaria, Czechoslovakia, Germany, Hungary, Italy and Yugoslavia.
   Gold bloc: Belgium, France, Netherlands and Switzerland.
3. Figures are unweighted averages.
4. 'The world' is the weighted sum of Maddison's 16 capitalist countries.
5. For most countries the output measure used is real GDP.

periods. During the 1929–32 depression, 'world' output declined by more than 6% per annum; however, the experience of the various policy regime groups varied markedly. The sterling bloc exhibited the mildest contraction, with output falling by an annual rate of less than 2% per annum, and just 0.5% if Canada is excluded from the sample (Canada was particularly adversely affected by its large agricultural sector and its links with the United States). This suggests that devaluation policies may have helped to mitigate the adverse effects of the depression. Leaving gold provided less help for the 'other devaluers' group, although there is evidence that those which devalued early experienced a milder depression than those which delayed and devalued late. Thus, the timing of the policy response was important.

For the period of recovery, 1932–37, most countries exhibited reasonable cyclical growth. The exception was the gold bloc countries. Constrained by their commitment to their exchange rate parities they had to adopt tight monetary and fiscal policies to maintain internal and external balance. Thus although output was depressed, the French government in the early 1930s adopted contractionary fiscal policies to prevent destabilising exchange rate speculation.

A simple comparison of growth performance during recovery can be misleading as it will include both a cyclical component (the automatic recovery from a deep depression) and policy-induced effects. An alternative is to examine inter-period, peak-to-peak growth performance. Table 5.6 reports the change in the annual rate of growth of output during 1929–37 relative to 1924–29.[17] The results of the 'world' economy indicate a retardation of the growth path. This is consistent with other findings (Perron, 1989) that the shock of the Great Depression had persistent effects on the level of output. The performance of the different policy regimes, however, provides important contrasts. The countries that devalued, particularly those that devalued early, experienced only a small (or zero) fall in trend growth. Those countries that had the limited benefits of exchange controls experienced a deterioration in annual growth of 3.3%. The poorest performing group was the gold bloc, which had little flexibility to initiate policies for domestic recovery.

Further evidence of the striking contrasts in performance of different policy regimes is shown in Table 5.7, which presents figures for the annual growth of industrial production. These results indicate that those countries that devalued, and to a lesser extent those that introduced exchange controls, had a milder industrial depression, faster recovery and a better inter-period growth performance.

Table 5.8 presents some evidence on the unemployment performance of the different policy regimes. The reliability and availability of interwar unemployment data is limited, and such data should therefore be used with caution. What is apparent, however, is that the high unemployment that developed during the Depression persisted throughout the period of recovery. Only for the sterling bloc was average unemployment lower for the recovery period compared with the average for the Depression

Table 5.7. Performance of different policy regimes: annual growth rate of industrial production.

	Depression	Recovery	Inter-period
Sterling bloc	−5.3	9.5	−2.0
– (excluding Canada)	−3.7	9.3	−0.5
Other devaluers	−8.3	11.9	−2.1
– early devaluers	−4.7	12.8	—
– late devaluers	−11.8	11.0	—
Exchange control	−11.2	10.3	−4.1
Gold bloc	−10.9	6.0	−7.1

Sources: Mitchell (1975, 1983).
Notes:
1. *Phases*: See Table 5.6.
2. *Countries*: As Table 5.6, except 'Sterling bloc' excludes Denmark from inter-period estimates. 'Other devaluers' excludes Columbia and Japan. 'Exchange control' group excludes Bulgaria, Yugoslavia and Hungary from inter-period estimates. 'Gold bloc' excludes Switzerland and includes Poland.

period; for the other regimes unemployment, although falling, averaged more during the 1933–37 period. In part this will reflect employment lagging output, plus changing activity rates and demographic shifts. More importantly it may be evidence of the persistent effects of the Great Depression, the long-term unemployed having difficulties re-entering the labour market (Crafts, 1987).

Table 5.8. Performance of different policy regimes: average annual unemployment rate.

	(i) Depression 1930–32	(ii) Recovery 1933–37	(ii-i)
Sterling bloc	10.3	9.5	−0.8
– (excluding Canada)	9.9	8.8	−1.1
USA	16.0	19.5	+3.5
Exchange control	9.3	9.4	+0.1
Gold bloc	4.4	6.8	+2.4

Source: Maddison (1991).
Notes:
1. *Phases*: See Table 5.6.
2. *Countries*: As Table 5.6, except 'other devaluers' excluded due to lack of data. 'Exchange control' group excludes Bulgaria, Czechoslovakia, Hungary and Yugoslavia.
3. French data are for benchmark years only.

Growth and improved economic performance during the 1930s was dependent on countries untying themselves from the strictures of the gold standard and adopting independent policies. Additionally some countries also reaped the advantages of increased protectionism and fiscal expansion. What is apparent, however, is that the cooperative regime failed and uncoordinated policies were a vast improvement.

The role of wages

Beenstock, Capie and Griffiths (1984) argue that it was real wage movements that accounted for the cyclical fluctuations in output, during both the Great Depression and the subsequent recovery. It is true that wages did move counter-cyclically over the 1929–37 cycle in Britain – rising relative to trend in the recession and then falling relative to trend during the recovery – but the causes of the output fluctuations lay elsewhere, and the timing of the fluctuations do not actually fit the Beenstock *et al.* story.[18] We have shown elsewhere (Michie, 1987) that this wage–output correlation itself does not hold outside those particular years – a finding which reinforces the argument of Worswick and Dimsdale that the output and wage series are more likely to have been independently generated.[19]

The Economic Consequences of Mr Major

The similar experience of deep slumps and widespread unemployment has led to comparisons between the interwar period and recent economic events, including by analogy between the ERM and the interwar gold standard: both resemble adjustable-peg systems in theory, but rather less adjustable in practice; both failed to deal with external shocks; both suffered adversely from speculative attacks; and both limited the flexibility of domestic policy. As in 1931, Britain disengaged itself from the exchange rate system, allowed the exchange rate to fall, and introduced cheap money. As in 1931, policy initiatives reflect crisis management rather than any coherent strategy, although the benefits of devaluation were more fully discussed 60 years ago than they were prior to September 1992. Similarly, the French 'franc fort' policy resembles the ultimately misconceived French commitment to gold in the 1930s.

Despite the historical similarities, some important differences remain. First, the potential for policy independence is now more limited: international capital markets are more integrated, making it more difficult to engineer unilateral reductions in interest rates. Recent British experience does show, however, that such unilateral action is still possible, with the leaving of the ERM allowing interest rate cuts despite claims prior to September 1992 that interest rates would actually have to increase in such circumstances to compensate for loss of confidence and credibility. Second, there is now the problem of inflation, whereas from the mid-1920s prices were falling. The problem today is to identify precisely what the current inflation constraint is. The objective of the British government of keeping inflation below 4% seems to reflect political rather than economic considerations. Third, current price and wage-setting structures may limit the potential for trade policy to alter relative prices, limiting the gains in competitiveness. This contrasts with the interwar period, when nominal wage resistance was more important than real wage resistance. And fourth, the present economic problems faced by European economies have different causes and different characteristics from the interwar period. For instance, depressed demand in the British economy today reflects the high level of debt in the private sector, resulting from supply-side mismanagement in the form of the unrecognised impact of financial deregulation in the mid-1980s. Allowing for the different economic conditions prevailing in the two periods, some important lessons can still be drawn.

Macroeconomic management

Macroeconomic policies which retard growth may have persistent effects on the real economy. The magnitude of the Great Depression did lasting damage to the level of world income. We have yet to observe the long-term impacts of the early-1990s recession. What is apparent, however, is that governments should react to external shocks quickly by using accommodating monetary and fiscal policies and that internal deflation is an inappropriate tool for permanently reducing inflation.

Policy regimes

Policy regimes which are based on trying to achieve convergence of inflation rates can have adverse real effects. They fail to accommodate different initial conditions, tend to have a deflationary bias and fail to successfully accommodate shocks. The experience of the gold standard supports this, as does more recent evidence. The notion that because Germany had a strong economy and a strong currency, imposing a strong currency on Britain would thereby strengthen the domestic economy, was fatally flawed. Causation runs from the real economy to the exchange rate, not vice versa. Britain's decision to joint the ERM at DM2.95 served to weaken Britain's trading sector as well as removing the policy options required to deal with domestic recession. As with the collapse of world trade in 1929, the problems of German unification and the Danish response to Maastricht produced a major shock to the exchange rate system. Where the collapse of the gold standard led to the introduction of uncoordinated policies, the full impact of the 1990s breakdown have yet to fully unravel. Those countries that have left the ERM, such as Britain, should, however, resist the temptation to enter into any cooperative regime which would further exacerbate the problems of slow growth and high unemployment.

One of the keys to economic growth during the 1930s was the use of independent and uncoordinated policies. This is not the same as saying that coordination *per se* is ineffective. What is ineffective is coordination based on convergence towards monetary and financial targets, which has adverse impacts on the real economies of the participants. During the 1930s, coordination based on structured reflation and the effective redistribution of resources to regions or countries of the world with difficulties would have been appropriate. The limitations of such regimes is that the level of cooperation required is significant and the rules required are complex and not easily enforced. In the absence of such a regime, independent policies were the next best option, and as such proved successful during the 1930s. Unless current European economic policy is reorientated towards the objective of full employment, embracing an active industrial and regional policy, rather than with the myopic concern with zero inflation, the route forward must once again be based on independent national growth strategies which would not only allow countries to help themselves, but by doing so would help each other. Competitive deflation is the real 'beggar thy neighbour' policy of the 1990s.[20]

The unemployment problem

Despite economic revival in the 1930s, unemployment remained high. It was a constant cause of poverty, disease and malnutrition. The implementation of a growth strategy today, whether it be of a national or European variety, is a necessary condition for tackling unemployment, but may not of itself be sufficient. It is important, therefore, first that the pursuit of market flexibility does not further erode the welfare system upon which the basic needs of so many depend; and second that policies for employment are pursued alongside those for economic recovery and growth. These need to include measures such as reducing the length of the working week and year; expanding employment-intensive public services and public works, such as a major environmental programme; and supply-side measures on education and training, and on research, development and design to see through new products and production processes.[21]

Conclusion

The European economies in the 1930s experienced differing degrees of employment growth, and the cause of this growth also differed across countries. What was common to many of the countries, however, was the breaking of the exchange rate constraint on monetary policy. In addition, some countries benefited from fiscal expansion, a policy shift often associated with the publication in 1936 of Keynes's *General Theory*, although in reality it had more to do with rearmament and, in certain countries, fascist economic policies.[22]

Today, mass unemployment and economic stagnation have been brought about by monetarist policies pursued by governments in the European Community operating under the labels 'Conservative' and 'Socialist' alike. The operation of the ERM caused high interest rate policies, producing widespread unemployment throughout the 1980s in many of the participating economies.

National income fell by 2.4% in Britain in 1991; growth remained negative throughout 1992; and 1993 growth is likely to be so weak as to be unable to prevent unemployment remaining near 3 million. When Britain joined the ERM in October 1990, why, though, was an overvalued exchange rate, at 2.95 Deutschmarks, chosen? The stated objective was squeezing inflation; what was not stated was the route by which it was hoped it would work, by deliberately making things hard for British firms, thereby forcing them to try to cut costs by cutting wages and introducing more intensive working practices. As detailed above, this is not the first time that governments have allowed the currency to be overvalued in this way. Winston Churchill as Chancellor took Britain back onto the gold standard in the 1920s at an overvalued rate, with Keynes warning at the time, in his pamphlet *The Economic Consequences of Mr Churchill*, of the disastrous likely consequences of this policy – consequences which were to include the General Strike of 1926. Similarly, the recession of 1979–81 was exacerbated by a high exchange rate caused not only by North Sea oil, but also by the high interest rates which followed from the Thatcher government's monetarist experiment.

In the interwar period, Britain was indeed forced to abandon the gold standard. And the exchange rate similarly fell after 1981, depreciating nearly 30% by 1986, helping fuel the recovery. Likewise, the overvalued rate at which Chancellor Major entered the ERM meant that our membership was always doomed to failure. Yet those who pointed this out at the time were dismissed out of hand. The leadership of all three major political parties supported continued membership at the overvalued rate. Even if this had been a genuine option, it would have been a disastrous one, but in reality it was not even an option.

But the problems of the ERM lie deeper than just having joined at the wrong rate. The ERM was and is a high unemployment mechanism, because all the pressure is on the weak economies to take action, rather than on the strong ones. And worse, that action is designed more to prop up the currencies of the weak economies than to strengthen those economies' productive potential, which is the only sustainable basis for maintaining a healthy currency. Interest rates are thus increased. These depress investment plans and leave the economy in question further weakened. Yet it is most likely the weakness of the economy which underlay the weakness of the currency in the first place. So a weak economy produces a weak currency; the ERM then requires the government in question to raise interest rates; and increased interest rates squeezes the country's economy, leaving it still weaker. If this high interest rate policy proves inadequate, then government spending cuts are required, further accelerating the cumulative process of relative decline.

Instead, what is needed is, first, the dropping of the Maastricht Treaty's convergence criteria for PSBR levels in a recession, and second, the overcoming of the ERM's deflationary 'fault lines'. Keynes himself had argued that the Bretton Woods system should have put more onus on the surplus countries to reflate rather than deficit countries to deflate, but knowing that the United States – the main surplus country – would not agree, the British negotiating team did not even pursue Keynes's full proposals, provoking his response that since the Americans would not listen to sense, the British proposed talking nonsense.

6

The Mitterrand Experience[1]

Serge Halimi, Jonathan Michie and Seumas Milne

The leader who deserves the monetarist palm is François Mitterrand . . . Mr Mitterrand's Socialist government allowed real wages to rise by less than 6 percent between 1983 and 1989 . . . Perhaps the main policy legacy of the 1980s will turn out to be neither 'Reaganism' nor 'Thatcherism', but 'Mitterrandism'. (*Financial Times*, 20 April 1990.)

The crushing electoral defeat of the French Socialist Party in March 1993 poses a challenge not only to any left or reforming government in the Europe of the 1990s, but to the whole process of rapid west European integration embodied in the Maastricht Treaty. Although the socialists were damaged by the general aura of corruption, sleaze and patronage that had come to characterise their administration, there is little doubt that the impact of their economic policies – particularly on jobs – was the decisive factor in their defeat. Seventy per cent of French voters cited unemployment as the reason for the Socialists' decimation at the polls.

And yet there are few governments in Europe that stuck as closely to the financial orthodoxy codified in the convergence criteria of the Maastricht Treaty. None could claim such a fervent adherence to the Exchange Rate Mechanism and their currency's position within it. The guiding principle of all the post-1983 French socialist governments was the 'franc fort', pegged in the narrow band, as the only reliable path to 'competitive disinflation'. All else was sacrificed at the ERM's altar, notably French employment.

In common with other west European social democratic parties, the French socialists attempted to imitate the German 'social market' model, complete with large-scale vocational training programmes, regional devolution and banking reorganisations on German lines. The programme on which the British Labour Party fought the 1992 general election closely shadowed latter-day French socialist policies. The decisive rejection of these policies in practice by the French people – and the parallel price being paid for similar approaches in Italy and Spain – must raise doubts as to their long-term political worth or viability.

But the post-1983 French economic orientation was itself the result of the failure of the more radical, reflationary policies of the previous two years. For many – and not just in France – the collapse of the 'Mitterrand experiment' of 1981–83 was the final nail in the coffin of go-it-alone, 'reflation in one country' economic strategies. The common programme on which the socialist-communist government of 1981 was elected closely reflected the left reflationary policies then dominant in the British Labour Party, associated with the 'alternative economic strategy' of the late 1970s and early 1980s. The adoption of austerity measures in France in 1982–83, combined with Labour's devastating defeat in the 1983 general election in Britain, helped convince a broad section of progressive opinion that independent national alternatives were no longer viable technical or political options.

The failure of precisely those austerity policies – which were seen subsequently as the only option – leaves a political and economic policy vacuum. It demands a reassessment of both the 1981–82 experience and the reasons for the disastrous effects of later French socialist policies. There is no question of a simple return to the strategies of the early 1980s in different – and more difficult – political and economic conditions. But the lessons of the first years of the Mitterrand administration are, in our view, not at all those which are usually drawn.

This chapter begins by setting out the tasks and dangers facing the incoming Mitterrand government, as viewed by the Socialists themselves before taking office. We then examine the 'Mitterrand experiment' of 1981–82, and assess why it was blown off course; we question the conventional wisdom that the experience means that all such attempts at national expansion are doomed to failure. We then consider some of the legacies of the Mitterrand experiment, including the extension of public ownership, as well as the 'alternative' policies pursued from 1983 to 1993, with some final comments on the 1993 election which so decisively rejected that 'alternative'.

The Socialists' Diagnosis of 1981[2]

For the Socialists, the escalation of unemployment (which had risen fourfold between 1974 and 1981) constituted the key failure of the Right's economic policy. For them, Giscard d'Estaing had neglected the 'industrial imperative' by adopting an anti-Keynesian and monetarist approach. Provided Giscard's strategy of interdependence through specialisation was rejected and provided it was understood that jobs had to be created in industry, not in the 'parasitic service sector', then 'yes, full employment is possible'.[3] In fact, full employment was claimed to be a moral obligation: for François Mitterrand, 'a country like ours with 1,500,000 unemployed ceases to be a free country'.[4] With full employment would come high wages: 'True competitiveness rests, not on the exploitation of an underpaid labour force, but on the capacity to sustain competition with high levels of wages.'[5]

The French Right was blamed for having misunderstood the nature of the economic crisis, first by agreeing to the 'theorem of [German Chancellor] Helmut Schmidt', and second by endorsing the 'equation of [French Commissioner] Michel Albert'. According to Schmidt, 'the profits of today make the investments of tomorrow and the jobs of the day after'. But, for the Socialists, profits could not translate into investment unless domestic demand remained strong and international demand ceased to fall. As for 'the jobs of the day after', these would not materialise in the face of rationalisation and delocalisation. The 'equation of Albert' stated that 'employment is linked to growth, growth to a favourable balance of trade, and a favourable balance of trade to the adjustment of industry'. But here too, 'the premises were false and, therefore, an economic war waged on these bases could only be lost'. First, because 'major companies with an export vocation create fewer jobs than the ones they suppress'; second, because 'high-tech industries hardly make up for the loss of jobs resulting from the decline of traditional industries'.[6]

Thus the Socialists rejected the assumptions underlying mainstream liberal economic theory. They saw in the contest for international specialisation 'an obstacle race favouring the strong and the big'. And they advocated a reduction in the openness of the French economy and the use of the state to regenerate industries, subsidise research, and ease the process of restructuring. The Left's strategy borrowed many of its features from Japan: a state-sponsored industrial policy whenever useful, trade protection whenever necessary. But the extent of their political victory, the scope of the institutional and economic instruments they controlled and the time they seemed to have on their side led them to under-estimate the problems caused by the fact that their strategy would have to be implemented in an international recession, with deregulation spreading around the world. In a sense, what saved Keynesianism for France in 1981 was the failed monetarist policies of Giscard-Barre after 1976. But if this failure helped to conceal the Left's lack of creativity in attempting to revive the past, the Left's electoral victory could not recreate the old virtuous circles.

According to Mitterrand at the time, 'The Right plays its own game. It is the same as that of the multinational corporations.'[7] For the Left, the fraction of the French bourgeoisie represented in power by Giscard was no longer national. It had acquired a stake in an international division of labour leading to 'the disembowelling of the French economy on the altar of multinational capitalism'.[8] For the Socialists, this choice resulted in 'the progressive abandonment of essential economic sectors (shipbuilding, textiles, steel, consumer electronics), which represents a considerable economic and social cost'.[9] Foreign trade's share of GNP had risen steadily from 10% in 1960 to 22% by 1978. French industries had not held up well in the face of this competition, in part because of a profit squeeze which acted as a disincentive to invest. At the same time, 'Raymond

Barre's policy of overvaluing the franc had hurt the competitive position of already weak French industries.'[10]

International specialisation was thought to favour the US, Germany and Japan – with which France ran a large trade deficit – because the French market was smaller than those 'from which the industries of our three principal competitors (USA, Germany, Japan) operate'.[11] And the linkage of the franc with the strong mark through the EMS 'worsens a policy of austerity which chokes off our economy and aggravates social inequalities'.[12] In other words, the Socialists of 1980–81 were rejecting the openness of the French economy and the overvaluation of the currency. The protracted debate on the issue of the EMS embodied both these arguments. One of the products of Giscard's legacy had, in the words of Alain Lipietz, been that:

> Any succeeding government was condemned to subordinate its social policy to external constraints . . . all growth of French consumption gave rise to a disproportionate rise in imports. The trend was even more marked for French investment . . . [This situation set the stage for] a collapse of the economic basis for a modernist social democratic compromise.[13]

The Socialist Party's *Projet Socialiste* (1980) did contain an awareness of this potential conflict between the economic policy the Socialists wanted to implement and the external constraints France had accumulated:

> A strong growth rate will not be possible without an external imbalance and an increased economic dependence, unless French industry is able to handle by itself the burst in demand that will result from the rise in purchasing power. This involves the indispensable reconquest of the domestic market . . .
>
> The French understand that the balance of trade will be a key to the success of the Left. *A failure in that area would lead us either to call into question the 'Projet Socialiste' or to run into depreciation and debt* . . .
>
> Free-market logic depends on a deceleration of economic activity to slow down the growth of imports. It is the worst possible solution. A country that makes the effort to stimulate its economy must avail itself of *the necessity to curb an unlimited swelling of imports* which would abort the re-ignition of its expansion. Its responsibility is to *take the necessary steps so that a recovery of demand can be met by domestic production* without risking inflation.[14]

Since the problem had been identified, what steps did the Socialists have in mind to address it? One answer was economic and industrial, the other monetary. On the economic front, the idea was 'to stop the increase *and then to reverse* the share of GNP attributable to foreign trade'.[15] Point 20 of Mitterrand's programme spoke of bringing back that share to 'below 20 percent by 1990'. This objective entailed 'industrial intervention for the reconquest of the domestic market' (Point 15). For the Socialists, it was 'urgent to reduce the abusive penetration of our market by products coming from our major industrial competitors . . . by investing in the sectors to make them competitive'.[16] However, since this would take time, and since a balance of payments deficit might threaten the whole strategy, protection was not excluded. It is true that the Socialists had asserted 'a fundamental choice in favour of the opening of borders to foreign competition', but only in the context of 'neither *indiscriminate* protectionism, nor *unconditional* free trade':[17]

> The free flow of trade *is a means that can be justified insofar as* it contributes to growth and to better jobs, *but not when* its effect is . . . inflation, deflation and unemployment.[18]

In other words, the upholding of the process (free trade) was contingent on the nature of the outcome (growth, jobs). And the Socialists had said time and again that, as of 1980, process and outcome had become contradictory for France. In a sense, they would demonstrate this contradiction when, in 1983, they reaffirmed free trade while slowing growth and cutting jobs. As for the EMS:

> At the European level, *the PS cannot agree to the existing EMS* which entails the alignment of weaker currencies on the Deutschmark and, therefore, short of a new emergency exit from the system [like that of 1976 when the franc was devalued by 30%] requires a toughened policy of austerity.[19]

In other words, before it took office, the French Left had assessed the pitfalls of a policy of reflation. And to avoid them, it had, either implicitly or explicitly, accepted the need to consider trade protection and currency devaluation. How far these steps would have helped remains debatable. What is clear, however, is that by not enacting them, the Socialists ran into precisely the problems which they themselves had anticipated.

1981–82: Reflation in One Country

François Mitterrand and his socialist-communist government came to office in May and June 1981 on the basis of the *Programme Commun* of the 1970s – the most radical economic and social strategy envisaged by any French administration since the immediate post-war period. In economic terms, the programme was avowedly reflationary. It aimed to boost demand through higher public spending, wage increases and transfer payments to the less well-off in order to stimulate growth and cut the dole queues. Inflation was to be contained through a combination of money supply restrictions and incomes policy. Nationalisation of private banks and major industrial groups was intended to provide a motor for investment, for technological change and for restructuring, aimed at recapturing the domestic market.

In an echo of the experience of the British Labour government during 1974–75, the Mitterrand experiment began in the depths of a longer than expected international economic recession, but also at a time when the other advanced capitalist countries were pursuing disinflationary – and in the case of Britain, outright deflationary – economic policies.

The first stages of the programme were duly implemented, albeit modified insofar as the parity of the franc was not to be touched and no protectionist measures were to be used. Twelve major industrial firms and 38 smallish financial institutions were nationalised. Income transfers were increased by just under 13% in 1981–82 and disposable income by 6.3% (compared with a 2% drop in both West Germany and Britain).[20] Although taxes on the better-off were raised to pay for extra expenditure, the continuing slow-down forced up the budget deficit to 2.6% of GNP in 1983. But this was relatively modest. The original OECD estimate in 1984 suggested a fiscal stimulus of 1.4% of GNP during 1981–82. Revised estimates in 1991 put it higher, at 2.3% of GNP.[21] Either way, it was not out of line with the 2% of GNP French expansion in 1977–78, or the United States' 1.8% of GNP stimulus in 1982–83.

Various measures were taken to cut the labour supply (shorter working week, overtime restrictions, lower retirement age) and 88,000 jobs were created in the public sector in 1981–83. The minimum wage was raised sharply and pro-labour employment legislation enacted.

Disappointing results

The overall results of this package were sluggish growth, a continuing rise in unemployment, balance of payments problems and an acute exchange rate crisis. In the circumstances of international recession and the defence of the franc inside the ERM, this was an entirely predictable outcome.

French growth was 0.3% in 1981, 1.6% in 1982 and 0.7% in 1983 – compared with West German figures of −0.1%, −1.0% and 1.3%, and an EC average of −0.3%, 0.5% and 1.0%. The French outcome is undramatic, but significantly better than that of its competitors. Similarly, the rise in unemployment was not halted, but it was slowed: joblessness increased from 7.5% in 1981 to 8.2% in 1982, and to 8.4% in 1983. That was again better than, say, Britain or West Germany, where unemployment doubled between 1980 and 1982, as against a French increase of 28%.[22] Comparing the performance of European countries over the seven years 1979–86, Andrew Glyn found that France showed the greatest degree of 'employment spreading' (a variable made up from the sum of the absolute values of changes in the share of state employment and of falls in average hours worked), due to the Mitterrand government's early policies of hours cuts and increases in state employment with explicit employment objectives, but at the same time a poor overall employment performance.[23] By contrast, French inflation – which started off well above the EC average – rose further in 1981 and fell slowly during 1982 and 1983.

Not surprisingly, the key problems emerged over the balance of payments, capital flight and massive pressures on the exchange rate. The trade deficit increased from $4.7 billion in 1981 to $12.1 billion the following year, as French growth met EC-wide recession and imports were sucked in. Speculation against the franc had begun even before

Mitterrand's election, but the new government stubbornly resisted the inevitable devaluation for a crucial six months, while it jacked up interest rates and tightened capital controls. In October 1981, the franc was devalued by 3% within the ERM and the mark revalued by 5.5%. But the pressures continued. In March 1982, interest rates were raised again to try and stem the massive outflow of capital. In June, the franc was devalued by 5.75% and the mark revalued by 4.25%. But although the volume of exports rose and the volume of imports fell, the devaluations did not immediately redress the trade deficit.[24] The government did not wait to find out how long the devaluations would take to feed through: a four-month wage freeze was introduced and monetary and fiscal policy sharply tightened.[25]

From devaluation to 'franc fort'

In May 1981, the new President had both the technical justification and political support for a policy of not only realigning the parity of the franc, but also of challenging the validity of a European Monetary System which imposed on its members the constraints of economic orthodoxy along West German lines.

The technical justification was, first, that the French franc had maintained the same parity against the West German mark since February 1978, and given the inflation differential, this had entailed an overvaluation of the franc of almost 20%; and second, after February 1981, and especially after Mitterrand's election, France suffered a massive capital flight (including between four and five billion dollars in the week of May 11–18 1981), its foreign currency reserves shrank dramatically and the franc came under attack. A devaluation or a floating of the currency would have avoided the squandering of the reserves accumulated under Giscard-Barre, as well as avoiding the raising of interest rates to prohibitive levels. Three devaluations occurred in any case, but only later, thus fuelling the accusations of the Right that they were sanctions for mistaken economic policies. The critical monetary decision, made on the very day of President Mitterrand's inauguration, is described by Prime Minister Mauroy as follows:

> 21 May 1981. I look at François Mitterrand saluting the crowd from a convertible car driving us to the Elysée. . . . Since May 10th, the franc has lost value and our foreign currency reserves have dwindled. . . . In the car, I size up the situation with François Mitterrand. Capital exports may amount to $1.5bn for this one day alone. . . . A rapid decision must be made. Some, like Michel Rocard, favour a floating of the franc, that is to say an immediate devaluation. Jacques Delors, on the other hand . . . wishes a defence of our currency and its staying in the European system. I share that position. The President, who distrusts the dramatisation of monetary affairs estimates that *political common sense dictates the solution: one does not salute the victory of the Left with a devaluation.* . . .

> I affirm our will to defend the franc. . . . When he entered the Elysée [in
> 1974], Giscard was not able to maintain the franc in the EMS. We accept the
> challenge. . . . We must not repeat the mistakes of past experiences. I know
> that it is often because of the difficulty to control monetary and financial
> balances that the Socialists have failed in the past.[26]

Each of these three arguments – 'political common sense', the desire to do
'better' than the Right and the intent to improve on the Left's past
performance – are questionable. From a political standpoint, it is true that
Mitterrand was about to call new parliamentary elections (for June 14th
and 21st), hoping for a solid Socialist majority. Given the mood of his
inauguration, it is understandable that the new President did not wish to
break with his 'force tranquille' by being the bearer of bad news: he
preferred 'saluting the crowd' to a 'salute of the victory of the Left with a
devaluation'. It is not obvious, however, that a devaluation would have
done more to alter the 'state of grace' than capital outflows or rising
interest rates: the devaluation could be justified as a clearing of the decks
before a new presidential term. At any rate, after 21 June and the Socialist
parliamentary landslide, the imperatives of short-term political expedi-
ency had disappeared. Second, the desire to 'accept a challenge' which the
Right had failed to meet, meant that instead of being solely concerned
with the implementation of its programme – a difficult task already – the
Left also wanted to beat the Right at their own game. As Lipietz noted at
the time:

> To accept that the strength of the franc should be the criterion for good
> management, is to accept the challenge of the adversary on the worst
> possible terrain, to bend before a constraint he himself never subscribed
> much to, and to maintain high interest rates.[27]

And third, on the desire not to 'repeat the mistakes of past experiences', if
Edouard Herriot – who led a left of centre government in 1924 – and the
Popular Front government of Léon Blum made a mistake (or several of
them), it had been in adhering to a set of priorities that could not be
sustained (a ceiling for monetary creation in 1924, a high parity of the franc
in 1936).[28] And, as had been the case in 1936, the Left's 'mistake' of 1981
would be to sacrifice its stated industrial strategy on the alter of an
improvised monetary policy. Ironically, the results of that choice would
prove almost identical: Blum took office in May 1936, Mitterrand in May
1981; the first devaluation of the Popular Front took place in late September 1936, the first devaluation of Mitterrand's presidential term in early
October 1981; the second devaluation of the Popular Front was decided in
June 1937, that of Mitterrand in June 1982.[29] Had Pierre Mauroy intended
'to repeat the mistakes of the past', he could hardly have planned it better.
And, if the denouement was not to prove identical, it is only thanks to the
political and institutional arrangements that allowed the Left in 1981 to
survive the devaluations of the franc, a string of electoral defeats, and
abysmal ratings in the polls.

One last explanation for the non-devaluation of May 1981 foreshadows the 1983 debate on the issue of the EMS. According to Jacques Delors, Mitterrand's decision was based on the desire not to jeopardise 'the necessary correspondence between his economic policy and a foreign policy set on speeding up European construction'.[30] The point is certainly a critical one. But it can be interpreted in two ways. A first interpretation would equate Mitterrand's choice in 1981 with de Gaulle's in 1944: instead of taking a dramatic – or at least difficult – economic step, he chose to concentrate on his foreign policy objectives. But 1981 differed significantly from 1944: in 1944, there was more plausibility in prioritising the defence of France's 'rank' in the world. De Gaulle could therefore arguably be excused for not being too interested in the monetary steps suggested to him by Pierre Mendés-France.[31] The international situation confronting Mitterrand in 1981 was not nearly as dramatic, and unlike de Gaulle, he had set economic and social policies as his priorities. A second interpretation is that if the French Left thought that the chances for a successful implementation of its economic strategy resided in a 'European social space' then a 'correspondence' between European construction and progressive Keynesianism could be proclaimed. In fact, however, neither Kohl nor Thatcher had any interest in a 'social space' or a Keynesian reflation, not to mention a 'rupture with capitalism'.

In the same way as by following monetarist policies the Left was forced to abandon most of its industrial dreams, by being 'pro-European' in the context of 1981 (or of 1993 for that matter) François Mitterrand would have to sacrifice many of his social priorities. Thierry Pfister, Mauroy's political adviser, implicitly confirms the extent to which 'a speeding up of European construction' constituted a major constraint, not a help, for the Left's initial strategy. The non-devaluation of 1981 represented an attempt to reassure hostile partners who would keep on demanding further reassurances:

> The first signal given on the international scene [by a devaluation or by a withdrawal from the EMS] would have been a recoiling from European solidarities. But the victory of the Left in France already arouses surprise and distrust in most of the Western capitals . . . And this apprehension is likely to be compounded when the Communists will join the new majority [after the parliamentary elections of June 1981].[32]

In other words, as early as May 1981, the Socialists wanted not only to do better than the Right when it came to the defence of the franc, they were also set on appeasing conservative EC partners by remaining in a monetary system that was known to constrain the economic strategy advocated in 1981. As in the case of its relations with business, the Left would not fully reassure its European neighbours before it would accept their priorities and adopt their policies.

All of this should not be taken to imply that an immediate withdrawal from the EMS, and hence a substantial devaluation, would not have entailed serious economic consequences. During the first few months, a devaluation increases the trade deficit, since its effect over the flows of products are not as immediate as those over their prices (exports are less profitable, import costs rise). Moreover, given the openness of the French economy, some imports could not easily be replaced by domestic production. These problems were further compounded by France's dependence on imported oil, the price of which was denominated in (then rising) US dollars. Lastly, the export advantage that was to be gained by a cheaper franc was limited by the existence of depressed world markets for French goods (recession in the West, debt crisis in the Third World). However, all these difficulties arose in any case. The only result of the rearguard struggle begun in May 1981 was to draw out the effects of the economic crisis over three devaluations instead of one, all of them approved by Germany, France's major trade partner. And since each devaluation was timid and delayed, they could hardly do much to stimulate exports:

> A withdrawal from the EMS was likely to succeed immediately after May 10th, 1981. It would have entailed a sharp drop in the franc. But then, the French government would have acquired the latitude to choose the parity it wanted between the franc and the mark. It would have availed itself of the necessary margin, as proven by the successful devaluations of 1958 [17%] and 1969 [12.5%], without which French devaluations are almost always ineffective.[33]

The introduction of 'austerity' policies in June 1982 marked the end of the experiment, but the pressures on the franc remained. In March 1983 – in a striking echo of the divisions in the British Labour government over the IMF loan in 1976 – the government split over how to cope with the 'external constraint'. The left, led by Jean-Pierre Chevènement – who, like Tony Benn, was industry minister[34] – wanted an abandonment of austerity and a turn to more radical measures to continue the expansion. Jacques Delors took the opposite line, insisting on the vital importance of sticking with the ERM. Delors prevailed. The franc was devalued for a third time – by 2.5%, the mark revalued by 5.5% – and in return the original programme on which the socialists were elected was comprehensively abandoned. From then on, the fight against inflation, rather than unemployment, was to take precedence. The French socialists never looked back – or, rather, forward – again.

From Reflation to Austerity

The traditional story of the reflation of 1981–82 is of a mistaken dash for expansion, provoking, through the influx of imports, a massive trade deficit. In important ways, this account is not satisfactory. First, the reflation was not politically avoidable; second, although economically risky, it remained modest in scope; and third, the trade deficit of 1982 was not principally caused by the reflation of 1981.

On the first point, coming to power after several decades in opposition, the Left had to satisfy the demands of a constituency victimized by a policy of austerity; although substantially weakened, the Communist Party could have proved a powerful opposition. The Socialists, whether they believed in the efficacy of the measures they were about to take, or whether they made 'a last concession to their political culture',[35] had no choice. Having promised change and having run so hard against the incumbent, they could not emulate Giscard and Barre without destroying at once their 'state of grace'. As Mauroy explained later: 'The policy of reflation was inevitable. It was the condition of our staying in power for five years'.[36]

Although risky, the reflation was modest in its scope. François Mitterrand had proclaimed his refusal 'to remain immobile in a lethargy that would precede death'.[37] Accordingly, his government behaved like 'a transmission belt attempting to ignite a lagging private investment'.[38] With the deteriorating supply-side conditions of French industry (declining profits) and import penetration high, any reflation entailed the risk of reflating imports before domestic production. But it was not necessary that the policy should succeed instantaneously: France's foreign currency holdings were very large, maybe sufficient to sustain the first few months of what could only be bad trade statistics.[39] Instead, these holdings were squandered in a futile attempt to maintain the parity of the franc. And the trade figures deteriorated sharply, in part because no protective steps were taken. Yet the so-called 'dash for expansion' remained relatively sluggish. Pierre Mauroy even acknowledged that:

> The reflation of consumer demand was more limited than I would have hoped. We had to be prudent. We could not take the risk of a brutal, inflationary flare-up.[40]

The figures bear him out. In 1975–76, Giscard's Prime Minister Jacques Chirac had initiated his own reflation through a rise in public spending and a cut in interest rates. The package amounted to a proportion of GNP comparable to that of Mitterrand's. However, the first attempt took place amid a global expansion, while the latter did not. And Mitterrand had to accommodate rising interest rates.[41]

These two differences bring us closer to the crux of the issue. The failure of the 1981 reflation was not principally caused by the reflation itself. The trade deficit of 1982 owed most of its size to the world-wide recession, the escalating value of the dollar, and the global trend to higher interest rates. As early as January 1982, *Le Nouvel Observateur* noted that: 'If the US recession continues, it risks causing the whole reflation package to fall apart.'[42] That is what it did. The need to follow the American rise in interest rates (for fear of renewed attacks on the franc) jeopardized a policy premised on a resumption of growth; it provoked a larger than expected budget deficit (due to loss of revenue); and it made any upsurge in investment unlikely because of the depression and the cost of capital. The sharp rise in the value of the dollar multiplied the cost of French imports (especially energy), without helping French exports to the US much (a limited amount in a very competitive market). Thus the domestic contribution to the 1982 trade deficit[43] amount to 27 billion francs; whereas international factors (a soaring dollar and rising interest rates) represented 57 billion francs.[44]

The political impact of the shift towards austerity was severe. Between February and October 1982, confidence in the government moved from a surplus of 24 percentage points (59% favourable, 35% unfavourable) to a deficit of one point (46% versus 47%). The shift was especially striking among workers and the young. The renaissance of the Right, a growing perception that the government was not keeping its promises, and a string of electoral setbacks all testified to the end of Mitterrand's 'state of grace'. In this, the retreat of June 1982 foretold the subsequent débâcles: during the referendum on Maastricht (September 1992), the 'no' vote was especially strong in the same areas of the country (Seine Saint-Denis, Nord, Limousin) and among the same social groups (employees: 58% 'no', industrial workers: 64% 'no') which had given François Mitterrand his largest winning margins in the presidential elections of 1981 and 1988. Lavishly praised by the media, the Left's 'new realism' has been repeatedly disavowed by its electorate.

Lessons of Failure

The reasons for the failure of the Mitterrand experiment are quite straight-forward. Once the political decision had been taken to put the ERM (and, by extension, the alliance and integration with West Germany) above all other public policy goals, the U-turn of March 1983 was unavoidable. The commitment to the narrow band of the ERM meant no independent fiscal and monetary policy could conceivably be followed. Even with the three small-scale realignments that were agreed, the *quid pro quo* – austerity policies to bring French inflation down at least to the EC average – meant an abandonment of expansion, growth, redistribution and anti-unemployment policies.

Ironically, by the end of 1983, the effects of devaluation had fed through and the current account deficit was well below its 1980 level. But the size of the devaluations only just matched the inflation differential with France's ERM partners.[45] The devaluations, as in the case of the British Labour government of 1964–70, were too little, too late. Consequently, their impact was felt long after the decision to abandon the socialist-communist programme had been made.

The international recession of the time meant that the room for manoeuvre was much reduced. Sharp devaluations (and probably some form of protection of the kind advocated by Chevènement) were necessary.

But in addition, the recession meant that – as has been argued by a number of analysts – the reflation was in fact much too timid. Far from being the reckless 'dash for growth' that is often portrayed, the expansion was too weak to offset the contractionary influences from outside. In 1982–83, the world recession cut demand for French exports by 5%. Given that exports were then about 20% of GDP, the contractionary effect was about 1% – or at least half the fiscal stimulus of 1981–82.[46]

It is widely argued among mainstream economists that the main reason for the failure of the 1981–82 reflation was supply-side factors – notably, relatively high employers' social security and labour costs – and that France had a non-accelerating inflation rate of unemployment of 7–8%.[47] However, real unit labour costs only increased marginally between 1980 and 1982 and fell steadily throughout the 1980s, while unemployment rose. The clear implication is that the rise in joblessness owed far more to contractionary policies and the franc fort policy than to supply-side factors in the labour market.

A more telling point is that the flight of capital and investment strike would have caused serious difficulties for the first Mitterrand administration even without the international recession and the self-defeating defence of the franc: between the first quarter of 1981 and the second quarter of 1982, 81% of the deterioration in the balance of payments was due to the capital, not the current, account;[48] and private investment fell sharply from 1981 to 1983.[49]

In reality, such a response to any radical reforming government is likely to be hard to avoid. The only way to have ridden it out in the French case would have been to have devalued sharply, pulled out of the ERM and called the speculators' bluff – knowing that the consequent fall in the exchange rate would soon become self-defeating and thus self-correcting. The investment strike required more decisive government intervention and a larger increase in public investment. But none of this amounts to the evidence of a hopeless cause finally exposed. Instead, the experiment of 1981–82 exposes a government implementing a strategy it was less than wholeheartedly committed to and which it abandoned at the first whiff of grape-shot.

The Legacy of 1981–82

There are few areas of the Mitterrand experiment of 1981–82 which have been subjected to greater criticism than the nationalisation programme. At the extreme, it is held to have been simply a hangover from the Common Programme with the Communist Party, which owed everything to political dogma and nothing to any genuine economic rationale.[50] We would argue that, on the contrary, the nationalisations were one of the few planks of the original 1981 platform that, despite the 1983 U-turn, can be said to have been a limited success – limited partly because with the U-turn the 'industrial policy had no time to become effective'.[51] In addition, 'the poor state of some nationalised firms meant they required unexpectedly thorough restructuring', and some of the sectoral plans ran up 'against Common Market regulations (e.g. subsidies to the textile industries)'.[52] From Spring 1983 'the government's industrial policy entered a more market-oriented phase . . . . The sectoral plans were scaled down or abandoned'.[53]

Despite this, the enlarged public sector did protect France's manufacturing base in a way that privatisation of industries in Britain did not, and allowed them generally to perform well at the cutting edge of industry, transport and communications. Thus although spending on investment and R&D in electronics fell short of the original plan, it still represented an increase over the 1970s, permitting the French electronics industry to reach a rate of growth of output of 8% in 1983.[54] And in some areas the planning contracts and increased subsidies seemed effectively to reverse decline.[55]

However, following the U-turn these achievements were also limited by political and economic choices which led the new public sector to mimic the strategies of privately-owned multinationals – investing heavily overseas while cutting jobs at home – rather than providing the originally intended motor of domestic industrial and social reconstruction. Nationalisation thus allowed a systematic restructuring of French industry on transnational lines. Ten years on, French publicly-owned industry is more competitive, but part of the price has been a level of joblessness which has sunk the government which turned industrial balance-sheets round.

The concerns nationalised in 1982 employed around 800 000 – of whom a quarter of a million worked abroad – and meant that of France's 20 main industrial groups, 13 belonged to the public sector.[56] Of the 12 industrial companies taken over in 1982, seven were among France's 20 biggest firms and five – Compagnie Générale d'Electricité (electrical), Thomson-Brandt (electronics), Saint-Gobain (glass and electronics), Pechiney-Ugine-Kuhlman (metals and chemicals) and Rhône-Poulenc (chemicals and textiles) – were major international groups. Three were subsidiaries of US and West German multinationals. Together, they brought 16% of industrial employment and 20% of industrial output under state control. They joined a public sector that was already large by Western standards. After 1982, the nationalised sector represented 24% of industrial employment, 32% of all turnover and 60% of investment. Half the production of companies of more than 2000 employees was in the public sector.[57]

The original aims of the public ownership programme were to generate employment and investment, lead the drive to rebuild French industry and recapture the domestic market, kick-start growth and create a new social dialogue. With the exception of CGE, the private industrial giants brought into the public sector were losing money on a huge scale and were highly vulnerable to foreign competition. In the context of the collapse of the government's macroeconomic expansion policies, the prospects for using the new public enterprises as the motor of growth evaporated. The costs of compensation were relatively small, given that asset-holders were essentially exchanging shares for government bonds.[58] But with the failure to achieve macroeconomic growth, losses grew inexorably. In 1984, the government initiated a massive restructuring programme, including large-scale redundancies and site-closures. Usinor and Sacilor were merged in 1986; the new company is now the second largest steel producer in the world after Nippon Steel. A major reorganisation of the chemical industry, for example, led to greater specialisation by Rhône-Poulenc and Pechiney (which was left to concentrate on the nuclear and electro-metallurgical industries). Thomson has narrowed down its operations to concentrate mainly on military electronics.[59]

The restructuring process was paid for by massive injections of state capital: 80 billion francs between 1982 and 1992 (mostly during the 1984–86 period) and total dividends, which now exceed investments, have so far been only 14.6 billion francs.[60] In the period of 'cohabitation' (between a right-wing government and President Mitterrand) from 1986–88, three of those companies natinalised in 1982 were privatised: CGE, Saint-Gobain and Matra. Although the weight of the public sector has fallen back – both as a result of the privatisations of the Right and the partial, creeping privatisations of the socialist government – it still remains the second largest public sector in the European Community after Italy. Using an index which combines employment, net value added and investment, the public sector now accounts for 18% of the French economy (set against 23% in 1982), compared with 6% in Britain (16% in 1982).[61]

In the words of Elie Cohen, research director of Paris's Centre National de la Récherche Scientifique, the 1982 nationalisations 'have made an essential contribution to the renewal and modernisation of French capi-talism'; whatever government had been in power in the early 1980s would have had to intervene heavily to modernise French industry.[62] Both the old and new public sectors are now in a far healthier state from the narow point of view of their balance sheets, though they are increasingly heavily indebted because of ambitious international acquisition policies.

Nationalisations which some viewed as having been 'more nationalist than socialist' have ended up at the forefront of French industry's rush to internationalisation, with a huge programme of expansion and acqui-sition.[63] Bull, the French chip manufacturer, is now joining forces with its greatest rival, the US giant IBM. State-owned Renault has taken a stake in Volvo. And Aérospatiale is forging ever-closer links with Daimler-Benz. More than half the sales of the nine largest nationalised industrial com-panies are overseas.

The French state sector has been increasingly active in buying up private sector companies abroad – in effect, creeping nationalisation on an inter-national scale. Keen though the British government has been to attract inward investment, including acquisitions of British firms by foreign ones, the European Commission had to intervene to stop the British government's practice of discriminating against French public sector firms taking over British private sector firms.[64] Rhône-Poulenc, for example, bought a majority stake in the profitable US pharmaceuticals company, Rorer, in 1990. The process of forging international joint ventures with other large nationally-based industrial groups is the product of necessity. In the aerospace, automotive and electronics industries, research and development costs and industrial investments are so huge, they increasingly need to be shared by even the largest companies.[65] The successful Airbus consortium – three of whose four participating companies were state-owned until British Aerospace was privatised – is an indication of the potential for public sector international cooperation.

Aérospatiale, Usinor-Sacilor and Thomson – all the product of companies nationalised in 1982 – now rate number two in the European aerospace, world steel and world defence electronics industries respectively.[66] The fate of Britain's attempts to establish a presence in electronic components is indicative: the company Inmos was founded in 1978 by the National Enterprise Board, but was sold off to Thorn EMI in 1984, who in turn sold it in March 1989 to SGS-Thomson, the Franco-Italian joint venture. Significantly, the partners in SGS-Thomson are the Italian state-owned IRI group and the French electronics group Thomson, also state-controlled.[67]

From the mid-1980s, the French socialist government began cautiously to retreat from public ownership by selling batches of shares in the nationalised sector. In 1988, when François Mitterrand was re-elected for a second seven-year term, the government established the so-called 'ni-ni' policy: 'ni nationalisations, ni privatisations' (neither nationalisations nor privatisations). By 1992, the Socialist Party had committed itself to 'opening up' the capital of public enterprises, and to a policy of 'privatisations *and* nationalisations'. The new government of the right is committed to privatisation in the so-called 'competitive sector', but is still cautious about selling off the public utilities. On both sides, the case for privatisation is made almost entirely on the basis of the need to raise cash, rather than from any suggestion that the private sector is inherently more dynamic or efficient.[68] There is no doubt in France that state capitalist enterprise can work effectively (although that of course was not all that was intended originally in 1981–82); indeed, when the conservative Balladur government unveiled its privatisation programme in the summer of 1993, the nationalised firms put up for sale – including those brought into the public sector in 1982 – were described as 'some of the world's finest blue-chip companies' (*Guardian*, 17 May 1993) and 'robust industrial concerns' (*Financial Times*, 27 May 1993).

The 'alternative' policies pursued through to 1993

By the end of 1992, after ten years of 'competitive disinflation' (the purpose of which was to create jobs by increasing market shares), unemployment in France had increased from 7.4% in May 1981 to 10.3% – a rise of almost 40%. There had also been a widening of income and wealth inequalities.[69] An official study of French incomes under Mitterrand's presidency reported that:

> Since 1982, the disposable income of all households has progressed much slower than national income: 8% versus 15%. . . . The rate of return for capital improves every year. This improvement has absorbed 60% of the gain in productivity and almost half of the growth of national income. The returns for labour, on the other hand, have improved very slowly. . . . A stabilisation if not a decline of wages, a sharp progression of property incomes, a slowing down of the growth of social entitlements . . . these are the great trends which have determined the evolution of household disposable income since the beginning of the 1980s.
>
> In constant francs, the total of all wages increased by only 5.8% between 1982 and 1988. It had grown by 63.5% between 1970 and 1982. [And taking into account an 18.7% increase in social security taxes] net wages fell by 1.4% from 1982 to 1988.[70]

Confronted with this study, Prime Minister Rocard acknowledged that 'a cultural revolution rehabilitating the enterprise' and a distribution of income more favourable to business were paid for by 'a decline of purchasing power, massive lay-offs, and growing job insecurity.'[71]

According to Blanchard and Muet (1993), the 'competitive deflation' pursued since 1983 would only eventually succeed in lowering the rate of unemployment by three percentage points if a 30% competitiveness gain could be accumulated – which France's trading partners would in any case be unlikely to accept. Indeed, several years' gain from France's deflationary pain were lost overnight when sterling and the lire were driven out of the ERM in 1992. Blanchard and Muet also cast doubt (pp. 31–2) on whether the increased profit rate forced through in the 1980s actually led to increased investment; even if investment does respond better to demand when profits are high, the growth of demand remains key.[72]

The 1993 Election

'The world of money is all-powerful. It won everything,'[73] Michel Rocard declared in 1993. He should know: between 1981 and 1993 he was a cabinet member or Prime Minister for seven of the 12 years when GNP grew by 30% while the average purchasing power of wage earners increased by only 5%. Were the profits reinvested towards the 'jobs of tomorrow'? The profits of the 66 largest industrial groups grew by 2.8% in 1991, 2.1% in 1992 and, it is estimated, will grow by 2.5% in 1993. Employment fell by 2.1% in 1991, 3.5% in 1992 and, it is estimated, by 2.6% in 1993.[74]

A few days before the 1993 election, Dominique Strauss-Kahn, the then socialist minister for industry, was asked by the *Wall Street Journal* 'what will change if the Right wins?', and answered: 'Nothing. Their economic policy won't be very different from the one we are conducting.'[75]

The Maastricht referendum of 1992 had reflected a divide between two constituencies: one working class, the other middle and upper class; one traditionally republican, the other traditionally Catholic; one opposed to a market-oriented Europe, the other promoting it. In the 1992 referendum and 1993 general election the Socialist Party was widely perceived as having abandoned its electoral base; in 1993, 15% of those who had voted Socialist in 1988 switched to the ecologists, 14% to the conservatives, 6% to the Communists and far left, 3% to the National Front and 19% abstained. In the space of five years the Socialists managed to lose more than half their voters. Their monetarist policies, despite being universally praised by the media, brought them the most severe electoral setback the Left had ever suffered in French history.

> The Left loses its way when it chooses a policy consisting in the sole play of market mechanisms in order to reassure the moneyed interests. Not only does it compromise its mission, but it also succeeds less well than would the adversary. In that case, it would be preferable to leave it to the adversary.[76]

Those words were written in 1977 by a young history professor in a book called *A History Lesson for the Left in Power*, analysing the failure of the Left government of Edouard Herriot in 1924, a government too weak to confront the 'wall of money'. By March 1993 the same writer had himself become a Minister in the Socialist Government and was running for a seat in the general election. He did not get elected and is no longer a Minister.

Conclusion

The French socialist experience has far-reaching implications for radical and alternative economic policies. The record of the public sector and industrial intervention in the 1980s offers important lessons for others. Even though the original industrial strategy was not fully pursued, there were clear examples of the benefits of public sector investment, for example in telecommunications.[77] They are indicative of the central role which the public sector can play in the creation of a modern productive infrastructure, in the development of successful industrial districts and in driving up the rate of industrial investment – all prerequisites for a return to sustainable full employment.

The French socialists' economic record also seriously undermines the case for the ERM and the single market as the wave of the future and a plausible basis for a return to anything remotely resembling full employment at national or at European level. This point is in any case becoming more widely accepted in the context of a process of European economic integration that is at the very least stalled, if not actually breaking down.

Crucially, the failure of the 1981–83 French reflationary experiment cannot legitimately be used to justify the widespread claim that effective national macroeconomic and industrial policies are no longer viable. The dangers of attempting to prop up the value of the currency, the deflationary pressures exerted by the ERM, the threat of capital flight, the certainty of balance of payments problems if demand was reflated were all anticipated by the French socialists before they took office. Their own programme specifically warned of the certain collapse into the deflationary policies that actually took place unless commitment to expansion was put above commitment to trade liberalisation and the ERM. There is nothing that happened in 1981–83 which could not be – and was not – foreseen or which was fundamentally different from the experience of the British Labour governments in the middle 1960s and 1970s. Quite simply, there was no political will to take the economic measures (and pay the political costs) necessary to maintain the expansion and carry out the original programme.

Certainly there are greater constraints on European governments today because of globalisation – notably of financial markets, but also because of the effects of the single market and closer trade integration. But the role for economic and industrial policy at national level remains massive. The breakdown of the ERM has widened the scope for such a role. Spending by the 12 EC national states is about 50 times the size of the European Commission's entire budget. In the absence of a coordinated European-wide expansion – and even in conjunction with one – large-scale action at national level is essential. Indeed, greater international economic integration means that the impact of successful national intervention is paradoxically greater than before. Conversely, a resigned abdication from active macroeconomic and industrial policy which allows a loss of competitive advantage, whether by one European country or by Europe as a whole, will have disastrous effects, magnified by global markets into a far faster loss of world and domestic markets, production and employment.

No More Jobs for the Boys

Edward Balls

The long-term unemployed are the main casualties of the economic changes that have hit Europe, and indeed most of the developed world, over the last two decades. Most have been out of work for years rather than months. Predominantly men, usually poorly educated and with few marketable skills, they did not find work when the economy was booming in the late 1980s. And they are unlikely to get jobs when the recovery finally arrives and job vacancies start to reappear. But Europe's unemployment problem is more severe than the unemployment statistics suggest. By focusing on 'unemployment' – people who are available and actively looking for work – OECD unemployment statistics exclude a group that should be of great importance to policy-makers: people who have no jobs and who have given up the search for employment. Developed societies ignore the non-employed at their peril, as the OECD has repeatedly stressed to developed country finance ministers over the past two years. OECD internal papers describe the growing links between joblessness and economic deprivation and their consequences: drug use and abuse, racial tensions and a rising tide of crime and violence. Yet, while the OECD's diagnosis is correct, its standard prescription – cuts in the level and duration of unemployment benefits – is flawed. The international evidence suggests that removing the ability of people without jobs to claim welfare benefits risks compounding rather than solving the problem, by pushing the unemployed off the official jobless count into economic inactivity rather than employment. It may succeed in reducing the measured unemployment rate, but the risk is that it will merely suppress the problem until it re-emerges in more damaging ways.

Unemployment and Non-employment

Unemployment rates rose in almost every OECD member country in the 1980s; the rise was concentrated among men, not women; it has remained persistently and exceptionally high in Europe. But rising unemployment is only part of the story. Male labour force participation has dropped sharply over the past decade, as many men have shifted from being 'unemployed' to 'economically inactive'. The common characteristic of these two groups is that they do not have jobs; all can be classified under the general heading of 'non-employed'. The pattern of unemployment and non-employment rates is very different. The US may be a low 'unemployment' country, but it is also a low employment country. Figure 7.1 shows the international pattern of non-employment rates in the 1980s: the sum of the unemployed and the economically inactive as a percentage of the total population. They cover men only, as males constitute the bulk of the unemployed, and they include people of prime working age, to exclude the impact on inactivity rates of higher educational participation among young people and early retirement among older men.

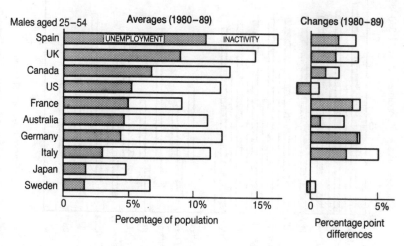

Figure 7.1.   Unemployment and non-employment in the 1980s.
Source: OECD *Employment Outlook* 1992.

Two patterns emerge: first, non-employment rates are much more constant across countries than are unemployment rates. The US, Canada and Australia have non-employment rates similar to those in Europe. Only Japan and Sweden have low non-employment rates by OECD standards. And second, non-employment rose during the 1980s in almost every OECD country. In continental Europe, this rise was largely reflected in the unemployment statistics. Elsewhere – the UK, Australia, Canada and Sweden – the rise in inactivity was at least as important as the rise in unemployment. The US is the exception: its non-employment rate fell slightly, after rising in the 1970s. But it was the standard around which the rest of the OECD converged. The non-employment rate of men aged 25–55 had doubled in the US since 1970, but tripled in the UK, France and Germany. This rising trend of male inactivity has been more than matched by increased employment of women. Figure 7.2 compares the percentages of men and women that had jobs on average across the 1980s. It covers the 25–54 age group only, to avoid complications caused by education or early retirement.

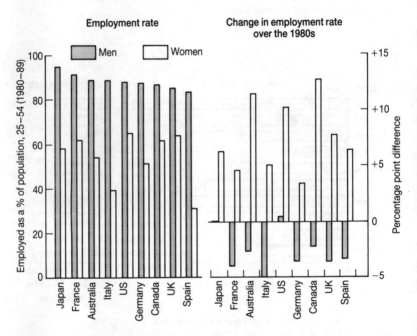

Figure 7.2. The employment battle of the sexes.
Source: OECD *Employment Outlook*, July 1992.

Male employment rates are universally higher than female employment rates. But, roughly speaking, those countries with lower male employment rates have higher female employment rates. The US, for example, has a male non-employment problem at least as serious as in the main European countries. But the US also has the highest rate of female employment, followed closely by the UK and Canada. Women are catching up fast. Female employment rates rose in every country between the beginning and the end of the decade, while the male employment rate fell everywhere except in the US and Japan. Again, the rise in female employment was relatively rapid in those countries where the male employment rate was lower: the US, UK and Canada.

Why do so few men work?

When the focus of attention is shifted from unemployment to non-employment rates, many of the standard explanations of the persistence of unemployment rates in the 1980s appear to break down: first, the rise in unemployment in Europe over the past few years is undoubtedly due, in large part, to the high interest rates and slow growth that the European exchange rate mechanism transmitted from Germany across the Continent. But while lower interest rates and more expansionary fiscal policies might reduce Europe's unemployment problem, they will not solve it. For slow growth cannot explain why non-employment remained so high throughout the period of strong economic growth in the latter half of the 1980s. Even a robust European recovery over the next few years will leave European unemployment rates at twice their level of two decades ago.

Second, the pace of real wage growth across Europe in the 1980s was rapid in light of the overhang of unemployment, especially in the UK. Maybe the employed insiders have prevented the unemployed from getting back into jobs. But why did this rise in non-employment in the UK occur when trade union membership was falling and labour market regulations were being relaxed? Nor did America escape the rise in non-employment, despite relatively weak labour unions. UK unemployment remained above 1.5 million in the late 1980s, despite a high level of vacancies in all regions of the country, for unskilled as well as skilled jobs. (See Balls, Katz and Summers, 1992).

And third, countries which have limited unemployment benefits do appear to have faced less serious unemployment problems. Both the US and Sweden have relatively low unemployment rates and restrict the duration of unemployment pay: to 26 weeks in the US and one year in Sweden. Britain's Restart programme, introduced in 1986, was intended to have similar effects; the evidence appears encouraging. Unemployed people were required to attend regular interviews, the eligibility requirements for unemployment benefits were tightened, and the male unemployment rate, as measured by the OECD, fell from 11% to 6.3% in just four years. But to conclude that limiting unemployment benefit durations will increase male employment is to misread the evidence of the 1980s. Once unemployment rates are replaced with non-employment rates, the simple correlation between benefit duration and joblessness breaks down. US men without jobs are less likely to say they are actively seeking work, because they do not receive welfare payments if they do. The duration of benefits does not appear to affect total joblessness, only how that joblessness is allocated between unemployment and inactivity. The same criticism applies to Britain's Restart programme: the unemployment rate for men aged 45–64 fell from 7.4% in 1984 to 5.5% in 1989, but the non-employment rate actually rose over the same period from 18% to 19.4%. Many of these men were reallocated from unemployment to sickness and disability benefits. The number of men claiming these benefits rose by 6% between 1980 and 1986, but by a third between 1986 and 1990, adding nearly 400,000 new claimaints (see Schmitt and Wadsworth, 1993).

Trade, brains and brawn

Variation across countries in rates of economic growth, wage-bargaining institutions, benefit levels, and active support for the unemployed is large. But these national differences disguise a feature that all developed countries share the collapse in the demand for unskilled male labour in manufacturing industry. The fall in the share of manufacturing in total employment has affected all OECD countries. Between 1970 and 1987 the share of industrial employment in total employment fell by 7.3 percentage points in the US, by 8.4 percentage points in France and by 14.9 percentage points in the UK. In the UK, employment of unskilled manual workers fell 9.7% between 1979 and 1989 and the employment of partly skilled (and more highly paid) manual workers fell even faster – by 13.6% over the same period. This fall in manufacturing employment has particularly hurt unskilled men who could in the past demand relatively high wages. In the modern and competitive era, high-wage, low-skill, 'good' jobs are a thing of the past. Unemployment rates are much higher for workers with low educational qualifications. Demand for unskilled labour has fallen for two reasons: increased competition from the developing world and a shift within manufacturing industry towards higher skilled, white collar employment as the result of technological change.

Is developing country competition to blame?

The popular view that competition from low-cost producers in developing countries poses a growing threat to jobs and incomes in industrial countries is gaining ground. Both Ross Perot, one of the 1992 US presidential candidates, and senior Democrats in the US Congress have latched onto this fear. Nor is it surprising that Perot managed to strike a raw nerve. In the minds of many blue-collar Americans, the North American Free Trade Agreement spells lower wages and fewer jobs. The experience over the last two decades suggests that low-wage, low-skill workers do have reason to worry about their economic security. Developing country exports to the developed have certainly grown rapidly over the past three decades, and exports from the East Asian economies have grown even faster: by an average 9.2% between 1965 and 1980, and 10.2% a year between 1980 and 1990. The share of developing country goods in total developed country consumption of manufactures has more than tripled in the last 25 years. Yet developing country trade is still too small to have significant negative effects on wages and employment in developed countries. The penetration of developing country imports into developed country markets may be growing, but it remains low. Developing country

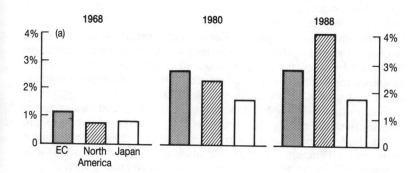

Figure 7.3(a). Imports from developing countries as a share of consumption (all manufactures).
Source: World Bank: *Global Economic Prospects* 1992.

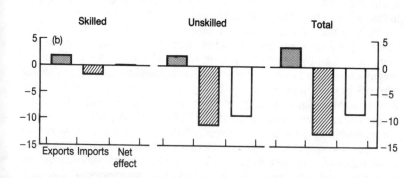

Figure 7.3(b). Cumulative impact on manufacturing employment in industrial countries, 1990 (million jobs per year).
Source: Wood (1991).

exports account for less than one-tenth of the manufacturing imports of developed countries, and only 3.1% of total manufacturing consumption. Even if all developing countries had achieved South Korean-style export growth in the 1980s, this share would have been a mere 0.6 percentage points higher. The impact of trade on labour-intensive manufacturing industry in developed countries, however, has been more pronounced. The share of developing country trade in industrial country imports of these goods has grown from 9.8% in 1965 to 18.7% in 1989, and developing country clothing producers now account for 22.1% of total clothing consumption in industrial countries. Adrian Wood of the Institute of Development Studies at Sussex University argues that the cumulative effects of developing country trade on manufacturing employment in industrial countries over the last 30 years are much higher than the conventional wisdom suggests. Skilled employment has increased very slightly – the extra jobs created by higher exports outweighed the jobs displaced by imports. But for unskilled employees, the losses have swamped the gains. By 1990 total manufacturing employment was a net 9 million jobs lower for the industrial countries.

Still, estimates of the manufacturing employment cost of developing country trade are not so large compared to the actual decline in manufacturing employment that has occurred. The decline in the share of manufacturing in total employment in industrial countries, from 29% in the mid-1960s to 22% in the mid-1980s, implies a loss of 20 million jobs.

Victims of the high technology age

Labour-saving technological change is a second and probably more important reason for the decline in blue-collar employment. In the UK, for example, productivity grew rapidly in the 1980s – by an average 5% a year, compared with just 0.9% between 1975 and 1980, and among the main industrialised countries, only Japan had faster productivity growth – but the bulk of the gain in output per head was achieved by shedding jobs, rather than increasing output and investment. Manufacturing employment has fallen by more than a third since 1979, while the real value of manufacturing output is below its 1979 level. The share of craft and skilled workers in total manufacturing employment fell from 31.3% in 1971 to 28.1% in 1990, while the share of plant and machine operatives fell from 24.6% to 21.7% over the same period. Evidence of this shift in demand for labour within manufacturing in favour of skilled and educated workers is most readily available in the US. Berman, Bound and Griliches (1993) show that over the past 30 years, the growth of manufacturing output, capital and raw materials in US manufacturing has consistently outstripped employment. But while the number of non-production workers has continued to grow, blue-collar employment has stagnated since the mid-1970s (Figure 7.4).

Figure 7.4. US manufacturing output and input volumes, percentage change since 1959.
Source: Berman, Bound and Griliches (1993).

Between 1979 and 1989 employment of US production workers fell by 2.2 million to 12.3 million, while non-production employment increased by 0.2 million to 6.7 million, raising the share of non-production employment from 23% in 1973 to 29% in 1989. While the share of imports in total US manufacturing shipments also doubled over that period, Berman, Bound and Griliches estimate that less than a third of the increase in the share of non-production workers in total employment in the 1980s occurred because old, labour-intensive industries were replaced by new, high-tech industries. More than two-thirds of the increase in non-production employment occurred within existing industries as they upgraded their technology and expanded the use of computers. Not surprisingly, non-production workers – engaged in supervision, management and administration, technology and product development, sales and delivery – are more likely to have educational qualifications and are better paid than their blue-collar counterparts. More than 90% of non-production workers graduated from high school in 1987, compared with 70% of production workers. Only 17% of blue-collar workers attend further education, half the average for all manufacturing employees.

A more unequal world

This structural shift has left a residue of poorly educated, unskilled male labour in Europe and the US whose market value has fallen sharply. Not surprisingly, wage inequality has grown across the industrialised world over the past two decades. The wages of young, inexperienced and poorly educated workers, particularly men, have fallen relative to better educated, high-skill workers. Lawrence Katz and Gary Loveman of Harvard University tracked the changes in wage inequality in the UK, the US and France, finding the relative wages of low-paid workers to have fallen sharply in the US and the UK over the past two decades, although in France the difference between earnings of the lowest and highest-paid workers narrowed from the mid-1970s, before rising again from 1984 (Figure 7.5).

The wage inequality index shows changes in the difference between average wages of the top and bottom 10% of adult males (with 1970 as a base year). The differential itself was wider in France than in the UK in 1970, and remains so today, while wage inequality remains highest in the US.

Falling demand for unskilled labour had different effects on wages and unemployment because of cross-country differences in labour markets. The US and UK have seen similar increases in overall wage inequality over the past two decades. The US rise was spread evenly over the entire period, while in Britain the rise was concentrated in the 1980s, since the incomes policies of the 1970s reduced wage inequality. In the US, relative wages rose for non-manual, educated and experienced workers. In the UK the relative earnings of non-manual and educated workers also rose, but the relative fall in unskilled wages was greater for men aged over 40 than for younger men. But there was one important difference between the US and the UK: the real wages of the lowest-paid 10% of workers fell by 10% between 1979 and 1987 in the US (and by 30% since 1970), but they rose by 10% in the UK. In France, earnings inequality fell from the mid-1970s to the mid-1980s, though it has risen again since. Young and unskilled workers in France did not experience a decline in their relative wages, while real wages also rose, particularly for manual workers. But France has not escaped these forces. The wages of the top 10% of French workers have risen rapidly relative to the average. But the combination of a relatively high minimum wage and unemployment benefits has put a floor to wages at the bottom of the wage distribution. Instead, poorly educated French workers have been progressively priced out of work, leading to persistently high rates of unskilled, youth and female unemployment. In

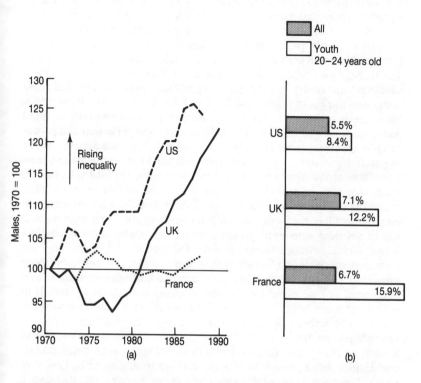

Figure 7.5.(a). Wage inequality index (log difference between the average weekly wage of the top and bottom decile of adult males wage-earners).
Source: Katz and Loveman (1990).

Figure 7.5.(b). Male unemployment rates, 1990.
Source: OECD. Standardised unemployment rates.

France, then, the rise in labour market adjusted mainly through quantities rather than prices, and inequality widened occurred between the employed and the unemployed. Katz and Loveman argue that the French statutory minimum wage, and the practice of negotiating industry-wide minimum wage levels, prevented a fall in wages of the unskilled and young. The level of the minimum wage has remained above 60% of the mean non-agricultural wage over the past two decades and has risen relative to unskilled earnings. The failure of relative wages of the unskilled to fall caused the employment prospects of less-skilled young people to deteriorate sharply in the 1980s. Consequently, youth and female unemployment has been consistently higher in France than in both the UK and the US.

This difference helps explain why, when the fall in male employment has been universal, the rise in female employment occurred more rapidly outside continental Europe. Anglo-Saxon deregulated labour markets have done better at job creation. In these countries, the demise of heavy industrial, highly paid, 'good jobs' has been more than offset by the growth of less well paid, often part-time, employment in the service sector. The share of part-time employment in total UK employment was 21.8% in 1990, up from 16.4% in 1979. The US part-time share was 16.9% in 1990, compared to 12% in France and 5.7% in Italy. Women have proved to be both cheap and flexible relative to men. They take the bulk of these part-time jobs – 87% in Britain, 78% in Australia, 68% in the US – and often at lower wages than men would command. Part-time female workers are more likely to have children, and while single women tend to earn at least 90% of the hourly wage paid to single men, married women earn much less: 69% in Australia and 59% in the US and UK.

But the collapse in unskilled wages in the US and the growth of female employment has not solved the male non-employment problem. The US has as severe a non-employment problem as France. Lower unskilled wages may allow more women to enter the labour market, but they also encourage more men to find alternative sources of income elsewhere. Very low relative wages for unskilled jobs and a lack of income support have been cited as one cause for the rise in crime committed by American youths who are officially 'inactive' but unofficially active outside the system. The rather sketchy US evidence suggests that badly educated young men can triple their take-home pay though crime. A survey in Boston in 1989 found that over two-thirds of young men believed they could make more money 'on the streets', up from a third in 1980. The LSE's Professor Richard Freeman points to the way the increase in incarceration has been concentrated among the uneducated, and there-fore among blacks who are much less likely to finish high school. By 1986, 7.4% of US male high school drop-outs aged 25–34, and 26% of black male drop-outs, were in prison. One-fifth of all black men aged 16–34 had a criminal record in the 1980s, compared to 7% of all men in that age group.

The UK is increasingly taking the US route. The real wages of the low paid have not fallen, but wage inequality rose more sharply than in Europe as labour market regulations were dismantled. Unemployment benefits, though permanent, are low compared with the rest of Europe. Little wonder then that the UK is taking on other US characteristics: high vacancies and rapid female employment growth alongside a rising pool of non-employed, and increasingly unemployable, men 'active' outside the system. *Regional Trends* highlights the rise in crime and drug-related crime that has occurred, particularly where unemployment has been high over the past decade.

Only Sweden appears to have bucked the trend, maintaining both relatively low unemployment and non-employment rates and a relatively equal wage distribution, despite a fall in manufacturing employment. Sweden's average unemployment rate actually fell by 0.2 percentage points between 1968–73 and 1985–90, compared to a rise of 5.1 percentage points in Germany and 5.9 percentage points in the UK. Yet the conventional explanations for Sweden's success – its retraining schemes for the unemployed – do not seem satisfactory. While Sweden's active labour market programmes pushed a quarter to a third of outflows from unemployment into relief work and training, the OECD has not been able to find empirical evidence to suggest that they actually improved the job prospects of participants. In any case, they absorbed on average less than 3% of the labour force in the 1980s. Perhaps the key element in Sweden's success story is public sector employment – Sweden has traditionally had a larger government sector than other European countries (Figure 7.6).

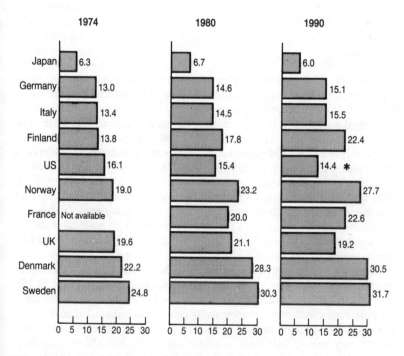

Figure 7.6. Government employment as percentage of total employment, 1974–90.
Source: OECD.
*1989 figure.

While the share of government employment in total employment rose by 2.1 percentage points in Germany between 1974 and 1990, and actually fell marginally in the UK, it rose by 6.9 percentage points in Sweden over the same 16-year period. Sweden was not alone. Aside from the dramatically small size of Japan's government sector, the striking feature of Figure 7.6 is the rapid growth of public sector employment across the Nordic countries, all of which, with the exception of Denmark, maintained very low unemployment rates by European standards in the 1980s. This growth of public sector employment also helps show how the Nordic countries were able to avoid the rise in wage inequality that plagued many other developed countries as a result of the declining demand for unskilled labour. The growth in part-time employment among unskilled workers in the UK and US in the 1980s, largely in the private sector, required a large relative fall in the wages of low-paid workers. In Sweden, the burden was borne not by low-paid workers, but by taxpayers who financed the growth in better-paid public sector jobs. By 1988, total Swedish taxes had risen to 55% of gross domestic product, compared to a European average tax share of 41%.

Conclusion

The OECD and the European Commission are increasingly worried about the impact of high unemployment on economic efficiency and social stability: 'High unemployment entails economic waste and widespread individual hardship' (OECD 1992 *Employment Outlook*). And the costs are not just economic. Internal OECD briefing papers write of the links between joblessness and economic deprivation: drug abuse, racial tension and a rising tide of crime and violence: 'The accompanying process of economic and social exclusion can endanger social cohesion'. The OECD fears that the current economic slowdown, and ensuing increase in unemployment, will make these problems both more perceptible and acute, with dangerous consequences for social cohesion and political stability. Yet these trends will only be accelerated if the OECD's recommendation that unemployment benefit be curtailed is adopted. It may succeed in reducing the measured unemployment count, but men will merely be encouraged to earn a living outside the system, as has occurred in the US. The more relevant question is how OECD countries can subsidise unskilled men in a more economically efficient manner. Supporting the unskilled unemployed to do nothing through the unemployment benefit system may be wasteful; the available evidence suggests that paying them to retrain has little impact on their chances of employment; and paying them decent wages to work in the public sector is very expensive, as Sweden has discovered. But developed countries cannot afford to ignore the non-employed. The risk in stopping benefits or replacing them with poorly paid workfare schemes is that the young unemployed will be driven not into employment but into the criminal economies of modern cities. A better option is to subsidise employment, so closing the gap between what the illegal economy offers young people and what the market will pay. Subsidising their employment, in either the private or public sectors, makes more sense than leaving the long-term unemployed to decay.

8

European Integration and Growth[1]

Horst Reichenbach, Guillermo Davila Muro and
Stefan Lehner

The European Community is going through a phase of slow growth which is proving longer and more severe than expected. Instead of the hoped-for recovery, 1993 will bring a third year of slow growth, with a return to healthier rates of expansion expected for 1994 at the earliest. Unemployment is increasing and cannot be expected to stabilise until well into 1994.

Unfortunately, the scope for economic policy to stimulate growth in the short term is very limited. Budget deficits have swollen and are already higher than at the beginning of the 1980s. Consequently, the margin of manoeuvre for fiscal policy is severely constrained in most countries. Nevertheless, member states and the Commission have made a serious attempt to put together a credible growth initiative as requested by the 1992 Edinburgh European Council.

The conclusions of the April 1993 Ecofin meeting provide a synopsis of these efforts. This chapter does not describe or comment on the Edinburgh growth initiative, but rather addresses the more medium- and long-term issue of the relationship between European integration and economic growth. The proposition is that this relationship is positive in both senses. On the one hand, deepened integration has furthered economic growth, and, on the other hand, during expansion periods it has been easier to further accelerate the integration process. In addition, growth and deepened integration have had a positive impact with regard to the objective of cohesion, i.e. regional income differentials have been reduced. As this holds for the past, there are good reasons to be also optimistic for the future in a medium-term perspective of three to five years.

This chapter provides a synopsis of trade and economic growth effects of European integration by a selective reference to the existing literature,[2] examining the link between integration and the reduction of regional income disparities in the Community. Further integration potential from the internal market and Economic and Monetary Union (EMU) is indicated, and against this background of the medium-term integration process, the potential economic impact of the transition to EMU is analysed.

Trade and Growth Effects of European Integration

Economic analysis points to both static and dynamic welfare gains from economic integration. Typically these arise from the elimination of cost-increasing barriers to trade, improved resource allocation, the pro-competitive effects on market structures and business practices, the attraction of foreign direct investment and finally positive psychological effects on the expectations of economic agents. Ultimately, economic integration should increase intra-regional trade and economic growth.[3]

Trade and economic growth in the European Community since 1957

The steady increase in intra-EC trade can be categorised into three distinct periods which closely correlate with the intensity of integration efforts. The first period (1957–73) saw intra-EC trade as a percentage of total trade rise from some 35% to above 50%. High economic growth alone throughout this period cannot account for so rapid a reorientation of trade patterns. Rather, the dismantling of trade barriers and construction of a customs union were crucial determinants. During the second period (1973–84), the level of intra-Community trade stagnated, albeit subject to fluctuations. An unfavourable economic climate put a halt to meaningful integration efforts, and led to a proliferation of non-tariff barriers between the member states. Throughout the third period (1985–92), the share of intra-EC trade jumped 10 percentage points, from 50% to some 60%. European integration initiatives throughout this period were intense, following the publication of the Commission's White Paper in 1985, the adoption of the Single European Act and the successful realisation of the 1992 single market programme.

Much of the growth in intra-EC trade has been intra-industry trade, an indication of the exploitation of economies of scale, factor mobility and the harmonisation of consumer preferences in Community markets (Greenaway, 1989). Some 63% of intra-EC trade was of an intra-industry nature in 1987; 70% if Portugal and Greece[4] are excluded (Sapir, 1992).

The degree of trade openness provides a further indication of the effects of integration, i.e. the average ratio of total (intra+extra) EC imports and exports as a percentage of GDP. It has increased substantially for all member states: for the EC as a whole it jumped from 15.3% over the period 1961–70 to 23.3% during 1980–90 (Commission of the EC, 1992). Furthermore, the share of EC trade in world trade flows increased from 24.9% for the EC6 in 1957 to 41.4% for the EC12 in 1990. According to evidence presented in de Melo, Panagariya and Rodrik (1992), accessions to the Community only account for a part of this change, implying a positive impact of integration on the Community's overall trade activities.

This latter feature provides an important indication that regional integration in the EC is not imposing significant trade diversion costs on third countries. The Community remains the largest world trading partner, with extra-EC trade of goods and services accounting for 20.7% of world trade in 1990, compared with 16.8% for the US and 9.7% for Japan (Commission of the EC, 1993b). Between 1986 and 1991, the volume of extra-EC imports rose by 40.3%, compared with 30.7% for intra-EC imports, suggesting that foreign producers have been able to exploit the single market opportunity. Some authors (Messerlin, 1992; Lawrence, 1991; Hufbauer, 1990) argue that the existence of the EC has been a key factor in the realisation of successive GATT rounds.

The EC's share in world GDP has increased from 22.5% in 1965 to 23.5% in 1989 (Winters, 1993).[5] Moreover, economic growth, like trade, has closely matched the periods of successful integration initiatives, with the causality likely to be operating in a two-way fashion. On average, EC GDP grew by 4.8% p.a. during the period 1961–70, well above the trend level of 3.4% for the entire period 1960–90. Thereafter, the rate of economic growth declined and only rebounded after 1985. From 1986–90, growth averaged 3.2% p.a. compared with 1.4% between 1980 and 1985. The favourable performance of the Community is even more striking when one examines the growth in the levels of GDP per person employed. For the EC, this grew at a rate of 3.0% p.a. from 1960 to 1990, much higher than the 1.1% recorded by the US.

Ex-ante studies on the effects of economic integration

A static approach was employed in the Cecchini Report (Commission of the EC, 1988) to estimate the potential gains from the single market programme, which concluded that the removal of all barriers to trade and production would yield an increase in EC GDP of between 2.2% and 2.7%. However, when the effects of economies of scale from restructuring and increased production were accounted for, as well as the competitive effects on X-inefficiency and monopoly rents, the potential gains amounted to between 4.3% and 6.4% of GDP, depending upon the underlying assumptions. Haaland and Norman (1992), using a general equilibrium model with imperfect competition, attempted to forecast the impact on Scandinavian countries of accession to the EC. They estimated that EFTA countries would benefit from accession by some 3% of their expenditure on tradeable goods.

More recent research has focused attention upon the dynamic effects of integration, and points to very large additional gains. Baldwin (1992) considers that static growth effects ignore the endogeneity of capital. Trade liberalisation, by raising the return to capital over the medium run, may induce greater capital accumulation. Using the Cecchini estimates for the static gains from the 1992 programme, Baldwin concludes that the indirect benefits from integration due to an endogenous increase in capital accumulation are considerable for all member states, ranging between 0.6% and 8.9% of GDP. Combined, the static and dynamic benefits of the single market programme range between 3.1% and 15.4% of GDP.

Dornbusch (1989) highlighted the influence of the integration process on the expectations of economic agents (so-called 'animal spirits'). For example, a credible announcement of a move to a single market will induce increased investment. Producers will anticipate additional competitive pressures from external competitors and hence increase investment, either for defensive purposes (to defend domestic market share) or as part of an offensive strategy (to exploit the additional opportunities associated with larger markets). Entrepreneurs will rush to first-mover advantage and thereby gain temporary oligopolistic rents.[6]

Ex-post studies on the economic effects of integration

Ex-post evaluations of the welfare effects of economic integration were traditionally measured in a static partial equilibrium framework in terms of trade creation and trade diversion.[7] For example, Balassa (1975) concludes that trade creation far outweighs trade diversion, although the net effect is relatively small, 1% of GDP.[8] This positive outcome is confirmed in most other studies of a similar nature, which are reviewed by Ohly (1993).

An alternative approach is to compare the growth experiences of industrialised countries which have experienced integration with those which have not. Maddison (1987), using the neoclassical growth theory, examined nine structural factors[9] for economic growth in six countries: the US, France, Germany, the Netherlands, the UK and Japan.[10] On average, these factors explain only 65% of the growth rate in the European economies, leaving a much larger unexplained residual compared with the US and Japan. This residual could be attributed to European integration as a specific factor of growth in European economies.[11] Crafts (1992) provides a revised version of Maddison's research. The thesis that integration favours economic growth is supported through the faster convergence of labour productivity in Europe with US levels than was recorded by other industrialised countries (excluding Japan).[12] A possible explanation for the growth residuals estimated by Maddison and Crafts is provided by de Melo, Panagariya and Rodrik (1992), who stress that technological diffusion is more prevalent in an integrated economic area with adequate competitive pressures.

Using a dynamic version of the foreign trade multiplier, Marques Mendes (1986) decomposes the global effects of economic integration into several components[13] for two periods: EC6 for 1961–72 and EC9 for 1974–81. During the first period, the Benelux countries benefited most from integration, with half their growth rate attributed to EC member-ship. For the second period, the contribution to growth is also substantial, ranging from 59% for France to 8% for Ireland, with export growth being the dominant force in integration effects.

Conclusive evidence of the positive effect of European integration on French economic growth is provided by Coe and Moghadan (1993). They suggest that 0.7 percentage points out of a 3.0% annual average growth rate over the period 1971–91 is attributable to European integration. They further predict that 0.5 percentage points out of a forecast growth rate of 2.9% for 1992–97 will be due to the European single market. Furthermore, EC integration will positively impact upon investment and R&D and thereby substantially enhance the potential output.

Integration and the Reduction of Regional Disparities

A key question for the Community is whether economic integration leads to the reduction of regional income disparities. Levine and Renalt (1992) tested the robustness of explanatory variables for economic growth. Only a few were found to be significant, namely the investment/GDP ratio, initial levels of human capital and the degree of trade openness, all of which suggest that some convergence should take place in the EC. Ben-David (1992a) confirms decreasing levels of income disparity in the EC, a trend which does not arise in other regional groupings.[14] The close link with the timing of tariff reductions allows Ben-David to conclude that a strong relationship exists in the reduction of intra-EC income differentials and the functioning of the common market. For EFTA, Ben-David (1992b) finds that income convergence lags behind trade liberalisation by more than seven years. Hence, trade liberalisation within the Community had a greater impact on income convergence among EFTA countries than had their own internal trade reforms.

Cingolani (1993) obtains a Theil index of per capita income disparity of 0.00753 among the EC12 for 1989. This figure increases with the level of disaggregation. Cingolani concludes that half of the variance is due to inter-country differences. After declining sharply during the 1950s and 1960s, income disparities hardly changed over the period 1970–90. However, the structure of the differences has altered, with inter-country disparities declining (from 0.0095 to 0.00753) while the intra-country regional component was virtually unchanged. The decrease in cross-country disparities coincided with periods of integration, 1970–75 and 1985–90. Finally, Cingolani finds evidence that regions which are initially less developed showed a tendency to grow faster than developed regions.

The Internal Market

By the beginning of 1993 the internal market programme which the Community had embarked upon in 1985 had been largely achieved; 95% of the 282 measures foreseen in the White Book had been adopted at Community level, over 80% of the programme had entered into force and member states had transposed 75% of the measures into national law.

The analysis of the economic impact has to take into account the time profile of the completion of the internal market. Few changes had come into effect before 1992. Nevertheless there are indications that between 1987 and 1991 the growing credibility of the internal market programme had already considerably changed the strategies of many Community enterprises: a strong increase in intra-Community trade (the share of which in total Community imports plus exports increased from 50.6% in 1984 to 60.1% in 1991), a wave of Community-wide mergers and acquisitions by the 1,000 largest Community enterprises (1984/85: 44, 1989/90: 257), a strong increase in foreign direct investment and growth rates of real gross fixed capital formation in equipment close to 10% p.a. from 1987 to 1989, some of which was explicitly motivated by preparation for the internal market. In sectors which had been characterised by particularly strong non-tariff barriers, intra-EC exports increased dramatically.[15] It would therefore appear that a significant part of the favourable economic development in the Community in the second part of the 1980s can be attributed to anticipatory effects of the internal market.

Short of a repetition of the Cecchini Report exercise,[16] no reliable quantification of these effects can be provided. A comparison of actual GDP and employment growth from 1987 to 1992 for the EC, the United States and Japan with the trend rates for 1981–90 indicates that the Community was subject to a positive shock in this period far larger than its trading partners. A more sophisticated approach comparing observed values of GDP and employment with a 'no change' forecast indicates similarly that since 1988 a structural and positive effect on GDP and employment has occurred independently of the cyclical upturn.[17] The cumulative impact on GDP may have reached 3.5% by 1990 (1.5% on employment), remaining at that level during 1991 and 1992; i.e. it is still present underneath the current recession.[18] A similar conclusion can be inferred for the Community labour market using the Prognos projections for Community employment until the year 2000, without the internal market as a baseline. The second half of the 1980s saw record expansion of Community employment (9.5 million additional jobs between 1985 and 1991) exceeding the Prognos baseline by some 2 million persons employed in 1992 (1.6% of total employment).[19]

Most measures have only come into effect from 1992 onward, and important changes are to be expected in the regulatory framework for several important sectors during the 1990s (insurance, financial services, automobiles, air and road transport). It is therefore quite likely that an important part of the efficiency enhancing and growth stimulating effects of the internal market will still be realised during the 1990s.

Economic and Monetary Union

While the effects of the completion of the internal market are working their way through the system, the Community has already defined the way ahead for further economic integration. The second stage of Economic and Monetary Union (EMU) will start for all member states on 1 January 1994 and provides for a period of transition and preparation of at most five years[20] to successfully launch a stable EMU. From the beginning of stage two a newly created European Monetary Institute will coordinate the monetary preparations for the final stage of EMU. Furthermore, new rules against monetary financing of budgetary deficits, privileged government access to financial markets and the 'bail out' of member states by the Community or other member states will come into effect and strengthen the direct link between the individual budgetary situation of a member state and the risk premia it faces in the financial markets. Furthermore, market constraints on public deficits will be complemented by a Community procedure to avoid 'excessive deficits' (see below). For most member states, the predominant task in this transition will be to continue and, where necessary, reinforce economic policies to meet the convergence criteria which would give them access to the third stage of EMU.

In the Treaty and attached protocols, four 'convergence criteria'[21] have been specified:

(1) a high degree of price stability – interpreted to mean an average rate of consumer price inflation that does not exceed by more than 1.5 percentage points that of the three best performing member states;
(2) an exchange rate within the normal band of the Exchange Rate Mechanism (ERM) for at least two years without severe tensions;
(3) a long-term interest rate indicative of durable convergence, i.e. which does not exceed by more than 2 percentage points that of the three best performing member states in terms of price stability; and
(4) a sustainable financial position – the member states must not be subject of a Council decision that an 'excessive deficit' exists.

While the first three criteria are rather straightforward, assessment of a sustainable financial position is more complex.[22] It starts from two identifiable quantitative thresholds. The first asks whether the ratio of the government deficit to GDP exceeds 3%, unless either the ratio has declined substantially and reached a level that comes close to 3%, or alternatively, the excess over 3% is only exceptional and temporary, and the ratio remains close to 3%. The second asks whether the ratio of government debt to GDP exceeds 60%, unless the ratio is sufficiently diminishing and approaching the reference value at a satisfactory pace.

Both thresholds set ambitious quantitative targets, but allow room to take into account the dynamic development of the budgetary situation of a member state, as well as to a certain extent the play of automatic stabilisers.

There has been considerable debate going back to the 1970s whether any *ex-ante* convergence would be required for a monetary union. On the one hand, according to the 'monetarist' view, nominal convergence (of prices, budget deficits, interest rates, etc) is not a prerequisite for monetary union because this convergence would be brought about automatically following a credible announcement of a date for a monetary union. Proponents of this theory rely on the credibility of the announcement, adequate changes in expectations and the effective functioning of the financial markets to deliver 'converging' developments of wages, prices and interest rates. The Treaty measures to strengthen the constraints imposed by the financial markets are inspired from this view.[23] On the other hand, the 'economist's' view holds that a stable monetary union can only succeed if a sufficient degree of convergence has been achieved beforehand. Proponents of this view point to inefficiencies in the financial markets when the assessment of the credit-worthiness of governments is concerned and to external effects, if heavily indebted governments directly or indirectly force the common central bank to relax its monetary policy. These arguments have led to the inclusion of the explicit *ex-ante* convergence criteria.

It is certainly impossible to argue that the specific criteria chosen describe some magical threshold, beyond which the stability of EMU is threatened. But they provide a rather unambiguous test to reveal member states' preferences for a 'hard currency' EMU.[24] The credibility of the new and therefore unproven European Central Bank (ECB) will be significantly enhanced if it is only controlled by member states which have successfully passed this test. It may thus avoid having to establish its credibility and independence at potentially very high cost.[25]

The current situation is illustrated in Table 8.1, which presents recent data on variables relevant to the convergence criteria.[26] In 1992 the three member states with the lowest rates of inflation were Denmark, Belgium and France, with rates ranging from 2.1% to 2.6%. The reference value for the inflation criterion would therefore be between 3.6% and 4.1%. Six member states currently meet this criterion, with (unified) Germany, the United Kingdom, Italy and Spain somewhat above and Portugal and Greece far above the threshold. First Commission 'status quo'[27] projections for 1994 would expect Germany, the United Kingdom and Italy within the thresholds, Spain only marginally above and also Portugal and Greece converging fast. Long-term interest rates present a similar picture, with Germany still setting the floor. Their convergence may, however, be slower than for inflation. After the turmoil in the EMS since autumn 1992 and the devaluation of the Irish punt in February 1993, currently only a hard core of six out of the seven countries which from the beginning of the

European Monetary System applied the narrow band for their currencies in the Exchange Rate Mechanism fulfil the exchange rate criterion. In 1992 only in Luxembourg, Denmark, France and Ireland were budget deficits below 3% of GDP, with Germany and the Netherlands as border cases and Italy and Greece in double digits. Public debt still requires attention in Denmark and the Netherlands, whereas Germany, Spain and the United Kingdom have a larger margin of manoeuvre from this point of view. The very high levels of debt in Belgium, Greece, Italy and (in spite of significant improvements in recent years, see below) in Ireland force major adjustments. The 'status quo' projections for 1994 show hardly a different picture.

Discretionary policy adjustments are therefore required for most member states to meet the convergence criteria. To assess the economic impact of the transition to EMU is, however, a difficult exercise. Already the objectives are not yet fully determined, questions remain for example concerning the choice of indicators. More important, the decision on participation in the third stage contains elements of political judgement both for Commission and Council as they have to propose and adopt a decision whether a member state has an 'excessive deficit'[28] as well as for heads of state and government which have to arrive at an overall judgement – by qualified majority – whether a member state fulfils the conditions for participation in a single currency. Furthermore there remains a margin concerning the timing of the beginning of stage three. Structural breaks resulting from a growing credibility of EMU are also difficult to take into account.

In addition, assumptions have to be made for the policies the member states would follow in the absence of the prospect of EMU, the baseline problem. Doubts have, for example, been expressed about the sustainability of the EMS over a longer period with completely liberalised capital movements.[29] It would appear quite probable that without the perspective of EMU, exchange rates would be subject to more frequent realignments. As the recent controversy about 'competitive devaluations' has shown, this could even threaten the internal market itself. In addition to the question of the sustainability of the current monetary, exchange rate and trade regime, assumptions have to be made about which major policy changes would be executed in the absence of the convergence criteria. Particularly in the area of public finance, several member states would in any case have to take measures to prevent public debt explosion and/or to reduce inflation – in particular, Greece, Italy, Portugal and Spain.

If such measures were postponed, confidence in these economies would be further eroded, threatening them with a snowballing destabilisation effect, in particular because of higher risk premia on long-term interest rates. The importance of this effect can be illustrated from the recent development of long-term interest differentials between individual member states and Germany. The crisis of confidence in EMU which

Table 8.1. Convergence in the EC in 1992.

	Inflation (private consumption deflator)	Public finance			Participation in the EMS Exchange Rate Mechanism[a]	Long-term interest rate
		Net lending of general government (% of GDP)	Gross public debt (% of GDP)			
			1992	Annual change 1991–92		
Belgium	2.4	6.7	132.2	1.1	NB (1979)	8.7
Denmark	2.1	2.3	74.0	1.8	NB (1979)	10.1
Germany	4.8	3.2	43.3	1.3	NB (1979)	8.0
Greece	16.0	13.4	106.7	4.7	No	21.3[b]
Spain	6.0	4.6	47.4	1.8	WB (1989)	12.2
France	2.6	2.8	50.1	1.6	NB (1979)	8.6
Ireland	2.9	2.7	99.0	−1.9	NB (1979)	9.1
Italy	5.3	10.5	106.8	5.5	suspended	13.6
Luxembourg	3.4	0.4	6.8	0.7	NB (1979)	—
The Netherlands	3.1	3.5	79.8	1.5	NB (1979)	8.1
Portugal	9.1	5.6	66.2	−2.3	WB (1992)	15.0
UK	5.1	6.1	45.9	4.8	suspended	9.1
EC	4.6	5.3	62.8	2.4		10.0

Source: Commission Services (1993).
Notes: [a] Participation in the narrow (NB) or wide band (WB) of the exchange-rate mechanism since (year). (The EMS was established in 1979).
[b] Only short-term interest rate available.

emerged after the negative result of the first Danish referendum in June 1992 reversed the process of downward convergence of recent years. Italy, for example, suffered a 2 percentage point increase in this differential between spring 1992 and spring 1993 which, given the high level of debt with a rather short maturity and the current borrowing requirement, directly worsened Italy's economic performance. The comparison between France and the United Kingdom is also instructive: while both had narrowed their differentials to 0.5 percentage points in spring 1992, these deteriorated considerably more in the United Kingdom (to 1.6 percentage points in spring 1993) than in France (1.0 percentage points). This would indicate that the 'costs' of non-convergence are substantial, which would explain why all member states have maintained their commitment to the convergence objectives.[30]

So far, no estimates of the impact of convergence exist which address comprehensively these baseline problems. To provide nevertheless an estimate of the orders of magnitude involved, Italianer (1993) simulates the effects on EC GDP of six member states (Belgium, Germany, Greece, Spain, the Netherlands and Portugal) reducing their deficits to 3% of GDP by 1996, using the EC Commission QUEST model. To get somewhat closer to a realistic baseline the simulations disregard Italy, on the assumption that it would have to adjust in any case, and consider the current British deficit strongly cyclical and therefore not requiring structural adjustment. In one scenario where nominal interest rates are kept fixed, deficit convergence would reduce the level of Community GDP in 1996 by 0.3 percentage points. In another scenario it is assumed that the convergence process would gradually make the long-term interest rate differentials with Germany disappear for the five other countries. Due to credibility effects, this interest rate decrease would not have an immediate effect but would reduce the losses in the level of EC GDP by 1996 to 0.1 percentage point.

IMF simulations of July 1992[31] using the Multimod model made no baseline adjustments at all, and included Italy and the United Kingdom. They arrived at an EC GDP in 1996 of −0.5% below the baseline if risk premia are not reduced. With risk premium adjustment, however, the Multimod simulations indicate an EC GDP in 1996 0.1% higher than without convergence, as investment picks up. Nominal and real depreciation as inflation rates fall also contribute to the eventual compensation of the initial contractionary effects. It should be noted that the Multimod simulations expect further expansion after 1996.

While the impact on the Community would appear small and transitory, it will certainly be more significant for individual member states. They could, however, find some encouragement from the experience of the two most extreme cases of fiscal rectitude of the 1980s – Denmark and Ireland.[32] Denmark succeeded between 1982 and 1985 in reducing its public deficit from 9.1% to 2.0% of GDP. At the same time its economic growth reached 4.4% and 4.5% in 1984 and 1985 respectively – a performance not achieved since the early 1970s, and far above the Community average. Possibly even more surprising was the performance of Ireland, which reduced its deficit from 1986 to 1989 by nearly 10 percentage points to 2.2% of GDP, while at the same time moving from economic recession in 1986 to a boom in 1989. Giavazzi and Pagano (1990) retrace these cases of 'expansionary stabilisation' to the announcement of durable pegging of the domestic currencies to the German mark permitting sharply lower interest rates, an increase in asset prices and a surge in private consumption. The credibility of the shift in the fiscal policy stance appears to have played a crucial role. This aspect is also stressed by Nicoletti (1988), who finds that a history of inflation, high public deficits and debt – he stresses the cases of Italy and Belgium – leads to compensating private sector saving behaviour. To the extent that such experiences can be credibly replaced by expectations of stability, reductions in private saving could attenuate the disinflationary effects considerably.

The assessment of the transition to EMU should finally not overlook that the realisation of EMU will create considerable efficiency gains and reduce uncertainties.[33] The gains in transaction costs alone of having a single currency have been estimated at 0.3–0.4% of Community GDP. Therefore the microeconomic savings of a single currency could more than compensate for any temporary GDP decrease due to convergence, not to mention the other benefits in terms of price stability, disappearance of exchange rate uncertainty, optimal investment allocation and dynamic growth effects.

Conclusion

The analysis of the economic effects of regional economic integration has some way to go, in particular with regard to dynamic effects and integration which goes beyond the liberalization of trade. From the existing analysis it appears that EC integration has stimulated growth for all its member states and that the contribution of integration to growth may have been quite substantial. Contrary to some worries, the peripheral member states appear to have benefited more than proportionally from integration. Further Community integration provides a valuable potential for further growth. Many cost savings and efficiency gains from the internal market remain to be realised. It will be a Community policy priority during the 1990s to make the internal market work. Economic and Monetary Union opens up new dimensions for gains from integration. As soon as the credibility of its realisation is restored, anticipatory effects should be felt before the third stage actually comes into effect.

To be able to join EMU, some member states will have to undertake major budgetary adjustments during the 1990s. The overall effect of the transition to EMU for the Community will be limited and could actually turn out to be positive, as each successful adjustment in a member state enhances the credibility of the overall project. From the point of view of the member states concerned, EMU provides a unique opportunity to achieve budgetary consolidation in a Community context which facilitates politically the taking of unpopular decisions and rewards credible commitments to convergence with reduced interest costs. Much more adjustment should have been achieved during the period of strong growth and employment creation experienced throughout the Community in the second half of the 1980s, but even in today's circumstances credible pursuit of the EMU objective remains the best option for the Community and each individual member state.

Part III

Regional and Industrial Policies

9

Regional Disparities, the Single Market, and European Monetary Union

Jane Collier

In the last five years, European integration appears to have taken a giant step forwards. The internal market is being completed, monetary union is in prospect, and European countries outside the EC are either already becoming more closely associated, or are seeking association with the core group of countries. But as integration becomes a reality, so economic and social disparities within Europe become more apparent, giving rise to increasing concern. This is not merely because disparities threaten political consensus, it is also because it is now realised that the very forces which generate integration will widen those disparities, and hence set up processes which threaten the achievement of integration itself. The dynamic effects of freer markets may disadvantage weaker regions, which will be unable to compete once the protection afforded by non-tariff barriers (NTBs) has been removed, and regional competitiveness will become polarised by regional specialisation. These effects will be reinforced by monetary union, which will remove the option of using exchange rates to cushion weaker competitors and to offset the effects of external shocks. Furthermore, monetary union will limit existing powers of national governments to use public sectors deficits to reflate the economy or to increase aid to weaker regions.

A smooth transition to an integrated Europe will only be achieved if there is increasing economic and social cohesion. Cohesion is a political concept; it has to do with how people feel about disparities and the efforts being made to reduce them (Begg and Mayes, 1991). Economic convergence has several facets (Anderton, Barrell and in't Veld, 1991); *nominal* convergence of inflation rates was largely achieved at country level in the EMS during the 1980s, but only at the price of high unemployment. *Real* convergence, on the other hand, requires not merely convergence of overall inflation rates, but also convergence of per capita incomes and levels of employment measured at the regional level. This in turn will require some degree of structural convergence.[1] Whereas nominal convergence is a necessary but not sufficient condition for real convergence, pronounced regional disparties will constrain the possibility of securing nominal convergence.

Convergence is a necessary element of social cohesion, not because it implies greater equality, but because it alters perceptions. However, social cohesion does require a commitment to equity. Attempts by policy-makers to build cohesion will thus need to take account not merely of disparities between regions, but also of poverty levels within them. In other words, the issue of interregional and intraregional distribution is at the heart of the problem of cohesion. It is for this reason that this chapter focuses on regional disparities in employment rates, rather than regional income disparities. Per capita income measurements for a region can be close to the Community average but can hide large intraregional disparities; regional unemployment rates give a clearer indication of welfare differences within and between regions.[2] Convergence of unemployment rates is the basis of social cohesion; it matters in human terms, in Community terms and in political terms.

Regional Disparities

Current measured disparities are the outcome of cumulative causation processes, as well as of 'spread' and 'backwash' effects (Myrdal, 1957). Two measures of disparity are normally used: per capita GDP and employment levels. GDP disparities are measured in terms of purchasing power standards (PPS), which express an identical volume of goods and services for each country, taking account of differences in price levels. However, other indicators of regional disparity are also informative; these include demographic factors (high birth rates, ageing populations, dependency ratios), the sectoral structure of employment, productivity and wage differentials, infrastructure indicators such as the adequacy of water supplies, or welfare indicators such as the existence of primary health care, or secondary education attainment.[3]

There is no evidence that regional convergence is happening in Europe. Such convergence as took place in the post-war period only happened because of the differential growth rates of richer and poorer countries. Evidence on the two major indicators shows that although the position of some regions improved during the 1980s, regional disparities have in general shown no tendency to decline, in spite of the growth in employment and output experienced in the Community as a whole after 1985. Twenty per cent of the EC population still live in regions where the per capita GDP is less than 75% of the Community average, and interregional disparities in the Community are at least twice as great as those in the US.

Table 9.1. Country-level per capita PPS, 1980–90 (EUR = 100).

	1980	1990
Greece	52	47
Spain	72	75
France	114	112
Portugal	53	56
UK	97	101
Ireland	61	68
Italy	102	102
Luxembourg	115	124
Denmark	106	107
Germany	119	117
Belgium	106	105
Netherlands	108	101

Source: *Eurostat* (1993a).
Note: Figures for Germany exclude the former GDR.

Table 9.2. Regional per capita PPS, 1980–90 (EUR = 100).

	1980		1990	
	Lowest	Highest	Lowest	Highest
Greece	35	71	34	58
Spain	45	91	49	98
France	87	182	79	166
Portugal	44	69	35	76
UK	74	114	74	154 (121)
Italy	58	135	61	135
Germany	85	187	81	183
Belgium	83	166	78	166
Netherlands	87	208	61 (82)	135

Notes: 1. Ireland, Luxembourg and Denmark are classed as single regions for purposes of these data.
      2. Because the 1980 data are incomplete, the figures comparable to the 1980 data are given in brackets.
Source: *Eurostat* (1993b).

GDP

Per capita GDP in the top ten regions in 1990 was more than three times greater than the GDP of the bottom ten regions. During the 1960s and up to the mid-1970s, GDP disparities converged both between countries and between regions, but since then, although there has been some convergence at the country level, interregional disparities have marginally widened.

GDP trends over the 1980s show convergence towards the European average in all countries with the exception of Greece and Luxembourg. Within countries, regional inequalities are tending to widen rather than converge (see Figure 9.1). Only 40% of regions in 1990 had a per capita income that was closer to the Community average than it had been in 1980 (CEC, 1991c).[4]

Unemployment

By the end of 1992 the unemployment rate in the EC as a whole had reached 9.5%, having averaged 8.7% over the year, and 8.4% in 1991. (This compares with 1992 figures of 7.4% for the US and 2.2% for Japan). The EC figure re resents a total of 14.1 million people currently out of work (based on the ILO definition), an increase of more than 1.2 million compared with the previous year. The most significant increases in unemployment occurred in France (+9%), Germany (+9%), the UK (+8%), and Spain (+8%) – in other words, in economies where the structure of employment is recession-sensitive. This development reverses the favourable trend in employment growth shared by all EC countries since the mid-1980s, which was primarily due to a growth in service employment (+12%, 1983–88) which more than compensated for the decline in industrial employment (−1.5%, 1983–88) (CEC, 1991a).

However, the overall employment figures hide substantial disparities at the regional level. Regional disparities in employment are wider than those in GDP; unemployment rates range from 1.5% to 29%. During the first half of the 1980s regional disparities widened because of job losses, especially in manufacturing. In the second half of the 1980s this trend began to be reversed. But although output growth of between 1% and 2% was sufficient to create jobs because productivity levels had fallen from previous years, unemployment in the weaker regions fell by less than the number of new jobs, and by less than in the stronger regions (Figure 9.2). There are two reasons for this. The first is demographic: the weaker regions of the Community have higher birth-rates, which gives rise to a faster growth in the working age population. It is estimated that 85% of the job requirements for the Community as a whole in the period 1990–95 are represented by those currently unemployed, and 15% by growth in the labour force – largely in areas where unemployment is already high. The second reason is that activity rates vary cyclically due to the existence of a hidden labour supply, largely female. The effect of these two factors is to understate the severity of rising unemployment – the unemployment figures understate the 1992 position by something like half a million.

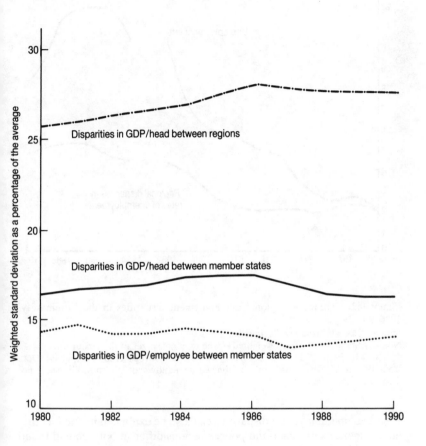

Figure 9.1.   Trends in regional income disparities in the Community, 1980–90.
Source: CEC (1991c), *The Regions in the 90s*.
Note: Disparities are measured by the weighted standard deviation of regional values for
GDP in purchasing power standards.
To avoid giving the same weight in the calculation of standard deviation to both large
and small regions, it is weighted by the size of the population in each region (or each
member state as appropriate). The weighted standard deviation is given by:
$s = \sqrt{\Sigma (Xr\text{-}X)^2\ Wr/W}$. Here X is the average GDP per head $(= 100)$, Xr is the regions
GDP per head (expressed as % of EC average) and Wr and W are the size of population
in the region and the Community as a whole respectively.

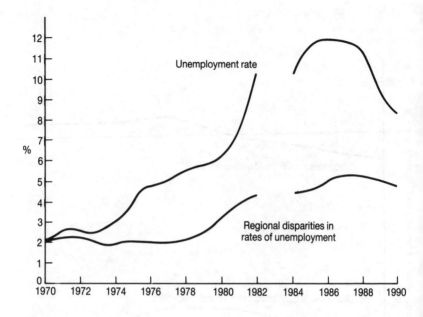

Figure 9.2. Trends in regional unemployment disparities in the Community, 1970–90.
Source: CEC (1991c). *The Regions in the 90s.*
Notes: 1.Standard deviation weighted by the regional shares of the labour force.
2. *NB:* Data from 1970 to 1982 are based on statistics for registered unemployed. Data from 1983 to 1990 are based on harmonised unemployment statistics. Greece is not included before 1983.

Regional unemployment disparities can also be explained by the fact that labour markets in richer and poorer regions differ in both demand- and supply-side characteristics. Employment/working age population ratios are lower in poorer regions, particularly among women, and dependency ratios are higher. Hidden labour supply was over 20% in these regions in 1989, as opposed to under 13% in other parts of the Community. The population of working age increased by 3% in the poorer regions over the period 1985–89; in the rest of the Community it increased by just over 1%. During the period, fewer jobs were created in the poorer regions, and part-time work was less available. In these regions, employment in industry and services has to grow at a higher rate than in the developed regions, not just to cater for the increases in the working age population and the higher numbers of unemployed (both visible and hidden), but also to mop up the unemployment caused by the decline in the agricultural sector (CEC, 1991c).

Regional Effects of the SEM

The internal market will have different effects, depending on the type of region in question. Regions are characterised as advanced, lagging (Objective 1), and traditional-industry (Objective 2). It is difficult to estimate the likely outcome for any one region; the best that can be done is to base estimates on recent economic development trends in a particular region, and calculate the probability of that development trend being strengthened or broken by the advent of the SEM (Peschel, 1992). In other words, the existing character of the region is as least as important a determinant of the changes which the SEM will bring as is the impact of the SEM itself.

Post-SEM changes can be analysed in several ways. The first is to use a sectoral approach and to analyse by:

(1) Identifying the industrial sectors most affected by NTBs to intra-Community trade, where such barriers prevent the exploitation of economies of scale or permit the existence of price discrepancies. Forty such industries have been identified (Buiges, Ilkovitz and Lebrun, 1990). They account for over half of the total manufacturing employment and about one-eighth of the total employment of the Community, and represent a higher share of employment in weaker than in advanced regions.
(2) Identifying the regions where these sectors are represented.
(3) Looking at the ways in which the lifting of NTBs might result in the exploitation of regional comparative or absolute advantages, as well as in the achievement of economies of scale and successful product differentiation in the industries affected. Regional winners and losers should thus in theory be fairly easy to identify.

However, such a 'top-down' model does not include any information as to how these changes will happen, nor about the factors which will both enable and constrain a region's ability to exploit its comparative or absolute advantages. It says nothing about the attitude of companies to new challenges, nothing about the ability of factor markets to respond. It ignores the dynamic aspects – the effects created by linkages, forward or backward, or by production-oriented service industry development (Peschel, 1992). It says nothing about the cumulative processes which will become operative as a consequence of scale economies, agglomeration economies, synergies, or technical progress. Nor does it consider possible regional limits to growth due to pollution or land scarcity.

An alternative approach is to start with the regions themselves. The impact on any given region of the 'array of events' (Steinle, 1992) which constitute the completion of the internal market will depend (a) on regional sensitivity – i.e. the extent to which a region is affected by any or all of the possible factors, and (b) on regional competitiveness – the extent to which it is sufficiently adaptable to take advantage of them.

Regional sensitivity might be measured in a number of ways; Steinle suggests using measures of the intensity of cross-border freight transport (tonnes per capita), or measures of the share of employment in a given region in sectors most likely to be affected.

Regional competitiveness will depend on the ability of a region to respond flexibly to the new opportunities. A high degree of competitiveness will imply that entrepreneurs are willing to act on the opportunities presented, that companies are prepared to innovate and diversify in product terms so as to expand trade and increase value added, and that the region can supply the skilled and qualified labour required. Regional competitiveness is likely to be higher, the lower is company size, the higher is the R&D intensity and the innovative capacity, and the greater is the export orientation. Regions likely to fit this picture include regions which are growing faster than the national average, where there are new development areas, and where existing regional policies have had an impact.

A third approach sees the completion of the SEM as bringing the advantages of freer trade. It builds on the structural characteristics of regions – capital intensity, labour intensity and R&D – and uses this to predict structural and locational outcomes (Quevit, 1992). The factors which will determine the industrial, structural and locational outcomes of the SEM – and hence the revealed comparative advantages of the regions – are industrial typology, factor intensity, and the technology base, because these determine the possibilities of gain from economies of scale, product and process development and market potential. The diversity of productive systems, together with the dynamic industrial effects of the SEM will combine together to produce one of two possible scenarios; regions may be characterised by one or the other, or neither:

(1) Inter-industrial scenarios where economies of scale and comparative advantage combine to concentrate production geographically. Regions where such concentrations occur will be those where the productive sector in question is already efficient, and/or where it uses factors of production with which the region is well endowed. Wine, clothing, footwear and machine tools are examples of industries where such concentration will occur; they tend to be based in the weaker regions.

(2) Intra-industrial scenarios where product differentiation causes production to be dispersed across the Community. The industries in question here tend to be capital- and technology-intensive, and to be based in the more advanced regions of the Community.

The notion of revealed comparative advantage might suggest that once the internal market is completed, weaker regions should deepen their speciali-sation in inter-industrial low-technology production, whereas central regions should specialise in intra-industrial capital- and technology-intensive sectors. This might bring short-term benefits, but in the longer term it would only accentuate regional disparities (Neven, 1990). Weaker regions will therefore need to exploit local advantages by looking for niche markets in specialised sectors which become profitable in the context of the larger European market, particularly in view of the fact that many of their more traditional industrial sectors will become increasingly vulnera-ble to competition from Eastern Europe.

Employment effects of the SEM in the weaker regions will depend on the balance of job gains and losses as a result of the widening of markets, and these will be different in kind for Objective 1 and Objective 2 regions. They will also be determined by the abolition of protectionist structures and procedures. In overall terms the outlook for employment will be more favourable:

(1) If existing small and medium-size enterprises (SMEs) can respond to the opportunities of the SEM. Multinational investment is more likely to be both capital intensive and footloose; also, such investment does not necessarily create linkages with indigenous firms, and can result in the perpetuation of a 'dual economy'.[5]
(2) If niche specialisms can be developed to counter problems of distance from markets.
(3) To the extent that successful market initiatives result in production linkages in industrial and service sectors.

These gains have to be set against:

(1) Job losses due to rationalisation in labour-intensive sectors such as financial services, as well as in pharmaceuticals and other high-tech industries due to deregulation and harmonisation of standards.
(2) Job losses in MNEs due to rationalisation which follows competition in public procurement.
(3) Job losses in customs employment, and in multistage procedures (wholesaling, distribution) which become redundant on completion of the SEM.
(4) The effects of new forms of work, where for instance employers move to contract/part-time work in order to reduce employee costs, or where increases in tertiary employment increases the availability of part-time and flexi-time work.

Finally, employment prospects in the weaker regions will be threatened to the extent that companies in these regions are pushed to restructure and achieve productivity gains at the expense of employment, or to achieve economies of scale by increasing the capital labour ratio. The first of these developments has already been seen in countries such as Italy in the 1960s and Spain in the 1980s, where attempts to close the gap with other countries have led to a widening of regional disparities and migration from non-competitive regions. The competitive pressures of the internal market will make it more difficult for regions to choose a development path characterised by low productivity and high employment, even though in regional terms this strategy might make more sense (Camagni, 1992).

Regional Disparities and EMU

From a regional point of view, European monetary unification will have the effect of widening the single currency areas in which regions currently exist. The effects of EMU on regional employment will be contingent in the first instance on whether or not Europe is an optimum currency area (OCA) i.e. one in which (a) all areas are symmetrically affected by external shocks, and (b) there is perfect mobility of labour combined with wage flexibility (de Grauwe, 1992). In an OCA the loss of national monetary policy autonomy will be unimportant, because since all countries are identically affected by external shocks, a common policy response will be sufficient to counter their effects. Any localised unemployment problems will disappear as labour moves from low-wage to high-wage areas. Also, capital mobility will even out asymmetric effects even if labour is imperfectly mobile (Ingram, 1973). One determinant of the symmetry of disturbances is the structural comparability of the areas within the OCA. When regions are specialised in the production of goods whose prices are differently affected by external supply-side shocks, then asymmetric effects are more likely than when regions are similar in structure (Kenen, 1969). Similarly, demand-side shocks will cause asymmetric effects unless the composition of output is identical in all countries.

Evidence on Europe in the 1980s points to substantial variability of real exchange rates between countries indicating that Europe is not an OCA. This variability is greater than that shown between states within the US (Bayoumi and Eichengreen, 1992). This may to some extent be explained by the fact that supply shocks have tended to be larger, and less correlated across countries, than within the US. It may also be the case that European real exchange rate (RER) variability in the 1980s was biased by variations in nominal rates; there is evidence (Edwards, 1989; Eichengreen, 1989) that the variability of RERs increases with the variability of nominal rates, and European RERs have certainly been subject to such variability due to monetary disturbances in a way which RERs in the US common currency area have not. Furthermore, the speed of adjustment to shocks is greater in the US, for reasons discussed below. If it is also true, as the above study found, that supply shocks are larger and more idiosyncratic at the periphery than at the core, it would imply (a) that there may well be good arguments for a two-speed Europe, and (b) that EMU will have substantial regional implications.

The regional implications of EMU will arise from the fact that variations in inter-country RERs will imply changes in the relative prices of traded and non-traded goods (Eichengreen, 1991b). The consequences for any given region will reflect the bias of these two types of activity in the region. Suppose that an external shock causes a rise in the RER of country A, so that its exports become more expensive and imports cheaper. Unemployment will rise in the regions which produce exports and import substitutes. One study which attempts to estimate the elasticity of the regional unemployment response to changes in the RER for the UK and Italy respectively (Eichengreen, 1991b) shows that regional disparities which arise as a result of RER changes are greater in Italy than the UK, but comparable between Italy and the US, given the level of national unemployment (an important proviso). However, if the RER between the two countries is held constant, cyclical fluctuations create the same level of regional disparity in both countries. This would appear to confirm the hypothesis that it is the regional pattern of production which determines the employment response to external shocks.

If Europe is not an OCA, so that RERs will need to vary between countries, regional unemployment disparities will arise. The fact that these disparities are no greater than those in the US for any given national unemployment rate is not particularly reassuring; adjustment possibilities are very different. The US has fiscal autonomy to alter the national unemployment rate in a way which will be denied to post-EMU countries. Not only that, but federal fiscal systems in the US provide interregional transfers which cushion the impact of regional disparities. If incomes in any US state fall by $1, tax payments fall by 30 cents and transfers from Washington rise by 10 cents (Sala i Martin and Sachs, 1991). In addition, labour mobility in the US is higher than in Europe. Nor can the weaker regions take comfort from the fact that the EMU will bring potential benefits. The estimate for static gains from EMU is about 1% of GDP, and the dynamic gains – which it is estimated will be greater – are likely to impact in the stronger regions. The weakest regions are those with the highest inflation rates – Greece, Portugal, Italy – and those with the highest unemployment – Spain and Ireland. The convergence criteria involving fiscal tightening will worsen disparities and threaten cohesion.

The completion of the internal market will increase regional differentiation by (a) favouring the regions which can most easily benefit from the opportunities it offers, and (b) encouraging regional specialisation which will in turn widen employment disparities. The completed internal market will therefore lead to regional concentration of industrial activities because of the existence of economies of scale and the multinational character of large companies (Krugman, 1991; Bayoumi and Eichengreen, 1992). This will cause Europe to move further away from being an OCA as countries become even less similar in their response to external shocks. In addition, the loss of the nominal exchange rate as a policy instrument, as well as the stricter disciplines imposed on budgetary policies, will have a greater impact on those economies which are undergoing structural change because of the completion of the internal market.

Convergence and Cohesion

The conclusion to be drawn from the foregoing argument is that the completion of the internal market and monetary unification will set in motion powerful forces which will widen rather than reduce regional employment disparities. How then can cohesion be achieved in an economic climate subject to 'divergent regional evolutions' (Blanchard and Katz, 1992: 69)? Regional economic theories give no grounds for supposing that the free play of market forces will reduce disparities. However, a number of possible adjustment mechanisms exist; some are more desirable than others.

Migration

Migration is triggered by job possibilities as well as by wage differentials. In the US, labour mobility is high, and the regional unemployment problem is insignificant in consequence. Growth rates differ between states; any disturbance to existing growth paths is met by a combination of adjustment in relative wages, small shifts in participation, and migration. For every 100 workers who lose their jobs, 30 stay unemployed, five leave the labour force, and 65 leave the state. Relative wages fall in response to demand shocks, and have a weak positive effect in terms of attracting jobs to the region, although this is not sufficient to reverse unemployment (Blanchard and Katz, 1992). However, most of the migration in the EC is represented by immigration from other countries. On average each year only 1.5% of the Community's population decide to move to another region; that figure is less than half the figure for US interstate migration (CEC, 1987).[6] Migration will be encouraged by the completion of the internal market, but linguistic and cultural barriers will hinder it. This is fortunate, because migration is not desirable in social terms. It widens disparities as the workforce in weaker regions is depleted, and adds to congestion and environmental problems in the stronger regions. Emigration, if it occurs, will take the best trained and the youngest, so that weaker regions will fail to attract capital, even if wages are low, and will in the end become economic 'deserts'.

Factor market flexibility

Wage flexibility has become much more important at the macroeconomic level during the 1980s, as exchange rate flexibility between EC countries has been progressively reduced (CEC, 1991b). At the beginning of the 1980s all EC economies achieved reductions in wage and price inflation by tightening monetary policies and restructuring their economies; this included the introduction of more flexible and performance-oriented pay strategies (Barrell, 1990). Most governments also attempted some form of direct intervention in the wage-setting process; in the UK the government resorted to legislation to reduce the power of the unions. The loss of the exchange rate as a shock absorber after EMU will mean that the burden of adjustment at the national level will fall on wages, costs, and ultimately prices. At the regional level, realignments of RERs which vary because of the differential effects of external shocks will only be achieved by wage flexibility. However, the move to equalise pay and conditions across Europe by the unions, as well as the reduction in employee cost differentials brought about by the Social Chapter, may reduce flexibility. On the other hand, there has been a retreat from indexation in wage bargaining, but flexibility in this respect – merit payments, productivity-related increases, profit-related payments – has been limited by collective bargaining structures.[7] Capital flexibility will also have a role to play in ironing out interregional differences in competitiveness due to differences in productivity, and the SEM and EMU will encourge this. However, flexibility may not be so easy to achieve. The IFO survey (1990) identified a number of structural problems which currently reduce capital mobility – interregional disparities in the cost of credit, a shortage of flexible financing instruments, differences in infrastructure, labour market rigidities in declining industrial regions which lead to the maintenance of high wages by 'insiders', and variations in the supply of qualified labour. Also, capital flexibility brings its own problems in terms of overall adjustment: by moving to regions with low labour costs, it may tend to inhibit the development of more skill-intensive activities.

Fiscal federalism

Existing economic federations provide examples of mechanisms for redistribution in a monetary union, so that real exchange rate parity does not have to be bought at the cost of high levels of unemployment (MacDougall, 1992). Whereas in unitary states, such as the majority of EC countries fiscal redistribution happens automatically, in that citizens in the richer regions pay taxes and those in poorer regions receive benefits, in federal systems intergovernmental grants and tax-sharing play an additional and more important part in redistribution.[8] Also, in existing monetary unions such as the US, federal tax and transfer systems help cushion the effects of regional shocks; in the US, declining federal tax payments and increasing transfers provide a one-third offset to region-specific reductions in activity (Sala i Martin and Sachs, 1991). At the moment the Community budget is tiny, and has at best a weak redistributive effect. MacDougall estimates that with a Community budget of the order of 2–2.5% of GDP it would be possible to reduce inequalities by 10%, while a budget of 5–7% of GDP would achieve a reduction of 40% in inequalities.[9] However, a much larger budget, and a more proactive fiscal policy would be necessary to cushion weaker regions against cyclical effects. If a European monetary union assumed the character of a federation in fiscal terms, the Maastricht restrictions on national budget deficits would assume less importance, because fiscal revenues from the stronger regions could be transferred to the weaker. In the case of countries where regional performance varied considerably, weaker regions could be supported by fiscal redistribution within countries, but in cases where variation in performance is not great, or where economies are on the whole weaker than their neighbours, fiscal redistribution needs to be centralised if the costs of monetary unification are not to exceed the benefits. Unless Europe develops the same kind of redistributive and equalising mechanisms as there are in existing economic unions, successful integration will not happen.

Structural assistance

Structural funds were doubled in 1992, and are to be further increased after Maastricht. There has also been a major shift in the emphasis of regional policy; the aim now is to make poorer regions more competitive. Prior to 1987 investment in infrastructure accounted for 80% of total Regional Fund expenditure, whereas it now represents only 55% of expenditure in Objective 1 (O1) regions, and 16% of expenditure in Objective 2 (O2) regions. In future, 40% of O1 expenditure and 80% of O2 expenditure will be used to support productive investment (CEC, 1991c). The emphasis varies by country, and whereas this can be seen as evidence of EC problem-sensitive flexibility (Hall and van der Wee, 1992), it can also be seen as evidence of the Commission's awareness of the threat of a polarised development in Europe as a consequence of the SEM (Amin, Charles and Howells, 1992). This assistance will be devoted mainly to supporting SMEs and providing training, transport and communications infrastructures. No strategy is likely to be optimal on all counts, but the Commission's current plans raise several questions. To what extent does the emphasis of this type of policy disadvantage poorer areas which lack entrepreneurship? Do policies to improve efficiency and competitiveness advantage the already advantaged regions? Will these measures encourage coherent growth in these regions, given the fact that the necessary institutional structures may not exist? Since these regions lack an established industrial base, how realistic is it to attempt to build up SMEs in these areas – particularly as a permissive merger policy and existing technology policy both favour large firms?

Conclusion: Cohesion with Diversity

This chapter has argued that the political drive to unite Europe has taken insufficient account of the problems posed by regional disparity, and that efforts to encourage convergence are in effect attempts to impose uniformity of economic performance. The Single European Act articulates the requirement for integration as economic and social cohesion. Another way of thinking about the most desirable future scenario for the regions of Europe is in terms of their sustainable development combined with an equalisation of employment opportunities (although not necessarily per capita incomes), recognising that regional preferences may differ and may contain elements such as uncrowded roads and unpolluted air, and accepting the fact that not all regions are capable of being equally competitive. Redistributive fiscal policies which allow diversity to exist may in the end be the best way of optimising overall welfare in Europe.

10

Regional and Industrial Aspects of Unemployment in Europe[1]

John Tomaney

> The Community shall have as its task . . . to promote throughout the Community a harmonious development of economic activities, a continuous and balanced expansion . . . an accelerated raising of the standard of living. (Treaty of Rome, Article 2.)

> The Commission is, however, conscious that there may be risks that, by increasing the possibilities for human, material and financial services to move without obstacle to areas of greatest economic advantage, existing discrepancies between regions could be exacerbated and therefore the objective of convergence jeopardized. (White Paper on the Single European Act, 1985.)

Article 2 of the Treaty of Rome is frequently cited as evidence that a concern with regional inequalities is at the heart of the European project. Regional policy has been expanded at each enlargement of the European Community and the '1992' project was accompanied by a doubling of the size of the Structural Funds, the main means by which the EC has attempted to address regional disparities. Most recently, the proposed creation of a 'Cohesion Fund' for the four weaker member states – Portugal, Spain, Ireland and Greece – and the establishment of a 'Committee of the Regions', as required by the Maastricht Treaty, has given further weight to the impression that the Community regards the reduction of regional inequalities as one of its central tasks.

This chapter, however, emphasises how current patterns of industrial restructuring are likely to adversely affect the employment prospects of the less-favoured regions (LFRs) of the EC. The completion of the internal market and a range of associated EC policies, together with plans for economic and monetary union, are likely to accentuate the processes which are disadvantaging the weaker regions. The chapter presents a brief review of the regional dimension of the unemployment problem in Europe and some other aspects of regional inequalities, identifying the tendencies in industrial restructuring that are working to disadvantage the weaker regions and exploring the reasons for this. The process of restructuring in one industry is examined in detail to understand the actual ramifications of industrial change for the prospects of LFRs, and the limits of EC regional policy in the face of these tendencies are highlighted. Finally, the chapter examines the ways in which economic and monetary union will further undermine the position of LFRs in the emerging 'new Europe'. The basic contention of this chapter is that while reflation and a higher rate of growth in Europe are a necessary condition for an improvement in the prospects of the LFRs, reflation will not by itself ensure that these regions are able to achieve self-sustaining growth trajectories.

The extent and nature of regional disparities

The European Commission's own analysis (CEC, 1991c) of the trends in GDP per head and in GDP per person employed reveals two distinct phases in the emergence of the current pattern of disparities:

(1) A period of convergence between member states and between regions, which came to an end with the economic recession of the mid-1970s.
(2) A period when this convergence process, arrested by the low growth and by the recessions which took place at the national and Community levels, gave way to a regressive phase which returned inter-regional disparities to the levels of the beginning of the 1970s, or even earlier.

During the late 1980s overall rates of economic growth in the four least developed member states were higher than the EC average, and this translated into an improvement in GDP per head in Spain, Portugal and Ireland, although this was not the case in Greece. Economic growth in Spain, Portugal and Ireland reflected increased flows of foreign investment. In Portugal, for instance, rates of foreign investment increased forty-fold in the period after accession (Amin, Bradley *et al.*, 1993). Despite these improvements, however, regional disparities increased within these member states. In Portugal, for instance, the bulk of new investment was concentrated in the Lisbon/Setubal region. Even within some northern member states, there is evidence that regional inequalities widened during the growth period of the late 1980s. For instance, in the UK the per capita GDP of the North East region fell relative to the national average during the 1980s (Bradley and Tomaney, 1992).

The most recent data show that the rate of unemployment for the Community as a whole (excluding the five new German *Länder* and the four French Overseas Departments) rose from 8.5% in April to 9.4% in April 1992, largely because of increasing unemployment in Spain, Greece, Ireland and the United Kingdom (*Eurostat*, 1993a). The rate of unemployment was above 20% in certain regions of southern Italy and Spain.

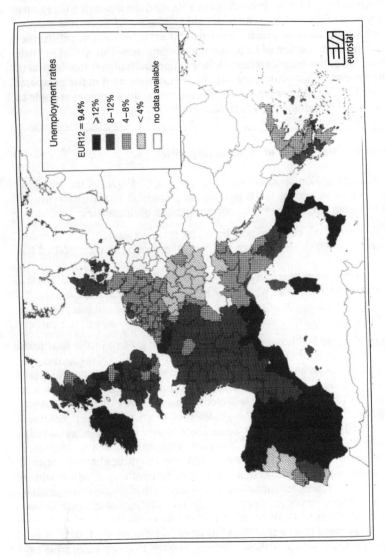

Figure 10.1. Unemployment in the EC, April 1992, by region.

Unemployment rates

EUR12 = 9.4%

- >12%
- 8–12%
- 4–8%
- < 4%
- no data available

eurostat

On the other hand, despite a rise, the figure remained below 5% in the south of Germany, in Luxembourg, in northern Italy and in Portugal. Figure 10.1 illustrates the spatial pattern of unemployment.

Inequalities in per capita GDP in the Community are, if anything, more pronounced than disparities in unemployment (*Eurostat*, 1993b). At the national level, Greece and Portugal had per capita GDPs of less than 60% of the EC average in 1990, when expressed in terms of purchasing power parities. On the other hand, Luxembourg's GDP per head is 124% of the EC average, while Germany's is 117% of the average. There is a clear core–periphery pattern, with richer regions concentrated in the centre of the Community and poorer regions in the southern and western periphery, especially in the extreme south and west. For instance, there was a small group of regions with a GDP per head in 1990 more than 125% of the EC average: Bruxelles and Antwerpen; Stuttgart, Oberbayern, Mittelfranken, Bremen, Hamburg and Darmstadt (and Hesse as a whole); Île de France; Valle d'Aosta, Lombardia and Emilia Romagna; Groningen; and Greater London. On the other hand, 20% of regions had a per capita GDP of less than 75% of the EC average, including all of Greece, most of Portugal, large parts of Spain and southern Italy, Ireland and Northern Ireland. These disparities are illustrated in Figure 10.2.

What are the mechanisms by which such inequalities are generated? EC analysis identifies pathological characteristics of regions as explanations of poor performance and as guides to policy counter-measures. It is the quantity and quality of the resources possessed by LFRs that are seen as the reason for their poor performance relative to that of the EC as a whole. EC analyses and policy identify two main types of problem regions: 'lagging regions' (Objective 1 regions) and 'declining industrial regions' (Objective 2 regions) together with 'rural regions' (Objective 5b regions). Objective 1 regions comprise the southern European regions and Ireland and Objective 2 regions generally comprise areas of northern member states, while Objective 5b comprise mainly remote mountain areas. Overall, Objectives 1, 2 and 5b cover respectively 21.5%, 16.25% and 5% of the population of the Community. Generally, EC analyses and policy responses identify a lack of infrastructure as the main problem in Objective 1 regions. A skills mismatch is seen as the main problem in Objective 2 regions, although a proportion of EC expenditures in Objective 2 regions also goes into supporting new productive capacity (CEC, 1991c). Recently, the term 'infrastructure' has come to be defined more widely. For instance, the Commission has begun to recognise that improving the technological base of LFRs should be a focus of policy, although expenditure in relation to this objective remains small as a proportion of total regional expenditures.

Official analyses of the unemployment problem in the peripheral regions treat them in isolation, rather than analysing underdevelopment in the periphery in relation to the strength of what might be termed Europe's 'core' regions. The regional disparities in unemployment and per capita

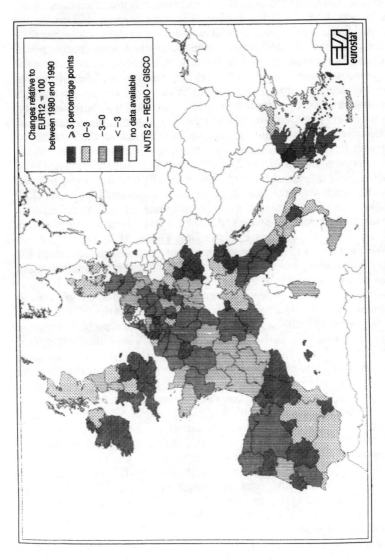

Figure 10.2. Per capita GDP in the EC, 1980–90 change by region.

income reflect a major imbalance in the spatial division of European industry, which favours a band of core regions. For some reason this zone of economic strength has come to be known variously as the 'hot' or 'blue' 'banana'. The zone runs from southern England through Flanders and Randstad-Holland/Limburg, western Germany and south-eastern France and on into northern and central Italy (Figure 10.3). Most of Europe's leading firms are headquartered in this zone and, as such, it is the economic decision-making centre of the EC. A disproportionate amount of Europe's industrial output comes from this area. Perhaps the most obvious manifestation of the dominance of this core zone, and the easiest to measure, has been Germany's trade surplus with its EC partners over recent years (IPPR, 1989; Grahl and Teague, 1990; Williams, Williams and Haslam, 1991), although the analysis of disparities suggests this over-simplifies the picture somewhat.

There is important evidence that the historical dominance of this core is being reinforced by changes in the nature of production which place a greater premium on scientific and technical innovation. This core area is home to many of the commercially-exploitable research and technology

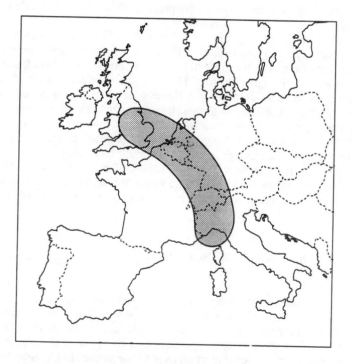

Figure 10.3. The economic core of the EC.

strengths of the EC. A recent study of the European Commission (*Fast/ Monitor*, 1992) suggested that many of Europe's public and private scientific and technical strengths are concentrated in what it terms 'islands of innovation', contained in the major cities of these regions. The study identified ten such 'islands' – based on an analysis of centres of innovation in biotechnology, artificial intelligence, aeronautics and space and textiles – which it describes as 'knots' in a European 'web of cooperation'. The quality of cooperative links between these islands and the rest of Europe was comparatively poor. The study concluded that the growing importance of scientific networks and their apparently closed nature pointed to 'an ever stronger core of innovation constituted by the major islands of innovation'.

The scientific and technical strengths of the core regions and the infrastructure that supports them (especially in terms of human capital provision) amount to a powerful 'pull-factor' for the location of new investment. While a significant amount of mobile investment flowed into low-wage areas of the EC in the late 1980s, there is evidence that mobile investment with a significant technology content was being attracted to the core regions of Europe (Amin, Bradley *et al.*, 1993). The existing spatial division of labour tends to be reinforced by this process. An example is Sony, which has located its assembly plants in Wales but has located its strategic functions (including R&D) in Stuttgart.

Neoclassical analyses of the alleged benefits of economic integration predict convergence in per capita GDP, occuring through market mechanisms as diminishing returns to capital in core regions set in and low income economies exhibit higher returns. However, such evidence as that just described appears to confirm that there is no such tendency towards automatic self-stabilisation in the social system. On the contrary, existing evidence suggests that a process of 'circular and cumulative causation' is under way which is reinforcing the already dominant position of core regions. The idea that such processes are normally characteristic of market economies has been an important justification of regional policies in the past. This view stresses the likelihood of tendencies toward divergence rather than convergence in the absence of countervailing measures (Kaldor, 1970; Myrdal, 1957).

Centripetal tendencies in the New Europe

The project of European integration, based on the creation of 'European' capitals designed to meet competition from South East Asia and the USA, is unleashing forces which will accentuate rather than reduce regional disparities. The promotion of a unified European economy is in large measure a response to what is perceived as the poor performance of European industry in global markets over a long period. In EC analyses a very important role is ascribed to fragmentation of the European market in explaining this poor performance. This concern underlies the measures in the Single European Act that were concerned with removing non-tariff barriers to trade. Related to this is the notion that national capital increasingly needs to organise on a European-wide basis. This might seem to run against some of the analyses based on 'perfect competition' that are used to justify the single market project, and there might be doubts as to whether the promotion of oligopoly serves consumer interest:

> In line with the EC proposals, the initiatives which have flowed from the revival of the project to complete the Single Market have far more to do with the reshaping and support of the Euro-multinationals, as gladiators representing the Community in the global market amphitheatre, than with the promotion of more 'perfect' competition after models of orthodox neoclassical economics (Ramsay, 1992: 27).

Cecchini (1988) and Emerson (1988) stress the degree to which the single market will promote restructuring and rationalisation, leading to greater scale economies. Some 80% of the postulated GDP growth arising from the effects of the single market is seen as deriving from the achievement of scale economies as a result of restructuring through rationalisation of product lines, mergers and acquisitions and increased use of joint ventures.

Other aspects of EC policy have served to reinforce this support for large firms. For instance, the strengthened competition policy, including the introduction of a new Merger Regulation, has not prevented further concentration of European industry. In the period to September 1992, there were over 100 applications for clearance under the provision of the Merger Regulation; only nine went to the full investigation stage and only one (Aerospatiale/De Havilland) was blocked. The power of large firms has also been further reinforced by EC technology policy which has emphasised pre-competitive research programmes aimed at major national or EC 'champions'. Relatively little effort, by contrast, has gone into encouraging effective utilisation and diffusion of research and technological development aimed at a much broader spread of firms and regions (Amin, Charles and Howells, 1992).

The 1980s saw a massive 25% annual average increase in the number of industrial mergers and majority acquisitions (excluding distribution, banking and insurance), with a steadily rising proportion of Community and international mergers after 1982–83. Until the late 1980s, the majority of mergers were *within* member states (e.g. 70% in 1984–85 and 1986–87). By contrast, the share of mergers *between* Community member states rose from 19% in 1983–84 to 40% in 1988–89, with non-EC international mergers accounting for the remaining 13%. Merger activity was particularly evident in high growth sectors. This growth in intra-EC merger activity was accompanied by a proliferation of joint ventures during the same period. In 1982–83, industrial joint ventures registered by the Commission totalled 46, while by 1988–89 this figure had risen to 129.

The clear message . . . is that, especially in the most dynamic sectors, Europe's industries are becoming more integrated at an EC-wide level through increased merger activity and collaboration in the hands of larger firms seeking to establish global presence. Deploying a variety of means – mergers and takeovers, alliances or new investment – it appears that, on the eve of, and perhaps even in response to the Single Market, the MNCs (both European and non-European) will reinforce their position as the real shapers and shakers of the Community economy. (Amin, Charles and Howells, 1992: 324.)

A key concern for policies aimed at the creation of full employment in Europe then, is to understand and respond to the use of space by the strengthened large firm sector. The Commission's own analyses are less than optimistic about the immediate impact of the single market on the industrial performance of LFRs, although there is always a belief that medium-term prospects are positive. An analysis of 40 sectors likely to be affected by the removal of non-tariff barriers (NTBs), including both sectors where public procurement tended to benefit national enterprises and sectors which tended to supply local markets, found that there were significant differences in the share of manufacturing for which these sectors accounted and that shares were highest in LFRs, reaching as high as 60% in Portugal and Greece. The study concluded that trade in these sectors will expand as a consequence of the removal of non-tariff barriers, and many firms, especially in LFRs, will collapse as demand is met by transnational companies. Thus, the costs of adjustment are likely to fall most heavily on the LFRs, as they are most poorly placed to survive the intensified competition (Buiges and Ilzkovitz, 1990).

Another examination of the prospects of seven sectors (agri-food, pharmaceuticals, textiles, shoes, construction, financial services and transportation) which are important components of the industrial structures of Greece, Ireland, Portugal and Spain predicted that implementation of the single market is likely to stimulate modernisation in many industries in the southern member states and Ireland, resulting in considerable productivity gains and output gains in the medium term (Booz Allen and Hamilton, 1989). However, the study also showed that the likely short-run effect of restructuring and rationalisation would be employment loss. The study suggested that the industrial problems of these member states were structural rather than sectoral, and highlighted inadequacies in workforce and management skills, as well as poor infrastructure and R&D networks relative to competitors elsewhere.

A separate study (Cegos-Idet, 1989) which examined the likely regional impact of the opening of public procurement, predicted takeovers of firms in southern member states by firms from northern member states. The study expected such acquisitions to lead to the modernisation of productive capacity, but expected this to be accompanied by job loss. Moreover, a number of establishments in lagging regions were seen as being vulnerable to closure in the long run, although in the medium term technical and cultural differences and entrenched purchasing habits of utility companies were seen as representing possible obstacles to a full integration of public procurement markets.

Cecchini (1988) identified the pharmaceutical industry as one where significant rationalisation could occur as a result of convergence and harmonisation of standards and regulations. In particular, Cecchini predicted rationalisation of secondary stage manufacturing, which is labour intensive and in which many separate plants were established in different localities to gain favourable pricing deals from national governments. This rationalisation favours large firms and disadvantages LFRs. In the southern member states of the EC, for instance, the sector comprises a large number of small companies producing traditional pharmaceuticals for the indigenous market and the secondary production facilities of transnational companies attracted by favourable state pricing agreements. Both of these look fragile against the forces of restructuring unleashed by the single market and wider forces of globalisation impelled by the increasing cost and scale of R&D. The sector has already been characterised by a wave of mergers and by a process of plant rationalisation. For instance, the merger of SmithKline and Beecham, undertaken in conjunction with the preparations for the single market, has led to large-scale plant closures. In 1989 the two companies had over 50 manufacturing plants world-wide, many of them in Europe. In 1991, this number had been cut to 20 and has been projected to fall to around six by 1994/5 (Howells, 1992).

Restructuring at the sectoral level and its employment and regional implications: a case study

It is worth examining in a little detail how industrial restructuring associated with the single market is occurring in practice. Railway equipment is an interesting case, being a sector which is represented in most member states, in particular in the LFRs; it is a sector in which the European Commission hopes and expects to see significant rationalisation as a consequence of the single market, and is seen as being characterised by overcapacity and low levels of profitability. The main obstacle to rationalisation in the sector is seen as the procurement practices of railway utilities which favour national producers (Cecchini, 1988; Emerson, 1988). Restructuring in railway equipment is not solely a response to the completion of the internal market, but also to the globalisation of markets and technological changes such as the need for large companies to provide integrated railway technology systems, not just single items of equipment such as locomotives or signals. In some respects significant restructuring was underway before the publication of the White Paper on the single market, although it increased during the late 1980s and has continued apace.

The merger of the large electrical companies Asea and Brown Boveri was announced in 1986 as an explicit response to the creation of the single market. Asea is Swedish-owned, while Brown-Boveri is Swiss-owned with a large number of its plants in Germany. The merger of the companies was followed by a series of acquisitions of railway equipment firms. Major acquisitions included the CCC group, Spain's largest electrical engineering group, as well as a number of companies in Scandinavia and the UK. For instance, ABB now controls 80% of the former state-owned UK rolling stock producer BREL (renamed ABB Transportation). In 1991 ABB merged its rail interests with those of the Thyssen group (Figure 10.4). At the time of writing ABB is undertaking a major review of its railway equipment division which is likely to lead to rationalisation and a 'reconfiguration' of manufacturing capacity.

In France the restructuring of the railway equipment sector began with

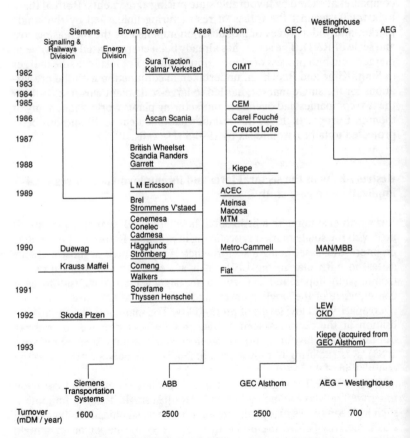

Figure 10.4. Merger, acquisition and joint venture in the European railway equipment industry.
Source: Industry journals, press reports, company interviews.

the emergence of Alsthom as the principal producer of rolling stock, following its acquisition of the rail activities of Jeumont Schneider. (The only other significant supplier, ANF-Industrie, was acquired by Bombardier of Canada.) Between 1980 and 1989 Alsthom shed around 12 000 workers and closed seven major plants as part of a radical restructuring programme. In 1988 Alsthom and GEC announced the merger of their electrical engineering activities (including their railway equipment divisions), stating that this merger was an explicit response to the merger of Asea and Brown Boveri. From 1989 GEC-Alsthom has made a series of acquisitions, beginning with the Belgian locomotive manufacturer ACEC. In late 1989 GEC-Alsthom acquired an 85% interest in the Spanish rolling stock manufacturers Atiensa and MTM, after a debt write-off by the Spanish government. Privately-owned Macosa agreed to contribute its railway interests in return for a minority share in the new group. The deal was a prelude to the closure of works in Barcelona and the run-down of plants in Valencia and Alcazàr de San Juan. Subsequently, GEC-Alsthom acquired Metro Cammell in the UK and then the rail interests of Fiat.

This process of concentration continued virtually unabated during the 1980s and early 1990s, although recently the German cartel office rejected a plan by AEG and Siemens to merge their railway equipment interests, because of the dominance this would have given the new company in the domestic market – AEG had already acquired the rail interests of MAN and MBB, while Siemens had already acquired control of Deuwag, a manufacturer of light rail vehicles and multiple units. The market for rail equipment in Germany has a low import penetration due to the historical procurement patterns of the federal railway authorities. AEG and Siemens had hoped to form a single company, in order to better compete with GEC-Alsthom and ABB. Despite this setback, the companies still plan 'partial collaboration' in order to overcome the competition authorities' objections. Siemens has shown a preference for this type of link-up in the past, as evidenced by its cooperation agreement with the main Italian manufacturer, Ansaldo Transporti.

Most recently, the main railway engineering groups have begun to move into eastern Europe. This began with acquisitions in the former East Germany. AEG acquired the massive LEW locomotive works in Henningsdorf, while GEC-Alsthom is negotiating to acquire Deutsche Waggonbau from the Treuhand. Elsewhere, AEG has acquired the CKD works in Prague, while Siemens is in negotiations with Skoda Plzen to acquire its rail and electrical engineering interests and ABB controls the Polish traction manufacturer Dolmel.

This restructuring has resulted in the emergence of a railway equipment industry in Europe dominated by four very large companies whose main R&D and production activities are located in the core regions of Europe. For these producers the acquisition of capacity in the periphery can either provide access to low-cost, skilled labour (especially true of eastern Europe) or knowledge of local markets – or both. For the LFRs, restructuring means at best loss of ownership and control, at worst plant closure and job loss. Robert Peron, Executive Director of Bombardier Eurorail, has pointed to a general problem of the current pattern of restructuring:

> Governments promoting the single market will need to pay attention, particularly in the smaller countries, to ensure that their market is not opened up in isolation. There is a possibility of local industry being invaded by foreign suppliers able to offer low prices because they enjoy numerous domestic orders in their own countries. The local supplier dependent on domestic orders will in such circumstances have little chance of competing in other markets.

In the short-term, persistent national market differences (in terms of particular technologies and so on) will ensure the survival of some local producers in the LFRs, but beyond this there is likely to be further restructuring. This evidence tends to support the notion that adjustment processes are likely to impact heavily on the LFRs, but tends to undermine the basis for medium-term optimism that characterises official analyses.

Limits of regional policy

In the face of the processes that appear to threaten the employment base of the LFRs, EC regional policy is modest in both scope and scale. This is hardly surprising. Delors (1989) argues that there is no inevitable process of 'circular and cumulative causation' and rejects the idea that subsidies on capital and labour should form a part of regional policy. For Delors such measures are not in keeping with the free market ethos that underpins the creation of the single market and the wider process of European integration – they serve merely to distort market mechanisms and hence the allocation of resources, and delay the adjustment process in the regions. Delors rehearses many of the common criticisms of traditional regional policy measures and expresses support for those measures that he regards as having the least impact on market mechanisms. He advocates investment in physical infrastructure and the upgrading of human capital as the main functions of regional policy, more or less reflecting the current activities of the EC Structural Funds. Delors instead advocates the value of 'decentralised', local entrepreneurialism as a solution to regional problems.

The reform of the Structural Funds in 1988 was designed to assist the adaptation of the LFRs to the conditions of the single market. There is some evidence that reform has led to greater coordination between different arms of the fund and that in some regions they have supported innovative and worthwhile projects. However, despite a doubling of the resources available for the period 1989–93, total expenditure on the Structural Funds remains small in relation to the nature and scale of the problems in the LFRs, amounting to only 0.24% of EC GDP. As Doyle (1989) notes, the Funds remain small relative to the alleged welfare gains derived from the single market – the source of the adjustment problems that the increased Funds are supposed to address (see also Perrons, 1992). Moreover, the reluctance of the northern member states to agree in full the Delors II package will limit the effectiveness of the Cohesion Fund agreed at Maastricht. To the degree that regional policy does operate, there is a danger that the infrastructure improvements which are to be financed through EC regional policy, especially the transborder links financed through the Cohesion Fund, may serve merely to provide large markets for companies whose main production will remain in the European core regions. In Spain, for instance, a large portion of the ECU620 million European Regional Development Fund expenditures earmarked for transport, is to support the TGV link between Paris and Madrid (which largely uses the technology of GEC-Alsthom).

More generally, such infrastructure improvement might merely serve to promote easier penetration of markets in the LFRs by firms in the core regions. Recently, for instance, Lyons has become a focus for large investments in distribution logistics activities as firms such as IKEA and Volvo Trucks have sought to enter southern European markets without actually locating there (Amin, Bradley, *et al.*, 1993).

Patterns of EC expenditure are characterised by major anomalies. The current structure of the EC budget does not automatically assist cohesion, largely because about 80% of the price support expenditures made through the Common Agricultural Policy goes to 20% of farmers in the north and centre of the Community. This reflects the fact that such expenditures are made not in relation to 'cohesion' criteria but on the basis of farm output. Research suggests that, overall, the impact of the EC budget on LFRs is broadly neutral (Franzmeyer *et al.*, 1991). Ireland, Greece and Portugal have been net beneficiaries, but so too is Denmark. By contrast, Spain does relatively badly. For instance it finances 8% of the EC's research and development budget, but receives only 5% of the spending, partly because its research base is too low to absorb more resources (*Financial Times*, 18 June 1991).

Structural Funds have been used to attract mobile investment into LFRs, as a means of job generation; the focus in the 1980s has been on 'high technology' inward investment, often in the face of heightened competition for such investment. This has often been preferred to a strategy of improving the technology base and utilisation rates of indigenous firms and plants, or supporting the development of local supplier networks. Such inward investments have been attracted into LFRs at considerable public expense, yet often there is little local research and technical contact between the new high technology investment and the local economy. Such investments add little to the capacity of regions to achieve self-sustaining growth of the local economy and are more likely to confirm the LFRs in the role of low-skilled, low-wage assembly outposts (Amin, Bradley *et al.*, 1993).

Moreover, the rationalisation of branch plants described earlier reinforces the power of large firms in relation to LFRs. In such a situation
there is even more scope for large firms to play off region against region in
order to retain existing investment and secure new funds. There is a
danger that an ever-larger proportion of regional policy expenditure is
given over to the attraction of ever fewer flows of mobile investment, while
simultaneously conditions of employment are eroded in the LFRs. These
trends are exemplified by the recent relocation of production by Digital
from Galway in Ireland to Ayr in Scotland, leading to the loss of 800 jobs
in Galway and inflicting a social and economic disaster on the city (*Financial Times*, 2 March 1993). The planned relocation of production by
Hoover from Dijon to Cambuslang follows the acceptance by the Scottish
workforce of diminished working conditions and the preparedness of Scottish Enterprise to provide funds to support the relocation (*European
Industrial Relations Review*, March 1993). In the absence of countervailing
measures, this moving of jobs between assisted areas seems a more likely
scenario in the new Europe than any major relocation of key activities
from the core regions (so-called 'social dumping').

Economic and Monetary Union

As currently constituted, plans for economic and monetary union are
likely to further widen regional disparities. One of the chief means by
which monetary union will impact upon regions is through the removal of
exchange rates as an instrument of economic policy. Fiscal policy will
therefore have to become the main means for the regional distribution of
income and employment. The stringent fiscal discipline which is stipulated
in the Maastricht Treaty poses a severe threat to the regions which will
have the greatest burden of adjustment in relation to the series of nominal
macroeconomic variables (inflation and interest rates, public deficit and
debt). Clearly the most serious threat is to weak regions in member states
with weak fiscal capacity and running large deficits. For instance Greece
has a deficit of 15% of GDP, while Italy has public debt of 100% of GDP
(Begg and Mayes, 1993).

The German experience of uniting two economies with widely differing
productivity levels gives some indication of the likely effects economic and
monetary union can have on indigenous production and the costs of infrastructure development which the EC will have to confront in order to meet its
objective of balanced development. Ultimately, the achievement of convergence is only possible with long-term transfers. The MacDougall Report on the
role of public finance in European Integration argued that a Federal Europe
would need inter-regional resource transfers of around 20–25% of GDP and
that a 'looser' federation would require expenditures of around 5–7% of
Community GDP (CEC, 1977). As we have already seen, the Community
Structural Funds represent only a fraction of 1% of GDP.

Under Maastricht, economic and monetary union will not, however, be accompanied by the creation of automatic fiscal stabilisers of the type that have characterised German unification. The Maastricht Treaty did not require the creation of new institutions to guarantee the achievement of cohesion, implying, as Godley (1992) notes, that the only new institution required by a unified Europe is an independent central bank. The EC has no plans to become a direct tax-raising authority which would have allowed the transfer of funds directly to individuals in LFRs through the tax and benefit system. The EC budget remains tiny as a proportion of EC GDP (1.2%) and, despite pleas from the Spanish government in 1992 for the creation of a system of automatic transfers to the weaker member states, the negotiations surrounding the Delors II funding package designed to accompany economic and monetary union suggest that automatic resource transfers on a European scale are an unlikely scenario (Hughes Hallet and Scott, 1992). Begg and Mayes (1993) note that even if the Delors II package were to have been implemented in full, the proportion of income derived from transfers in most recipient regions would remain modest, reaching only 8.9% in the most intensively assisted regions, compared to the net fiscal transfer to the Mezzogiorno from the Centre-North of Italy representing around 22% of the income of the South.

Structural policies in the new Europe

The fall-out from the completion of the internal market and the transition to economic and monetary union is likely to impact heavily on the LFRs. There is little doubt that Community regional policies themselves will have a limited impact on cohesion over the period of transition to monetary union, while the ability of member state governments, especially in southern Europe, to respond to growing regional problems will be limited by Maastricht's convergence requirements. In such a situation it is difficult to be optimistic about the prospects for Europe's disadvantaged regions. There is, therefore, an overwhelming case for the abandonment of the convergence requirements in order to allow Member states the necessary latitude to be able to deal with their specific regional problems.

At the same time the evidence presented in this chapter suggests that there is a strong justification for adopting a European rather than a wholly nation-state based view of regional problems. The emergence of a distinctively European spatial division of labour appears to be reinforcing existing regional disparities both between and within member states. This strengthens the case for EC regional policy and suggests the need for an expansion in its scope. Certainly, there appears to be little justification for proceeding to full economic and monetary union without a massive transfer of resources from the stronger regions to the weaker ones.

Historical experience suggests that a high rate of economic growth will be a necessary condition for the reduction of regional disparities in Europe. However, the evidence presented in this chapter suggests that this alone will be insufficient. So long as EC industrial policy is constituted around the principles of market liberalisation and the promotion of 'European champions', there is likely to be a major imbalance in the development of the European economy. As Doyle (1989: 79) has pointed out, a true commitment to cohesion 'should mean a regional dimension to every European policy'. This suggests that the prospects for the LFRs would be served by a more active industrial policy which had as a central tenet the decentralisation of industrial activity from the European core.

11

Industrial Strategy and Employment in Europe[1]

Malcolm Sawyer

There appears to have been an outbreak of recognition recently of the need for some form of interventionist industrial strategy to bolster industrial performance. The breadth of support for an industrial strategy is perhaps suggestive that the scope and nature of such a strategy is often ill-defined, with a strong element of meaning all things to all people. The notion of an industrial strategy can cover the range from paying attention to the demands of manufacturing industry through to a comprehensive, if outline, plan of the future development of an economy. The term 'industrial strategy' is used here, rather than 'industrial policy', to convey the idea that a strategic stance is adopted by the government concerned with a published, if outline, view of the future course of the economy. Industrial policy is often used to mean little more than competition policy (e.g. policies on monopoly, mergers and restrictive practices), whereas industrial strategy involves a wide range of policy instruments and objectives. Indeed, the key element of an industrial strategy is intentions rather than instruments: for example, low interest rates used to promote investment and industrial development would count as an instrument of industrial strategy. The essence of an industrial strategy is that the government seeks to pursue a range of economic and industrial policies which are consistent with the overall strategy.

There is, however, a deeper and more profound difference between industrial strategy and competition policy. The former usually relies on the view that the government can play a positive enabling role in the economy and that institutions (such as unions, employers and organisations) can have a beneficial influence on the workings of the economy. In contrast, competition policy is based on some perceived desirable properties of competition and the unfettered market mechanism. In general, institutions such as firms and trade unions, and agreements between firms would be seen as 'market imperfections' which harm the operation of a market economy, and hence the focus of competition policy should be geared towards the removal of those imperfections.

The case for an industrial strategy

An industrial strategy (along with a wide range of other policies) is a necessary component of a package of policies to combat unemployment. This general line of argument is based on two basic assumptions. The first is that a market economy does not tend to automatically generate full employment and that it is not just inadequate aggregate demand and/or macroeconomic policy mistakes which generate unemployment. The second (and related) one is that unfettered market mechanisms tend to perpetuate inequalities and disparities. Such disparities involve high levels of unemployment in the less prosperous regions, and industrial and regional strategies are required to overcome those disparities.

The contribution of an industrial strategy towards the achievement of full employment can be seen to arise from easing supply-side constraints and thus the balance of trade constraints, and improving the distribution of economic activity across regions (a point to which we return below). An industrial strategy could improve the inflationary performance of an economy by, for example, reducing supply bottlenecks, and thereby it may permit a higher level of economic activity. In some respects though, little direct effect can be expected from industrial strategy in terms of reducing unemployment: indeed faster productivity growth which would be expected, *ceteris paribus*, from a successful industrial strategy may increase unemployment. Hence appropriate demand management policies are also required to sustain employment levels.

An industrial strategy is only one arm of economic and industrial policy, though it may consist of numerous policy instruments and many objectives. But even on a broad definition, an industrial strategy would need to be complemented by a range of other appropriate policies. In particular, policies designed to sustain the level of aggregate demand would be required, for there is little reason to think that adequate demand would otherwise be forthcoming. A high level of demand is required not only for reasons of employment creation but also to underpin confidence necessary for the industrial strategy to operate. Investment would be enhanced by high levels of capacity utilisation, and the changes in employment patterns arising from industrial development are less painful for those involved when demand is high.

The general notion of an industrial strategy can be linked with that of the developmental state – a state organised and concerned to promote economic and industrial development. There will be, of course, other types of activity undertaken by such a state, but a central concern of its economic and industrial policies would be that of industrial development. In contrast, competition policy is based on the notion of a regulatory state – one which constrains economic activities, whether or not such constraints are perceived to be in the general social interest. The form of regulation may vary over time. For example, nationalisation and privatisation may be used as alternative modes of regulation of public utilities.[2]

Although industrial policy has generally been viewed as the preserve of central government within the nation state, it is by no means self-evident that it must be so, and the issue of the appropriate tier of government to deal with industrial policy becomes an issue in the context of the EC single market (Geroski, 1990). In particular, there is the question of which aspects of industrial policy should lie within the province of the European Commission, which aspects with national governments and which aspects with regional government. Competition policy and the completion of the single market are clearly Community-level activities. But many of the policies which could form part of an industrial strategy – such as the encouragement of small businesses and of networks between firms – can (and should) be implemented at the regional or local level of government. A regional policy is still required to provide some overall balance between regions, and that is essentially a Community-level activity, for the redistribution would need to operate across the Community.

I have argued elsewhere (Sawyer, 1992) that there is a set of theoretical ideas which can be used to underpin the idea of an industrial strategy. Two are particularly relevant here. The first is the linked notions of cumulative causation (Myrdal, 1957) and centripetalism (Cowling, 1987, 1990) which arise from the operation of market (and other) forces. With increasing returns, 'change becomes progressive and propagates itself in a cumulative way'. Further 'no analysis of the forces making for economic equilibrium . . . will serve to illumine this field, for movements away from equilibrium, departures from previous trends, are characteristic of it' (Young, 1928, quoted in Kaldor, 1972). Static economies of scale pose the dilemma of the choice between efficiency and monopoly power. Dynamic economies of scale pose the dilemma that these arise from the process of growth and the creation of new resources, but the process generates disparities between regions and nations. While those regions which prosper make good use of their resources, the depressed regions exhibit unemployment of labour and capital. Thus, cumulative causation involves underutilisation of existing resources in the process of resource creation through investment etc. It also means that the economic resources of the 'weak' are underutilised and undervalued.

Cowling (1985) extends the argument on the effects of cumulative causation into the social and political arena. Cumulative causation at the level of the firm leads to concentration. Cowling argues that:

> growth in sheer size is not the only threat to democratic control; there are also parallel changes in the organisation of big business which will tend to undermine democracy. Two tendencies which stand out in this regard are transnationalism and centripetal developments. . . . Centripetal economic tendencies become centripetal political and cultural tendencies and the community enters a vicious circle of relative decline. Thus whole communities lose effective control over their own lives – the essence of true democracy.

This centripetalism arises from the interactions of firms and markets, and while there may be some counteracting forces at work, there is a degree of inevitability in these tendencies. Thus, some non-market forces, notably the actions of governments, are required to offset the tendencies. An area which is suffering from relative decline will find great difficulty in recovering, and such recovery would require deliberate action to offset or reverse these centripetal forces, say through local or national government. Some element of removal from the global market system may be required through trade protection and similar measures, and these are measures which are no longer available to national governments within the European Community. The policy dilemma here is how to preserve the creative functions of markets while restraining their centripetal tendencies. It perhaps suggests that policy restraints by government (such as trade protection) will harm the creative functions, while developmental policies by government will enhance them.

Relatively backward regions suffer from unemployment and underemployment: workers in the secondary labour markets suffer from underutilisation of their skills and talents. This suggests that unemployment will always be a feature of market economies, at least in the relatively backward regions. But as Myrdal argued, it is not only market forces that generate cumulative causation, and the socio-political forces may exacerbate rather than ease these problems. A broadly conceived industrial strategy would have to offset these forces towards disparities and underutilisation of resources: regional policies, training and education of disadvantaged groups are thereby included under the ambit of industrial strategy.

The relevance of these notions for industrial strategy and the single market is straightforward. Insofar as these forces of cumulative causation operate, they will benefit the core areas (e.g. many parts of France, Germany, northern Italy, southern England) to the (relative) detriment of the peripheral areas (e.g. Greece, Ireland, southern Italy, Portugal). In this view, the operation of the single market will, at a minimum, maintain existing disparities and may well reinforce them, and it has to be remembered that there are large disparities between regions within the European Community. The core areas will, of course, have more resources at their disposal to pursue, *inter alia*, an industrial strategy than will the peripheral areas. Regional policy, involving a major redistribution of resources, is thus also required to redress the balance and to enable the attainment of something approaching full employment in the peripheral areas. It clearly suggests the need for redistribution of resources at the Community level, and the need for some Community-level policies.[3]

The second idea of relevance here is the need to dispense with the dichotomy between allocation through markets and allocation through planning which has plagued the debates on economic organisation. This dichotomy has been strongly influenced by the equivalence in static general equilibrium theory of the two forms of allocation. But that theory ignores important elements of the real world such as competition through new products, strategic planning and uncertainty. Yet it is such forms of competition and planning (whether by firms, governments or whoever) which are viewed here as crucial to competitive economic strength. There is a degree of complementarity between the market mechanism and industrial strategy. For, as Best (1990) argues:

> The first element in a successful industrial policy is a creative use and shaping of the market. Industrial policy fails when it overrides or ignores the market and is based upon the presumption that plans and markets are alternative means of economic coordination. The purpose is not to substitute the plan for the market but to shape and use markets.

In a rather similar vein, Amsden (1989) distinguishes between state policy which is market-conforming and that which is market-augmenting.

Towards a high-wage economy

I indicated above that a successful industrial strategy would only be an indirect creator of employment, but would be seen as required for a successful and competitive economy. There is a broader consideration here, namely the question of the type of employment created. Much recent discussion has made reference to notions such as high-wage/high-productivity economies. 'High' and 'low' are not defined with any precision in this context, except by reference to other countries. The underlying argument is clear: namely that an economy cannot permit its unit labour costs to diverge substantially from those in other countries so far as traded goods are concerned, but that unit labour costs depend on both wages (including indirect labour costs) and productivity.

The dispute between the British government and the other European Community governments over the Social Chapter can clearly be interpreted in these terms, with those supporting the Social Chapter seeking to pursue the high-wage/high productivity route.

A high-productivity regime (if it is to be maintained over time) requires mechanisms to ensure high levels of productivity (given the resources available) and the creation of resources over time. It is convenient first to discuss the level of (labour) productivity and then second to consider the growth of productivity and technological change.

In the neoclassical analysis of markets, the level of labour productivity is determined by the extent of cooperating factors and technology, and technical efficiency is assumed to be present. While it is widely recognised that technical efficiency is not generally achieved, the thrust of the neoclassical literature is that competition restrains the degree of inefficiency and that efficient institutional and contractual arrangements emerge. In the Austrian tradition, following Alchian and Demsetz (1972), a residual claimant is required for technical efficiency and that is generally identified with private ownership. Competition and private ownership are then viewed as mechanisms for the enforcement of work discipline and of technical efficiency.

Some interesting recent analysis has cast doubt on the validity of that general approach, and Bowles and Gintis (1993) make a range of propositions, many of which are relevant to this discussion. These include:

(1) 'Cost-minimising contingent renewal enforcement strategies are inefficient';
(2) 'The employment relationship of the capitalist firm is inefficient, in the sense that a redistribution to the workers of ownership of the firm and control over enforcement strategies generally permits compensation of the former owners while making the workers better off';
(3) 'The survival of hierarchical over polyarchical or democratic firms be explained by their efficacy in enforcing distributional claims, and does not require their efficiency in allocating resources';
(4) 'Anonymity in market exchange fosters norms hostile to the efficient solution of coordination problems'.

But they argue that:

a closer approximation of the real world to Walrasian assumptions might do more harm than good. The reason is that efficient and otherwise desirable solutions to coordination problems often are facilitated by social norms valuing such things as cooperation, truth-telling and non-aggression towards others. A Walrasian world would undermine the evolutionary processes supporting these norms.

In other words, the search for the 'perfect' market would not lead to generally more beneficial outcomes.

This can be linked with the gains which are possible from worker participation in decision-making and production. Bowles, Gordon and Weisskopf (1990), for example, argue that 'the keys to high-productivity work performance are commitment and cooperation. The keys to commitment and cooperation, in turn, are participation in the design and execution of work and a share in the gains of a job well done'. The Austrian approach emphasises the use of information by entrepreneurs but identifies the entrepreneur with property ownership and the requirement for a residual claimant. However, much information and knowledge resides with workers, individually and collectively, who in the right institutional setting can use that information and knowledge fruitfully. The ability of workers to exploit their specialised knowledge would enhance efficiency.

These arguments are suggestive of the general notion that an unfettered market system would not be efficient and hence would not be a high productivity system. It should be noted here that the term 'market system' may be difficult to define with any precision. The neoclassical concept involves an arm's-length relationship between firms, based on parametric prices with little role for government other than provision of public goods, correction of market failure and enforcement of contracts and property rights. Market systems in practice involve many forms of relationship between firms, and a more extensive role for government. But the argument here is that attempts to replicate the 'pure' market economy would involve opting for the low-wage economy route.

It is perhaps uncontroversial to say that the growth of productivity will require, *inter alia*, investment in machinery and people, technological change and its implementation. In each case there are well-known reasons why the unfettered market system would not perform as well as one involving some forms of intervention. Education and training are widely quoted examples where the difference between private and social returns would lead firms to under-invest. Investment in machinery can be adversely affected by inherent uncertainty about the future, which may be exacerbated by an unfettered market system and by the short-termism of the finance capital markets. Research and development may also be inhibited by a significant divergence between private and social returns and by long-term and uncertain pay-offs. The development of new products and processes is likely to require a degree of cooperation between firms: for example, the development of a new aircraft involves a wide range of firms supplying the component parts to the aircraft constructor.

These arguments point to the general notion that a high-productivity economy will not be one based on an unfettered market system. A high-productivity economy requires the effective use of its workforce; while a market system may enforce work discipline, it does not permit the full use of the knowledge and skills of its workforce. Further, a high productivity economy requires the creation of resources which a market economy is likely to underprovide (e.g. for reasons of lack of confidence in an uncertain world, and the short-term pressures imposed by financial markets).

Although there are clear suggestions that some forms of inter-firm cooperation are beneficial, there appears to be an absence, as yet, of clear guidelines on how to judge the suitability of different forms of cooperation. Some forms, such as price-fixing and market-sharing agreements, are likely to be harmful (which has been the traditional view). But others, particularly where there is mutual support of research and development, appear beneficial.

Plans and markets

Two features of the traditional market/plan dichotomy discussed above are significant here. The first is that the analysis is essentially static in nature, and its focus is on the coordination of the production and distribution of a predetermined range of goods and services. Little attention is given to the development of new products, so that firms in the market system have to accept the prevailing market conditions and cannot mould those conditions to their own advantage. The plan has been seen as akin to central planning, whereas planning by government (and others) can, and generally does, take the form of adopting broad strategic aims for the future evolution of the economy. Information is assumed to be readily available in both cases, and there is a duality between the decentralised market solution and the centralised planning solution.

The second feature is the counterposing of market *or* plan (paralleling that of allocation through price *or* through the firm), whereas the underlying view here is that market and plan (and also that role of price mechanism and the firm) are to some degree complementary. Anglo-American economic analysis has focused on the essential *opposition* of market and plan, thereby leaving a yawning gap such that analysis of the complementarity of market and plan is difficult to undertake. The complementarity arises from the government setting the general framework within which firms operate, and seeking to aid firms to fulfil the strategy.

It is often argued that governments have to provide goods which have some of the properties of 'public goods'. The difficulty presented by such 'public goods' is not only that they will tend to be under-provided by the private sector, but also that each private agent will face incentives in the short term which undermine the provision of these quasi-public goods in the longer term. Then, as Streeck (1991) argues, 'a lack of appropriate non-market institutions on the supply-side may thus stand in the way of an optimal use of productive resources'. But these 'individually non-appropriable factors' are more extensive than usually described in orthodox economics and include social peace, competence and ecological synergies, as well as knowledge and skills (Streeck, 1991: 42–45). In this type of approach, there are ambiguities and contradictions in the relationships between government and enterprises. Any element of monopoly or restrictive practices legislation places government in opposition to the immediate interests of the enterprises. The intention to foster industrial development requires cooperation between government and enterprises (though with questions of whose interests are being pursued). Although it is possible to place too much stress on the demands of consistency, nevertheless a policy of cooperation and a policy of restraint do involve different perspectives on government–business relationships.

It is difficult to believe that a set of strict rules could be drawn up for the provision of aid to enterprises such that a non-discretionary policy could be operated. The thrust of the 'new competition' literature and some of the arguments advanced above is that there is a need for a flexible approach by government to match a wide range of situations. A supportive government policy which provides aid to enterprises on a discretionary basis will clearly run into problems of consistency and the potential for corruption (though anti-trust policy is not immune from either of those problems).

Industrial strategy and the European Community

The Treaty of Rome (particularly articles 85 and 86, dealing with cartels and restrictive practices and with monopoly respectively) and the policies which flow from it appear to run counter to the developmental state approach and to be consonant with the 'market failure' approach. In view of the economic policies pursued in the member states (and this would have been even more the case when the Treaty of Rome was signed), there is a considerable paradox here.[4] Member countries agreed to policies at the Community level (e.g. on monopolies and restrictive practices) which they did not pursue at the national level (Germany being an exception), and built in impediments to industrial policies at the Community level which were pursued at the national level. But this may reflect the existence of national industrial policies 'based on different ideologies and power structures between the government, trade unions and employers in each member state' (Hitiris, 1988). Further, the arrival of the single market places limitations on government interventions and does not create the institutional apparatus for a Community-level industrial strategy.

The notion of a single market is clearly one in which there are no significant barriers to trade and there is a strong tendency towards a uniformity of price across the single market. This notion lends itself to competition policy designed to lower those barriers and to remove any perceived monopoly impediments to trade.

The implementation of an industrial strategy faces (at least) three sets of obstacles. The first set is the political and intellectual climate, particularly evident in Britain, which appears to often find it difficult to comprehend that markets do not and cannot in practice operate in a perfect manner. Neoclassical economics starts from a conception of a perfect market, with many features of real economies seen as imperfections impeding the operation of markets and to be removed if possible. In contrast, the starting point for an industrial strategy is that free markets (if such a concept can be defined) would not operate in any sense in a perfect manner. Further, there is clear hostility among most industrialists to the general idea of state intervention and to the political parties which would seek to intervene in industrial matters. Subsidies with few strings attached are generally welcomed (and sought by industrialists), but an industrial strategy would require government involvement in decision-making as well. Yet the cooperation (to some degree) of such industrialists would be a key ingredient for the success of an industrial strategy. The second set of obstacles arises from the need for the relevant institutional arrangements for an industrial strategy, which probably means a variety of corporatist-type structures. There have to be mechanisms through which government, business and workers can interact, make and implement decisions. Even such structures which do exist have been undermined in the past decade or so. The Treaty of Rome (articles 85 and 86 especially) embodied a competition policy and the corresponding institutions have been put in place.

The single market extends the operation of competition policy. But there has not been any corresponding creation of the types of institutions which would be required for an industrial strategy.

The third set of obstacles is the absence of a set of clear policy proposals as to what would constitute an industrial strategy and how it could be operated in practice in the current economic and social circumstances. Policies such as enhanced training programmes to ease skill shortages, the promotion of technology transfer networks, etc. can be identified as possible policies within an overall industrial strategy. Reference can also be made to successful industrial strategies, as in Japan and Korea, but the strategies pursued in those countries not only had a range of undesirable features but also were implemented in economies where protection from international forces was possible.

The idea of 'national champions' is often associated with industrial strategy, with French governments in particular having adopted such an approach. This is not an inevitable feature, as the Japanese and Korean experience indicates where policy has often favoured two rather than one 'national champion' in an industry. The adoption of a single 'national champion' creates a monopoly problem, not just in the usual sense but also in that the government becomes reliant on that particular firm for success in the sector concerned. The 'national champion' approach is likely to play less of a role in the future. In part, the fostering of 'national champions' will become more difficult within the single market, though that would not necessarily stop such a policy, nor prevent the idea of 'European champions'. A further consideration comes from the significance of economies of scale. Although a substantial part of the benefits of the single market are supposed to come through the further exploitation of economies of scale (Cecchini, 1988), other commentators have been rather more circumspect in this regard (e.g. Davis *et al.*, 1990). The case for a single 'national champion' is, of course, undermined by the absence of any economies of scale.

The phrases 'national champions' and 'spotting winners' are frequently used to deride industrial strategy. In that regard, I prefer to draw on the argument advanced by Cowling (1987) to the effect that it is not a matter of 'picking winners', but rather of 'creating winners'. Thus there is no reason why specific firms have to be selected for aid but rather that some sectors (e.g. selected high technology industries) and some types of activity (e.g. research and development) receive support from the state. It is to create the climate within which firms flourish. Or, as Tomer (1993) argues, '[i]f athletic team members are not learning and responding appropriately, it is up to the coach to correct the situation. If too many firms in the economy are failing to learn and perform satisfactorily, there is obviously a need for an "economic" coach'.

An important question in this area relates to the appropriate level of government (European Community, national, regional or local) at which an industrial strategy should be operated. A rather Utopian answer would be that the design of the strategy would be a Community level matter, though many decisions could be delegated to a lower level of government, where the decisions would be taken within the context of the overall strategy. This answer overlooks, of course, the political constraints in the adoption of such an approach as well as its informational and other requirements. When an industrial strategy is viewed as the support of a range of particular industries, then it can be argued that it is only when there are economies of scale which are comparable in size to the European economy that it is necessary to operate the policy at the European level. However, if policy instruments such as interest rates are used for industrial development purposes, then they may well be essentially Community-level policy instruments for, even in the absence of monetary union, there is little discretion at the national level over interest rates.

There are many elements of an industrial strategy for which implementation at a local or regional level would be appropriate. The provision of infrastructure and of training could be cited as two fairly obvious examples. However, this decentralisation raises (at least) two problems. First, there is the degree to which there is counter-productive competition between localities: the obvious example here being the use of subsidies to attract inward investment. Second, the more prosperous localities can expand more on their industrial strategies than the less prosperous regions, thereby exacerbating disparities between localities.

Conclusion

The general theme of this chapter is that the achievement of full employment requires, *inter alia*, an industrial strategy to mould the way in which market forces operate, since those forces left to themselves will not generate full employment. However, the development and implementation of such a strategy requires an enormous shift in the political and intellectual environment, as well as the creation of appropriate institutional arrangements.

12

European Employment Policies

Andrew Glyn and Bob Rowthorn

Employment experience and policies in Europe have varied widely since 1973, comparing both different countries and various sub-periods. Employment performance was particularly bad in the first half of the 1980s in what may be labelled the European core (Germany, France, Belgium, the Netherlands and the UK).[1] As can be seen from Table 12.1, per capita output of the market sector stagnated, growing by a mere 0.4% p.a. over the period.[2] Since hourly productivity grew quite rapidly, the result was a fall of over 2.6% a year in the total number of hours worked in the market sector of these economies.[3] This loss of work opportunities in the market sector was only partly offset by job creation in the state sector and by cuts in the working week (sharing the available work amongst more people). The net effect was that employment fell at nearly 1.5% p.a., leading to a massive rise in unemployment.

There are three routes to a rapid increase in total employment: one in

Table 12.1. European employment patterns, 1979–90.
(average annual percentage changes)

	European core 1979–85	European core 1985–90
Market output (MO) per head of pop of working age (Pop)	0.4	2.9
− Productivity	3.1	1.8
= Total hours in market sector/Pop	−2.6	1.0
+ Share of state employment	0.4	0.2
+ Fall in hours per worker	0.9	0.1
= Employment/Pop	−1.4	1.0
Memorandum item		
Post-tax real earnings/worker	−0.3	1.5

which a dynamic market sector generates additional work, a second in which an expanding non-market sector (typically the state) provides additional work, and a third in which the total amount of paid work available in the economy is shared out among more people through cuts in working time. The former route is exemplified by the European core in the later 1980s. As Table 12.1 shows, output in the market sector grew quite rapidly at around 3% p.a. over the period 1985–90, while productivity growth slowed down to less than 2% p.a. As a result, total hours of work performed in the market sector rose by 1% p.a. This was the major factor behind the observed increase in total employment during the period. The extreme case of this pattern was the UK, where productivity grew so slowly (0.6% p.a. in the market sector as a whole) that employment actually rose at 2% per year faster than the population of working age, outdoing over this period even the US 'jobs machine'.

Over most of the period since 1973, the so-called corporatist economies in the Nordic group have been far more successful than their neighbours in the EC at maintaining employment levels (see Rowthorn and Glyn, 1990, and Pekkarinen, Pohjola and Rowthorn, 1992). During the 'intershock' period (1973–79) they exemplified an alternative high employment model, whereby total employment was increased despite a major decline in work opportunities in the market sector. This outcome was achieved by increasing state employment and reducing hours of work. Table 12.2 presents the data for Sweden, which is particularly striking in that the total number of people in employment was not just maintained but greatly increased, above all through the rise of state employment.[4] Several of the Nordic countries are suffering very severe employment problems at present (Finland as its vital USSR market has crumbled, Sweden after the credit-based boom of the later 1980s has collapsed). However, their intershock experience provides lessons as to the possibilities (as well as the pitfalls) of the public sector playing a much more central role than in the more

Table 12.2. Employment patterns 1973–79, European core and Sweden. (average annual percentage changes)

	European core 1973–79	Sweden 1973–79
Market output (MO) per head of pop of working age (Pop)	1.5	1.2
− Productivity	3.4	2.8
= Total hours in market sector/Pop	−1.8	−1.6
+ Share of state employment	0.4	1.2
+ Fall in hours per worker	0.8	1.3
= Employment/Pop	−0.6	0.9
Memorandum item		
Post-tax real earnings/worker	1.6	−0.7

market-oriented model which has spread from the US into much of
Europe in the 1980s. There the main policy focus has been on supply-side
measures, such as labour market deregulation, to boost employment in
the market sector.

Keynesian Policies

Traditional Keynesian fiscal and monetary policies promote employment
by expanding demand for market sector output (interest rate cuts to
stimulate investment, tax cuts to stimulate consumption, public spending
to raise demand for supplies from the market sector); they also increase
employment in the non-market sector if they include higher expenditure
on public services. Such policies encounter a number of objections, on
the grounds that one or other of the following constraints on expansion
will be breached.

Inflation

Under certain conditions, the risk of inflation may seriously restrict the
scope for Keynesian policies designed to create employment by stimulating demand. For example, if there are bottlenecks in the economy, the
resulting increase in demand may lead to severe shortages of certain
types of capacity or skilled labour, causing a demand-led wage-price
spiral. If unions are well-organised and militant, falling unemployment
may soon cause unsustainable wage pressures to develop well before the
point of full employment of labour or capacity is reached. However,
under these conditions it is not merely Keynesian policies which are ruled
out by the risk of inflation. The same objection will then apply with
almost equal force to any increase in demand, however caused, including
a spontaneous recovery in consumer spending or a boom in exports.
Even an expansion led by investment would face identical problems until
the new capacity came on stream. To the extent that additional demand
leads to unacceptable inflation, any increase in demand, no matter what
its origin, is unsustainable and will have to be choked off by government
policy. Under these conditions, if there is a spontaneous recovery in
consumer demand or a boom in exports, the government will have to
tighten fiscal or monetary policy so as to restore aggregate demand to its
former level.

Those who oppose Keynesian policies on the grounds that they are
inflationary are, in effect, arguing that a demand-led recovery of any
kind is impossible. Under certain conditions this may well be true, but it
is important to recognise that there is nothing uniquely, or even especially, inflationary about government measures to stimulate demand.
Where they are valid, the inflationary objections to Keynesian policies
derive not from the fact that government measures are involved, but

simply from the fact that such policies increase aggregate demand under conditions where such an increase has an unacceptable impact on the price level.

To the extent that wage bargaining plays a role in the inflationary process, inflation cannot be understood in narrowly economic terms, but must be seen as a political problem demanding a political solution. The recent experience of Germany has illustrated that, where the situation demands that the exercise of bargaining power is moderated, then trade unions have to be brought into an effective form of social contract where the sacrifices (including forgone improvements as well as actual cuts) have to be allocated in a way which commands broad social support. If this is impossible, and inflation constitutes a binding constraint, then no form of demand expansion (including those discussed in this chapter) offers any hope of reducing unemployment.

Balance of payments

In the present situation of the UK in particular, but also other European countries with weak external positions, the balance of payments represents, in our opinion, a more serious constraint on expansion than does inflation. This constraint applies to any generalised expansion because of the implications for imports. It is obviously related to the question of inflation since real exchange rate adjustments, which would ease payments problems in an expansion, may be ruled out because of their implications for import prices and therefore inflation. Even so it is conventional to think of them as somewhat separate, and in practice it may be one rather than the other problem which appears first and frustrates a generalised expansion. Moreover if trade elasticities are low, or if international economic relations (within the EC for example) make necessary adjustments in exchange rates difficult to achieve, then it is more useful to think of the balance of payments as a constraint in its own right.

Public debt

Limits to the financing of deficits are often seen as an independent constraint on expansion because of the fear of an explosive and unsustainable growth in the ratio of public debt to GDP. In a purely demand-constrained economy, this fear is unjustified. As the appendix to this chapter argues in more detail, in such an economy *any* rise in government spending or cut in tax rates will eventually cause output and income to rise to the point where additional tax revenue is sufficient to contain or eliminate the budget deficit. In a purely demand-constrained economy, Keynesian fiscal measures are ultimately self-financing because of their highly expansionary impact on output and national income and thereby on tax revenue. However, if the balance of payments is weak, then the induced expansion in domestic output and national income following a Keynesian stimulus will eventually become unsustainable because of its effect on imports and the country's external financial situation. In this case, the initial stimulus will have to be reversed through either expenditure cuts or higher tax rates. Failure to do so will lead to the feared explosion in public debt and to a deteriorating external situation as the country's overseas debts accumulate.

The point is that an economy facing a binding balance of payments constraint is not purely demand-constrained. In a balance of payments constrained economy, Keynesian fiscal policies to stimulate demand are not self-financing and may be unviable in the medium term because of their impact both on the country's external position and the public debt. This may not completely rule out their employment as a short-term pump-priming or countercyclical measure, but it does place severe limitations on their use.[5]

Employment Creation in a Balance of Payments Constrained Economy

This chapter is concerned with how employment can be increased in a situation where conventional Keynesian measures are inappropriate for balance of payments reasons, which we believe represent the immediate constraint in many economies such as the UK. We focus on two policy packages which correspond very broadly to the market/non-market routes to employment growth identified earlier. The first is a scheme for self-financing wage subsidies (as in Snower's recent proposal that unemployment benefit and tax lost from unemployment should be paid as a temporary and declining subsidy to employers taking on unemployed workers). This policy relies on stimulating the employment-creating capacity of the market sector by reducing the cost of certain kinds of labour to employers. The second policy is a programme of greater government expenditure on public services and infrastructure. Such a programme stimulates employment throughout the economy by increasing both government purchases from the market sector and increasing the output of public services by the non-market sector.[6]

Pattern and Predictability of Employment Effects

In order to compare the two policies it is helpful to visualise their having the same effect on employment. It should be said that the impact on employment of a wage subsidy is rather uncertain. It depends on the extent to which both: (a) total output in the market sector is constrained by the cost of labour, and (b) a wage subsidy will encourage more labour-intensive methods of production for any given level of output. If the scheme is to be self-financing, it must generate sufficient employment so that the unemployment benefit saved and extra tax received are at least equal to the immediate cost of the scheme to the government. To achieve such an outcome the scheme must overcome the formidable problems of monitoring (so that those taken on really are additional workers) and displacement (of other workers by those receiving the subsidy). These problems are well known and make the impact of wage subsidies rather unpredictable.[7]

Additional expenditures on the welfare services or infrastructural programmes have a much more predictable impact on employment. The responsible authorities face a hard budget constraint, in the face of insistent demands for improvements in the services provided, and may therefore be relied on to expand spending with little or no delay when finance is made available. Whether the employment takes place within the public sector (NHS cleaners, school teachers) or the market sector (construction workers on infrastructural projects), there is little or no problem of either monitoring or displacement and thus of deadweight costs of spending on intramarginal jobs. Nor is there a problem of insufficient capacity, since the physical capacity for expanding public service employment (mainly buildings) is available and there is massive excess capacity in the construction industry, where many jobs would be created by infrastructural programmes.

While the impact on employment of increased public expenditure programmes is predictable, it is also expensive. Instead of being self-financing, as in our benchmark case of a truly marginal wage subsidy equal to the exchequer cost of unemployment, the government has to pay the excess of the wage over the cost of unemployment. To preserve budgetary comparability with the wage subsidy case we should assume, therefore, that any net increase in government expenditure is financed by higher taxation. This implies, in effect, that personal consumption in aggregate is held constant: those who were previously employed face higher tax rates to pay for the net cost of supporting the extra people employed on public expenditure programmes. The extra cost, of course, excludes savings on dole payments and the like and any taxes paid by those employed on the programmes. The tax-financed expenditure programme described here is, in effect, a redistribution of the national wage fund. The post-tax wages of those already in employment are reduced and the revenue thereby obtained is used to support people who were previously unemployed. Many of the former experience a reduction in their personal consumption, while many of the latter experience an increase.[8] In aggregate, though, personal consumption remains unchanged. In terms of personal consumption, some people gain and some lose. The whole population, however, gains from improved public services, which clearly helps to increase the political feasibility of the project. In addition, the required tax revenue may be raised more or less progressively, which is another issue bearing on the political feasibility of the project (feelings of appropriate sacrifice, etc.).

Balance of payments

When it comes to the balance of payments, the fact that the tax-financed expenditure programmes involve a redistribution, rather than expansion, of personal consumption of market sector output is a decisive advantage. In contrast, the expansion of market sector production, inherent in the wage subsidy policy, will inevitably lead to higher imports. On the one hand intermediate imports will be sucked in as inputs into the general expansion of market sector output; on the other, aggregate personal consumption will increase, and this will involve substantially more imports of finished goods. Such a deterioration in the balance of payments may not be sustainable. It is true that there is an offsetting factor. The fall in marginal production costs arising from the wage subsidy should have some effect on exports (and import competing sectors). In principle a wage subsidy should function like a devaluation of the currency to increase cost competitiveness. But the effect on cost competitiveness may be rather weak (elasticity pessimism), especially if the reduction in costs refers only to marginal production, depriving firms of the much more generalised rise in profits on exports which may explain a good part of the effect of a devaluation. There is no guarantee this will have a big enough effect on the current account. 'Supply-side policies', specifically encouragement to fixed investment, training, R&D and so forth, may hold out the only hope of breaking the balance of payments constraint on the growth of market sector output. Marginal employment subsidies, even though they may increase the labour intensity of market sector output and encourage some switching towards domestic production, may still be quite insufficient to allow the desired expansion of employment without balance of payments problems intervening.

Does such a balance of payments constraint on market sector expansion imply an absolute ceiling on the generation of jobs? Not necessarily. Expanding employment in the welfare services involves very little if any additional import requirement. Sixty-six per cent of general government non-military consumption is on direct employment; the import content of the rest is rather low, as major suppliers are business services, pharmaceuticals and construction, all with relatively low import requirements.[9] Providing the expenditure is financed by taxation, then total consumption is left unchanged; its redistribution towards the previously unemployed, with relatively low incomes, will if anything reduce imports as their expenditure will be on goods with lower import content than those bought by taxpayers, especially if the tax increases are on higher incomes (Borooah, 1988). If public expenditure flows to private construction firms, the demand for imported inputs will rise, but with some half of construction output representing value-added, and the import content of purchases by the industry being rather low (timber being an exception), the expansion of imports would be limited provided there is the relevant excess capacity. In effect, public expenditure of this sort is targeted on activities with a very low import intensity, something which is impossible to organise in the context of general incentives for the market sector to expand. Moreover, to the extent that the public expenditure increases involve some improvements to the economic infrastructure (improved educational services, training programmes, transport investment, for example), they will actually contribute to the universally desired improvement in the supply side, something not directly touched by employment subsidies.

Balance of payments weakness may rule out the classic remedy of expanding demand across the board (such as occurred in the later 1980s with the credit-based consumer boom in many European countries); what is required is rather the policy advocated in *How to pay for the War*, where Keynes analysed the measures necessary to restrain consumption while employment was expanded in the munitions industries and the armed forces. Between 1938 and 1942 total employment rose by around 3.3 million, but market sector employment fell as additional workers were deployed to the armed forces.[10]

Such a drastic programme is not required in the present situation. The public expenditure programme advocated here would lead to some increase in market sector employment. Moreover, additional public sector employment would not be in the armed services, but in health, education and other services which contribute directly to the standard of living. There would be no reduction in aggregate personal consumption, as Keynes envisaged, but merely a redistribution of personal consumption within the population. The need to limit aggregate personal consumption does not arise in the present context from the need to release labour into other uses, as it did in the war, but from the requirement to prevent imports rising excessively. With across-the-board import controls no longer a credible option, and with the likelihood that trading partners would object equally to marginal employment subsidies which had a comparable effect in preventing a deterioration in the trade balance, the only feasible approach might be to ensure that the expansion is targeted on the least import intensive sectors. These are precisely the sectors of public works and public services which have been so drastically run down recently and whose expansion could command much popular support.

Inflation

At first sight the impact on inflation seems more serious if employment is increased by tax-financed spending on public services rather than by a self-financing wage subsidy. The latter involves no reduction in the post-tax real wages of existing workers, since the subsidy is financed entirely out of exchequer savings on dole payments and the like, together with the taxes paid automatically by any additional workers employed. In contrast, tax-financed spending on public services does involve an increase in tax rates and therefore reduces the post-tax real wage of existing workers. In this case, the exchequer must meet the full cost of employing extra workers, which is normally greater than any savings from reduced dole payments and the like. Thus, public services or public procurement are typically more expensive than wage subsidies as a way to create employment. From this point of view they are more inflationary.

However, this is not the end of the story. The unemployed are expensive to maintain and when they gain employment through public expenditure programmes they pay taxes like any other workers. These represent considerable savings which must be taken into account when evaluating the net cost of such programmes. Because of these savings the net cost of employing additional workers is well below the wage paid to existing workers. If the cost of unemployment is half the gross wage, then for every £1 raised from current tax payers, public services costing £2 can be financed and will be received (broadly) by those who pay the taxes. Provided the extra workers in the public services are efficiently used in ways which visibly improve the standard of these services, many existing taxpayers will undoubtedly feel better off, despite the increase in their tax bill. Surveys frequently indicate that people are willing to pay higher taxes to finance improved public services. In times of mass unemployment, this finding is likely to be reinforced by the fact that these services can be obtained on the cheap because of the enormous savings to the exchequer involved in taking people off the dole. Given the relatively modest rise in taxes involved, increased expenditure on public services could prove quite popular at the present time since it would increase the standard of living of so many people, including many already in employment. For this reason, it might be less inflationary than a wage subsidy of the type advocated by Snower, which reduces unemployment but has virtually no effect on the standard of living of the existing workforce.

The corporatist countries show extended periods in which real consumption out of earnings fails to rise, or even falls so as to finance increased employment in the public services. In Sweden during 1973–79 consumption from earnings fell at over 1% p.a., despite a 3% p.a. growth in hourly productivity. Much of the additional productivity was diverted into support for greater employment in the welfare services.[11] There are obvious limits to such a process, and overstepping these limits has undoubtedly contributed to the current problems in Sweden (see Pekkarinen, Pohjola and Rowthorn, 1992). But Sweden is an extreme case, and in most of Europe both tax rates and public expenditure are much lower. Besides, these limits are not immutable; the key surely is, that very strong political support has to be built up for expanding the public services and infrastructure, emphasising its twin advantages of reducing unemployment and increasing welfare.

Temporary or Permanent?

Both the policy options discussed thus far – wage subsidies or expansion of public services/infrastructure – have a certain self-liquidating potential. If the wage subsidies are effective, and by one means or another market sector investment rises, then the increased capital stock will help to obviate the need for the subsidies by increasing productivity (provided real wage pressure is kept in check). While there is no reason to see expansion of the public services as essentially temporary (smaller class sizes are permanently desirable), a sharp increase in public investment contains the potential, once the most urgent reconstruction is met, for room to be made for additional market sector investment, should it be forthcoming. It is of course highly desirable that the latter *should* come, since a balance of payments constraint is likely to imply the existence of insufficient competitive capacity. To achieve its full effect, infrastructural investment by the government (including improvements in education) needs to be complemented by fixed investment in new products and processes by the market sector. Specific incentives for private investment are especially necessary in this case, since the investment must anticipate rather than simply follow a rapid rise in market sector output.

Summary and Conclusion

Two major policies, designed to achieve a given increase in employment with no change in the balance of the budget, may be compared thus:

	Wage subsidy	Public services
Market sector output & employment	Large increase	Small increase
Public services output & Employment	Unchanged	Up
Post-tax wage rate	Unchanged	Down (tax rate up)
Aggregate consumption	Up	Unchanged
Predictability of employment effect	Low	High
Balance of payments	Imports up a lot; lower marginal costs raise competitiveness?	Small effect on imports
Long-term competitiveness	Higher market output stimulates investment	Infrastructure and human capital improvements
Inflation	Fall in U raises wage pressures	Fall in U raises wage pressure; cut in personal consumption exacerbates; improvement in public services basis for social contract?

The arguments above as to the benefits of increased public expenditure programmes do not depend on the output being provided directly by the public sector. The key is that the output should be *purchased* by the public sector (which makes predictable both the type of goods and services produced and the amount of employment created) and that the output concerned should have a low import content. While it has been convenient to speak of it as non-market sector output, and there are in our view powerful efficiency and equity grounds for keeping public services publicly produced, it is the fact that the expenditure is publicly financed and directed which is essential here. The employment implications would be broadly similar if instead of hiring, for example, additional NHS staff, the money were used to finance private treatment for NHS patients.

It is well-known that an expansion has a more severe effect on the trade balance if it is carried out by one European country than at the level of the Community as a whole (for the average EC country 58% of imports are from other EC countries, and for Western Europe as a whole the figure is 69%).[12] This suggests that the degree of *necessity* for public sector 'bias', in a programme for high employment would be less at the Community level than for an individual country. But agreement at the Community level for serious expansionary packages seems some way off yet.[13] In the mean time it is important to be clear that there is a viable programme for raising employment in a single country, provided the political support can be generated not only for expanding the public services and infrastructural spending, but most importantly for 'paying' for them by severe restraint on the growth of real take-home pay (including possible reductions in the early stages).

The contagious impact of a major, public sector-led expansion of employment in a single country should not be underestimated. Just as the collapse of the Mitterrand expansion in 1983 seemed to signal the final collapse of traditional Keynesian policies, so a successful expansion of employment would do more than anything else to build up support for EC-level expansion. Such a universal expansion would help relax the balance of payments constraint facing individual countries and thereby reduce the need to restrain personal consumption, since the increased imports arising from higher personal consumption within any individual country would be partly offset by increased exports to other European countries. There would be less need for higher taxes to restrain personal consumption, and any political problems associated with the whole project would be that much weaker.

Appendix: The Dynamics of Public Sector Deficits and Debt

by *Wynne Godley and Bob Rowthorn*

This appendix is an edited version of a paper submitted by the authors to the UK Treasury panel of economic advisors. The model presented is highly simplified and cannot do justice to the full complexity of the problem. However, it does bring out clearly the central issues.

The main conclusions are as follows. Consider an economy in which neither inflation nor the balance of payments is a constraint on output, so that any permanent increase in demand leads to an equal and permanent rise in output. In such an economy, tax cuts or additional government expenditure are eventually self-financing. They lead to some increase in government debt, but not to an explosion, since this debt will ultimately stabilise. The factor stabilising the debt is the behaviour of output. Following a fiscal stimulus, output will rise and tax revenue will automatically increase. Moreover, the expansion will continue to the point where additional tax revenue is sufficient to halt government borrowing and stabilise the debt. In an inflation-constrained economy, the expansionary process will lead to an unsustainable inflation and the government will be compelled to half the expansion before tax revenue has increased sufficiently to stabilise the government debt. In a balance of payments constrained economy, the government debt will grow without limit because the output multiplier will be too small to generate the tax revenue required to stabilise government debt. The counterpart to expanding government debt will be an expanding national debt to foreigners.

Comparison with other models

To illustrate how it is that public expenditure will, on certain assumptions be self-financing, we present the following model, which closely resembles models already presented in the classic article by Blinder and Solow (1973). Like their model, ours takes output as entirely demand-constrained. Any increase in demand is matched by an equivalent rise in output, with no prohibitive costs in the form of unacceptable inflation or a balance of payments deficit. However, our model differs from theirs in several ways.

(1) *Interest rates*: Their model was designed to compare the effects of monetary and fiscal policy, and to this end the stock of money is taken as exogenous and the interest rate is endogenous. By contrast, we take the interest rate as exogenous and assume that the authorities adjust the stock of money so as to keep the interest rate at this level.

(2) *Investment*: Their model includes an investment function, but this is not central to their analysis and merely serves to complicate the exposition without adding anything central. In our model, investment is ignored, although it could easily be included.

(3) *Inflation*: Their model ignores inflation. Our model takes inflation

into account. Inflation has a number of effects. In a stationary economy, inflation allows the government to finance part of its expenditure by issuing money (seigniorage). And in a growing economy, inflation increases the ability of the government to finance expenditure in this way. (In a growing economy, even without inflation, the government will normally finance some of its expenditure by issuing money to keep up with the growing demand for 'real' money.) Inflation also increases the effective tax rate on interest receipts, since taxes are normally levied on nominal interest, not real interest. This is a manifestation of 'fiscal drag'. Finally, inflation affects the choice between money and bonds in the portfolios of wealth-holders. With reasonable parameter values, the overall effect of inflation in our model is to reduce the government expenditure multiplier and thereby dampen the effects of fiscal policy.

(4) *Foreign trade*: Their models ignore foreign trade. Foreign trade is taken into account in our model, where it plays a crucial role. It sets an upper limit to the level of government expenditure which can be permanently sustained. If this limit is overstepped, the result is an unsustainable increase in both government debt and national indebtedness to foreigners – a 'New Cambridge' insight (Featherston and Godley, 1978). In this respect our model resembles that of Branson (1976).

The basic mechanism

The crucial mechanism regulating the government deficit and the accumulation of government debt is, in true Keynesian fashion, the level of total income. When government expenditure first increases, or when tax rates are first cut, the result is an increase in government borrowing. However, there is also an increase in output which generates more tax revenue and reduces both the deficit and the accumulation of government debt. Indeed, output eventually rises to the point where tax revenue is sufficient to stabilise the ratio of government debt to GDP. In the simplest case, where inflation is zero, a once and for all increase in primary government expenditure will lead to an increase in output such that the additional tax revenue is exactly equal to the extra primary government expenditure plus any interest payments arising from government borrowing during the transition period. Thus, a rise in primary government expenditure (or a cut in taxes) has no long-term effect on the government deficit since tax revenue will eventually rise to close the gap. Note that this argument assumes that output is demand determined. Where output is constrained in some way, tax cuts or extra government expenditure may not be sustainable.

The basic model

The basic model is described by equations (12.1) to (12.11).

Notation

Y	=	real GDP
C	=	real consumption
G	=	real government expenditure
Y_d	=	real disposable income
B	=	real stock of government bonds
M	=	real stock of money
$\hat{W}$	=	target wealth
M_n	=	nominal money stock
P	=	price level
D	=	overall government deficit
D_p	=	primary government deficit (i.e. deficit excluding interest payments)
f	=	proportion of bonds in net wealth
θ	=	tax rate
π	=	inflation rate
r	=	real interest rate
z	=	average real post-tax rate of return on net wealth
ω	=	target wealth-income ratio
λ	=	wealth adjustment coefficient
X	=	exports
m	=	import propensity
B^{gov}	=	total holdings of government bonds (including holdings by foreigners)
L^{for}	=	net national debt to foreigners
G^*	=	warranted level of government expenditure (i.e. maximum permanently sustainable with existing trade performance and tax rates).

Income expenditure

$$Y = C + G \tag{12.1}$$

Disposable income (with fiscal drag on nominal interest receipts)

$$Y_d = (1 - \theta)Y + \left[r - \theta\left[r + \frac{\pi}{1 + \pi} \right] \right]B_{-1} - \pi M_{-1} \tag{12.2}$$

Target wealth

$$\hat{W} = \omega Y_d \tag{12.3}$$

Wealth accumulation

$$W - W_{-1} = \lambda(\hat{W} - W_{-1}) \tag{12.4}$$

Savings

$$W - W_{-1} = Y_d - C \tag{12.5}$$

Wealth

$$W = B + M \tag{12.6}$$

Portfolio composition

$$\frac{B}{W} = f(r, \pi) \qquad f, f_r, f_\pi > 0 \qquad (12.7)$$

Real money stock

$$M = \frac{M_n}{P} \qquad (12.8)$$

Inflation

$$P = (1 + \pi)P_{-1} \qquad (12.9)$$

Government deficit

$$D = G + \left[r - \theta\left(r + \frac{\pi}{1 + \pi} \right) \right] B_{-1} - \theta Y \qquad (12.10)$$

Primary deficit

$$D_p = D - r B_{-1} \qquad (12.11)$$

Note that disposable income can be expressed as follows:

$$Y_d = (1 - \theta)Y + z W_{-1} \qquad (12.12)$$

where

$$z = \left[r - \theta\left(r + \frac{\pi}{1 + \pi} \right) \right] f_{-1} + \pi(1 - f_{-1})$$

Note also that z is the average real post-tax rate of return on wealth.
After manipulation, we get the following difference equation for wealth:

$$W = \beta W_{-1} + \gamma G \qquad (12.13)$$

where

$$\beta = \frac{\lambda\omega[1 - \theta + z] + \theta[1 - \lambda]}{\theta + \lambda\omega(1 - \theta)}$$

$$\gamma = \frac{\lambda\omega(1 - \theta)}{\theta + \lambda\omega(1 - \theta)}$$

Suppose π and r are constant. Then $f = f_{-1} = f(\pi, r)$. The condition for stability in equation (12.13) is as follows:

$$\frac{\theta}{z} > \omega \qquad (12.14)$$

This will be satisfied for most reasonable parameter values. For example, with $\theta = 0.25$ and $z = 0.05$, the inequality is satisfied for $\omega < 5$.

Growth path

Assume π, r are constant and

$$G = (1 + g)^t G_0 \qquad g \geq 0 \tag{12.15}$$

The behaviour of W is given by:

$$W = \beta W_{-1} + \gamma(1 + g)^t G_0 \tag{12.16}$$

where β, γ are as above. The solution is

$$W = \left[W_0 - \frac{(1 + g)\gamma}{(1 + g) - \beta} \cdot G_0 \right] \beta^t + \frac{(1 + g)\gamma}{1 + g - \beta} \cdot (1 + g)^t G_0 \tag{12.17}$$

Assuming $|\beta| < 1$, the first term on the right-hand side goes to zero and in the long run

$$\frac{W}{G} \to Lim \frac{W}{G} = \frac{(1 + g)\gamma}{1 + g - \beta} \tag{12.18}$$

Or, in full:

$$Lim \frac{W}{G} = \frac{(1 + g)\lambda\omega(1 - \theta)}{g\theta + \lambda\theta + \lambda\omega(g(1 - \theta) - z)} \tag{12.19}$$

It can also be shown that

$$Lim \frac{Y}{G} = \frac{1}{\theta} \left[1 + \left(\frac{z - g}{1 + g} \right) Lim \frac{W}{G} \right] \tag{12.20}$$

and hence

$$Lim \frac{Y}{G} = \frac{g + \lambda - \lambda\omega z}{g\theta + \lambda\theta + \lambda\omega(g(1 - \theta) - z)} \tag{12.21}$$

Since $B = fW$ and $M = (1 - f)W$, it follows from (12.19) that

$$Lim \frac{B}{Y} = \frac{(1 + g)\lambda\omega(1 - \theta)f}{g + \lambda - \lambda\omega z} \tag{12.22}$$

and

$$Lim \frac{M}{Y} = \frac{(1 + g)\lambda\omega(1 - \theta)(1 - f)}{g + \lambda - \lambda\omega z} \tag{12.23}$$

Note that B/Y and M/Y both stabilise. Hence the debt to GDP ratio does *not* explode. Also real money stock rises in line with GDP, and nominal money stock grows in line with nominal GDP. This gives the government seigniorage to help finance the deficit. From equation (12.10),

$$Lim \frac{D}{Y} = Lim \frac{G}{Y} + \frac{\left(r - \theta\left(r + \dfrac{\pi}{1 + \pi} \right) \right)}{1 + g} Lim \frac{B}{Y} - \theta \tag{12.24}$$

and

$$Lim \frac{D_p}{Y} = Lim \frac{D}{Y} - \frac{r}{1+g} Lim \frac{B}{Y} \qquad (12.25)$$

Hence both the overall and the primary deficits stabilise as fractions of GDP.

Note that the primary budget balance adjusts automatically so as to stabilise the debt to GDP ratio. This spontaneous adjustment occurs through induced variations in GDP. The government cannot directly determine the primary balance. It can only control r, θ and G, and once the time path of these is fixed as above, the variable Y will automatically evolve so as to stabilise the ratio B/Y. If this ratio is too large, Y will grow rapidly and generate sufficient tax revenue to bring this ratio down.

There is a standard proposition that the government cannot permanently maintain a primary deficit if the interest rate is greater than the growth rate ($r>g$). This proposition ignores the seigniorage arising from growth in the nominal money stock (= inflation + rise in the real money stock). Moreover, even when true, the statement is misleading. In a demand-constrained economy, the level of Y relative to G will automatically adjust so as to produce the primary balance (deficit or surplus) required to stabilise the ratio B/Y. If seigniorage is not sufficient to finance the deficit, a primary surplus will be required. This surplus will arise automatically under the conditions assumed in the present model.

Comparative statics

In this section we assume that $g = 0$ and examine the stationary equilibrium positions. The transition between these equilibria is ignored.

From the four equations (12.19), (12.21), (12.22) and (12.23), taking $g = 0$, we obtain the following stationary equilibrium relationships:

$$W = \frac{\omega(1 - \theta)}{(\theta - \omega z)} G$$

$$Y = \frac{1 - \omega z}{\theta - \omega z} G$$

$$\frac{B}{Y} = \frac{\omega(1 - \theta)f}{(1 - \omega z)}$$

Differentiating, we obtain[14]

$$\frac{\partial Y}{\partial G} > 0, \qquad \frac{\partial Y}{\partial \theta} < 0$$

$$\frac{\partial(B/Y)}{\partial G} = 0, \qquad \frac{\partial(B/Y)}{\partial \theta} < 0$$

Hence, a rise in government expenditure or a cut in tax rates both increase GDP. In the former case, the equilibrium ratio of government debt to GDP is unchanged.

In the case of a tax cut, the debt to GDP ratio increases but eventually stabilises. This conclusion holds no matter what the real interest rate. The factor which stabilises government debt is the behaviour of output. Following an increase in government expenditure or a cut in the tax rate, output will expand to the point where sufficient tax revenue is generated to produce the primary surplus required to cover government interest payments on bonds (net of any gain from seigniorage on new money).

Open economy

Let us extend the above analysis to the case of an open economy. Let B denote the net stock of bonds, government and foreign, held by domestic residents. Assume that exports, X, are endogenous, imports are a constant fraction m of domestic production, and that the real exchange rate is fixed. Assume also that the real rate of return on overseas borrowing is equal to the domestic rate.

In this open economy case, equation (12.1) must be replaced by the following equation:

$$Y = C + G + X - mY \qquad (12.1a)$$

It can be easily shown that the behaviour of W is given by the following equation:

$$W = \tilde{\beta} W_{-1} + \tilde{\gamma}(G + X) \qquad (12.13a)$$

where:

$$\tilde{\beta} = \frac{(m + \theta)[1 - \lambda(1 - z\omega)] + \lambda\omega(1 - \theta)(1 + z)}{m + \theta + \lambda\omega(1 - \theta)}$$

$$\tilde{\gamma} = \frac{\lambda\omega(1 - \theta)}{m + \theta + \lambda\omega(1 - \theta)}$$

Suppose π and r are constant. The condition for stability in equation (12.13a) is that $\tilde{\beta} < 1$, which after rearrangement can be written as follows:

$$\frac{m + \theta}{(1 + m)z} > \omega \qquad (12.14a)$$

For reasonable parameter values this will be satisfied. For example, with $\theta = 0.25$, $z = 0.05$ and $m = 0.25$, the inequality is satisfied if $\omega < 8$.

Comparative statics: quasi-steady state

Assume that government expenditure G is constant. Provided the stability conditions are satisfied the key variables converge to the following values:

$$W = \frac{\omega(1 - \theta)}{\theta + m - \omega z(1 + m)}(G + X)$$

$$Y = \frac{1 - \omega z}{\theta + m - \omega z(1 + m)}(G + X)$$

$$\frac{B}{Y} = \frac{\omega(1 - \theta)f}{1 - \omega z}$$

Note that the expression for B/Y is the same as in the closed economy case.

Let us now consider the behaviour of government and foreign debt. By definition:

$$B = B^{gov} - L^{for} \qquad (12.26)$$

where B^{gov} is the total amount of government bonds outstanding, including those held abroad, and L^{for} is net national liabilities to foreigners by the private sector and government combined.

Government bonds are issued to cover that part of the budget deficit which is not covered by money creation. Hence, in the 'quasi-steady state' we are considering:

$$\Delta B^{gov} = D - \pi M \qquad (12.27)$$

where $M = (1 - f)W$ and D is given by equation (12.10). Since B is constant in the quasi-steady state, it follows from (12.26) that:

$$\Delta L^{for} = \Delta B^{gov} \qquad (12.28)$$

Using (12.27), it can be shown after manipulation that:

$$\Delta B^{gov} = \frac{[m(1 - \omega z) - (1 - \theta)\omega\pi]G - [(1 - \omega z) - (1 - \theta)(1 - \omega\pi)]X}{m(1 - \omega z) + \theta - \omega z} \qquad (12.29)$$

The expression on the right-hand side is zero when $G = G^*$ where

$$G^* = \frac{(1 - \omega z) - (1 - \theta)(1 - \omega\pi)}{m(1 - \omega z) - (1 - \theta)\omega\pi}X \qquad (12.30)$$

This is the level of government expenditure which is 'warranted' by the country's trade performance. If $G > G^*$ then $\Delta L^{for} = \Delta B^{gov} > 0$. In this case government debt will increase indefinitely, as will the net indebtedness of the country as a whole to foreigners. Note that the problem of exploding government debt is intimately related to external trade performance. For example, suppose that trade performance is improved by means of a devaluation which increases X and reduces m. Then the 'warranted' level of government expenditure, as given by equation (12.30), will increase.

For reasonable parameter values $\partial G^*/\partial\theta > 0$. The implications of this are as follows. Suppose that $G = G^*$, so that government expenditure is at the maximum level which can be permanently sustained with the given trade performance and tax rates. Equation (12.30) tells us that government expenditure can still be increased, provided the tax rate θ is raised.

PART IV

Combating Unemployment in Europe

PART IV

Combating Unemployment in Europe

13

The Coordination of Macroeconomic Policy in the European Community

John Eatwell

The case for macroeconomic policy coordination within the European Community seems to be obvious. The economies of the European Community are so highly integrated (at least 20% of national expenditure in each state being derived from exports to other member states) that the overall performance of each of the member states is highly dependent on the performance of the others. The degree and direction of dependence is clearly a function of size, as well as the other components of economic strength (productivity, market share, industrial composition, financial and monetary institutions, and so on). But nowhere is the impact negligible. In these circumstances the efficient conduct of economic policy would suggest that policy be coordinated. Not only does the policy stance of one country have an impact on the rest of the Community, but there is a reciprocal, second round influence back on the first country. The task of coordination is to internalise these externalities.

Given the potential efficiency of policy coordination, and, more importantly, given the national self-interest which would seem to be present in policy coordination, the interesting question is: 'Why doesn't it happen?'. The history of policy coordination is one of ample rhetoric, many learned arguments, and very little action.

The exception has, of course, been the *imposed* quasi-coordination in monetary policy. Within the ERM, at least post-1987, free capital movements meant that equilibrium interest rates in the member countries differed only by the expected changes in exchange rates. Interest rates were 'coordinated' by the market. This coordination of monetary policy, at least as far as the determination of short-term interest rates was concerned, was achieved asymmetrically, the foreign exchange markets imposing German interest rates (determined by German domestic policy priorities) on other ERM members.

Even following Britain's departure from the ERM, a similar effect might be expected to hold so long as free capital markets are preserved. Expectations as to the future movement of the exchange rate will have a much greater variance outside the ERM, so that interest rates may diverge for substantial periods of time, but in the long-run interest rates 'should' converge. They do not. The daily fluctuations in the exchange rate mean that daily capital gains and losses dominate the determination of the overall return on holding sterling, and relative interest rates are far less important – except, of course, in so far as they affect expectations as to future movements of the exchange rate. The 'coordination' of short-term interest rates is no longer imposed.

As far as fiscal policy is concerned, the contrast between the theoretical benefits of policy coordination and the lack of any significant action is most striking. The French experience in the early 1980s is often cited as an example of the dangers of going it alone. Britain may well provide another example over the next 18 months or so. Yet despite the available examples, and despite the power and simplicity of the argument that higher rates of growth and higher levels of employment may be attained without excessive growth of international indebtedness if national growth rates are coordinated, coordination simply does not happen. It is this paradox, the failure of governments to pursue policies which would apparently be in their best interests, which I attempt to explore in this chapter.

There are a number of possible explanations of the paradox which I want to deal with first before moving on to the main part of my analysis.

First, it might be argued that while governments recognise that macroeconomic policy coordination is desirable, it is simply too difficult to put into practice. This may well be true. Even under the most stable circumstances the outcomes of economic policy are only predictable within broad ranges. Moreover, the complexities of international interactions are even more difficult to incorporate into decision making than are domestic effects, of which policy makers have far more experience, and over which they believe they have greater control – a belief, by the way, which is often contradicted by events. And domestic pressures may well absorb too much time and too high a proportion of the available policy-making and policy-implementation skills.

Second, the expected gains from coordinated action may be too small to warrant the effort required for effective international coordination. The experience of pre-1973 growth in the OECD suggests that this is not the case, however. Although there was no active coordination of policies, the fact that all OECD countries grew relatively rapidly over a sustained period clearly produced significant externalities for each country. It is difficult, for example, to imagine that the UK could have maintained a trend growth rate of around 3% per year in the 1960s, if other OECD countries had not been growing at equivalent or faster rates. If those conditions could be replicated, at least as far as relative rates of growth are concerned, then an essential ingredient of higher growth and employment throughout the EC would be in place.

Third, the expected gains from coordinated action may be very unevenly distributed, making a policy consensus difficult to achieve. Indeed, it is possible that for some countries there is little or no benefit to be had from policy coordination. This would be the case of countries which are entirely unconstrained by either their foreign balance, or international monetary conditions. The unconstrained countries then set their policy stance with concern only for domestic economic circumstances, and feel no need to pay any attention to the likely impact on other countries. This is, of course, the story of German monetary policy in recent years. The Bundesbank appears to have pursued German monetary policy on purely a domestic basis, the impact on other EC member states being ignored. The Bundesbank's position does appear to have changed, however, with the rescue operation for the French franc in September 1992, and with the development of Franco-German monetary cooperation since then. These changes are clearly connected with the perception by the German authorities that the collapse of the ERM, which might follow a forced devaluation of the franc, would not be in the interests of either the current or the future conduct of German monetary policy. The asymmetry has, at least partially, broken down, and recognition of the need for some sort of coordination of monetary policy is the result.

Fourth, it might be argued that economies operate in such a way that policy coordination is an empty notion anyway. If, for example, economies are essentially self-adjusting, in the manner of neoclassical general equilibrium models, and deviations from equilibrium are due simply to short-term market failures, then the task of the policy-maker is to create the circumstances under which the powerful equilibrating forces of the market can operate more effectively. In other words, the task of the policy-maker is to eliminate, as far as is possible, the short-term imperfections. It would not be appropriate to devote space in this chapter to make the case against this characterisation of the operation of modern market economies, but it is worth noting that this theoretical stance seems to have determined the position of the British government, at least in the early 1980s when they rejected the need for any policy coordination. That position was theoretically consistent. A similar point of view seems to inform some of the economic arguments of the Maastrict Treaty. For although there are various provisions for mutual surveillance through Ecofin and associated committees, and, of course, for discussion of the interactions of monetary policy at the secretive Monetary Committee, the goals of coordination are all defined in terms of a self-adjusting model. All that matters is the stance of monetary policy. Fiscal policy is not, for example, seen as an active means of securing a given level of employment or rate of growth. It is a policy for balancing the budget. For the purposes of this chapter I will adopt the position which I myself believe to be true, namely that economies are not naturally self-adjusting to equilibrium levels of employment and growth; that active policies, especially active fiscal policies, may be required to secure socially desired levels of employment and growth; and that the interdependence of national economies can impose constraints on the exercise of those policies.

A 'stylized' European Community

In discussing the problems of policy coordination I will make a number of assumptions about the character of macroeconomic balance within the Community. These are my 'stylized facts'.

The level of unemployment within the Community is now about 17 million. From the perspective of some of the individual nation states, some of this is probably 'structural' in the sense that, due to the sheer lack of competitive domestic capacity, an expansion of domestic demand will have only limited effect on domestic employment, with demand being predominantly for imports. I will ignore this structural aspect of European unemployment, and assume that unemployment throughout the Community is 'Keynesian', i.e. attributable to a lack of effective demand.

A striking fact about the Community, taken as a whole, is that it seems to be persistently at, or near, external balance. External surpluses or deficits seldom exceed 1% of Community GDP, and are typically much less. In this respect the Community stands in stark contrast to the US and to Japan, both of which have persistent imbalances in current account in excess of 4% of GDP. Even supposing, however, that the overall external balance was maintained as the level of EC activity increased, the fact that this balance is arrived at by netting out individual imbalances imposes a potential balance of payments constraint on EC growth. The EC could achieve higher growth if it had the means of providing the financial transfers from surplus countries to deficit countries to net out the imbalances. Instead, surpluses accumulate in some member states, while the counterpart deficits constrain growth in others.[1]

I will examine the potential for effective policy coordination in the context of three 'stylized' cases, representing different exchange rate regimes:

(1) Fluctuating exchange rates between EC member states, the ERM having been assumed to have collapsed completely and replaced by a regime of floating rates.
(2) A full ERM, with different national currencies moving within very narrow bands relative to one another, with no realignments, and monetary policy in the hands of national authorities, though constrained by free capital movements.
(3) A monetary union, with a single currency and monetary policy, but with distinct national fiscal policies, and no tax and benefit transfers between nation states.

Fluctuating Exchange Rates

The advent of fluctuating exchange rates at the collapse of Bretton Woods, 1971–73, and the consequent privatisation of foreign exchange risk, has acted as both carrot and stick, enforcing the liberalisation of international capital movements and the increase of speculative currency flows.

Before the collapse, foreign exchange risk had been borne by the public sector. The immediate effect of the privatisation of risk was a remarkable transformation of the financial sector. In order to be able to provide the 'products' which permit firms to offset foreign exchange risk, financial institutions had to become bigger, more diverse, and acquire ready access to all the financial markets across which they wished to spread risk. The result was a rapid deregulation of the banking system, a wave of bank amalgamation (especially in the US), and the rapid abolition of exchange controls (all controls on US capital exports were abolished on 1 January 1974). Privatisation of risk was the stick behind the creation of a massive infrastructure of foreign exchange dealing. The carrot was the huge profits that could now be made from fluctuations in exchange rates.

The main impact of the expansion of speculative flows (now representing about 95% of all foreign exchange transactions) has been that countries have pursued very conservative financial policies in the hope of avoiding the policy disruption which can be the consequence of international speculation. The potential for financial instability has been a major factor behind the steady ratcheting upward of real interest rates, and has contributed to the sharp trend toward fiscal conservatism. These factors have been vital elements in the sharp slowdown in growth in the OECD countries since the collapse of Bretton Woods, and consequently in the persistent growth of unemployment. The deflationary effects of the fluctuating exchange rate regime have far outweighed any beneficial effects which might have arisen from any balancing of relative competitiveness by exchange rate changes.

Further doubt is cast on the efficacy of exchange rate changes to balance relative competitiveness by Nicholas Kaldor's observation (Kaldor, 1978) that changes in price competitiveness, brought about by both exchange rate changes and differential inflation rates, tend in the medium term to be *inversely* related to changes in national shares of world trade in manufactures – not positively related, as might be deduced from simple price theory. This counter-intuitive result suggested to Kaldor that it was the factors underlying the changing shares of manufactured trade which were influencing changes in relative competitiveness (as conventionally measured), rather than the other way round.

The idea that exchange rate variations might be an effective means of changing the distribution of demand between countries must therefore be regarded with some scepticism. However, if the balancing role of exchange rates is accepted for the purpose of argument, then if the overall level of demand in the Community is given, varying exchange rates are simply a means of redistributing employment and unemployment within the Community.

If the fluctuating exchange rate regime operated in this idealised form then it would obviate the need for any fiscal coordination, since countries can pursue whatever domestic fiscal policy they wish and current account balance will be maintained.

Simply to pose the now discredited idea that fluctuating exchange rates will enable countries to pursue whatever domestic policies they wish, suggests that the theoretical characterisation of the impact and potential role of exchange rate movements does not correspond to reality. Instead, exchange rate changes are means of competing for jobs. This effect may be offset by an increase in activity if loosening of monetary policy is associated with changes in exchange rates. For example, if the recent devaluation of sterling secures for Britain a higher share of total European employment, but that is not offset by some stimulation of the British economy, and of British imports, then there will be no net increase in EC jobs. Community partners may then prove to be unwilling to countenance a sustained British devaluation. Indeed, an exchange rate regime which, by its very nature, creates an environment in which member states *compete* over the allocation of employment between them is hardly conducive to fiscal policy coordination.

In sum, the potential which changing exchange rates may have for redistributing employment – whether in orthodox or Kaldorian 'perverse' manner – renders clear estimation of the *national* benefits of coordination, virtually impossible. Fluctuating rates and fiscal coordination are accordingly incompatible. The very notion of fiscal coordination would therefore seem to be something appropriate to a world of fixed or managed exchange rates or a monetary union.

Fixed Exchange Rates

The combination of fixed exchange rates and free capital movements which characterises the ERM creates strongly mercantilist pressures among the members states – each would like to maintain a surplus on current account to minimise the likelihood of disruption deriving from the activities of the international capital markets. This new mercantilism in turn creates a strong deflationary bias within the trading bloc.[2] That bias has been reinforced by the pursuit of a conservative monetary policy appropriate, if at all, only to circumstances in Germany. The challenge for fiscal policy coordination is to overcome this deflationary bias.

If the European economy is characterised by a system of fixed exchange rates and (roughly) similar rates of inflation, then it might be assumed, for the sake of argument, that import propensities are fixed. Given the structure of import propensities, there will be a given set of ratios between levels of national output which would maintain current account balances between member states. Higher levels of activity in these proportions will not lead to imbalances in intra-EC trade.

But the EC is not a closed system. The overall external balance is the result of netting out third party transactions. In the coordinated expansion, the relationship with third parties will contribute to the pattern of surpluses and deficits. The UK, for example, might maintain a balance with EC partners, but suffer a severe deficit with non-EC countries, the counterpart of which might be a German surplus with non-EC countries. The UK deficit might then force abandonment of its part of the growth strategy, bringing down the entire, interdependent effort. So policy coordination is made difficult within the EC, simply because member states have substantial trading relationships with economies which are not part of the coordination process.

Another problem with this coordinated expansion, even if third-party problems can be ignored, is that it does not solve the employment problem. The ratios of output referred to above will not necessarily correspond to the ratios of available capacity. One country could be left with high unemployment while another operates at full, or over-full levels of employment. This problem would be mitigated by the fact that import propensities are non-linear, rising sharply at high levels of capacity utilisation. So higher levels of employment may be attainable if more competitive countries are prepared to operate at high levels of capacity utilisation, forcing up their own import propensities.

To these difficulties must be added the problem of accurately determining the outcomes of macroeconomic policy mentioned above. The experience of West Germany, when encouraged to take on the role of the 'locomotive' pulling Western expansion in 1978, subsequently derailed by both the lack of reciprocal action (for a variety of reasons) by other major countries and by the second oil crisis, casts considerable doubt on the ability of policy-makers to deliver the planned balanced expansion.

These arguments suggest some reasons why it has been difficult to devise a coordinated expansion as part of a programme to secure full employment through the Community. Of course, the difficulties should not be overstated. Coordinated expansion would be a lot better than nothing, and the need to avoid the accumulation of debt does not require that the external account be balanced precisely, especially in the short run.

The problem is exacerbated if we consider the balance not in terms of levels of activity, but in terms of growth rates which are compatible with external balance. Since competitiveness will tend to be a positive function of the rate of growth of demand (and hence the relative import propensities will be a negative function of relative trend growth rates) not only will external balance be achieved only by different levels of activity at any one time, but it will be preserved only by rates of growth which will tend to diverge. This will have severe cumulative consequences for unemployment in the slow growth countries.

The difficulty in securing medium-term coordination will be

compounded by the fact that competitive success tends to follow upon the ability to secure a rapid growth of markets abroad, i.e. to secure export-led growth. If the home market is consumption-led then investment will be geared toward home consumption. Moreover, investment will only grow at the rate of growth of the domestic economy. If, on the other hand, demand is export-led, then not only will the composition of investment be export-led too, but also the growth of investment, and the growth of tradables (notably manufactures) can exceed the growth of the domestic economy. But if the EC is in external balance then clearly it is impossible for all countries to enjoy export-led growth. The trend growth rate of those that do will tend to diverge from the growth rate of those that do not.

All this suggests that a short-run fiscal coordination designed to achieve, say, a general boost to demand in a recession is problematic. But it is possible, assuming that some countries would be willing to countenance a short-term deterioration in their external position, a deterioration which would be less severe than if they had attempted the same boost to demand alone, without coordination. However, it would be very difficult to organise longer-term attempts to sustain growth by coordinated action without the persistent accumulation of debt by some trading partners, and without some countries being condemned to persistently low relative rates of growth.

So policy coordination cannot simply be fiscal coordination. It will also require management of import propensities to secure a set of relative growth rates which are acceptable to the member states, and maintain substainable balances with third parties. Of course, it is exactly this sort of 'management' which is achieved by an idealised fluctuating exchange rate system. Unfortunately fluctuating rate systems do not work in the idealised manner.

The problem can be thought of the other way around, as Kaldor (1978) suggested. The observed changes in competitiveness are the consequence of the need to adjust import propensities to limit the divergence of growth rates, a divergence sustained and even strengthened by diverging market shares. Kaldor's paradox that market shares are inversely related to measured competitiveness is, at least in part, due to the qualitative changes in products and processes which are an essential part of enhanced competitiveness, and for which productivity growth is an imperfect surrogate. In these circumstances the divergence would only be reversed by an 'excessive' adjustment of exchange rates, which overcompensate for dynamic differences in competitiveness as conventionally measured. Indeed, in these circumstances securing a pattern of growth rates which sustain full employment may well require the use of trade policy instruments other than exchange rates. What is necessary is to maintain high rates of growth in domestic demand to provide the foundation for higher productivity growth in the weaker countries – not export-led growth, but growth-led exports.

The Bretton Woods era of fixed exchange rates was not a period of policy coordination. The fixed rate system was buttressed by strict capital controls and by active trade policies, against which the dominant economic power, the United States, did not retaliate.[3] Individual countries were therefore able, within bounds, to pursue national economic objectives. That these added up to a reasonably coherent set of growth rates is to a substantial degree attributable to the combination of (a) managed trade, and (b) a persistent US deficit on combined current and long-term capital account which sustained the growth of world demand. The persistent high levels of employment were the result of the resultant structure of national policies: interdependent, yes; coordinated, no.

A similar reliance on national policies was the basis of the recovery from the recession of the 1930s. The recovery heralded by the abandonment of the gold standard, and the successive devaluation of currencies against gold, was not due so much to the devaluations (after all it was not possible for all countries to devalue against each other, and the countries which did not devalue were not big enough relative to the world economy to act as deficit-absorbing engines of world demand). It was instead due to the adoption of national expansionary policies – notably cheap money policies, fortified by capital and trade controls, once the need to maintain the monetary orthodoxy of the gold standard had been abandoned.[4]

Monetary Union

The great virtue of a monetary union is that it eliminates, at least as far as EC currencies are concerned, the deflationary pressures which derive from the structure of international finance in a multi-currency system. In so far as the origins of the new mercantilism are to be found in speculative currency flows, then the desire for a current account surplus, and the pressures for deflationary monetary policies will be eliminated. Moreover, the abolition of individual currencies will mean that the surpluses and deficits external to the EC will be netted out. The deflationary pressure exerted by the deficits of the weaker countries in the multi-currency ERM will also be eradicated. Thus the short-run barriers to coordinated action to achieve full employment will be removed. The difficulties of determining policy outcomes accurately may still be considerable, but the costs of mistakes will be far lower. Monetary union provides, therefore, the environment most favourable to coordinated fiscal expansion policies. These policies are likely to be most effective if combined with a monetary policy determined by EC, rather than German priorities.

In the medium term, however, the mercantilist pressures which derive from the real characteristics of the growth process will still be present in a monetary union. When high rates of productivity growth are associated with high output growth, and high productivity growth breeds competitive success, then those countries which are already most competitive will tend to enjoy a rate of growth of tradables output in excess of the rate of growth of their national economies, and in excess of the rate of growth of the EC taken as a whole.

These centripetal forces in the process of accumulation will concentrate industry in particular regions of the monetary union, and such forces will tend to be so strong as to overcome any price effects which attend relative regional decline. Since there will be no currency markets, the competitive weakness of industries in a particular country will not become generalised throughout the national economy via monetary policy. Instead, competitive weakness will be manifest in the accumulation of debt by individual families and companies within the weak region, and, of course, by declining fiscal revenues. That accumulation of debt will impose a slow growth of demand in the weaker region.

Overcoming that slow growth via a coordinated growth strategy is likely to be only a short to medium-term expedient. In the longer term, the only way to achieve economic balance is to take action to change the trade propensities. But, being in a monetary union, that can only be done by there being significantly lower rates of wage and price inflation in the weaker regions. The experiences of West Virginia within the US 'monetary union', or of the maritime provinces within the Canadian 'monetary union', suggest that such price effects will not be strong enough to offset regional weaknesses.

This brings us to a conclusion which seems to be a contradiction in terms: the most effective way to sustain a high rate of growth throughout the Community, and at the same time to maintain balanced growth as between member states (in other words, to solve the employment problem by means other than large-scale migration) would be a combination of a single currency and an active intra-EC trade policy. The single currency is the means of overcoming the deflationary mercantilist pressures which are typical of multi-currency trading systems with free capital movements. The active intra-EC trade policy is the means of overcoming (or at least spreading the benefits of) the self-reinforcing centripetal dynamics of capitalist accumulation.

In the heyday of the gold standard, this was exactly the way in which differential growth was maintained within the 'monetary union' of gold. In 1904 the average level of tariffs on industrial products imported from Britain was 25% in Germany, 34% in France, 73% in the United States, and 131% in Russia.

The contradiction of mixing EMU with an active trade policy may be overcome by recognising that resort to tariffs is not the only way an active policy could work. There might be labour subsidies for weaker regions, rather like the old Regional Employment Premium, or other transfers via regional and structural policies designed to enhance competitiveness in the weaker regions as well as maintain effective demand in the manner recommended in the MacDougall Report (Commission of the European Communities, 1977). Whether these would be sufficiently powerful to achieve the distribution of employment is another question. But they would certainly be better than nothing.

Summing-up

On the basis of the argument of this chapter, the pursuit of full employment policies requires a stable international monetary framework. Without such stability the deflationary pressures created by massive potential flows of speculative capital will overwhelm any attempt at either coordinated expansion, or relatively autonomous national expansion. A flexible exchange rate regime reinforces instability, virtually ruling out the possibility of coordinated macroeconomic policies to achieve full employment. A fixed rate regime with free capital movements is also highly unstable.

A stable monetary framework may be secured by a suitably buttressed fixed exchange rate system with occasional exchange rate changes. In this case coordinated expansion will be difficult to attain, other than in the short run. The best hope for full employment is to devise measures to curb speculative capital movements, and the use of some active trade policies to permit the pursuit of national full employment policies. Such national policies will then be mutually reinforcing internationally. Even so, to operate successfully, a reasonably open Bretton Woods framework needs a successor to the United States to exercise the role of leadership – a gap which a united European Community might fill. In addition it needs the assurance that capital exports from any major countries with trade surpluses would be sufficient to avoid deflationary pressures on their trading partners. But it is impossible to imagine this system working for long with free capital movements, unless entirely new ways are found to diminish speculative pressures.[5]

If the stable monetary framework is attained by monetary union, then in the short to medium term, coordinated fiscal expansion to attain full employment is likely to be successful. In the long term, however, the absence of any means to change import propensities by changing the exchange rate (assuming that this would work anyway) will mean that other methods of discriminating in favour of weaker regions must be found.

14

A Framework for European Exchange Rates in the 1990s[1]

Ruth Kelly

Sterling's humiliating departure from the Exchange Rate Mechanism in September 1992 was inevitable. The 'fault lines' at the heart of the system were so marked that even the entire war-chest of the Bank of England was insufficient to stem the tide of speculation against the pound for more than a few hours. It quickly became clear to the entire economic establishment that sterling's value against the German mark had been unsustainable. Moreover, the mechanisms which had been in place to promote orderly realignments of the system had withered away – not as a consequence of neglect, but as a deliberate policy choice to secure 'Euromonetarism' and pave the way towards European economic and monetary union.

Within six months, the Governor of the Bank of England, Robin Leigh Pemberton, was admitting that the Government's strategy had been seriously flawed. Appearing before the Treasury and Civil Service Select Committee in March 1993, he acknowledged that the authorities had become 'mesmerised' by five years of no realignments and had allowed fundamental imbalances between parities to remain unaddressed. If there had been no devaluation of the pound, the Bank hypothesised that within months, Britain would have seen falling prices and a deep slump in production.

The problem was that in the latter half of the 1980s, devaluation for countries with huge trade deficits – such as Britain – was seen as an admission of failure. The exchange rate was artificially elevated from being a tool of policy to a national virility symbol. Nor was the one measure which could have eased pressures on the system – the upward revaluation of the mark in the aftermath of the reunification of Germany in 1989 – actively sought. Indeed, individual parities against the mark were regarded as sacrosanct, whatever the ensuing consequences.

Robin Leigh Pemberton's stark admission is encouraging. But so far there has been little attempt to paint a picture of an ERM with realignments inherent in its conception. Part of the reticence is understandable. A glance back at the ERM leaves the unpleasant image of high real interest rates, enforced deflation, exorbitant levels of unemployment and ill-concealed social and industrial unrest.

Why have an exchange rate system at all? Is not the socialist alternative freely floating currencies? First, history suggests that floating rates are unstable, prone substantially to overshoot both up and down. The experience of the dollar and the pound over the 1980s reinforces the point. In a world of global markets and industries, wildly fluctuating exchange rates mean that companies do not know whether to invest for the future, with the result that strategic decisions are often delayed. Trade is also disrupted, and fluctuating currencies in a single market could distort competition and lead to protectionism. Moreover, currencies which are vastly out of line with the requirements – or 'fundamentals' – of an economy lead to an inefficient use of resources. The overvaluation of the pound in the early 1980s led to the devastation of manufacturing capacity and speeded up Britain's deindustrialisation. Similarly, undervaluation leads to an overemphasis on industrial production.

Ultimately any exchange rate system should boost prosperity, by promoting higher growth, lower unemployment and a slower rate of price increases. These conditions manifestly were not fulfilled in the ERM, which had elevated the goals of monetary and political union above that of Europe's economic welfare – a policy which proved to be economically devastating, and ultimately self-defeating.

First and foremost, the ERM lacked a credible adjustment mechanism to bring countries, which differed markedly in economic performance, into line and correct fundamental imbalances in current accounts. Britain's current account deficit stood at £12 billion in 1992 – an unprecedentedly high figure for a country which was in the midst of its longest recession since the 1930s. Yet the Maastricht convergence criteria only lay down targets for inflation, interest rates and budget deficits. In fact, it can be argued that Britain needed a – possibly inflationary – fiscal boost at that time to restore growth and reduce unemployment.

The emphasis on financial criteria was reinforced by inconsistent national economic policy objectives and the lack of a central European force capable of enforcing the commitment of individual member countries to strategies compatible with the ERM's successful operation. Germany was allowed to impose a restrictive monetary policy on the rest of Europe, without any obligation to take the interests of its fellow ERM members into account, many of whom were suffering from declining output.

Before outlining a fixed-but-flexible system, however, it is necessary to ask whether the concept of such a system is coherent. Professor Alan Walters, previously economic adviser to Mrs Thatcher, argued stridently before Britain's entry to the Exchange Rate Mechanism that any adjustable peg system which was not buttressed by quantitative exchange controls was 'half-baked' and would lead to perverse results. His argument hinged on the fact that if exchange rates were assumed immutable by all operators, mobile capital ensured roughly similar nominal interest rates throughout the system – whatever a particular country's rate of inflation – so that countries with high inflation rates have expansionary policies, while those with low inflation have restrictive policies:

> the EMS forces countries to have the same nominal interest rate. If, however, Italy is inflating at a rate of 7 per cent and Germany at a rate of 2 per cent . . . then there is a problem of perversity. With the same interest rate at, say, 5 per cent, the real rate of interest for Italy is minus 2 per cent and for Germany plus three per cent. Thus Italy will have an expansionary policy, while Germany will pursue one of restraint. But this will exacerbate inflation in Italy and yet restrain further the already low inflation in Germany. (Walters, 1990.)

While favouring a freely floating exchange rate, Professor Walters agreed that if the goal of policy was to have currency stability, there were only two coherent possibilities: to have completely fixed exchange rates and a single currency, or to buttress fixed parties with exchange controls.

This chapter suggests third option, within which a coherent framework for exchange rate realignment could be formed. It argues that the market mechanism could be used to discourage short-term capital flows, by taxing transactions in the foreign exchange market. At the same time, this would avoid some of the worst effects of absolute controls on capital – which in any case would be all but impossible to impose today. It is an attempt to sketch out what a Keynesian alternative to 'Euromonetarism' might look like and to point out that a strategy which combines stability and flexibility could be used to promote traditional socialist goals. It argues that any viable exchange rate system would have to provide for:

(1) minimal agreement between members over realistic paths for inflation, unemployment and growth for the community as a whole;
(2) a supranational body charged with the periodic assessment of members' economic performance and their current place in the business cycle, and with the power to use sanctions to enforce behaviour in line with the goals of the system and to recommend realignments of currencies when required; and
(3) anti-speculative measures to smooth instabilities and allow exchange rate policies to be determined by criteria other than the movement of short-term capital flows.

Fundamentally, the system must be based on a recognition that membership entails symmetric and reciprocal rights and responsibilities between surplus and deficit countries. A group of countries can maintain relatively stable parities against each other only if they are reasonably compatible in terms of their economies, in the instruments available to governments to steer economic policies and in their central institutional frameworks. In what follows, the last two of these conditions are assumed to hold.

Targets for Inflation, Unemployment and Growth

The first charge to be laid against the Exchange Rate Mechanism is that it is deflationary – aiming to promote the lowest possible level of inflation throughout its member countries by curbing demand. Not only would zero inflation throughout Europe be counter-productive, however, destroying jobs and slowing growth, but in the long run, countries have to recognise that increases in money wages in excess of productivity must normally increase prices. That is, a degree of inflation is more or less inevitable. It would be totally unrealistic to expect individual inflation rates to converge around zero, as is fairly obvious when we consider the historical experience of the Exchange Rate Mechanism. On average, there will be an upward trend in the Europe-wide price level, with individual countries varying around that trend. Thus members of any exchange rate system need to come to an agreement as to what is a desirable and realistic growth path for the community's inflation rate. Countries with lower rates would then be classified as 'low' inflation countries, and those with rates significantly above the trend as 'high' inflation countries.

The next point which needs to be drawn out is the importance of the speed of adjustment. A short, sharp shock, as seen in Britain in the early, Thatcherite, 1980s tends to lead to a situation in which almost all of the burden of adjustment falls on employment. A decade later, adjustment to the demands of the ERM was also rapid – although it was partially a response to the errors of the Lawson boom – leading to another sharp rise in unemployment. Part of the ERM's problem was that the Maastricht timetable agreed between members imposed tough financial convergence criteria with a limited amount of time in which to comply. In Britain, inflation was brought down from 10% to 1.7%, at the expense of a huge burst of unemployment – leading to massive loss of capacity and skills and thereby endangering any subsequent recovery. If the country had been given generous finance and time to adjust, then we could have expected a milder recession and a smaller rise in the unemployment total.

If the group as a whole is willing to sacrifice employment for price stability, then European inflation will tend to be lower. This means that it is necessary to take a view on the economic and political acceptability of the measures required to meet agreed targets – in each country – or the system will remain fragile. The British recession was ultimately too deep and unemployment too high for the increases in interest rates required to defend the pound in 1992 to be credible. In France, the authorities were able to sacrifice output for lower inflation over a prolonged period, although the 1993 general election débâcle for the Socialists means that even here, the authorities' credibility in the foreign exchange markets is open to question.

Employment should be recognised as an explicit policy goal. In terms of exchange rate management, the level of capacity utilisation acts as a constraint on the effectiveness of devaluation and changes the circumstances in which realignment is an appropriate remedy. Sterling's recent drop on the foreign exchanges could be expected to bring rich rewards in terms of extra demand for labour, without reigniting inflationary pressures.

Criteria for Adjustment

In the light of these considerations, it is necessary to provide for an adequate and realistic adjustment mechanism, which expressly defines the reciprocal rights and responsibilities of surplus and deficit countries. A grid set out along lines suggested by US Nobel Laureate Professor James Tobin, in a paper entitled 'Adjustment Responsibilities of Surplus and Deficit Countries', could provide an appropriate framework (see Table 14.1). Each country fits into an appropriately defined category, according to inflation, employment and current account status. Countries are defined as 'high', 'moderate' or 'low' inflation economies at any given time, and similarly for unemployment status. We thus have nine categories of deficit countries and nine categories of surplus countries. In the summer of 1992, Britain would have been classified as a 'high unemployment, low inflation, deficit country'.

Economies with high unemployment and low inflation would be encouraged to take expansionary action with little time constraint, while at the other extreme countries suffering high inflation, but little unemployment would be under severe orders to deflate rapidly. Only those suffering the twin problems of high inflation and intolerable levels of unemployment would be considered as potential candidates for devaluation. Economies with low unemployment and high inflation would be permitted to undertake restrictive policies without any demanding time constraint, while at the other extreme, those with high unemployment and low inflation would be required to take immediate expansionary action. Only those countries with low inflation and low unemployment would be considered candidates for revaluation, if the situation was deemed likely to persist.

The Supranational Body

All this requires coordination. It also requires a loss of autonomy for national economic policy. The point is, however, that if this is not explicitly recognised, then the prospects of any viable exchange rate system emerging are significantly reduced. But the successful operation of the system necessitates a body which is capable of determining each country's position in the grid at regular intervals and enforcing the appropriate policy response. One possibility is that the coordinating body could, on a

Table 14.1. Tobin's inflation/unemployment grid.

Rate of increase of money costs and/or prices	Deficit Countries			Surplus Countries		
	Rate of unemployment			Rate of unemployment		
	Low	Moderate	High	Low	Moderate	High
High	I Must take restrictive monetary-fiscal measures regardless of reserve position. Must use own reserves. Low claim to finance.	II Must take restrictive measures as a condition of finance.	III Normal claim to finance. Should devalue if situation persists?	I May take restrictive monetary-fiscal measures. No special obligation to lend surpluses.	II May take restrictive measures without special obligation to lend surpluses.	III Normal obligation to give finance, the more so if restrictive measures are taken.
Moderate	IV Must take restrictive measures as condition of finance.	V Should take fiscal-monetary measures to maintain situation. Normal claim to finance.	VI May take expansionary measures. Normal claim to finance.	IV Should take fiscal-monetary measures to maintain situation. Normal obligation to give finance.	V Should take fiscal-monetary measures to maintain situation. Normal obligation to give finance.	VI Must take expansionary measures, or else give abnormally large finance.
Low	VII Should take fiscal-monetary measures to maintain situation. Normal claim to finance.	VIII High claim to finance.	IX May take expansionary measures. Entitled to generous finance while promoting structural adjustments.	VII High obligation to give finance. Should revalue if situation persists?	VIII Must take expansionary measures, or else give abnormally large finance.	IX Must take expansionary measures regardless of reserve position and lend surpluses.

Source: Tobin (1966).

month-to-month basis, be operationally independent from, but demoncratically accountable to, a body such as Ecofin – the European Finance Ministers. This does not rule out the possibility that any given country's position may be affected by national cultural factors, such as the willingness to tolerate high inflation or high unemployment. Germany, for instance, might insist that if its inflation position is the community average, that this be classified in its own case as 'high' inflation. Thus there would still be room for debate.

The lack of this authority was one of the prime reasons for the ERM débâcle in September 1992. For a start, sterling had joined the mechanism at an unsustainable parity against the mark. Then, there was no body capable of arranging an orderly realignment of the mark against other European currencies when this was needed, implying that member countries had to take unwarranted interest rate medicine to maintain the value of their parities at a time when their domestic economic conditions suggested they should be taking expansionary action.

More difficult is the question of the form and limits of sanctions which the central body could use. The next part of this chapter looks at one ambitious proposal to invest power in a central authority, and is developed from the concepts embodied in the initial formulation of the International Monetary Fund, set up to administer the Bretton Woods system of exchange rates.

A Reformed, Enhanced European Monetary Institute

At the moment, the Maastricht Treaty provides in Stage Two for the setting up of the European Monetary Institute as a stepping stone towards a European Central Bank, with responsibility for setting European monetary policy under EMU. Article 109f of the Treaty already charges the EMI with, among other things, monitoring the functioning of the EMS and overseeing the development of the ECU. Moreover the EMI, acting by a majority of two-thirds of the members of its council, may 'make recommendations to the monetary authorities of the member states concerning the conduct of their monetary policy'. This concept is a useful one, but the idea needs fleshing out. Under the following proposals, it could still be used as a bridge to fuller economic integration of European states, but the lines along which such an eventuality would occur would be markedly different. It is interesting to note, however, that, given unanimity, this could be decided by the EC Council under article 109f(7) of the Treaty: 'The Council may, acting unanimously on a proposal from the Commission and after consulting the European Parliament and the EMI, confer upon the EMI other tasks for the preparation of the third stage'. Instead of laying down fixed timetables for convergence, the new institution could act as an enabler, allowing a parallel currency to develop in the market-place.

Various Alternative Parallel Currencies – Strengths and Weaknesses

The parallel currency concept should be no stranger to the UK authorities, who flirted with the idea of a 'hard ECU' in the run-up to signing the Maastricht Treaty. Under the UK proposals, the new currency would be a member of the narrow band of the ERM and its exchange rate would be free to fluctuate within those constraints against each other member currency, in line with market demands – but it would never devalue, or more accurately, it would never allow any member currency to revalue against it.

Although the scheme has some attractions – it could for instance allow the EMI to have some experience of managing a real currency, setting interest rates, etc. – it would, I think, be strongly deflationary. Imagine if the hard ECU had been in place in 1988. Within a year, German reunification would have made the mark a prime candidate for revaluation against all other currencies. But the rules of the system would not have permitted a revaluation of the mark against the hard ECU, so the EMI would have been forced to raise ECU interest rates to make the ECU relatively more attractive than the mark – thus setting a floor for European interest rates.

Even if the member countries were to find the policy unbearably deflationary, and all were to devalue against the ECU, it is unlikely that they would be able to lower their interest rates. Under the rules of the system, their next change of parity could only be downwards, so they could in fact be forced to have an interest rate premium over the hard ECU interest rate. Thus the hard ECU system would be more deflationary than the present one, where at least the possibility of a future revaluation against the mark means that the interest rate premium does not have to be so large.

An alternative would be a soft ECU, and the EMI would permit other countries to revalue against it, when the situation suggested that was the right course. This would overcome some of the worst defects of the hard ECU system, while allowing the EMI to have experience of managing a real currency, and could eventually substitute for the currencies of member countries. Unlike the case of the hard ECU, it would not necessarily be deflationary. Nor, however, would it have the attraction associated with the hard ECU that people would choose to hold it rather than a harder member currency.

The current ECU is made up from a basket of existing European currencies, with weights of member countries roughly determined according to their economic strength, reset every five years. This seems to be the most appropriate vehicle for the EMI as a force for economic integration. The basket ECU would become stronger as the weights of one of the members grew relative to the average.

The EMI would first of all be charged with encouraging the acceptability of ECUs in the market-place. It would be helpful – but not essential – if

ECUs became legal tender in each country, although the main force behind their use would be their acceptability as a means of settling debts. Each nation would have to show a commitment to the currency and this could be done, perhaps, by using tax incentives to promote ECU trading – such as exempting movements into the ECU from a transactions tax.

As the monetary authority responsible for the ECU, the EMI would have responsibility for setting ECU interest rates – which would be roughly some form of weighted average of the interest rates in the countries of its constituents. Then the ECU would run in parallel with European currencies and act as a common rather than single European currency. At first, the EMI would need to be given a one-off allocation of ECUs – perhaps some proportion of member countries' foreign exchange reserves – but thereafter the stock of ECUs would be increased in line with intra-European trade or EC growth. In these circumstances, ECUs would become readily recognisable as another form of international money and could be used as an intervention currency on the foreign exchanges.

The power of the EMI would be found in its ability to lend reserves to national authorities to support their currencies and to be available to finance current account deficits. It is also possible that it could have a wing empowered to finance long-term structural adjustment programmes to bring down unemployment or break a country's inflationary psychology. Thus each country's obligations flowing from its position in the grid would be backed up by financial sanctions, or alternatively, an economy's classification might confer rights of EMI finance. The system is thus much more ambitious than a mere pooling of European reserves being advocated at the moment in some quarters to rectify the 'fault lines' in the ERM.

In its proposals for a hard ECU, the UK authorities came up with an idea which could act as an effective sanction on member countries who were following loose monetary policies. It was called the repurchase requirement:

> the main liabilities of the EMF would be hard ECU deposits. On the other side of the balance sheet, its assets would be the national currencies surrendered by purchasers of the hard ECU deposits. If the EMF were prepared to go on holding these currencies without limit, a potentially dangerous loophole in monetary discipline would be created. Normally, a monetary authority which pursues a loose monetary policy must expect downward pressure on its exchange rates in consequence, as financial markets react to the excessive supply of that currency. But if the EMF were to act as an unlimited buyer, that downward pressure would be attenuated if not eliminated. The lax monetary authority could go on with its loose policy knowing that the EMF would be a safety net.
>
> . . . there would be pre-set limits on the amounts of national currencies the EMF could hold – either absolute amounts or maximum proportions of any one currency held on its balance sheet. Once these limits were reached, the EMF would have the discretion to ask the monetary authority concerned to repurchase from its national currency in return for hard ECU or some other currency. (HM Treasury, 1990: 5.)

If this were applied stringently, the debtor country would use up all of its foreign exchange reserves, and ultimately be forced into a devaluation. This could act as an extremely powerful deterrent. In parallel, surplus countries could be forced to lend their reserves to the central pool to varying degrees, depending on their circumstances.

Fiscal versus Monetary Policy

Should the new European institution specify structural adjustment policies as a prerequisite of aid, in the manner of the IMF approach to the developing world? Or should nations be left to their own devices? I believe that policy prescription is an unnecessary infringement of national autonomy and few, if any, nation states would be prepared to participate in such a system. However, the European parities are dependent on the level of interest rates, and within reason these need to be equalised between economies, except if countries are perceived in the financial markets to be at differing stages of the business cycle, for example. This would suggest that the main instrument is fiscal policy. But to rule out the use of interest rates would be premature. Indeed, it is crucial to recognise that capital flows are as important in determining the appropriate level of interest rates – and policy stance – as imbalances on the current account. For this reason, I suggest that it is necessary to smooth disruptions to the economic system by imposing curbs on speculation.

Transaction Taxes

A 0.5% tax on foreign exchange transactions, levied by national governments, would act as a substantial deterrent to speculation. There would, for example, need to be an annual interest rate differential of 1% between countries for it to be worth while buying a currency and switching back at the end of the year. Alternatively, there would need to be a 4 point interest differential on three-month bills for it to be profitable to indulge in such trading. The present proposals envisage instituting the transaction tax in a European context, although it would be more effective if it were adopted on an international basis. It could indeed be one way of tying the dollar and the yen to the EMS and limiting world-wide currency fluctuations. (Transaction taxes would also limit fluctuations against floating currencies.) One obvious difficulty with the implementation of a transaction tax is that currency transactions would be driven offshore. But there are ways of overcoming circumvention of the rule, such as exempting all currency transactions not undertaken through regulated exchanges from legal status – thus unpaid debts would not be backed by the force of law. And as Professor Rudiger Dornbusch comments:

In this context it is worth noting that Japan and Switzerland do have a financial transaction tax. An appropriate response to the offshore problem is to develop such a tax in cooperation with other countries. (Dornbursch, 1990.)

Similarly, Germany's system of minimum reserve requirements can make banks in Germany more expensive to use than those abroad, yet Frankfurt remains an important trading centre.

A tax on foreign exchange transactions would provide a valuable source of revenue for the government. The Bank of England's latest foreign exchange survey showed that there are daily deals worth $300 billion on the London forex market, so, in the unlikely event that behaviour remained unchanged, a 0.5% tax would yield around $1.5 billion of revenue every day.

It is clear that the larger the size of the tax, the greater the deterrent to speculation, but equally the greater the costs imposed on international trade. An appropriate tax would leave virtually all trade profitable, however, while making the currency market less liquid. One result of a reduction in liquidity would be that it becomes more risky for commercial firms to engage in large-scale trade, unsure about their ability to off-load substantial sums of a particular currency in the market. But liquidity is merely one aspect of a market for foreign exchange, and is only desirable if all other parts of the economy are working efficiently. This is patently not the case.

In the second-best world in which we live, there are important trade-offs between on the one hand, liquidity, speed of response to new information and cost, and on the other, more stable foreign exchange markets, a more stable trading environment and a greater degree of national policy autonomy. One possibility is that in the initial stages, trade settled in ECUs could be made exempt – or partially exempt – from the tax. This would give an extremely powerful spur to the adoption of the ECU and would foster movement towards a single currency.

But any new tax on foreign exchange would require institutional reform to take account – and address – the worst aspects of a decline in liquidity. For example, the market at the moment is largely quote-driven, because liquidity is so great. That is, if a trader wishes to sell a currency he just has to offer it at the going rate and he will be certain to find a taker. Once liquidity is drained out of the system, however, it is almost impossible to run a quote-driven system. Indeed, deals have to be matched – a seller has to find a potential buyer before negotiating a price. If the institutional framework is not designed to incorporate fluctuation limits, this could lead to large swings in prices, rather than a reduction in volatility.

The other side to this argument is that it becomes much easier for a central bank to manage exchange rates by intervening in the foreign exchange market, if less speculative business is being transacted. So a workable transaction tax in Britain would seem necessarily to involve a greater role for national central banks and the EMI.

The reduction in liquidity would leave national Central Banks in a pivotal position. One consequence would be that they would be forced to act as a lender/buyer of last resort. That is, if there were prima facia evidence that a deal would be thwarted because of the foreign exchange difficulties, the Bank of England would have to accept the risk – maybe at a premium price. This would mean that the central bank assumed the role of 'market maker' in certain circumstances, determining the prices at which currency deals were undertaken.

The control of derivatives – futures, swaps and options which are nominally based on the underlying cash transaction – is also crucial to any attempt to regulate either the foreign exchange market or the stock market. In 1987, portfolio insurance – or the attempt by investors to use financial derivatives to protect and enhance the value of their assets – was blamed in large part for the collapse on Wall Street. In 1992, operations in financial instruments disrupted trading and added to the chaos. The 1987 stock market crash in the United States vividly exposed the fallacy that the cash market and the buying and selling of derivatives were mutually independent. It also showed that apparently high levels of liquidity are insufficient when all the buyers or sellers appear on the same side of the market. Both of these conclusions are relevant to the regulation of currency trading. Derivatives trading is a relatively new industry built on the cornerstones of rapid innovation in the foreign exchange market and the revolution in computer technology, which has meant that traders are able to deal 'over-the-counter' with each other, avoiding organised exchanges. By 1991 the value of turnover in futures contracts exceeded cash transactions by 440% in France and by 250% in Germany. The result has been the creation of a whole new industry – risk management – as business attempts to hedge its bets on future stock market and currency fluctuations, as well as to assess the underlying risk involved in trading in these new instruments.

But trading in derivatives can be destabilising for the overall market. This occurs if, for example, competition tempts exchanges to raise or remove maximum daily fluctuation limits or reduce prudential requirements – so-called 'margin'. Margin requirements for individual traders and capital adequacy ratios for banks can be seen as two sides of the same coin. Both are safeguards against risk and take the form of an obligation to deposit collateral against the value of deals to be undertaken. The difference is that margins concern individual transactions, while capital adequacy requirements are designed to protect against institutional risk of default.

One way in which a future crisis could be made less likely is by raising margin requirements on currency derivatives. This is because margin acts as collateral and determines the effective economic leverage any individual trader can control – and hence the volume of speculative activity. Margin in the forward market is the equivalent to a transactions tax in the cash market, because the amount of money any trader has to put up-front on a forward contract is one cost of the deal. In turn, the role of capital adequacy for banks has recently been underlined by the Bank for International Settlements, which is now proposing to introduce additional capital requirements on banks for currency-related risks. An increase in required ratios could serve to eliminate part of the speculation handled in the banking system.

These measures would need to be backed up by circuit breakers, which are a recognition of the fact that in a moment of crisis, no trading system is able to cope with the volume of selling and no amount of liquidity can forestall the gridlock. They provide a much-needed breathing space for potential buyers to assess the market and rework their portfolios. Circuit breakers were imposed on stock market trading in the New York Stock Exchange in 1988, although they have been called into play very infrequently. Price fluctuation limits are also used on the Paris Bourse. There is no reason why such a strategy of interrupting trading in an orderly fashion could not be applied to the currency markets. If price limits were incorporated unilaterally in the UK, their success would depend on how much trading was diverted from London at times of crisis, but it would seem unlikely that a system designed to alleviate panic and restore order would be widely circumvented.

Summary and conclusion

The experience of floating exchange rates in the 1970s suggests that Europe should aim for some form of exchange rate stability, but the Exchange Rate Mechanism was both theoretically flawed and practically unworkable. It has become increasingly clear that any viable fixed-but-flexible exchange rate system requires curbs on currency speculation. A tax on foreign exchange transactions could provide the necessary 'sand in the wheels' of the foreign exchange market, forcing market participants to take a longer-term view of the valuation of currencies, and allowing a degree of policy autonomy between participating nations.

A transactions tax could not be a substitute for policy coordination, however, and any strengthening of the government's hands against the market runs the risk of institutionalising unsustainable economic policies. It would, therefore, become paramount to develop mechanisms to promote orderly realignments and policy adjustments within a reformed exchange rate system. The European Monetary Institute envisaged in Stage Two of the Maastricht Treaty could oversee national economic policies and advise on realignments. It would be charged with ensuring that the burden of adjustment fell equally on weak and strong members of the system and would focus on relative inflation and unemployment performances.

The system would be inoperable if the EMI could not wield substantial powers to enforce compliance with its recommendations. It could oversee the development of the fledgling European currency – the European Currency Unit – and use it to intervene in support of member currencies in the foreign exchange market. It could also provide financing for current account deficits and lay down appropriate timetables for real economic convergence among member countries.

15

Strategies for Growth and Employment in the European Community[1]

Francis Cripps and Terry Ward

The European Community in the 1990s faces severe problems of low growth, inadequate employment creation and high and rising unemployment, without the policy means of addressing these problems effectively. During the present recession, which in 1992 spread right across Europe, the number of people out of work has risen virtually everywhere, in many places from levels which were already unacceptably high. Recovery is widely expected to be slow in coming and modest in scale. On the European Commission's own prognosis (in its Communication to the Council before the 1992 Edinburgh Summit), even under favourable assumptions about the Community's capacity to create jobs, there is a high risk that the rate of unemployment will be at least 10–11% in 1996 – back to the peak level of the 1980s. With slow growth and rising unemployment, social conditions are likely to worsen and standards of social welfare and justice, which have already come under pressure over the past two decades in many parts of Europe, will tend to decline.

Faced with this predicament, government leaders at the Edinburgh Summit made only a token gesture towards reviving the European economy. They failed to deliver the short-term measures urgently needed to stimulate demand and pull the Community out of recession. Equally importantly, they failed to make any progress towards establishing a framework for policy coordination at the Community level which is essential for sustaining growth and creating jobs in the longer-term.

Without such coordination it will be difficult, if not impossible, for the Community to play its proper role in supporting growth in the global economy and to cooperate effectively with the US and Japan in managing economic and financial developments at the world level. It will also be less able to assist developing countries, especially in Central and Eastern Europe, North Africa and the Middle East, where economic growth is critical for long-term political stability and security in the region as a whole.

Indeed, instead of agreeing on closer cooperation, national governments and institutions have reiterated the importance of national sovereignty over economic policy and have made it clear that immediate national interests will continue to have precedence over Community-wide considerations.

Without a change in the attitude of a number of key decision-makers, it will be impossible to secure the agreement on the fundamental changes in the conduct of both monetary and fiscal policy required to achieve sustained recovery in the next few years, during Maastricht Stage 2. Indeed pressure for budgetary consolidation on countries where public deficits and levels of debt exceed the Maastricht reference values threatens to slow recovery even further and make it more difficult to reduce unemployment.

The challenge is to establish a coherent framework for economic policy coordination at the Community level, with adequate democratic control over the decision-makers. In the short-term, the aim should be:

(1) To implement changes in the conduct of monetary and fiscal policies so that they support rather than impede growth;
(2) To strengthen structural policies in order to boost development and job creation in those regions which are most in need, to expand investment in backward regions and in areas of industrial decline and to enhance the role of cities and local authorities as critical agents of development.

The political background

In the 1980s, the Community was strengthened by new measures which provided an impetus and dynamism to the economy and which promised increased prosperity and more jobs in all regions. The most important measure was the resolution to achieve full integration of the internal market by 1 January 1993, to create the largest single market in terms of purchasing power in the world.

In parallel, there were major increases in Structural Funds to assist disadvantaged regions and increased emphasis on infrastructure links (Trans-European Networks), which together were designed to secure more balanced economic development across the Community, as well as the introduction of programmes aimed at coordinating technology development.

Widespread enthusiasm for the Single Market encouraged governments of member states to negotiate the Maastricht Treaty, which defines plans for a staged transition to full monetary union and reinforces the Community's commitment to economic and social cohesion.

The Maastricht Treaty, however, has proved far more contentious than the Single Market. Despite the fact that, in terms of objectives, it strengthens the Community's commitment to balanced economic development, with increased regard for the environment and social cohesion, it has neither been presented nor generally perceived as providing the same kind of impetus to growth nor the means of overcoming tangible problems – of lack of jobs and of social deprivation – which are of most concern to people in the Community.

The Treaty was heavily criticised by the European Parliament because it failed almost completely to address the problem of the lack of democratic accountability under existing institutional arrangements, let alone deliver any solution.

At present, the Community is effectively controlled by the Council of Ministers, a committee of national government leaders, in which policies are bargained in terms of competing domestic interests. In order to advance new initiatives the Commission is obliged to respond to the Council rather than to the European Parliament. At the same time, representation in the Council is confined to national groupings which participate in the national government, effectively excluding regions and interest groups which have different views and objectives.

By proposing increased powers for Community bodies without corresponding proposals to make these bodies more accountable, the Maastricht Treaty seems to distance policy-makers even further from the people and makes it even more difficult for the electoral process to have an influence on the decisions which are taken.

Public scepticism about the Maastricht proposals was reinforced by the disruption of the ERM in September 1992. The failure of the central banks to resist financial market pressure and maintain exchange rates within agreed bands, together with the failure so far to come up with any concrete proposals for making any repetition of the experience less likely in the future, has made monetary union seem a much more difficult and longer-term process.

Moreover at the Edinburgh Summit, governments of member states refused to accept increases in the scale of the Community budget which would have been necessary to give substance to the commitment to closer economic and social cohesion, which is a key aspect of the Treaty. The expansion in the Community budget agreed in Edinburgh will mean that, in relation to GDP, it will be only marginally larger at the end of the decade than now, making it difficult to expand the scope of Community actions by very much. Although assistance to the poorer regions will increase markedly over this period through the expansion of the Structural Funds and the introduction of the new Cohesion Fund, financial transfers to these regions will still represent less than ½% of Community GDP in 1999 – enough to have a perceptible effect but nowhere near sufficient to fund the expenditure required to bring levels of economic and social infrastructure and support services and standards of education and training up to those in the rest of the Community.

At Edinburgh also, governments failed to respond to the issues of recession and high and rising unemployment which are the principal concerns of most people in the Community. Despite the Commission's warning about the sharp deterioration in the short-term outlook and the need to take 'decisive measures to address the situation', they contented themselves with announcing a small-scale package of investment measures spread over a number of years which will have an imperceptible effect on economic activity. Nor did they take any significant action 'aimed at reinforcing growth fundamentals and at encouraging job creation' which the Commission had called for in response to the likelihood that unemployment would remain unacceptably high over the medium term.

The Community seems to have reached an impasse over policy precisely at a time when action is urgently needed. Most national governments are in the position of trying to restore their credibility with their electorates either because they face an imminent election or because they have suffered major recent setbacks. No major government in Europe at present possesses the popular support to take the initiative in advocating a Community perspective for policy or a strengthening of central institutions. On the contrary, each is being forced by electoral considerations to give overriding priority to the defence of national interests.

Even if Maastricht Stage 2 arrangements are formally introduced as planned, on 1 January 1994, whatever their potential benefit, it seems unlikely at present that a common monetary policy will emerge or that the new arrangements will provide the basis for any new dynamic of growth and job creation. Prime minister John Major has stated that sterling will not rejoin the EMS in 1993, leaving it unclear how and when UK monetary policy could be reintegrated. More importantly, the Bundesbank has made it plain that under Stage 2 arrangements German monetary policy would continue exclusively to reflect national considerations.

At the same time, the proposals in the Treaty, if interpreted narrowly, concerning the need to pursue policies in Stage 2 which are aimed at reducing deficits and debt levels in those member states where they exceed narrowly specified limits make low growth and inadequate job creation more likely.

Given the continuing fragmentation of monetary and fiscal policy and the differing problems facing individual member states, the Council has not been able to face up to the recession and the large-scale destruction of jobs now in process. Hopes for economic recovery rest largely, as too often in the past, on an upturn in the United States, supported by the expansionary policies now being taken in Japan, and on an eventual improvement in European consumer and business confidence.

By failing to establish a joint framework for the conduct of monetary and fiscal policy, the Council has, moreover, made it more difficult for the Community to cooperate with the United States and Japan in regulating international financial markets, smoothing exchange rate fluctuations and supporting global economic growth. It is less able to respond to the opportunity for achieving more effective global economic management which the advent in the United States of a new – and potentially more sympathetic – President could provide.

The Community as a slow-growth area

Economic growth in the Community has been inadequate over the past 20 years, causing persistent problems of high unemployment, eroding government budgets and obstructing the development of backward regions. In 1974–75 and again in 1980–81, the interruption of economic growth in Europe could be blamed on oil crises. It is now, however, well over ten years since the last oil crisis and it is by now clear that the loss of dynamism in the European economy has wider causes.

In the 1950s and 1960s, the Community was one of the most dynamic areas of the world economy, with fast-growing trade and industry. Huge numbers of low-income farmers and agricultural workers as well as refugees from the East and immigrants from the South were absorbed into industrial and service jobs, while at the same time substantial shifts of employment from old, declining industries to new expanding ones took place relatively painlessly. Infrastructure and living conditions in backward regions improved dramatically.

Since 1973, the Community has been one of the least dynamic areas of the world economy. Economic growth has averaged only just over 2% over this period. No member state has consistently succeeded in achieving a growth rate much above this, highlighting the high degree of interdependence between the national economies. During this period, unemployment has risen in most countries to levels not experienced since the inter-war years as the rate of job creation has failed to keep pace with an expanding labour force.

Although some backward regions have continued to converge, the majority have remained blocked. Limited advances during phases of economic recovery have been wiped out as backward regions lost ground during phases of recession. At the same time, many formerly prosperous regions have suffered deindustrialisation as traditional industries have contracted without being replaced by new growth sectors. Big increases in unemployment have been the result.

The continuing decline in agricultural employment in backward regions has barely been compensated for by growth of service employment. Industrial sectors generally have ceased to provide significant numbers of new jobs as growth of output has been no higher – and in many cases much lower – than growth of productivity, stimulated by technological advance and increased competition in the Community and world markets.

Despite the low rate of economic growth, social cohesion has advanced steadily. Younger generations in all member states aspire to similar life-styles. Population growth has stabilised, family sizes have fallen every-where and there has been a sustained increase in women's participation in the labour force throughout the Community.

Convergence of social patterns during past decades has brought considerable improvements in backward areas, at a considerable cost to public budgets. Public provision of services and infrastructure has become increasingly unpopular in many parts of the Community, not only because of its high cost but also because it has continued to embody forms of paternalism – and sometimes corruption – which are not acceptable to modern generations. Nevertheless, the backlash against welfare programmes and programmes to assist less privileged areas has a high cost in regional and social terms.

As electorates everywhere demand reductions in tax burdens and direct value for money in public expenditure it is becoming increasingly difficult for governments to fund investment projects and/or transfers between countries and regions, and even to redistribute income on a substantial scale between individuals.

In sum, the low rate of economic growth since the 1970s has created a vicious circle in which backward and deindustrialising regions experience high unemployment and have insufficient resources or opportunities to regenerate their economies.

More prosperous regions are suspicious of transfers in favour of low-income areas and reluctant to accept immigration. Yet stagnation of peripheral regions within and outside the Community deprives the wider European economy of a growth dynamic. This has greatly increased the problems faced by countries in Central and Eastern Europe, struggling with ambitious programmes of political and economic reform and attempting massive restructuring of their economies, as well as by those in North Africa and the Middle East dependent on trade with the Community to support development. The stagnation of these surrounding regions in turn depresses markets for exports from the Community's more prosperous areas.

The regional dimension of the unemployment problem

Low economic growth is reflected in enormous disparities across regions in unemployment and in the availability of resources to fund development. These disparities have long-run and deep-seated historical causes, cutting across businesses and social groups. In all cases, the key problem is inadequate rates of economic development and job creation, rather than any failings on the part of the individuals who are unemployed. The disparities can only be effectively tackled by recognising the political and social nature of the underlying problems – inefficient public administration, inadequate levels of law and order, deficiencies in education and training and in the provision of social facilities, for example – as well as the economic factors involved.

Some of the most developed and prosperous regions – Southern Germany and Northern Italy in particular – have succeeded in avoiding high unemployment completely because of their productive efficiency and capacity for generating income through both inter-regional and international trade. Most of the poorer, less developed regions, predominantly in the South of the Community as well as older industrial areas in the North have, however, suffered substantial increases in unemployment since the mid-1970s.

In these regions, rates of unemployment are in many cases around 15–20% and in some local areas even higher. A high proportion of these unemployed, moreover, have been out of work for a prolonged period – at least a year and often much longer. In many areas of Southern Italy, Ireland and Spain, as well as in deindustrialising regions of Belgium, 60–70% or more of those recorded as unemployed have been without a job for a year or more.

Substantial numbers of those out of work are young people under 25. Rates of unemployment for this age group now average over 32% in Objective 1 regions as a whole, with even higher rates in the worst affected areas. In these parts of the Community, the difficulties facing young people looking for a job, often for the first time, are acute and many have to resign themselves to a long spell of unemployment before finding work. In all Southern member states, people under 25 make up well over a third of the long-term unemployed, and in Greece and Italy well over 40%.

In the more industrialised Northern parts of the Community, long-term unemployment is more a problem of older age groups, particularly those losing their job in middle age who find it difficult to find alternative work because employers prefer to take on younger recruits, and because not enough new jobs are being created to replace those lost.

In most of the high unemployment regions, especially in the South, the true scale of the problem is disguised by people – especially women – being deterred by the acute shortage of work from entering the labour market at all. Recorded rates of inactivity in these regions tend to be much higher than elsewhere, concealing large numbers of people who are effectively unemployed even if they are not counted in the official figures. In addition, many of those who are employed work in low-paid and insecure jobs under barely tolerable conditions.

On reasonable assumptions (comparing inactivity rates with those in the most economically and socially developed areas), concealed unemployment can be put at around double the numbers actually recorded as unemployed over large areas of the Community. In the less developed regions as a whole, concealed unemployment is probably over 15% of people of working age, implying that over 25% of people of working age are probably either openly unemployed or forced to be inactive because of job shortages, and in parts of Southern Italy and Spain, over a third.

This gives an indication of the true scale of the problem which needs to be confronted. The problem, moreover, is made worse by the fact that, despite substantial falls recently in the birth rate in Southern European countries, the population of working age in the less developed parts of the Community is set to go on increasing significantly over the next ten years – and indeed longer – whereas in many of the more prosperous regions it is likely to grow very slowly or to decline. The rate of job creation which is required in coming years to have any substantial impact on levels of unemployment – concealed as well as open – in less developed regions is, therefore, considerable.

Growth and regional employment

Higher sustained growth in the Community is a necessary condition for narrowing regional disparities in job creation and unemployment. On past evidence, both less developed and deindustrialising regions are especially affected by cyclical fluctuations in the growth of the Community economy. Periods of high growth tend to be periods of convergence in income per head and employment – periods of low growth or recession are periods of divergence. This is a reflection partly of the structure of activity in these regions, partly of their peripheral location and their reliance on financial inflows from the rest of the Community.

Experience in the second half of the 1980s, when the Community achieved a higher rate of employment growth than at any time since the 1950s, is instructive in illustrating both what future recovery might achieve and the limitations of growth *per se* in securing employment objectives. (At the country level, there was some tendency over this period for employment to rise by more in those countries where GDP growth was highest, and no country with low growth managed to increase employment significantly – with the partial exception of the Netherlands where there was a major rise in part-time working. See Figure 15.1.)

In the first half of the 1980s, output in the Community grew only slowly, and unemployment rose in most places, especially in the areas of industrial decline – Objective 2 regions – where job losses in industry were substantial and unemployment went up significantly. In the second half of the

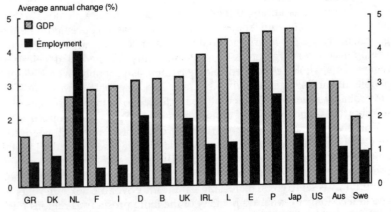

Figure 15.1   GDP growth and employment change, 1985–90.

1980s, however, when recovery occurred, employment increased significantly faster in the deindustrialising regions taken together than elsewhere in the Community, with growth generating significant job creation in services. As a result, unemployment fell by much more than in other regions. The reduction, however, was not universal. In some regions of France unemployment went up rather than down.

In less developed Objective 1 regions, the picture is more complicated. In aggregate, these regions experienced an increase in jobs in both industry and services similar in percentage terms to the increase in Objective 2 regions and higher than the more developed, prosperous parts of the Community. But large-scale job losses in agriculture, which remains an important occupation in these regions, meant that *in total* employment rose by much less than in Objective 2 regions and by no more than in the most prosperous regions.

There were, however, marked differences in experience between different areas, with regions in Spain and Portugal generally recording above-average growth of employment, those in Southern Italy, Greece and Ireland, below average. As a result unemployment in the latter regions either went up or fell by less than elsewhere, while in many parts of Spain and Portugal the unemployment rate came down by more than in prosperous regions. In aggregate, partly because of continued labour force growth, there was very little reduction in total unemployment in Objective 1 regions during the period or recovery.

Several lessons can be drawn from this experience. First, most regions in need of employment creation are likely to benefit from renewed growth in the Community, but it is not inevitable that all will. Second, because of the high proportion of employment which still remains in agriculture in the less developed regions, jobs have to be created there at a much higher rate in industry and services than elsewhere, just to provide work for those leaving the land. Third, because of higher prospective labour force growth – given both continuing growth of working-age population and increasing participation on the part of women – the overall growth of employment in these regions has to be especially high to prevent unemployment from increasing.

There are two further lessons. First high employment growth tends to mean far more job opportunities for young people and, therefore, the rate of unemployment for the under 25 age group is likely to come down by more than for older people, just as it tends to rise more in recession. This makes it easier to tackle the problem of youth unemployment. Second, employment growth will not necessarily mean any relative reduction in long-term unemployment. The average proportion unemployed for a year or more in the Community was only slightly lower in 1990 than in 1985. In Italy, Greece and Ireland, it was higher. This means that labour market action directed specifically at helping the long-term unemployed is essential to avoid significant numbers of people being deprived of work more or less permanently.

Obstacles to expansionary economic policies

The highly integrated nature of the Community economies and their close trading and financial links with the rest of the world are potential sources of economic strength. However, given the present fragmented state of policy-making in the Community, they can contribute to low growth and inhibit the adoption of more expansionary policies. At the same time, regional divisions profoundly condition politics at the national and European levels. The more prosperous countries and regions, particularly in a context of low growth, tend to be intent on protecting their own position and unwilling to transfer income to backward or depressed areas.

This division is reflected in differences in policy objectives, especially in the weight given to price stability as opposed to growth and employment creation. Until the balance of power in the Community shifts away from those areas giving overriding priority to stability – and therefore to low levels of credit creation and borrowing – any significant reorientation of policy will remain problematic.

Since the oil price crises of 1973–74 and 1979–80, emphasis on cautious monetary policies has generally held sway. The close trading and financial links between the Community and other parts of the world have meant that the Community economy has been greatly affected by fluctuations in activity elsewhere. Moreover, because of the highly integrated nature of the European economy, reinforced by the single market, a downturn or upturn in any one member country has spread quickly to other parts. Faced with a downturn in external demand, governments in the Community have often responded by reducing rather than expanding internal demand, cutting public expenditure and/or increasing taxes, in an attempt to contain increases in public deficits. By so doing, they have reinforced the recessionary impetus not only in their own economies but also elsewhere.

Such perverse action reflects a shift in the trade-off between internal and external policy considerations which has been reinforced by integration of trade and capital markets without parallel monetary unification. Action to stimulate internal demand is now more likely to benefit producers elsewhere than domestic businesses and creates disproportionate financial problems for the country which provides the stimulus.

Extreme caution in national fiscal and monetary policies has been encouraged by pressure from the international financial market which has become of increasing influence as the liquidity of foreign exchange transactions – and, therefore, the speed at which commitments can be converted from one currency to another – has grown. Rather than run the risk of provoking capital outflows, a possibly uncontrollable fall in their exchange rate, increased inflation and a financial crisis, governments have in general opted to follow 'strong money' policies.

The experience of individual countries – the UK in the mid-1970s and France in the early 1980s, for instance – which attempted to break out of recession by sustaining internal demand and which very soon encountered financial crisis, provides a powerful lesson of the dangers of unilateral attempts to resist international recession.

Initial steps towards monetary union, in particular, the commitment to maintaining fixed exchange rates for prolonged periods under the ERM and the abolition of exchange controls, have tightened the constraint on unilateral pursuit of more expansionary policies by individual member states. The result is that Community countries collectively have helped spread and intensify recession by the policy action – or lack of it – which they have taken in the past and have contributed almost nothing to stimulating recovery at the global level. Instead they have been content to wait for other regions of the world to take the lead in expanding demand.

Although the size of its market gives the Community the potential to play a major role in managing world economic activity – which would be an immense benefit not only to other countries, especially those in neighbouring regions to the East and South, but to the Community itself – this potential will remain unexploited so long as economic policy continues to be uncoordinated and so long as the priority in the more prosperous and powerful regions of the Community remains one of narrow short-term self-interest. The recent downturn in the German economy, the substantial fall in industrial production experienced over the past year and the rapid rise in unemployment may from this perspective be a favourable development insofar as these events may cause some reconsideration of policy objectives and priorities in the most prosperous parts of the Community.

It may, in particular, lead to a reassessment of the risk to inflation associated with the adoption of more than expansionary policies, a risk which in practice in a period of deep recession, with high unemployment, substantial underutilised resources and massive excess capacity, is likely to be low. (In the 1980s, faster growth in most countries was not accompanied by any significant rise in inflation.) More pertinently, it may also lead to a comparison of this risk with the misery created by unemployment and lack of opportunity and the near-certainty of increasing social and political unrest.

The need for policy action at the Community and local level

An effective response to slow growth and rising unemployment in the Community needs to emphasise the importance of policy action at two levels:

(1) At the Community level, to provide the necessary framework for accelerated economic development both within Western Europe and in neighbouring regions in Central and Eastern Europe, Africa and the Middle East;

(2) At the regional, local and city level where authorities have to deal
directly with the social consequences of low growth and inadequate
employment creation and must be the prime movers in any modern,
decentralised pattern of development.

Sustained recovery and increased convergence of levels of income and
employment must therefore incorporate, on the one hand, a strengthening
of Community institutions so that they become capable of managing
economic policy and of providing a coordinated monetary framework and,
on the other, increased resource transfers and the establishment of a
legislative framework to support investment and development at the
regional and city level.

The aim should be to sustain a rate of economic growth in the Community as a whole of 3–4%, instead of the rate of only just over 2%
achieved over the past 20 years, with higher rates in less developed regions
and areas of industrial decline and lower rates in the more prosperous
regions, where growth *per se* is not an overriding priority. A rate significantly lower than this is likely to make it impossible in practice to create
sufficient job opportunities to reduce unemployment to acceptable levels
within the next two decades. Nor would a lower growth rate in Western
Europe provide a viable context for reform and restructuring in Central
and Eastern Europe, North Africa and the Middle East. A lower growth
rate – and the inequalities associated with low growth – will also make it
difficult to fund social programmes within the Community and action to
protect and improve the environment, activities which are widely supported in their own right and are an important potential source of
employment.

A framework for monetary policy

Monetary stability is critical as a foundation for sustained investment and
growth of private and public sector spending. The monetary system as it
now exists, however, with only loose cooperation between central banks,
has failed to deliver the required stability. Moreover, by giving rise to high
real interest rates without removing uncertainty about future exchange
rates, it has served to depress growth in the Community. The aim should
be to ensure that, in a context of low growth and high unemployment,
monetary policy helps governments finance deficits caused by recession
and funds investment in infrastructure and new business development in
support of recovery.

Securing monetary stability and facilitating credit expansion require
close coordination in the operation of monetary policy. However,
although countries in the Community have problems in common, there
is no clear tendency, partly because of differing priorities, towards
increased cooperation in this area. These differences in priorities reflect

the substantial disparities in economic performance which still exist between member states and which stand to widen, the longer recession goes on. So long as they persist, they represent a major obstacle to monetary unification.

Recent upheavals in exchange markets make it clear that ECU parities for national currencies cannot be enforced arbitrarily in the face of divergent economic conditions in member states. Businesses and financial investors recognize that differences in inflation rates, public debt, unemployment and trade balances will sooner or later have to be compensated by realignment of exchange rates. The significant divergence in real exchange rates of major European currencies in the latter part of the 1980s and early 1990s, which resulted from maintaining nominal rates while rates of inflation and productivity performance differed, could not feasibly have continued for very much longer.

The implication is that full monetary union, with a single currency and, therefore, permanently fixed exchange rates, will only become feasible progressively as and when a greater degree of economic convergence – real as well as nominal – is achieved.

The present situation is difficult since the single market makes fluctuations in exchange rates and differences in costs of borrowing in different parts of the Community very important problems for business, while remaining differences in economic structure and national institutions prevent monetary unification. Ideally Maastricht Stage 2 should provide a framework for much closer coordination of national monetary policies in order to provide financial stability and prevent the kind of upheaval which occurred in September 1992. Despite reservations expressed by the Bundesbank and some national governments, risks to business could be much reduced through joint management of national currencies, respecting differences in national situations according to systematic criteria.

The formula for monetary policies in Europe must be flexibility, delivering effective stability of financial conditions, with a bias towards convergence. For example, there is an inevitable presumption that divergences in real (inflation-adjusted) exchange rates and real interest rates have to be kept within bounds by periodic adjustments of nominal rates. There are also lesser, but not entirely unreasonable, presumptions that countries with weak trade balances may require lower real interest rates and exchange rates for transitional periods, provided that lower real exchange rates do not feed back too strongly into inflation. Equally, countries with high inflation but relatively strong trade balances may benefit from higher real exchange rates, exerting pressure in favour of price stability.

During the 1980s, there was considerable emphasis on management of monetary policy according to quantitative targets for monetary aggregates, at the cost of rather wide fluctuations in interest rates in many member states. Disillusion with the results of 'monetarist' experiments has resulted in a more pragmatic attitude which ought to permit central banks to take a wider range of indicators into account. Doctrinal emphasis on monetary convergence carries risks similar to those implied by the former emphasis on monetary aggregates.

Provided that the need for flexibility is recognized, it should be possible for central banks, working closely together, to ensure reasonable stability of real exchange rates and real interest rates within the Maastricht Stage 2 framework, so long as the opportunity for coordinated monetary management which this provides is properly exploited.

Such cooperation is of major importance in supporting sustained recovery across the Community. While the action taken by the UK government in 1992 to disengage from the ERM and allow its exchange rate to depreciate may help stimulate domestic growth, it is an illusion to imagine that a freely floating rate represents a viable long-term strategy for the UK, still less an example to follow by other member states. Although short-term policy constraints may be weaker for a country with a freely floating exchange rate, uncertainty is substantially increased and businesses forced to gamble on week-to-week currency movements will have greater difficulty in making long-term commitments of investment and production. The UK government was in a position where it had no option but to devalue either inside or outside the ERM. It was also in a position where, with low inflation, the risk of increased price increases was less intimidating than the consequences of continuing slump and high and rising unemployment. As time goes on, the balance of priorities is likely to change and the need to ensure exchange rate stability will again become important. In practice, the UK example may demonstrate the defects of the current EMS. But it can also be interpreted as demonstrating the need to strengthen monetary cooperation and to operate the ERM in a more flexible manner, so that governments are not driven to take unilateral action which works against Community interests, and ultimately their own.

A framework for fiscal policy

The anti-growth bias of monetary policy has been compounded by a bias in attitudes to public expenditure and deficit-financing in particular, which has caused governments to seek to limit spending and reduce borrowing, even where increases were the direct result of recession and reduced private investment. In future, the aim should be to establish a framework for stable management of public expenditure and taxation over the long-term, to prevent policy reinforcing fluctuations in economic activity rather than smoothing them.

The slowdown in economic growth of the Community since the mid-1970s has created long-term fiscal problems in all member states. Revenue shortfalls in each cyclical recession have tended to push up the ratio of public debt to GDP, although in some countries this has been offset by privatisation (notably in the UK). In the Community as a whole the ratio of public debt to GDP has risen from 50% in the early 1980s to over 60% in 1992. In some member countries (Belgium, Italy, Ireland and Greece) public debt has risen to 100% or more of annual GDP.

At the same time, governments have in general tried to contain increases in budget deficits caused by slow growth. Although real interest rates have risen in the recent past to unprecedented levels, there is no evidence that these have been required to fund excessive budget deficits, or indeed that reducing deficits is necessary to bring interest rates down. Indeed real interest rates were lower in the first half of the 1980s than since then, despite budget deficits being higher (see Figure 15.2). Contrary to the widespread view which still dominates policy-making, the present high interest rates across the Community have little to do with levels of government borrowing. Instead they reflect the prevailing desire to limit credit creation, restrain demand, maintain a strong exchange rate and keep down inflation.

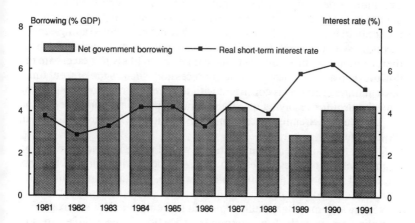

Figure 15.2. Net borrowing of general government and real short-term interest rates in the Community, 1981–91.

In the present recession, the reduction in revenue resulting from the erosion of the tax base and the increased expenditure caused by higher unemployment and lower activity are likely to be responsible for public deficits rising across the Community as a whole in 1993 by an estimated 3–4% of GDP – equivalent to ECU 225–300 billion.

These high levels of public debt, and the tendency towards large budget deficits which has caused them, increase the difficulties of managing monetary policy in the Community and of moving towards monetary union. The reaction in the Maastricht Treaty, if narrowly interpreted, is to impose ceilings on the scale of both debt and public deficits in relation to GDP, to monitor policy in the light of these levels and to establish an eventual procedure for compelling member states to eliminate excessive levels.

What needs to be emphasised are the repercussions of the required reductions in public expenditure and/or increases in taxes on economic activity, both in the country attempting to reduce its deficit and in the rest of the Community. Without member states with levels of public debt and budget deficits below the ceilings taking compensating expansionary action, there is a danger that the overall growth of demand in the Community will tend to be depressed, with consequent effects on output and employment.

To avoid curbing economic growth in this way, there are essentially three options. The first is to abandon the budgetary convergence criteria in Maastricht entirely and allow each member state to determine the level of deficit and debt which it considers appropriate, given its need for public services and investment in infrastructure. The second is to establish a financial instrument at the Community level, funded by the issue of Community debt and therefore not counting as a component of public debt of individual member states, to assist countries which are required to reduce debt levels. The third option, which could be adopted alongside the second, is to interpret the criteria as medium-term benchmarks and, therefore, not require governments to take action likely to exacerbate the downturn in activity during periods of recession, such as the present time. Such an interpretation is consistent with the Treaty provision establishing a mechanism for resolving questions about appropriate budgetary action in particular circumstances (in consultation with the European Parliament).

The first option seems unrealistic. It would place reliance entirely on financial market forces to restrain excessive borrowing and would carry the risk, if these were not sufficiently powerful, of undermining monetary management, confirming fears in the Bundesbank and elsewhere about moves towards monetary unification being accompanied by a relaxation of discipline on spendthrift governments and a flow of investable funds in their direction.

The second option has much to commend it. Debt creation at the Community level does not involve the same 'crowding out' objections levelled against increases in public debt at the national level and, since it has no implications for exchange rates between Community currencies, there is no reason why it should lead to any rise in interest rates. Moreover a significant facility – an amount equivalent to, say, 0.5% of Community GDP – could be created at comparatively modest cost in terms of interest payments.

At least eight of the EC member states now have public deficits in excess of the Maastricht guidelines (3% of GDP), and six have public debt well in excess of the Maastricht limit (60% of GDP). In most cases the size of public deficits and public debt is related to needs for expenditure on education, social services and infrastructure which exceed the national resources. In the absence of a Community debt instrument to assist debt reductions in member states, it is unrealistic to expect the Maastricht limits to be achieved in the present decade and it is liable to be highly damaging to economic and social cohesion if the member states concerned make a serious attempt to do so. (The Cohesion Fund established at Edinburgh for essentially the same purpose – though confined to the poorer countries – is far too small, at a mere ECU 15 billion spread over seven years, to ease the difficulties other than marginally.)

Debt financing at the Community level could also counteract the con-tractionary bias imparted to national policies by the existing multi-currency monetary system. The Community should be able to make good revenue shortfalls and support public authorities at national and local level through cyclical downturns by funding part of its own budget and rebating contributions from member states. The major obstacle to the creation of such a facility is political rather than economic. Governments have made it plain that they are unwilling at present to contemplate any substantial expansion of borrowing facilities at the Community level, a reluctance which seems to stem from the prevailing attitude towards public sector borrowing *per se* rather than the Community-level dimension of the proposal.

The third option of planning budgetary policy over the medium-term seems, at present, to offer the most promising basis for agreement and is consistent with orthodox economic thinking. During periods of recession, governments ought to experience little difficulty in funding the increased deficit which results from a downturn in economic activity and which, in practice, is a reflection of a reduction in private expenditure and a loss of confidence in private assets. Indeed by creating more debt they will in effect be compensating for the reduction in private sector debt which is likely to occur as the willingness of business to invest declines and, there-fore, 'crowding in' rather than 'crowding out' investment.

Moreover, by establishing a stable medium-term path for public expen-diture and tax rates, such an approach could make a major contribution to countering cyclical fluctuations in economic activity. It would allow public expenditure to expand and the revenue collected by government to decline as private-sector activity fell, so helping to offset this decline, while having a restraining effect if growth were excessive.

It is essential, however, that all governments within the Community agree on such an approach and support those whose deficits are increased by recession in order to provide protection against financial market pressure.

Problems of funding public expenditure

The bias against public debt, together with the failure of the monetary system to protect national currencies against financial market pressure, has not only prevented governments from sustaining spending during recession, it has thereby contributed to low growth and deprived less developed and deindustrialising regions of finance for public services, income support and investment, while making the cost of borrowing prohibitively expensive. This bias against public spending, and against raising the revenue from both taxes and borrowing to finance it, needs to be corrected if balanced development across the Community is to be supported.

During earlier decades tax revenues tended to rise as a share of GDP, providing rapid growth in resources for public expenditure. The reluctance of taxpayers to continue to support large public budgets has several causes. In a climate of recession or slow economic growth people are less willing to give up control over their income unless they know precisely how they personally will benefit. When public services come under financial pressure, standards tend to suffer and the confidence of those employed in the public sector is eroded.

In a context of increased competition, reinforced by the single market, and high unemployment caused by slow growth, people also fear that high taxes and social contributions will cost jobs. Reducing the tax burden and the cost of employment below levels in other countries becomes a means of gaining competitive advantage and of creating jobs, even though by damaging public services and infrastructure such a policy is liable over the longer-term to erode any advantage gained in the short-term.

During the past decade there has been little or no convergence of the fiscal systems of member states. The share of GDP taken by government revenue varies between around 50% in France and the Netherlands to around 35% in Spain and the UK, while the structure of taxation shows equally substantial differences. In particular, the level of social contributions and, therefore, the non-wage element of labour costs which employers face is two to three times higher in France, Italy and Belgium than in Denmark or the UK. Rates of taxes on business profits also vary markedly between countries.

The low level of the overall burden of taxation in the UK and Spain helps to keep costs of employment down in these countries, and may help attract businesses for which low labour costs are a major competitive factor. Conversely, high revenue shares in France and the Netherlands may reflect the relatively strong competitive performance of these countries within the single market – and indeed may contribute to strong performance, by funding higher expenditure on education and training and on infrastructure.

So long as major differences in competitive performance remain, it may be possible to sustain considerable differences in tax rates at the national level. The marked differences within member states in regional and local situations, however, make the national averages highly misleading and give rise to the question of to what extent high tax rates and social contributions in areas of high unemployment are a major impediment to job creation where it is most needed.

The regional perspective implies a need for more variation in effective burdens of taxation at local level and, possibly, greater harmonisation of national regimes, with national and Community transfer mechanisms to supplement resources for infrastructure and public services in low-income regions.

Structural policies and economic growth

Long-term funding for public programmes needs to be accompanied by specific measures to recycle present high levels of private savings into investment, especially in Objective 1 and Objective 2 regions where the need for job creation and the strengthening of economic performance is most acute. The effective use of such funds for the development, or redevelopment, of these regions requires partnership between the public authorities involved, local communities and business and international companies, which are a key source of technical and organisational expertise as well as finance.

During the past decade there has been an increasing accumulation of personal wealth in the form of pension funds and financial investments. The desire for personal financial wealth reflects higher incomes and declining confidence in public institutions. Since 1980 real rates of interest have been higher than in previous decades, offering a good return to private savers while at the same time raising the cost of funding the public sector.

Accumulation of personal financial wealth needs to be matched by investment in profitable assets in order to ensure the long-term security of financial funds and to sustain economic growth in line with savings. Low economic growth in the Community since the mid-1970s has reflected a failure to convert high savings into profitable investment. Instead, savings have been invested in growing public debt funded at high cost. As the public sector has become impoverished, it has become increasingly difficult to finance investments in infrastructure, environmental improvement, communal services and education which would be needed to provide the basis for more dynamic economic growth in backward and deindustrialised regions.

Given the reluctance of national governments to allow interference in monetary and fiscal policy, the Community's role in economic management has rightly focused on use of Structural Funds to assist investment in backward regions. But further development of structural policies is to a large extent frustrated by institutional factors – by struggles between member states over the allocation of funds, by questions of control over their deployment, by doubts about the competence, and in some cases integrity, of local administrators – as well as by lack of finance.

Without a new investment impetus, it is hard to foresee an improved rate of economic growth and job creation in backward areas within the Community or in surrounding regions of Central and Eastern Europe, the Middle East and Africa which are closely linked to the European economy.

The strongest political base for more dynamic structural policies is not the Community or national level, but the local or city level. Specific needs and opportunities are strongly felt by local communities, and the conciliation of business and social interests has to take place mainly at this level. A new dynamic to structural policies might, therefore, be given by a recognition of the primary role of cities and local institutions as the critical agents for development of backward and deindustrialised regions within the single market framework.

A second requirement for a strengthening of structural policies is a larger supply of funds. Institutions for finance of structural investment exist, both at Community level (EIB) and in many member states, but the prevailing high level of real interest rates remains a major problem. It is very difficult to justify long-term structural investments if they are required to generate real returns of 6% or 8% per year.

The widespread reliance of Community citizens on positive returns to their financial wealth, which is by now deeply institutionalised, makes a return to the zero or negative real interest rates experienced in the 1960s very unlikely. At the same time the accumulation of financial wealth can be expected to continue until the post-war generations begin to reach retirement age in the period after 2005. During the intervening period stronger incentives may be required to ensure that accumulating personal financial wealth is invested in infrastructure and business development.

The 1992 Edinburgh summit showed little support for large-scale borrowing by Community institutions to fund the Community's own operations or to finance transfers within or outside the Community's borders. The alternative is to provide increased stimulus for investment by local institutions, both public and private, especially in backward and deindustrialised regions where the existing economic base is least adequate.

Subsidies to investment in infrastructure, environmental improvement, education and training can readily be justified in terms of 'externalities' – i.e. non-revenue benefits to local areas and to the Community as a whole. Because of externalities, the direct returns to the organisation carrying out the investment will not necessarily cover the cost and, therefore, market forces, if left to themselves, will not ensure that such investment takes place. Public sector intervention is, therefore, required to correct the divergence between the private and social rate of return and, in the case of backward regions, in particular, to create the preconditions for attracting private investment on any significant scale.

For example, a 5% interest subsidy extended over the first ten years of long-term investments would greatly reduce the risk and improve the viability of projects. The cost of subsidising new investments equal to 1%

of Community GNP on these terms, building up to a subsidised capital equal to 10% of Community GNP after ten years – an amount which could make a significant impact in problem regions – would be about 0.5% of Community GNP – approximately the present size of expenditure on structural programmes.

At the present time there is a minor degree of integration between operations of the Community's Structural Funds and lending by the EIB. A more closely coordinated and more determined effort to promote investment is now badly needed. At the same time, much more scope should be given to private and public institutions at local level to act autonomously in carrying out investment programmes, in place of the present system of complex 'partnerships' largely between public bodies which tend to be dominated in many member states by Community institutions and national administrations.

Employment-creation programmes

In parallel with structural investment in regions where the pace of economic development has to be accelerated, there is a need to establish a framework of legislation to promote job creation through encouragement of small businesses and employment-intensive services. Even if GDP growth in the range 3–4% can be achieved over the rest of the decade, this in itself is unlikely to create enough jobs to bring down unemployment to acceptable levels and, at the same time, provide work for the substantial numbers of women forced up to now to be inactive.

Moreover, outside backward areas and regions of industrial decline, where the need for economic growth and large-scale investment is acute, growth of production *per se* tends in any event to be less of a priority. Even in many other parts of the Community, however, there are substantial underutilised resources, which if the constraints on putting them into production could be overcome, would add considerably to output, real income and employment. Nevertheless, in the more prosperous areas the challenge is to find alternative means of employment-creation other than high growth rates. This means accepting the need to manage market forces so as to direct resources into activities which are consistent with the desires of people living in these areas for improvements in the quality of life and, at the same time, to ensure that this is not at the expense of job opportunities.

There is no shortage of activities which can potentially provide jobs while helping to achieve a range of social and environmental objectives. For example, the environmental industry in the Community, which in many areas is still in its infancy, is estimated already to employ over 500,000. It offers significant scope for expansion, if finance were to be channelled into reducing pollution, waste management, water treatment, recycling and cleaning up both the natural and urban environment, and if the development of new production processes and new products in this area were encouraged. Programmes to save energy and to develop new sources and to provide improved education, health, recreation and cultural facilities could together create considerably more jobs.

At the same time, there is a need to encourage the development and growth of small and medium-sized enterprises. This is not only important for the job opportunities which are directly created – often in a more satisfying working environment than large companies are able to provide – but equally for the longer-term competitiveness of the Community economy. In many sectors, small businesses provide the research and innovations to feed larger companies, which need continuously to improve their productive efficiency and introduce new products in order to be able to compete on world markets, but which lack the flexibility and individual motivation required to develop new ideas in many areas.

Moreover, because they are local in scale, small and medium-sized businesses are better able to respond to local labour market conditions and demands, including developing and exploring more flexible working arrangements – which might enable, for example, a given volume of work to be shared among increased numbers of people. In the single market and in an increasingly unified financial market, however, small businesses will lose privileged access to local sources of funding and are likely to find it more difficult to develop.

An effective employment creation programme, combining support for small business and the development of locally-based services, requires the establishment of a Community-level framework which leaves as much discretion as possible over the choice of local actions but which, at the same time, defines the policy instruments which can be used and the rules governing their implementation.

The fiscal system, in the form of indirect taxes, tax concessions, exemptions and allowances, as well as public expenditure on grants and subsidies, is the primary means of implementing structural policies in market economies. But given the mobility of business within the unified Community market, it is difficult for national, regional and local governments to use fiscal instruments for structural purposes, in the absence of a framework defined at the Community level.

A good example is taxation designed to reduce environmental pollution and to increase the efficiency of use of limited natural resources. Although reduction of pollution and economising on scarce resources is of general benefit both to the country taking action and to others, any one member state which unilaterally introduces pollution or resource taxes faces the risk of losing business to others which are less careful. Similar arguments apply to tax incentives which favour small and medium-scale enterprises or taxes to fund improvements in education, health and social services, etc. The increased tax burden on larger enterprises again carries the risk that business will be displaced to other parts of the Community where tax rates are lower.

The enforcement of minimum standards of health and safety and of working conditions as proposed in the Social Chapter carries the same kind of risk. Unless these are applied across the whole of the Community, businesses may tend to shift to areas where the authorities are most lax. Indeed in the absence of an adequate mechanism for transferring income to problem regions to provide a significant incentive for business development, the responsible authorities may be tempted to use lax standards as a substitute means of attracting inward investment. The danger then is that, under pressure of competition, standards throughout the Community will gradually be reduced and the hard-won advances in working and social conditions will be lost.

Finally, the possibilities of work-sharing through both a general reduction in the length of the working week and increased part-time working need to be given more serious consideration. This is especially the case in those countries with relatively high levels of income per head. It would also apply more generally, however, if the constraints on achieving higher rates of growth cannot be overcome. In this case, work-sharing provides a means of distributing available employment more equitably. At present, for example, the average number of hours worked per person employed in the Netherlands is around 20% less than in Italy or France, countries with similar levels of *per capita* income, implying that there is substantial scope for bringing more people into employment in the latter two countries even in the absence of a significant growth of GDP.

The critical problem, however, does not so much concern how to share available work, but how to bring about the redistribution of income which this inevitably implies. In low wage countries, such as the UK as well as the less developed member states (average wages in the UK are only marginally above those in Spain), the key constraint on this kind of policy is that a high proportion of the workforce earn so little for the often long hours they now work that they are in no position to give up any significant part of their income.

Conclusion

The European Community is now entering a third decade of slow growth and high unemployment. The means of tackling the problem, which ought to be clear in principle to all those who believe in the necessity of economic management and which have been outlined above, have still to be developed in practice. What is lacking is the political will to establish the institutional framework required at the Community level for the coordination of monetary and fiscal policy which is essential for achieving the rates of growth needed to have a substantial and long-lasting effect on employment. Without such a framework, monetary policy will remain fragmented and, partly through maintaining high interest rates, partly through failing to secure a stable pattern of realistic exchange rates, is likely to continue to deter rather than to support investment and new business development; fiscal policy will continue to be directed at reducing budget deficits and cutting back public expenditure, rather than at managing demand to ensure adequate rates of growth; regional disparities, especially in terms of employment, are likely to widen and the various measures which could potentially create jobs or distribute work more equitably will tend to remain unexploited because of lack of income.

16

Policies to Reduce European Unemployment

John Grieve Smith

The high and rising level of unemployment is now the major economic challenge facing the European Community. Although the current recession has accentuated the problem, mass unemployment on a scale comparable with pre-war levels had already re-emerged in the 1980s. During the 1970s, unemployment in the Community crept up from 3% to 6%, but then rose to between 10% and 11% from 1983 to 1987. It dipped to 8% or 9% towards the end of the decade, before rising to 10% again in 1992. To reverse this process will require a fundamental revolution in prevailing attitudes of thought and approaches to economic policy.

Current levels of unemployment are as much a reflection of the political priorities attached to different objectives of economic policy as of a failure to comprehend the way such policies work, or technical errors of judgement. It was no coincidence that concern with rising levels of inflation at the end of the 1970s coincided with the spread of monetarism in various forms – a doctrine essentially concerned with analysing (albeit wrongheadedly) the problems of inflation rather than unemployment. Monetarist doctrine contributed to the growth of unemployment by suggesting that inflation could be squeezed out of the system without any lasting increase in unemployment. This encouraged the use of deflationary demand policies to combat inflation and, particularly in the UK, ruled out any form of collective incomes policy to deal with the wage/price spiral. Moreover by undermining the Keynesian consensus on the use of fiscal policy for demand management, but at the same time alleging that budget deficits were inflationary, they introduced a consistently deflationary bias in budgetary policy.

Reliance on monetary policy as the only legitimate weapon for demand management was also in itself a further move in a deflationary direction – partly because tight credit and high interest rates are more effective in curbing demand than low interest rates in stimulating it, but also because exchange rate considerations tend to exert more effective pressure to increase interest rates than to reduce them. The operation of the ERM reinforced this tendency. The switch in emphasis from budgetary to monetary policy has thus been inherently deflationary – and would have been more so if liberalisation of credit had not come to the rescue.

Low demand leads in turn to an erosion of the capacity to produce, so that any rise in demand can lead to supply constraints, even though unemployment remains high – as was the case in the UK in the 'Lawson boom'. One of the damaging legacies of the 1980s is that a decade of relatively low demand and high unemployment has had a lasting effect on Europe's effective capacity. Plant capacity, management structures, sales organisations, skilled and experienced labour, and the number of firms have all settled down at a level consistent with 8% to 10% unemployment. Higher demand, if it comes soon enough, will bring back into production some, though not all, of the resources thrown idle by the latest recession. But any more fundamental attack on unemployment must go further than merely reversing the effects of the immediate recession.

Reducing the level of unemployment by the 2% or so by which it has risen in the Community during the recession is only a start to tackling the problem. The need is to maintain a continued rate of increase in output faster than the trend rate of growth of potential output in order to reduce unemployment permanently. This depends first on demand management policies on which industry can confidently base long-term plans to expand their capacity and their labour force. Establishing such confidence will certainly be difficult in the UK after the experience of the 1980s and would mean avoiding transitory booms or too rapid a growth of demand before it could be matched by a corresponding growth of capacity. Such fine-tuning will never be 100% successful. More basically, confidence depends on setting a general policy regime both nationally, in the Community, and more widely, which will once again be seen as geared to achieving full employment. Unfortunately this is the very antithesis of the Treaty of Maastricht with the deflationary bias of its convergence provisions.

Integration and deflation

The Treaty of Maastricht raises the fundamental question of whether the movement towards economic and monetary union in Europe necessarily, or inevitably, conflicts with the goal of restoring full employment. Is full employment only attainable if we halt, or reverse the movement towards European fixed exchange rates?

In the simplest terms, the case for such a proposition is that exchange rate flexibility would allow some countries to have a higher inflation rate than others without running into balance of payments difficulties. The argument against it is that as countries have become more interdependent, with a higher level of intertrade, output in one country depends increasingly on the level of demand in its trading partners. It is therefore much more difficult to engineer full employment in one country alone: more-over, the attempt to do so will be more at risk from increasing imports leading to balance of payments difficulties. With the advent of a single market in the European Community in January 1993, the balance of the argument must have swung strongly towards the view that the countries of Europe have more chance of achieving full employment by acting together than on their own. But joint action does not depend on, nor need it await, the achievement of monetary union.

Policy Coordination

The establishment of a single market and the consequent growth of an already high level of intertrade within the Community strengthens the case for coordinated expansionary policies. If they all expand together, coun-tries' individual initiatives to expand demand and output will reinforce each other. Coordinated action will also ease the problem of expansion in two other important ways. In so far as expansion leads to any faster increase in prices, simultaneous expansion will minimise the dangers of individual countries' price levels getting out of line. In other words coordi-nated action to expand simultaneously will not aggravate the problem of price convergence, save in so far as inflation were to accelerate *more* in countries where inflation was already higher than average.

A further corollary of the greater effectiveness of coordinated expan-sion is that the likely 'multiplier' effect of fiscal action such as increased public investment is greater for the Community as a whole than for individual countries on their own – such stimuli will together raise output and incomes more than they would individually. This has important budgetary implications because it means that a temporary increase in deficits will result in a greater eventual increase in output and incomes and hence improvement in the budget balance. Coordinated budgetary action would maximise the eventual reduction in budget deficits in the recovery and minimise any continuing public debt problem.

What do we mean by coordinated expansion? At the least, it means a compact that allows each country to adopt expansionary policies in the belief that others will do likewise. But to have any further substance, it must involve some quantitative understanding of the expansion envisaged by each country, based in turn on a prior analysis of the possible effects on such things as their balance of payments, rates of inflation and levels of unemployment. It does not follow at the initial stage that the precise policies each country adopts to achieve its planned expansion are neces-sarily of mutual concern, but in certain instances they would be. Indeed in the case of monetary policy they would need to move together.

If, however, the members of the Community are to act together to achieve full employment and faster growth, we have somehow to extricate ourselves from the philosophy of the Delors Report and the convergence provisions of the Maastricht Treaty. The Treaty needs to be interpreted, and eventually amended, in such a way as to put the emphasis on economic policy coordination for expansion.

The first requirement then is that EC governments should individually and collectively reinstate full employment as a major policy objective, and reorientate post-Maastricht Community mechanisms so that they facilitate rather than hinder the achievement of this objective. For example, a statement that monetary union could not take place until unemployment in the Community was down to 5% could revolutionise assumptions about policy.

The first step along this road should be to draw up a set of guidelines directed towards full employment and faster growth. It would then have to be agreed that such guidelines would take precedence over the criteria for inflation rates, budget deficits, interest rates and exchange rates in the Treaty of Maastricht. The aim would remain convergence, but would include convergence towards lower levels of unemployment. Such a change would require some delicate political footwork, but without it the Maastricht process is likely to break up under the strain.

Article 103 of the Maastricht Treaty could provide the opportunity for such an approach by establishing the machinery for coordinating macro-economic policy, subject to the limitations imposed by the independence of the Central Bank. Article 103 provides that the Council shall draw up broad guidelines for the economic policies of member states and the Community. This broad statement of policy would be approved by a qualified majority of the Council and reported to the European Parliament; and to ensure closer coordination of economic policies, developments in each country would be monitored in the light of these guidelines and the need for convergence.

In the immediate future the most important point is to find a way round the 3% 'excessive government deficits' provisions, ruling out the use of countercyclical fiscal policy in the recession. Article 104c of the Treaty states that 'Member States shall avoid excessive government deficits', and that the Commission shall examine:

(a) whether the ratio of the planned or actual government deficit to gross domestic product exceeds a reference value, unless
— either the ratio has declined substantially and continuously and reached a level that comes close to the reference value;
— or, alternatively, the excess over the reference value is only exceptional and temporary and the ratio remains close to the reference value;
(b) whether the ratio of government debt to gross domestic product exceeds a reference value, unless the ratio is sufficiently diminishing and approaching the reference value at a satisfactory pace.

The reference values are specified in the relevant protocol as 3% and 60% respectively. Such arithmetical limits are (as is now widely recognised) conceptually erroneous. Budgetary policy should be evaluated on much wider criteria, in particular the macroeconomic situation prevailing at the time. But it could, if necessary, be argued quite convincingly that it would be reasonable to exceed the 3% limit temporarily by giving a deliberate stimulus to demand in current circumstances. It would be absurd for the Community to prolong the recession by calling in aid inappropriate and misconceived limits, whose only rationale was to avoid any danger of inflationary budgetary policies.

Since the policing of Article 104c depends on a report by the Commission which must 'take into account all relevant factors', it could be possible, if the Commission and Ministers were convinced of the need for expansionary policies, to permit higher deficits for a time without infringing the Treaty. While some influential member such as Germany might wish to keep these provisions intact as longer-term guidelines, there is a strong c: se for amending them when the Treaty next comes to be revised.

How expansion could affect the operation of the transitional provisions on price and interest rate convergence is uncertain, but the guiding principle in any new initiative should be that satisfaction of such conditions for monetary union must take second place to the needs of expansion. This may mean that a majority of countries will not qualify for monetary union and that no date can be set for the third stage when this is considered at the end of 1996 as required in Article 109j. The consequent provision that the adoption of a single currency shall start at the beginning of 1999 may then be amended, but that is sufficiently far ahead not to be a problem for now. The immediate problem is to reform the ERM.

The Future of the ERM

The emphasis in the 1980s on reducing inflation irrespective of the effect of unemployment was accentuated by European governments' masochistic attitudes to the ERM, with countries positively wishing to put external pressure on themselves to match the German rate of inflation, whatever the cost in unemployment. The ERM thus became a perverse and malign version of the Bretton Woods system of fixed exchange rates. The latter was set up to facilitate the achievement of full employment by avoiding countries 'exporting unemployment' by competitive devaluation. Fixed exchange rates were also seen as providing a stable environment for industrial investment and growth. The Bretton Woods agreement aimed (not altogether successfully) to avoid putting all the pressure for adjustment on deficit countries (viz. the scarce currency clause) and, in principle at any rate, did not expect deficit countries to deflate to the point of departing from full employment. There was specific provision for exchange rate adjustment in cases of 'fundamental disequilibrium'.

The greatest weakness of the Bretton Woods system in practice was the difficulty of making exchange rate adjustments solely by means of infrequent and fairly large devaluations. Exactly the same difficulty plagued the ERM in the second half of the 1980s. While the ERM was in principle more flexible, allowing for periodical adjustments by mutual agreement, in practice it came to be operated as a rigid, fixed rate system. Moreover, in tune with the spirit of the 1980s, no provision was made for taking account of the potentially deflationary effects of the system; and there was no recognition of the special responsibility of the major creditor, Germany, as there had been with the United States in the heyday of Bretton Woods. The proposed arrangements for transition to full monetary union set out in the Treaty of Maastricht would accentuate these deflationary pressures.

Can we find a better mechanism for keeping exchange rates as stable as possible, consistent with any divergencies in inflation rates and evolving balance of payments situations: in other words avoiding unnecessary fluctuations and smoothing out any longer-term adjustments? Should any revised ERM have some sort of 'crawling peg' mechanism, rather than leaving adjustments to be made in traumatic steps? If such a mechanism could be devised, it would obviate the large-scale speculation and political crises associated with the present system. One possibility could be to have fairly wide bands, and each month move the centre of the band to the level at which it finished the previous month. This would at least avoid the pressure of very short-term speculation.

The problem of such schemes, however, is that when it is clear that one currency is moving continuously downwards (or upwards), a corresponding interest rate differential will become inevitable. Individual countries would therefore have difficulty in operating interest rate policies designed primarily to suit their own internal macro situation. Of course, in so far as the exchange rate movements reflected disparate inflation rates, the interest rate differentials would tend to equalise real interest rates and would thus be a natural concomitant of a free market in credit. But if the interest rate differential reflected, say, a gradual devaluation to put right the UK balance of payments, the differential needed to equalise returns to investors would involve a higher real interest rate for UK borrowers (whether they borrowed in sterling or another European currency). For this and other reasons, it would thus be important, unlike our entry into the ERM, for countries to enter the new system at rates which were consistent with their longer-term balance of payments needs.

Further investigation is needed into what measures could be taken to minimise speculative currency movements. There are two main approaches. The first is to reinforce the mechanism for combating speculation by reducing the likelihood and expectation that it will be successful. The second is to make speculation itself more expensive. As regards the first approach, it is an obvious weakness of the original ERM that the task of countering speculative pressures depended on the agreement of central banks to take counter-action, in particular the Bundesbank. This limited the resources employed and created suspicion that the enthusiasm with which current parities will be supported will depend heavily on the Bundesbank's attitude to the currency in question. There is a case for a European monetary fund with greater resources which would automatically operate to preserve existing parities. (Indeed a similar case exists on a world-wide scale for a reform of the IMF.) The second approach is to consider whether financial regulation or taxation could be used to reduce the potential gains from currency speculation (see Chapter 14 of this volume, by Ruth Kelly). Europe has been so hypnotised by the supposed benefits of removing the presumed 'distortions' associated with the control of capital movements that it has not fully realised (as, for example, opinion in North America seems to have done) that large-scale currency speculation has become a major anti-social phenomenon that needs to be tackled. A major problem is the fact that movements between two European currencies can be made outside the jurisdiction of the Community.

Monetary Policy

The irony of the present situation is that as a hangover from the monetarist era governments are talking as if monetary policy is the main and most effective weapon for stimulating recovery in a situation where everything is conspiring to make it particularly difficult to use, and of only limited value. Those countries which have left the ERM have rather more room to manoeuvre than those which have remained in it, but the level of German interest rates inhibits reductions by either group. We are thus all left dependent on the Bundesbank's reaction to internal German developments as the main determinant of European interest levels. It is not surprising in these circumstances that France, in particular, should see the appeal of a European Central Bank whose policies would be more attuned to the needs of the Community as a whole. But if we are to consider monetary policy in the context of achieving full employment, the Maastricht proposals for a European Central Bank must be highly suspect.

The question of whether a European Central Bank or existing national central banks should be independent is not a marginal matter of judgement as to whether central bankers or politicians are likely to be the most competent arbiters of monetary policy, but goes to the heart of the objectives and philosophy of economic policy. The Maastricht concept of an independent central bank dedicated to the achievement of price stability is flawed in two ways. First, the argument for independence is that bankers will take more unpopular decisions than politicians; by this is meant, they will tolerate higher levels of unemployment in the pursuit of price stability. Second, the idea that price stability can be achieved solely by monetary policy is wrong, both in theory and in practice. In so far as price stability, or a low rate of inflation, is achievable by managing demand, both monetary and fiscal policy affect demand. There is no reason to suppose that curbing demand by the one means has intrinsically any more effect on inflation than curbing it by the other. But, of course, price stability is not achievable solely by manipulating demand, however high a price you are prepared to pay in terms of unemployment. Rates of inflation depend as much on the culture of pay bargaining as the manipulation of demand. Germany is a prime example.

The concept of an independent central bank dedicated to the achievement of price stability is thus inimical to the pursuit of full employment on two counts. Its governors have a formal objective which takes no account of employment considerations and whose pursuit will frequently be in conflict with them. In addition, the implication that the monetary authorities on their own, rather than monetary and fiscal policy acting together, should be responsible for demand management is totally misconceived. These objections are compounded in the case of the proposed European Central Bank by the fact that without any Federal government (or parliament) to lean on it, independence would be much more of a reality than the actual position in the United States or Germany, where the central banks' nominal independence is to some extent tempered by the political framework within which they have to operate.

This suggests therefore that in considering how to interpret or amend the Maastricht Treaty in a manner consistent with the pursuit of full employment, the proposed independence of the European Central Bank is a major obstacle to be overcome. The obligation to 'start the process leading to the independence' of national central banks is a more immediate problem, because it comes into the second stage of transition starting on 1 January 1994 (Article 109e.15), although we should presumably not be in technical breach of our Treaty obligation as long as the second stage was still in process. Making the Bank of England independent could seriously hinder the pursuit of an expansionary demand strategy in the coming years. The corollary is, of course, that if the Bank of England remains under national political control we cannot become members of the European system of central banks run by the European Central Bank. We would thus be tacitly vetoing membership of EMU as long as the European Central Bank remained independent of political control. This would be consistent with the view that monetary union is a corollary of full political union and should not precede it.

Postponing the creation of a European Central Bank would not necessarily mean a continuation of the degree of German dominance that we are experiencing at the moment. Germany hegemony reflects a situation where the Bundesbank wants rates higher than other countries would like if left to their own devices, rather than the size of the German economy or any predominance in financial markets. If for any reason other countries wanted to raise rates relative to Germany, they might find it easier to move in this direction, although they would on occasion be inhibited by the consequent upward pressure on their exchange rates. German influence is thus not a simple matter of the power or size of the German economy, but reflects its success in keeping down inflation combined with a desire to keep interest rates relatively high. It is not obvious that the Germans will always opt for high real interest rates. Their dominance might not be so marked if they wished to reduce interest rates as much, or to a greater extent, than other countries – because for instance they were experiencing a more serious recession.

It is an unfortunate accident of history that German reunification has been taken as requiring high interest rates at a time when the rest of Europe wants to reduce them. If demand in the German economy weakens, or if it is less successful in avoiding price inflation, the Bundesbank may no longer be so dominating an influence. Paradoxically, the greater the convergence of price inflation and the conjuncture of demand in Community countries, the less need there will be for a European Central Bank to establish a common European monetary policy. And without such convergence we shall in any event be well away from satisfying the conditions for monetary union. We need not therefore be too concerned at adopting policies which delay the emergence of a European Central Bank.

The first requirement for improving monetary conditions in Europe is greater exchange stability through reforming the ERM. The other major requirement as far as monetary policy is concerned, is a German recognition of the need for lower interest rates. It seems unlikely at present that the Bundesbank would be prepared to make any very significant long-term policy commitment. The best that can be hoped for is probably a vague statement in this direction subscribed to by the German government and some further operational lowering of interest rates by the Bundesbank.

Fiscal Policy

As long as European interest rates are effectively controlled by the Bundesbank it seems unlikely that an expansionary monetary policy will be the spearhead of any Community recovery programme. Moreover, lower interest rates in themselves seem likely to have only a limited impact in stimulating demand. In Britain, at any rate, the price of credit is not the main factor limiting private investment. The effect of the recession on profits and the uncertainties about future demand are probably more important. In addition for those, mainly small, firms who are reliant on bank borrowing to finance investment, cheaper credit does not mean easily available credit. The banks' bad debt experience has led them to be much more wary about making new loans.

The view that the recession can be cured solely by reducing interest rates has become a popular one with financial commentators who are reluctant to face up to the implications of taking budgetary action. But it is really evading the problem.

The main stimulus must come from fiscal policy. It is the apparent reluctance of European governments to take such action that presents the major obstacle to any effective programme. Willingness to use fiscal policy seems to depend on a balance of four factors. On the one hand, the extent to which the reduction of unemployment is seen as an economic and political priority; and the strength or otherwise of the belief in the efficacy of higher public expenditure or lower taxation as a stimulus. On the other, fear that any stimulus may lead to a renewal of inflation; and concern about running a larger public sector deficit – either because of possible reactions in financial markets or considerations about the longer-term growth of public debt.

As far as the efficacy of fiscal action is concerned, there seems little doubt that in present circumstances either an increase in government expenditure or a cut in taxation will lead to an increase in national expenditure and output, both directly in the short term, and then indirectly through the operation of the multiplier on personal consumption and the effects of higher activity in increasing investment. The longer-term effects depend on whether the economy would have eventually recovered to a similar level of activity of its own accord and what were the nature of the longer-term constraints on the level of activity.

Models which suggest that a fiscal stimulus will not alter the level of activity in the medium term tend to give a misleading impression of what is at stake. They seem merely to assume that the level to which unemployment can be reduced is set by some such constraint as its effect on the level of inflation or on the balance of payments, which would have come into effect in any event. Furthermore, they ignore the fact that a higher path of demand and output in the short term will avert the closure of capacity and loss of skills and lead to a higher level of industrial investment and new company creation. Thus the effect of a short-term stimulus is to lead to a higher level of effective productive capacity in the medium term. This will in turn lead to a higher level of exports. Most, if not all, models, tend to neglect this fact and assume that exports are merely a function of foreign demand and cost competitiveness; thus ignoring both the quality and quantity of the exporters' industrial capacity and range of products.

It is difficult to do justice to some of the arguments against the use of fiscal policy, because they are so riddled with inconsistencies. But since they have such a powerful sway on the politicians and officials who make the relevant decisions, it is important to meet them head-on. The most widespread is the popular view that budget deficits lead to inflation. In the Keynesian era it was widely recognised that this was only true if deficits led to general levels of excessive demand. But the monetarists have revived old beliefs that budget deficits automatically lead to price inflation (on their reasoning, through the money supply). It has therefore become necessary to keep reiterating the obvious fact that both budgetary and monetary policy may lead to either excessive or deficient demand. Whether any increases in budget deficits are appropriate depends on the state of demand. Many economists and others who accept this, however, assume that those who work in financial markets are incapable of absorbing such an elementary truth. They then too readily assume that the deliberate use of deficit budgeting must be constrained by the assumed prejudices of the markets – although what counts in the end in the markets is success or failure, not policy, whether it be at government or corporate level.

The next more sophisticated inhibition is that increased government borrowing will raise interest rates, and in the extreme case any such rise could 'crowd out' private investment and nullify any expansionary effects. The fact is that the general level of interest rates in any country is primarily set by its central bank subject to the constraints of international pressures i.e. other countries' interest rates and exchange rate considerations. The direct effects of changes in the supply of government bills or bonds is minimal and more likely to affect the yield curve than the general level of rates. This is particularly true now that there is a highly developed international bond market and differences in bond yields for the same maturity depend primarily on exchange rate considerations. Indeed increased borrowing by a government in its own currency will only have a significant effect in so far as it affects expectations of inflation and hence exchange rates.

Is there a public debt problem?

The latest, and currently most fashionable argument inhibiting counter-cyclical fiscal policies is concern about the effect on future interest payments on national debt. The OECD secretariat has been to the fore in making chilling statements about so-called 'structural deficits'. The OECD classify any change in budget deficits not directly attributable to recession as a 'change in the structural deficit'. Thus any counter-cyclical change over and above the operation of the automatic stabilisers is in their view a disturbing 'deterioration' in the 'structural deficit', rather than a welcome fiscal stimulus.[1]

A further major weakness in their approach is the concept of structural deficit being defined in terms of a trend, rather than full employment, level of activity. This means that a trend away from full employment (as in the 1980s) is regarded as creating a structural deterioration in public finances to be met by taxation or expenditure changes which are likely to aggravate such an adverse trend. Indeed the whole OECD approach is largely based on the fallacious assumption that the level of activity is unaffected by fiscal policy.

The most fundamental criticism of the OECD approach is to question the validity of a constant (or falling) debt to GNP ratio as a desirable policy objective.[2] It should be noted, incidentally, that the significant burden is not the volume of outstanding debt but the level of interest payments. A better measure would be the ratio of government interest payments to GNP.

There might appear to be a distinction between interest payable abroad, which could be seen as representing a real burden on the country, and interest payable at home, which merely involves transfer payments from the citizen as taxpayer to the citizen as *rentier*. But on closer examination it can be seen that merely selling bonds abroad does not affect the country's *net* interest payable abroad, unless it were at the same time to involve a corresponding increase in the balance of payments deficit. In other words, it is the balance of payments which determines the future burden of interest payments abroad, not whether a budget deficit is financed by selling bonds at home or to foreigners.

A country is in no sense poorer because it has a larger public debt. Indeed, greater public borrowing at a time when resources would otherwise be under-used will almost certainly make the country richer in future than it would otherwise have been. This is certainly true if the borrowing is spent on extra public investment; it will then have better public capital, such as schools, hospitals or roads. Thus if a higher public debt reflects a higher public capital stock, this should be greeted as a favourable, rather than unfavourable, indicator of national prosperity. Fear of increasing the future level of debt should not prevent us from using unemployed resources now to provide public facilities that will benefit us in future. Even if the extra borrowing merely reflected higher current public expenditure or lower taxation, but brought speedier recovery from the recession, it would have stimulated more industrial investment and a higher level of capacity than would otherwise have been the case.

The growth of public debt *per se* is a transfer problem of increasing taxation, or charges of various kinds, to meet the interest payments. The problem of financing future debt charges is merely part of the general problem of financing public expenditure in advanced economies. Once the peace dividend has been absorbed, we shall return to a position where expenditure on public services and infrastructure may tend to increase faster than national income, both because of an increase in relative prices and because of increasing standards. If these services are to remain predominantly in the public sector, this may lead to closer consideration of charges or contributions, with more rather than less emphasis on the 'insurance' principle for things such as health or social security benefits.

Much of the play made with debt ratios etc. is really based on antagonism towards the growth of public expenditure as such, and nothing to do with the real problems of public finance. The December 1992 OECD *Economic Outlook* gave the game away by holding up the present New Zealand government's dismantling of the welfare state as 'the leading example' of how to 'improve the efficiency and effectiveness of all forms of public spending'. It is unfortunate that this sort of political prejudice from an established international organisation should overlay any attempt to distinguish where, or to what extent, growing public debt could be a significant problem.

None of this is to deny that a growing interest burden on public debt may have undesirable consequences. But the irony of the present situation is that the consequence of failing to take expansionary action now is likely to be the perpetuation of the level of public sector deficits arising from the recession. It is only likely that these deficits will get back to lower levels if we can achieve a higher level of activity. Even in narrow public debt terms, there is thus a strong case for accepting a further increase in deficits temporarily in order to regain a higher level of economic activity.

Community-wide action

Fiscal action would necessarily be mainly national, but there could be a Community-wide element, such as the proposals for infrastructure projects financed by the European Investment Bank (see Chapter 15 in this volume, by Francis Cripps and Terry Ward). Since most projects will be national or regional in nature, the European element is more a matter of refinancing or window-dressing, than actual management. This is where a serious consideration of the debt problems of countries such as Italy could be constructive. The price other countries may have to pay for limited expansion, and avoiding residual areas of depression, may be to 'Europeanise' the debt problems of weaker members. The EIB proposals are a modest welcome first step. They suggest that floating 'European Recovery Bonds' with the collective financial backing of the Community to refinance part of the debt incurred by individual members should be carefully examined – whether on a project or more general basis.

In coordinating fiscal expansion by national governments, the main emphasis initially would be on the magnitude of the stimulus in each country, rather than on the particular measures to be adopted. But in the longer run it would be necessary to ensure that national action did not run counter to the inevitable move towards fiscal harmonisation inherent in the movement towards economic union. Thus there are practical, as well as specified limits on the extent to which indirect taxes can differ. Increasingly there will also be a need to harmonise corporate tax systems and rates, and tax regimes for the rich and mobile. On the expenditure side, there will be growing pressure to harmonise social security benefits, at least in terms of the rules and ratios of benefits to wages, if not in money terms. The same may eventually apply to services such as health and education, but that is in the more distant future.

The importance of fiscal expansion

There is a serious danger that unless European governments are prepared to take budgetary measures to stimulate demand, the Community will continue to experience heavy unemployment. Misplaced concern about the problems of public debt could have untold political and economic consequences. It tends to lead to self-defeating manoeuvres to reduce unemployment by public investment schemes or incentives to firms offset by increases in taxation or other cuts in expenditure.

The 'Clinton' approach, of combining longer-term measures to increase taxation and reduce expenditure with a short-term stimulus, is superficially attractive, and Mr Lamont was not the only European finance minister ostensibly to follow in his footsteps. But there are two major dangers – the first, as in the US, is that the stimulus may fall by the wayside, or as in the UK may never exist. The second is that the 'longer-term' deflationary measures may come into effect before there is any worthwhile recovery. It is important to distinguish between the medium-term need to avoid too rapid an increase in demand as present capacity limits are reached, and the longer-term necessity for demand to grow faster than trend for a number of years to ensure a return to full employment. This may well require a relatively 'relaxed' fiscal stance.

Pay bargaining

To shift emphasis convincingly towards restoring full employment it will be essential to find ways of keeping inflation in check other than by restricting demand. This is the most powerful lesson that we must learn from the 1980s. The need is twofold. The first is to avoid the general deflationary bias in the monetarist approach and Maastricht. The second is to minimise the difficulties arising from differential rates of inflation in countries such as the UK and Italy. Although the problem of the wage/price spiral has hitherto been regarded purely as a national one, its solution by non-deflationary means has now become a major European problem. The fact that the recession has temporarily slowed down the rate of wage increases has little bearing on the solution of the underlying problem, which will almost inevitably re-emerge with any sustained recovery.

The growth of European-wide bargaining will give the problem a new dimension. German unification provides a striking warning of the dangers of pressures to establish common wage levels while the absolute levels of productivity differ. If multi-country bargaining avoids this pitfall it could encourage uniform *percentage* rates of growth in plants in different parts of Europe. This might be an improvement, as the current tendency is for money wages to rise faster in countries such as the UK than in Germany. But for many years, at any rate, most pay-bargaining will remain national or regional. The objective must then be to bring to bear the same sort of general economic considerations as has been the case in major German negotiations. The precise method of attack must vary from country to country.[3] The reform of pay bargaining is, however, a key aspect of convergence with fuller employment and now needs to be brought firmly onto the Community agenda. It will have more significance for the average worker than the Social Chapter.

Supply side measures

So called 'supply-side' policies are very fashionable on both the right and left of the political spectrum – though with rather different measures in mind – and any discussion of policy would be incomplete without them. But a distinction needs to be made between the (albeit related) objectives of (a) speeding up productivity growth, the introduction of new products and so on, and (b) reducing unemployment. Encouraging the development and introduction of new technology will help one country or one group of countries, such as the Community, to survive in a competitive world and to avoid being held back by balance of payments problems. To this extent they will ease the problem of cutting unemployment. In addition, technological innovation tends to stimulate investment and improve employment, provided the new capital equipment is not largely imported.

Although measures to encourage technological development or improve education and training are highly desirable in their own right as important determinants of the long-term rate of growth, they are not basically a cure for unemployment. Nor is the need for them a particular phenomenon of the 1990s. They were as, or more, important in the post-war era of full employment.

The need to rebuild European capacity in order to ensure a continued reduction in unemployment after the recession is ended calls for new measures. The problem is to encourage firms to expand when they fear the risks of doing so. One of the legacies of the 1980s will be that cautious and conservative management will have survived where the more adventurous have gone to the wall. On the macroeconomic side, low interest rates and emphasis on a continuation of expansionary policies will be crucial. On the supply side, the need is for policies and institutions that ease the problems and risk of expansion. For example, in the case of small firms, a major need in the UK is for more equity finance and less reliance on overdrafts and loans. For larger firms in aerospace, for example, governments and the Commission can help by tackling policy questions such as defence programmes and airline procurement in such a way as to encourage and support major European companies. They should in particular be trying to preserve what is temporarily excess capacity during the recession, rather than encouraging its closure.

For too long the development of the Community has been conceived mainly in terms of removing constraints on competition, and not in terms of building up industrial cooperation and strong European-wide enterprises.

Summary and Conclusions

The high and rising level of unemployment is now the major challenge facing the European Community. To combat it will require not only action by individual national governments, but also collective action within the Community. Although the current recession has accentuated the problem, mass unemployment had already re-emerged in the 1980s. To reverse this process will require a fundamental revolution in prevailing attitudes of thought and approaches to economic policy.

The deflationary bias of the convergence provisions in the Treaty of Maastricht raises the question of whether the whole movement towards economic and monetary union necessarily, or inevitably, conflicts with the goal of restoring full employment. The concept of an independent European Central Bank dedicated to the achievement of price stability would hinder the combined use of monetary and fiscal policy as instruments of demand management in the pursuit of full employment.

The level of trade within the EC is, however, already so high that it has become difficult to engineer full employment in one country alone. The need is for coordinated expansionary policies. One country expanding on its own will experience a heavy leakage of higher demand into imports. But if they all expand together, countries' individual initiatives to expand demand and output will reinforce each other. There will be less danger of any one country running into balance of payments problems or its rate of inflation getting out of line. Coordinating expansion also has important budgetary implications because it means that a coordinated series of measures will result in a greater eventual increase in activity, and hence improvement in the budget deficit.

As long as European interest rates are effectively set by the Bundesbank it seems unlikely that there will be an expansionary monetary policy to spearhead any recovery programme. Moreover, lower interest rates in themselves seem likely to have only a limited impact in stimulating demand. The main stimulus must come from a Community-wide series of fiscal measures. The apparent reluctance of European governments to take such action is at present a major obstacle to any effective recovery programme. Concern about public sector deficits is in danger of becoming self-defeating. Unless positive action is taken to stimulate economic activity, high public sector deficits will continue throughout the Community. Increasing public expenditure or cutting taxes during the recession will lead to a temporary increase in deficits, but will reduce them in the longer term. Fiscal action would necessarily be mainly national, but there could be a Community-wide element, such as the proposals for infrastructure projects financed by the European Investment Bank. The option of issuing European Recovery Bonds with the collective financial backing of the Community to refinance part of the debt incurred by individual members should be examined carefully.

We need to devise a better mechanism for keeping exchange rates as stable as possible, consistent with any divergencies in inflation rates and evolving balance of payments situations. This points to some form of 'crawling peg' mechanism, combined with measures to reduce currency speculation. There is a case for a European monetary fund with the resources to counter speculative movements.

To shift emphasis towards restoring full employment it will be essential to find ways of keeping inflation in check other than by restricting demand. Although the problems of pay bargaining have hitherto been regarded purely as national ones, avoiding a wage/price spiral without resort to deflation has now become a European problem. The growth of European-wide bargaining will give the problem a new dimension. German unification provides a stark warning of the danger of pressures to establish common wage levels while the absolute levels of productivity differ.

One of the immediate tasks for industrial policy during the recession is to avoid the shutdown of plant and loss of workforces that will be needed once demand recovers. It should be recognised that such rescue operations are not at odds with the long-term pursuit of greater efficiency. Once recovery is well advanced, however, one of the most difficult problems in reducing unemployment below pre-recession levels will be to instil sufficient confidence in industry to expand its capacity and labour force. This is now one of the major tasks of industrial policy.

The machinery of European integration, with or without Maastricht, does not exist as an end in itself, but as a means of improving the operation of the European economy and hence safeguarding its political stability. Failure to tackle the unemployment problem would not only be an economic disaster of the first magnitude, but could lead to widespread dissaffection with the whole political framework of the Community.

Notes

Foreword

1 Another important point arises over the interconnection between budgetary and monetary policies. If public works are proposed, does *ceteris paribus* on monetary policy means no change in interest rates, or in the quantity of money?
2 More constructively, they might describe 'accompanying policies' which might be taken to accompany devaluation, so as to increase the chance of the whole package remaining effective – e.g. reform of the machinery for wage-determination. There are disadvantages in a country getting a reputation for over-frequent devaluation.

Chapter 1

1 We are grateful to John Grieve Smith and Brian Reddaway for comments.
2 See Michie and Wilkinson (1992).
3 While originally not acknowledging Rowthorn, Layard and Nickell have since done so.
4 The size of the market for the individual imperfectly competitive firm (and hence the employment it can offer) is determined by its price and the price of close substitutes. If the workers employed by that firm accept a lower wage so that the firm can retain its monopoly profits at a lower price, it will be able to increase its output and its market share, but only at the expense of other firms and the employment they offer. But of course if all firms lower their wages there will be no change in relative prices and no increase in demand.
5 Figures from De Sousa and Castro (1992:22).
6 See Singh (1987) and Rowthorn and Wells (1987).
7 See also McCombie and Thirlwall (1992).
8 See Joan Robinson's inaugural lecture, 'The New Mercantilism', Robinson (1966).
9 Datastream and WEFA, reported in the *Financial Times* of 26 April 1993. The figures for France and Italy are the latest available, referring to 1991.
10 For a detailed analysis of the Conservative government's labour market policies, see Deakin and Wilkinson, 1990.
11 The Department of Employment estimates that it is notified of approximately one-third of all job vacancies.
12 Firms involved include Tesco, Sainsburys and Safeways in retailing, Coats Viyella and Courtaulds in textiles and clothing and a range of leading firms in hotels, catering and leisure.
13 In 1982 the 'earnings related supplement' to the standard unemployment benefit was abolished; in 1984 the allowance for dependant children of those on unemployment

benefit went. The maternity grant which used to be available for all mothers giving birth was abolished in 1987. The industrial disablement benefit was abolished in 1986 for all those whose disability is assessed at less than 14 per cent. In 1987 the death grant was abolished. And the automatic link of pensions with earnings was broken by the Tories. For the financial implications of such policies, see Rowthorn (1992).

14 *Financial Times*, 13 May 1993.

15 As might be expected, the British government is pioneering this alternative. But Professor Dennis Snower, the self-proclaimed originator of the government Workstart scheme, fears that the government is not sufficiently ambitious, by only subsidising employers to the extent of £2,340 per year for each unemployed person found a job (*Financial Times*, 19 May 1993).

16 During the hard years of the mid-1790s the rulers of the countryside, following the example of Berkshire magistrates meeting at Speenhamland, decided to subsidise low wages out of local rates where the labourers' family income' fell below subsistence. See Hobsbawm and Rudé (1969) for a description and discussion of the system, from which this section draws.

17 Hobsbawm and Rudé (1969:47).

18 Polyani (1945:85), cited in Hobsbawm and Rudé (1969:48–9).

19 Hobsbawm and Rudé (1969:48).

20 Hobsbawm and Rudé (1969:50).

21 A May 1993 EC document on tackling unemployment proposed reducing employers' social security contributions for unskilled workers (see *The Guardian*, 14 May 1993). The dangers associated with such arrangements whereby private sector wages are subsidised from the public purse are also relevant for considering the relative merits of government employment creation policies of, on the one hand, expanding public sector employment and, on the other, subsidising employment in the private sector, as discussed in Chapter 12 by Andrew Glyn and Bob Rowthorn who find in any case that subsidising private sector employment is less desirable in terms of balance of payments and inflation constraints.

22 Hobsbawm and Rudé (1969:50–1).

23 It also needs to be stressed that these long-term economic costs from divisive labour market policies are quite separate from the additional direct costs associated with unemployment itself – estimated at roughly £60 billion a year for the UK alone, of which £24 billion is borne by taxpayers, £12 billion by lost profits and £24 billion by the unemployed (estimates by Richard Layard, reported in the *Financial Times* of 9 February 1993).

Chapter 2

This research has been financed by the ESRC Macromodelling Consortium.

1 For the most recent, and fullest exposition of the general approach to labour markets, see Layard, Nickell and Jackman (1991). As the framework is well known, we will discuss it only briefly here.

2 These issues are extensively discussed in Anderton, Barrell, in't Veld and Pittis (1992) and Anderton, Barrell and in't Veld (1992). We will keep our discussion brief and refer interested readers to these two papers as well as to Layard, Nickell and Jackman (1991).

3 In another simulation we examined the effects of relaxing the Maastricht criterion completely, by assuming that governments maintain the deficit ratio at its historical average of the last five years. The effects of this change in policy are dramatic and persistent. Output increases at its peak by 2–3% for all countries and unemployment drops by as much as a percentage point. However, in the short term there is a contraction in activity as long-term interest rates rise. Inflation is also higher in the

medium term, because higher interest rates are associated with a depreciating exchange rate.

Chapter 3

1 I am grateful to Robin Marris for discussions on this topic, and to Dan Corry and participants at seminars at the University of Manchester and at the University College Wales at Aberystwyth for comments on an earlier draft of this chapter. Many helpful comments were also made by my co-authors, to whom I am grateful and in particular to Andrew Glyn.

2 Annual data for prices and unemployment rates were used over the 1950–91 period. The analysis was actually started in 1952, to allow for the transition of many economies from the disruption of the Second World War. The data for the 1950s and early 1960s were taken from Maddison (1982), and for subsequent years from OECD sources.

3 Using the UROOT test in the TSP programme with a constant and one lag in most of the regressions, this being in general sufficient to obtain random residuals.

4 In the other eight countries, the calculated values of the test statistic range between -1.74 and -2.85, compared to the critical value at the 5% level of -3.50.

5 Ormerod (1992) gives a detailed account of the events in the UK in 1974–75 which led to the disastrous shifts which took place in that country.

6 As an indication of this, the Durbin-Watson statistics in these regressions are invariably well below 1.

7 Where Q(3) is the Box-Ljung Q-statistic for random residuals from one through three lags, N(2) is the Jarques-Bera test for normality, and RESET is the Ramsey test for linearity. The coefficient is stable using the Chow tests to test for breaks within the sample period.

Chapter 5

1 We are very grateful to Andrew Glyn, John Grieve Smith, Brian Reddaway, and Solomos Solomou for comments.

2 The estimates for the United States in Table 5.1 in the 'Galenson and Zellner' columns are actually taken from Lebergott (1964), as reproduced in Eichengreen and Hatton (1988).

3 Maddison (1991) has countered that Eichengreen and Hatton's criticisms of his data are unjustified as they wish to allow for underemployment in agriculture and services, which he considers is inconsistent with measures of employment and labour force.

4 That unemployment continues to cause such problems in the 1980s and 1990s is well illustrated by Burchell (1992); the psychological and other harmful effects of unemployment suggest that the unemployed are not simply enjoying leisure as a result of their intertemporal optimisation decisions.

5 The reconstructed gold standard consisted of various types of commodity money regimes. The commonest was the gold exchange standard, where central banks held some fraction of their reserves in foreign exchange rather than entirely in precious metals. Other types of regime included the gold bullion standard, the gold coin standard, the qualified gold standard and the silver standard.

6 As each country declared a parity against gold, this immediately established a network of fixed bilateral exchange rates. Only small variations in exchange rates were possible since an exchange rate could only rise or fall to the gold points (given by the costs of shipping, insurance and short-run credit) at which it became profitable to engage in gold market arbitrage (Eichengreen, 1989).

7 The balance of payments on current account was in surplus from 1924 to 1929, apart

from 1926 when the impact of the General Strike resulted in a small deficit (see Feinstein, 1972). The adverse impact of the overvaluation on competitiveness, however, led to smaller surpluses than in the immediate pre-war period.

8 During the period 1913–29, Britain's growth rate of 0.7% per annum was approximately one-third the world average (Kitson and Solomou, 1990a).

9 The chosen phasing for the policy-on period is 1924–29. As previously noted, the sequence of stabilizations makes it difficult to identify a clear start of the fixed exchange rate regime. This period was chosen as a suitable mid-point that accords with many peak-to-peak estimates. It excludes the depression period which is dealt with separately.

10 Cooper (1992:2125) observes that Friedman and Schwartz, 'having never met a central bank they liked, of course attributed the severity of the depression to the perverse behaviour of the Federal Reserve Board'.

11 See, for example, Eichengreen (1992) and Temin (1989).

12 The last major country to go into recession was Spain (1931Q1), which had a flexible exchange rate.

13 It should be noted that although many countries went into recession before the onset of world recession, their domestic problems were in part conditioned by developments overseas. Many of those countries that first went into recession were highly dependent on capital exports from the United States. When these funds dried up they had to adopt restrictive policies.

14 In his study of the gold standard and its lessons for European monetary union, Mića Panić (1992) demonstrates that monetary union today could prove even more damaging than was the gold standard, given the massive scale of migration which is unlikely to be accepted today, and the huge investments in colonial countries which again are unlikely to be mirrored by equivalent capital flows today.

15 The impact of the balance of payments constraint can be illustrated with a simple example. Take a country with national income (Y) of 100 units and exports (X) and imports (M) each of 20 units. The foreign trade multiplier can be expressed as $Y=X/m$ where m, the propensity to import, is 0.2. There is excess capacity and therefore an effective balance of payments constraint, in that unilateral reflation will raise imports and move the trade balance into deficit. A solution, therefore, is active trade policy which can raise output and maintain balance of payments equilibrium. If an effective devaluation is implemented, which, say left X unchanged at 20 units but which succeeded in reducing m from 0.2 to 0.18, the new trade multiplier would therefore be $Y=20/0.18$, so that national income increases to 111 units, and even with the reduced import propensity the final volume of imports will still be 20 units. Thus an independent trade policy has increased national income without affecting the volume of trade, although the openness of the economy has fallen. This example is obviously highly simplistic, as it does not take into account price effects, elasticities or other injections into the circular flow of income. What it does illustrate, however, is that active trade policy to alleviate an external constraint need not have adverse effects on other trading nations.

16 For an examination of the strengths and limitations of this argument, see Kitson and Solomou (1990a).

17 The choice of suitable peak-to-peak periods is complicated by the variable phasing of economic growth, and by data limitations. In particular the period 1925–29 may be considered too short; a separate exercise was therefore undertaken replacing this period with 1913–29, and the conclusions are broadly similar.

18 As argued in detail by, for example, Worswick (1984a, 1984b, 1984c) and Dimsdale (1984).

19 For evidence on the statistical correlations, and a discussion of the cyclical behaviour of wages and its policy implications, see Michie (1987).

20 'Of all bad-neighbourly conduct among trading nations, the worst is to go into a slump' – Joan Robinson (1966:4).

21 See Chapter 12 by Glyn and Rowthorn for a discussion of employment creation measures.
22 The relation between the *General Theory* and fascist economic policies is discussed by Keynes himself in his preface to the German edition of 1936. The version which appears in the *Collected Works of John Maynard Keynes* (published by the Royal Economic Society) is not complete, omitting, for example, Keynes's statement that his theory is 'applicable to situations in which national leadership is more pronounced' (see Schefold, 1980).

Chapter 6

1 We are grateful to Daniele Archibugi and Brian Reddaway for comments.
2 This section draws on Halimi (1993).
3 Parti Socialiste (1980:173).
4 Mitterrand (1980:303).
5 Parti Socialiste (1980:191).
6 Parti Socialiste (1980:88 and 90).
7 Mitterrand (1980:37).
8 Parti Socialiste (1980:18).
9 Parti Socialiste (1980:189).
10 Ross, Hoffman and Malzacher (1987:6).
11 Parti Socialiste (1980:91).
12 Mitterrand (1980:286).
13 Lipietz (1982).
14 Parti Socialiste (1980:190, 222, 224; emphasis added).
15 Parti Socialiste (1980:180; emphasis added).
16 Parti Socialiste (1980:189).
17 Parti Socialiste (1980:223).
18 Parti Socialiste (1980:223–4; emphasis added).
19 Parti Socialiste (1980:181).
20 OECD, *Economic Survey of France, 1985*.
21 OECD, *Economic Survey of France, 1990–1*.
22 OECD, *Historical Statistics, 1960–83*.
23 Glyn (1992:146).
24 Marc Lombard, 'A re-examination of the failure of Keynesian expansionary policies in France in 1981–3', unpublished paper, p. 23. The changes were not enough to offset the worse terms of trade and appear to reflect a standard J-curve effect.
25 The government also imposed a ban after 1982–83 on indexing wages to prices. In practice this led mainly to reduced wage increases in the public sector. It was achieved with the implicit agreement of certain unions, while others were too weak to contest it through strike action. See Hoang-Ngoc, Lallement and Michon (1992:7–8).
26 Mauroy (1982:17–19, 25, 28).
27 Lipietz (1985:179).
28 See Halimi (1993), who analyses the similar (monetarist) mistakes made by the Left in 1924, 1936 and 1981.
29 For a discussion of the lessons of the Blum experiment, see Halimi (1993) and Kalecki (1938). Kalecki (p. 39) argues that

> the increase in the budget deficit under the Blum Government, generally considered tremendous, was quite moderate in 'real' terms. To stimulate business activity appreciably a much greater deficit was needed. And the very recovery which this would have set in motion would have made possible an increase in tax revenues which would have balanced the budget in the following years. . . In order, however, to go forward with the stimulating of

production by budgetary deficit, the Blum Government needed a basis which they failed to secure from the very beginning: the exchange restrictions. The vulgar theory according to which the deficit – in particular when financed by the Central Bank – is an immediate peril to the currency, is deeply rooted among French economists, bankers and rentiers. Thus a 'large-scale deficit policy' must cause a tendency towards the flight of capital, followed often by a depreciation of the currency, which proves in turn the 'French deficit theory' at least, for France!

Even with the actual deficit – not sufficient to initiate recovery – the Blum Government had to face a steady pressure of capital flight which, to put it mildly, was by no means opposed by the leading financiers. Hence the vacillation of the Government between a wish to stimulate the economy and a willingness to reduce the budget deficit. The result was the fall of the Blum Government and the return to an orthodox financial policy.

30 Delors, quoted in *Le Nouvel Observateur*, 24 October 1981.
31 See Halimi (1993:Chapter 4).
32 Pfister (1985:242).
33 Professor Bourguinat, cited in *Le Monde* of 18 October 1983.
34 Chevènement was actually Minister of Industry and Research, the inclusion of 'Research' within the title reflecting the recognition of the need for an explicitly high-tech, high wage industrial policy.
35 Julliard (1988:90).
36 Mauroy, quoted in *Libération*, 11 May 1987. The 'five years' refer to 1981 to 1986, when the Right won the Parliamentary elections.
37 François Mitterrand, speaking on French television *TF1*, 8 April 1981.
38 Bauchard (1986:53).
39 Jacques Delors, the Finance Minister, conceded as much: 'We have some margin for play. We can sustain growth, stimulate the activity, and increase wages.' (quoted in Bauchard, 1986:24).
40 Mauroy (1982:28).
41 On the comparison between the reflation of 1975 and that of 1981, see *Observations et Diagnostics Economiques,* July 1985 (Publication of the Office Français de la Conjoncture Economique).
42 *Le Nouvel Observateur*, 23 January 1982.
43 93 billion francs in 1982 against 56 billion in 1981.
44 According to a study by Raymond Courbis and André Keller reported in *Le Monde* of 24 March 1983. They acknowledge that this attempt to estimate the domestic and international factors does not sum to the actual total (84 billion francs as against 93 billion francs respectively).
45 See Sachs and Wyplosz (1986).
46 See A. Fontenau and P. A. Muet, 'La Politique Economique depuis Mai 1981: Un Premier Bilan', *Observations et Diagnostics Economiques,* Revenue de L'OFce (Observatoire Français de conjuncture économique) No. 4. Similar points are made by M. Beudaert, 'L'année 1982 A Travers les Comptes Nationaux', *Economie et Statistique*, 1983.
47 See Sachs and Wyplosz (1986) and J-P Vesperini, 'L'Economie de la France', *Economica*, Paris, 1985.
48 Banque de France, *Bulletin Trimestriel*, 1981 and 1982.
49 See Lombard (1993).
50 See, for example, Balassa (1985).
51 Petit (1986:396).
52 Petit (1986:396–7).
53 Petit (1986:398).
54 Balassa (1985:316).
55 See Lauber (1987:34).
56 See Machin and Wright (1985:146).

57 Stoffaes, 'The Nationalisations 1981–84: An Initial Assessment', Chapter 6 of Machin and Wright (1985), pp. 144–146.
58 See Soskice (1985:170).
59 *Le Monde*, 10 March 1992.
60 *La Tribune de l'Expansion*, 16 June 1992.
61 Calculations by CEEP (Centre Européen de l'Entreprise Publique), quoted in *Les Accost*, 2 March 1993.
62 *La Tribune de l'Expansion*, 16 June 1992.
63 *Le Monde*, 10 March 1992.
64 As reported in the *Financial Times* of 11 June 1991, p. 4.
65 See Costello, Michie and Milne (1989:50 and 180–1).
66 See *La Tribune de l'Expansion*, 17 June 1992.
67 See Costello, Michie and Milne (1989:103–4). SGS-Thomson sold a 70% share to a Hong Kong electronics and property company, QPL International, in December 1992, after investing in similar plants in Grenoble and Milan.
68 See for example *Libération* of 12 March 1993, and *Le Monde* of 26 May 1992.
69 See Albert (1993:237).
70 Centre d'Etude des Revenus et des Coûts (1989:11, 16, 17, 19).
71 Rocard, cited in *Le Monde* of January 13 1990.
72 As with the modelling by Barrell, Caporale and Sefton (reported in Chapter 2), Blanchard and Muet's simulations of the effects of devaluation have unemployment rates returning to where they started from, but 'throughout the first seven years, unemployment is substantially lower than under the alternative' (p. 41).
73 M. Rocard, 'L'heure de Vérité', *France 2*, 25 April 1993.
74 Study by Crédit National, cited in *Libération*, April 9 1993.
75 Dominique Strauss-Kahn quoted in the *Wall Street Journal Europe* of 18 March 1993.
76 Jeanneney (1977:60).
77 See Costello, Michie and Milne (1989), especially pp. 153–4.

Chapter 8

1 The views expressed are personal and do not commit the Commission of the EC. The authors would like to thank D. Costello for valuable editorial help and Th. Delplace for secretarial assistance.
2 For a systematic review of measurement issues, see Ohly (1993).
3 The impact of economic integration on trade and economic growth should not be considered equivalent to the impact on welfare (in economic terms). Furthermore, the Community has evolved into an embryonic level of government in its own right (e.g. competences in the field of environment policy), the effects of which may not manifest themselves in trade figures or economic growth, but which do have an important impact on welfare.
4 The limited integration of these two economies into the EC economy in 1987, combined with their very different factor endowments *vis-à-vis* the other member states, points to greater scope for inter-industry trade to take place.
5 From 15.9% to 17% for the EC6.
6 Additional rents would arise from the fact that increased competition would raise the substitutability of products, thereby increasing the marginal return on investment. Firms would seek to develop new products and production techniques through higher R&D expenditure, leading to greater capital accumulation.
7 Subsequent refinements to Viner's methodology, such as trade suppression, the isolation of production and consumption effects, are reviewed in de Melo *et al.* (1992).
8 Balassa's study relates to manufactured goods, thereby ignoring the large trade diversion effects on agricultural products.

9 These included changes in sectoral structure, leader–follower convergence, foreign trade effects, economies of scale at the national level, energy effects, natural resource discovery, cost of government regulation and crime, labour (dis)hoarding practices and capacity constraints.

10 Three periods were considered: 1913–50, 1950–73 and 1973–84.

11 The fact that Maddison explicitly includes a foreign trade effect in his calculation does not substantially weaken this suggestion, given the bias towards the underestimation of the effects of economic integration on growth postulated by Baldwin (1992).

12 Growth in productivity is contrasted with the unconditional rate of convergence calculated according to Barro and Sala y Martin (1991).

13 These include growth of export volume, change in trade balance, labour remittances, foreign investment and net EC budgetary payments.

14 Ben-David proxies convergence by calculating the logged differences in member states' per capita income with the average of the EC.

15 Buigues and Sheehy (1993).

16 Which the 1992 European Council in Edinburgh requested the EC Commission to undertake in time to have results available in 1996.

17 Commission of the EC (1991).

18 Italianer (1992).

19 Lehner (1992).

20 A first decision on entry into stage three has to be taken before the end of 1996. At the latest, stage three will begin on 1 January 1999 with those member states which meet the convergence criteria.

21 Article 109j of the Treaty, which is explained in a protocol on convergence attached to the Treaty.

22 Details have been fixed in a protocol on excessive deficits which must be supplemented by secondary legislation before the start of stage two.

23 Some authors have proposed a further strengthening of market mechanisms, for example requiring that highly indebted countries lengthen their debt maturities and that prudential supervision is tightened by treating government securities as risky assets (Begg *et al.*, 1991).

24 It also became clear in the negotiations that the doubts concerning a shared view on policy priorities in EMU which remained in some member states (mainly Germany, but also the Netherlands) would only be overcome by such a convergence test, and the others eventually agreed. See also de Grauwe (1992).

25 Kenen (1992:79).

26 Data are from the European Community's 'Annual Economic Report for 1993', Commission of the EC (1993a).

27 Assuming unchanged policies. Unusually high uncertainties surround the winter 1992/93 economic forecasts.

28 The uncertainty will be considerably reduced once the first rounds of assessments beginning in 1994 have established the application of this criterion.

29 Giovannini (1991) and Portes (1993).

30 The United Kingdom has been granted a derogation from the commitment to join the third stage of EMU. It is therefore not bound by the convergence objectives. Denmark, however, which has a rather similar derogation, has declared it would nevertheless endeavour to meet the objectives.

31 These simulations were undertaken for the IMF Executive Board. Although they were not officially published, they were widely discussed in the press – see, for example, *Libération* of 28 July 1992.

32 For a detailed description, see Reichenbach (1992). If current forecasts are confirmed, Greece may have embarked since 1990 on a similarly successful adjustment.

33 For a full assessment of the economic effects of EMU, see Commission of the EC (1990).

Chapter 9

1 For instance, the institutional context of wage bargaining is important. The less centralised the bargaining process is, the more likely it is that labour will perceive a direct relationship between nominal wages and competitiveness, and between competitiveness and unemployment.

2 Assuming that incomes come from employment.

3 The CEC has constructed a weighted 'synthetic index' of regional disparity using GDP per person employed (0.25) as a productivity measure, per capita GDP (0.25), the unemployment rate adjusted for underemployment (0.40), and the projected labour force change to 1990 (0.10) (CEC, 1987). The problem with this index is that it hides more than it reveals.

4 Figure 9.1 also indicates that the convergence in productivity levels (GDP/employee ratio) which took place prior to 1986 was reversed after that year; this was due to the increases in employment which accompanied the growth of output in the second half of the 1980s.

5 Ireland is a good example; MNEs account for half manufacturing employment, have high export/output ratios and exist in high technology sectors. Indigenous firms account for 25% of manufacturing employment, are small-scale, low technology, and have low export propensities. Ireland's future in the SEM depends on the response of these firms. (Foley and Griffith, 1992.)

6 Eichengreen (1993) estimates the sensitivity of migration to shocks for the UK, Italy and the US. He finds that the elasticity of migration with respect to employment differentials is twice as large in the US as in the European countries.

7 The Social Chapter may adversely affect this flexibility. However, it is necessary for two reasons: (a) adjustment mechanisms may not be sufficient to ensure that weaker regions and groups do not suffer, and (b) the ability to compete in the labour market is not equal as between persons, either for reasons which are permanent (e.g. disability) or temporary (e.g. maternity). The Social Chapter is another way of increasing social cohesion, but it may permit social dumping. Given the low level of intra-European migration, it is unlikely that people will move in response to differences in social provision (Ermish, 1991) – which makes it all the more necessary that social provision is equalled across the Community. Furthermore, unequal provision will introduce further distortions into the labour market adjustment process.

8 Public expenditure at the federal level is usually about 25% of GDP, whereas in unitary states it is about 45%.

9 As opposed to the current level of 1.2% of GDP, and the projected 1997 level of 1.35%.

Chapter 10

1 The research on which this chapter draws was funded as part of the Economic and Social Research Council's 'Single European Market Initiative'. Thanks to James Cornford and Jonathan Michie for helpful comments.

Chapter 11

1 I am grateful to Philip Arestis and Jonathan Michie for comments on the first draft of this chapter.

2 I would see the privatisation programme in Britain since 1979 largely in terms of changing the mode of regulation (though there were clearly other aspects, such as the promotion of share ownership). The original nationalisation programmes may have

had elements of the promotion of industrial development, though arguments in terms of natural monopolies pose the state as a regulatory one.
3 For further discussion which is broadly in tune with the thrust of my argument here, see Arestis and Paliginis (1993, 1994).
4 Hitiris (1988) argues that '[t]he economic conditions of the 1950s and 1960s favoured the non-interventionist approach to industrial policy. Therefore it is not surprising that in the Treaty of Rome there is no specific reference to a need for comprehensive industrial policy'.

Chapter 12

1 Italy lacks the appropriate data for the calculations which follow, as do the so-called peripherals – Portugal, Greece, Spain and Ireland – most of whose employment performance has been even worse than in the core.
2 Throughout this section, statistics on output, employment and total hours of work are all expressed per head of population of working age.
3 This way of decomposing employment performance in order to isolate the contributions of market output growth, productivity, state employment and hours of work is explained in Glyn, 1992, which provides a detailed analysis of the period up to 1986.
4 The state also contributed to maintaining demand for the market sector via an extraordinary rise in transfer payments of more than 1% of market output per year from 1973 to 1979.
5 Somewhat different considerations apply in the case of an inflation-constrained economy, where the induced rise in output and income following a Keynesian fiscal stimulus would have an unacceptable impact on inflation. In this case, fiscal expansion does not lead to a public debt problem, and the increasing difficulties of the economy do not manifest themselves in an explosion of public debt, but in unacceptable inflation.
6 Cuts in working time which allow employment to expand without a rise in market sector output have similar costs to tax-financed increases in state employment (reduction in take-home pay per worker) but with different benefits (increased leisure time rather than improved state services). Problems with cuts in working time to create jobs have been widely discussed (see e.g. Dreze, 1986).
7 Snower's proposal does not go into any detail over these problems. For a discussion of the empirical evidence, see the recent report of the Employment Policy Institute (1993).
8 In multi-person households, the whole family may experience an increase in personal consumption if previously unemployed members of the family gain employment as a result of the public expenditure programme. The additional income from this source may outweigh any loss from higher tax rates on family members already employed. Thus, it is not the case that all employed workers will experience a reduction of personal consumption, although any public expenditure programme of the type described here will normally redistribute income and hence personal consumption between households.
9 UK Input Output Tables for 1989, *Economic Trends*, September 1992.
10 On that occasion aggregate consumption fell by 15%, as market sector output had to be diverted to munitions; this is of course not necessary now and means that the 'sacrifices' required are much less (although, unfortunately, so also is the sense of collective responsibility and discipline). Data from Feinstein, *UK National Income and Expenditure* 1865–1965.
11 As well as being channelled into very large increases in transfers.
12 GATT *International Trade 1990–91*, Vol II tables III.28, III.32.
13 In 1932 Kalecki discussed the possibility of increasing employment by 'major public

investment schemes, such as construction of canals or roads', financed by borrowing or increasing the money supply. Being very well aware of the effects on the trade
balance of increasing output (see p. 61) he pointed out that 'if it were to be carried
out on a large scale, it would have to be co-ordinated by an international agreement
of the individual capitalist governments, which, given today's quarrelling imperia-
lisms, is almost out of the question' (p. 53). Matters are at least a bit less bleak now!
14 The inequalities for B/Y assume that

$$\pi > -\frac{1}{1+\omega}$$

Chapter 13

1 In Chapter 15 of this volume, Francis Cripps and Terry Ward address this problem by
proposing a Community-level financial instrument to 'counteract the contractionary
bias imparted to national policies by the existing multi-currency monetary system.'
2 For similar arguments, see Robinson (1966). Joan Robinson's argument is presented
purely in terms of current account flows. Today, the flow deflationary pressures she
identifies are reinforced by the need to pursue 'sound' monetary policies to encourage
the maintenance of stock balances in currency portfolios.
3 For a full account of the trade policies of this era, particularly the 'management' of
trade by Germany, France and Japan, and the response of the United States, see
Shonfield (1965).
4 See Temin (1989) and the Chapter by Michael Kitson and Jonathan Michie in this
volume.
5 See Chapter 14 by Ruth Kelly in this volume for some suggestions.

Chapter 14

1 This chapter draws on my 1993 Fabian paper, *Taxing the Speculator*.

Chapter 15

1 This is a shortened and updated version of a study commissioned by the Socialist
Group of the European Parliament. It formed the keynote paper for a conference
organised by the Group in Brussels in February 1993. We are grateful to other
members of ARCA (Association for Applied Research in the Community), in particular, Gerhard Leithäuser, Jacques Mazier, Pascal Petit and Enrico Wolleb, who
provided valuable advice and material.

Chapter 16

1 See for example the paragraph on 'Slippage since 1989' on p. 25 of the OECD's
December 1992 *Economic Outlook*.
2 See Blanchard *et al.*, (1990), and their previous working paper, No. 78, 'Indicators of
Fiscal Policy: A Re-examination', April 1990.
3 I have discussed possible approaches in the UK in some detail elsewhere (Grieve
Smith, 1990).

References

Chapter 1

Blaug, M. (1963), 'The Myth of the Old Poor Law and the Making of the New', *Journal of Economic History*, **23**: 151–84.

Borooah, V. (1988), 'Income Distribution, Consumption Patterns and Economic Outcomes in the United Kingdom', *Contributions to Political Economy*, **7**: 49–63.

De Sousa, F.F. and Castro, A. (1992), 'Towards greater European co-operation: a necessary but difficult road'. In A. Castro, P. Mehaut and J. Rubery (eds), *Integration and Labour Market Organisation*, London: Academic Press.

Deakin, S. and Wilkinson, F. (1990), *The Economics of Employment Rights*. London: Institute of Employment Rights.

Deakin, S., Michie, J. and Wilkinson, F. (1992), *Inflation, Employment, Wage-bargaining and the Law*. London: Institute of Employment Rights.

Hobsbawm, E.J. and Rudé, G. (1969), *Captain Swing*. London: Lawrence & Wishart. (Page references are from the reprinted 1993 edition, London: Pimlico.)

IDS (1993), *Report 639*, April, London: Incomes Data Services Ltd.

McCombie, J. and Thirlwall, T. (1992), 'The Re-emergence of the Balance of Payments Constraint'. In J. Michie (ed.), *The Economic Legacy: 1979–1992*. London: Academic Press.

Michie, J. (1993), *Maastricht – Implications for Public Services*. Manchester: NALGO.

Michie, J. and Wilkinson, F. (1992), 'Inflation Policy and the Restructuring of Labour Markets'. In J. Michie (ed.), *The Economic Legacy: 1979–1992*. London: Academic Press.

National Association of Citizens Advice Bureaux (1993), *Job Insecurity*, March, London.

Polanyi, K. (1945), *Origins of Our Time*. London.

Robinson, J. (1966), 'The New Mercantilism', *An Inaugural Lecture*. Cambridge: Cambridge University Press; reprinted in *Collected Economic Papers*, Volume 4. Oxford: Blackwell, 1973.

Rogers, G. and Wilkinson, F. (1991), 'Deprivation and the labour market: Research issues and priorities', *Labour and Society*, **16** (2): 219–29.

Rowthorn, R. (1977), 'Conflict, inflation and money', *Cambridge Journal of Economics*, **1** (3), September: 215–39.

Rowthorn, R. (1992), 'Government Spending and Taxation in the Thatcher Era'.

In J. Michie (ed.), *The Economic Legacy: 1979–1992*. London: Academic Press.

Rowthorn, R. and Wells, J. (1987), *Deindustrialisation and Foreign Trade*, Cambridge: Cambridge University Press.

Singh, A. (1987), 'De-industrialisation'. In J. Eatwell, M.Milgate and P. Newman (eds), *The New Palgrave Dictionary of Economics*. London: Macmillan.

Wilkinson, F. (1989), *Government Policy and the Structure of the Labour Market, 1979 to 1986*, Paper presented at the Economic Development and Labour Market Segmentation Conference.

Wilkinson, F. (1991), 'The structuring of economics and social deprivation and the working of the labour markets in industrial countries', *Labour and Society*, **16** (2): 119–38.

Wilkinson, F. (1992), *Why Britain Needs a Minimum Wage*. London: Institute for Public Policy Research.

Chapter 2

Anderton, R., Barrell, R. and in't Veld, J.W. (1992), 'Forward looking wages and the analysis of Monetary Union'. In R. Barrell and J. Whitley (eds), *Macroeconomic Policy Coordination in Europe*. London: Sage.

Anderton, R., Barrell, R., in't Veld, J.W. and Pittis, N. (1992) 'Forward-looking wages and nominal inertia in the ERM', *National Institute Economic Review*, **141**, August: 94–105.

Barrell, R. and in't Veld, J.W. (1991), 'FEERs and the path to EMU', *National Institute Economic Review*, **137**, August.

Barrell, R. and in't Veld, J.W. (1992), 'Wealth Effects and Fiscal Policy in NIGEM', *National Institute Economic Review*, **140**, May.

Britton, A. (1993), 'Two routes to full employment', *National Institute Economic Review*, **144**, May: 5–11.

Church, K. (1992), 'Properties of the FEERs in models of the UK Economy', *National Institute Economic Review*, **141**, August: 62–70.

Coe, D.T. (1985), 'Nominal wages, the Nairu and wage flexibility', *OECD Economic Studies*, **5**, Autumn.

Cushman, D.O. (1983), 'The Effects of Real Exchange Rate Risk on International Trade', *Journal of International Economics*, **15**: 44–63.

Hooper, P. and Kohlhagen, S. (1978), 'The Effect of Exchange Rate Uncertainty on the Prices and Volume of International Trade', *Journal of International Economics*, **8**: 483–511.

Layard, R., Nickell, S. and Jackman, R. (1991), *Unemployment: macroeconomic performance and the labour market*, Oxford: Oxford University Press.

Lucas, R.E. Jr (1976), 'Econometric policy evaluation: a critique'. In K. Brunner and A.H. Meltzer (eds), *The Phillips Curve and Labour Markets*, Carnegie-Rochester Conference Series on Public Policy, **1**: 19–46.

Pain, N. (1992a), 'The aftermath of "Black Wednesday", The economic impact of the sterling devaluation and the base rate cut', *National Institute Briefing Note*, **3**, September.

Pain, N. (1992b), 'The UK Economy', *National Institute Economic Review*, **142**, November.

Weber, A. (1991) 'Reputation and credibility in the European Monetary System', *Economic Policy*, **12**, April.

Whitley, J.D. (1992), 'Comparative simulation analysis of the European multi-country models', *Journal of Forecasting*, May.

Chapter 3

Blanchard, O. and Summers, L.H. (1988), 'Beyond the Natural Rate Hypothesis', *American Economic Review Papers and Proceedings*, **78**: 182–7.

Feinstein, C.H. (1972), *Statistical Tables of National Income and Expenditure and Output of the UK, 1855–1965*, Department of Applied Economics, Cambridge and Royal Economic Society.

Kalecki, M. (1943), 'Political Aspects of Full Employment'. In *Selected Essays on the Dynamics of the Capitalist Economy*. Cambridge: Cambridge University Press, 1971.

Maddison, A. (1982), *Phases of Capitalist Development*. Oxford: Oxford University Press.

Manning, A. (1992), 'Multiple Equilibria in the British Labour Market', *European Economic Review*, **36**: 1333–65.

Ormerod, P. (1992), 'Incomes Policies'. In M. Artis and D. Cobham (eds), *The Economic Record of the 1974–79 Labour Government*. Manchester: Manchester University Press.

Phillips, A.W. (1958), 'The Relationship between Unemployment and the Rate of Change of Money Wage Rates in the UK, 1861–1957', *Economica*, **25**: 283–99.

Chapter 4

Appellbaum, E. and Schettkat, R. (1991), 'Employment and industrial restructuring in the United States and West Germany'. In E. Matzner and W. Streeck (eds), *Beyond Keynesianism: The Socioeconomics of Production and Full Employment*. Aldershot: Edward Elgar.

Boyer, R. (1988), 'Europe at the crossroads'. In R. Boyer (ed.), *The Search for Labour Market Flexibility: European Economies in Transition*. Oxford: Clarendon Press.

Brown, W. (1993), 'The contraction of collective bargaining', *British Journal of Industrial Relations*, **31**(2).

Calmfors, L. and Driffill, J. (1989), 'Bargaining structure, corporatism and macroeconomic performance', *Economic Policy*, **6**, April: 13–61.

Cowling, K. (1989), 'A new industrial strategy: preparing Europe for the turn of the century', *Warwick Economic Research Papers*, **326**.

Freeman, R. (1988), 'Union Density and Economic Performance: an analysis of US States', *European Economic Review*, **32**.

Harrison, B. and Bluestone, B. (1990), 'Wage polarisation in the US and the "flexibility" debate', *Cambridge Journal of Economics*, **14**(3).

Hughes, K. (ed.) (1993), *European Competitiveness*. Cambridge: Cambridge University Press.

Marsden, D. and Silvestre, J.J. (1992), 'Pay and European Integration'. In D. Marsden, (ed.), *Pay and Employment in the New Europe*. Aldershot: Edward Elgar.

Minford, P. (1990), 'Corporatism, the natural rate and productivity'. In J. Philpott (ed.), *Trade Unions and the Economy: Into the 1990s*. London: Employment Institute.

Nolan, P. (1989a), 'Walking on water? Performance and industrial relations under Thatcher', *Industrial Relations Journal*, **20**(2).

Nolan, P. (1989b), 'The productivity miracle?'. In F. Green, (ed.), *The Restructuring of the UK Economy*. Brighton: Harvester Press.

OECD (1992a), *Historical Statistics 1960–1990*. Paris.

OECD (1992b), *Employment Outlook*. Paris.

O'Mahony, M. (1992), 'Productivity Levels in British and German Manufacturing Industry', *National Institute Economic Review*. **139**, February.

Oulton, N. (1987), 'Plant closures and the productivity "miracle" in manufacturing', *National Institute Economic Review*. **121**, August.

Streeck, W. (1986), *Industrial Relations and industrial restructuring in the motor industry*. Industrial Relations Research Unit, University of Warwick.

Streeck, W. (1991), 'On the institutional conditions of diversified quality production'. In E. Matzner and W. Streeck (eds), *Beyond Keynesianism: The socioeconomics of Production and Full Employment*. Aldershot: Edward Elgar.

Chapter 5

Beenstock, M., Capie, F. and Griffiths, B. (1984), 'Economic Recovery in the United Kingdom in the 1930s'. In Bank of England Panel Paper no. 23, April, *The UK Recovery in the 1930s*: 29–56.

Broadberry, S.N. (1984), 'The north European depression of the 1920s', *Scandinavian Economic History Review*, **32**: 159–67.

Burchell, B. (1992), 'Changes in the Labour Market and the Psychological Health of the Nation'. In J. Michie (ed.), *The Economic Legacy: 1979–1992*. London: Academic Press.

Capie, F. (1992), 'Trade Wars: A Repetition of the Interwar Years?', *IEA Current Controversies*, **2**.

Carre, J.J., Dubois, P. and Malinvaud, E. (1976), *French Economic Growth*. Oxford: Oxford University Press.

de Cecco, M. (1992), 'Gold Standard'. In P. Newman, M. Milgate and J. Eatwell (eds), *The New Palgrave Dictionary of Money and Finance*. London: Macmillan.

Cooper, R.N. (1992), 'Fettered to Gold? Economic policy in the interwar period', *Journal of Economic Literature*, **30**: 2120–8.

Crafts, N.F.R. (1987), 'Long term unemployed in Britain during the 1930s', *Economic History Review*, **40**: 418–32.

Crafts, N.F.R. (1991), 'Economics and history'. In D. Greenaway, M. Bleaney and I. Steward (eds), *Companion to Contemporary Economic Thought*. London: Routledge.

Cripps, F. (1978), 'Causes of growth and recession in world trade', In Cambridge Economic Policy Group, *Economic Policy Review*, March, no. 4. Cambridge: Department of Applied Economics.

Dimsdale, N.H. (1984), 'Employment and Real Wages in the Inter-war Period', *National Institute Economic Review*, **110**, November: 94–103.

Eichengreen, B. (1989), 'The comparative performance of fixed and flexible exchange regimes: interwar evidence', LSE Centre for Economic Performance, Discussion Paper 349, November.

Eichengreen, B. (1990), 'Relaxing the external constraint: Europe in the 1930s', LSE Centre for Economic Performance, Discussion Paper 452, September.

Eichengreen, B., (1991), 'The interwar economy in a European mirror', LSE Centre for Economic Performance, Discussion Paper 589, October.

Eichengreen, B. (1992), *Golden Fetters; The Gold Standard and the Great Depression 1919–1939*. Oxford: Oxford University Press.

Eichengreen, B. and Hatton, T.J. (eds) (1988), *Interwar Unemployment in International Perspective: Overview*. Dordrecht: Kluwer.

Fearon, P. (1979), *The Origins and Nature of the Great Slump*. London: Macmillan.

Feinstein, C.H. (1972), *Statistical Tables of National Income and Expenditure and Output of the UK, 1855–1965*, Department of Applied Economics, Cambridge and Royal Economic Society.

Friedman, M. and Schwartz, A. (1963), *A Monetary History of the United States*. Chicago: University of Chicago Press.

Friedman, P. (1978), 'An econometric model of national income, commercial policy and the level of international trade: the open economies of Europe, 1924–1938', *Journal of Economic History*, **38**: 148–80.

Galenson, W. and Zellner, A. (1957), 'International comparison of unemployment rates'. In National Bureau of Economic Research, *The Measurement and Behaviour of Unemployment*. Princeton, NJ: Princeton University Press.

Harris, B. (1988), 'Unemployment, insurance and health in interwar Britain'. In B. Eichengreen and T.J. Haton (eds), *Interwar Unemployment in International Perspective*. Dordrecht: Kluwer.

ILO (1940), *Year Book of Labour Statistics, 1940*. Geneva: International Labour Office.

Keynes, J.M. (1925), 'The Economic Consequences of Mr Churchill', *The Collected Writings of John Maynard Keynes, Volume IX: Essays in Persuasion*, pp. 207–230. Published for the Royal Economic Society by Macmillan.

Kindleberger, C.P. (1973), *The World in Depression, 1929–1939*. Berkley, Calif.: University of California Press.

Kitson, M. (1992), 'The move to autarchy: the political economy of Nazi trade policy'. Cambridge: Department of Applied Economics Working Paper 9201.

Kitson, M. and Solomou, S. (1990a), *Protectionism and Economic Revival: The British Interwar Economy*. Cambridge: Cambridge University Press.

Kitson, M. and Solomou, S. (1990b), 'The interwar trade dataset; a guide to the statistics, sources and definitions', *mimeo*. Cambridge: Department of Applied Economics.

League of Nations (1932), *World Economic Survey 1931–32*. Geneva.

League of Nations (1939), *Review of World Trade 1938*. Geneva.

Lebergott, S. (1964), *Manpower in Economic Growth*. New York: McGraw Hill.

Lewis, W.A. (1949), *Economic Survey, 1919–1939*. London: George Allen & Unwin.

Maddison, A. (1991), *Dynamic Forces in Capitalist Development*. Oxford: Oxford University Press.

Michie, J. (1987), *Wages in the Business Cycle: An Empirical and Methodological Analysis*. London: Pinter.

Mitchell, B.R. (1975), *European Historical Statistics, 1750–1970*. London: Macmillan.

Mitchell, B.R. (1983), *International Historical Statistics: The Americas and Australasia*. London: Macmillan.

Moggridge, D.E. (1972), *British Monetary Policy 1924–1931; The Norman Conquest of $4.86*. Cambridge: Cambridge University Press.

Nurkse, R. (1944), *International Currency Experience*. Geneva: League of Nations.

Panić, M. (1992), *European Monetary Union*. London: St Martin's Press.

Perron, P. (1989), 'The Great Crash, the oil price shock and the unit root hypothesis', *Econometrica*, **57**: 1361–401.

Redmond, J. (1984), 'The sterling overvaluation in 1925: a multilateral approach', *Economic History Review*, November.

Richardson, H.W. (1967), *Economic Recovery in Britain, 1932–9*. London: Weidenfeld & Nicholson.

Robinson, J. (1966), 'The New Mercantilism', *An Inaugural Lecture*. Cambridge: Cambridge University Press; reprinted in *Collected Economic Papers*, Volume 4. Oxford: Blackwell, 1973.

Romer, C. (1990), 'The Great Crash and the onset of the Great Depression', *Quarterly Journal of Economics*, **105**: 597–624.

Schefold, B. (1980), 'The General Theory for a totalitarian state? A note on Keynes's Preface to the German edition of 1936', *Cambridge Journal of Economics*, **4** (2) June: 175–6.

Temin, P. (1989), *Lessons from the Great Depression*. Cambridge, Mass.: MIT Press.

Worswick, G.D.N. (1984a), 'The recovery in Britain in the 1930s', in Bank of England Panel of Academic Consultants, *The UK Economic Recovery in the 1930s*, Panel Paper, **23**: 5–28.

Worswick, G.D.N. (1984b), 'The Sources of Recovery in the UK in the 1930s', *National Institute Economic Review*, **4/84**, November, no. 110: 85–93.

Worswick, G.D.N. (1984c), 'Two Great Recessions: the 1980s and the 1930s in Britain', *Scottish Journal of Political Economy*, **31** (3), November: 209–28.

Chapter 6

Albert, M. (1993), *Capitalism Against Capitalism*. London: Whurr Publishers.

Ambler, J.S. (ed.) (1985), *The French Socialist Experiment*. Philadelphia, Penn.: Institute for the Study of Human Issues.

Balassa, B. (1985), 'French Industrial Policy under the Socialist Government', *American Economic Association Papers and Proceedings*, **75** (2), May: 315–19.

Banque de France, *Bulletin Trimestriel, 1981–1983*. Paris: Banque de France.

Bauchard, P. (1986), *La Guerre des Deux Roses*. Paris: Grasset.

Blanchard, O.J. and Muet, P.A. (1993), 'Competitiveness through disinflation: an assessment of the French macroeconomic strategy', *Economic Policy*, April.

Centre d'Etude des Revenus et des Coûts (1989), *Les Français et Leurs Revenus; le Tournant des Années 80*. Paris: La Documentation Française.

Costello, N., Michie, J. and Milne, S. (1989), *Beyond the Casino Economy*. London: Verso.

Derbyshire, I. (1987), *Politics in France: from Giscard to Mitterrand*. Edinburgh: Chambers.

Fontenau, A. and Muet, P.A. (1983), 'La Politique Economique depuis Mai 1981: Un Premier Bilan', *Observations et Diagnostics Economiques*, Revue de L'OFce (Observatoire Français de conjuncture économique), **4**.

Friend, J.W. (1989), *Seven Years in France: François Mitterrand and the unintended revolution*. London: Westview Press.

Glyn, A. (1992), 'Corporatism, Patterns of Employment, and Access to Consumption'. In J. Pekkarinen, M. Pohjola and R. Rowthorn (eds), *Social Corporatism – A Superior Economic System?* Oxford: Oxford University Press.

Halimi, S. (1993), *Sisyphe Est Fatigué, les Echecs de la Gauche au Pouvoir (1924, 1936, 1944, 1981)*. Paris: Robert Laffont.

Herzog, P. (1985), *Un Chemin Pour Sortir de la Crise*. Paris: Messidor/Editions Sociales.

Hoang-Ngoc, L., Lallement, M. and Michon, F. (1992), 'Labour market regulation in France: topics and levels', *International Contributions to Labour Studies*, **2**: 1–15.

Jeanneney, J.-N. (1977), *Leçon d'Histoire pour une gauche au pouvoir; La faillité du Cartel*. Paris: Le Seuil.

Julliard, J. (1988), *La République du Centre: la Fin de l'Exception Francaise*. Paris: Calmann-Lévy.

Kalecki, M. (1938), 'The Lesson of the Blum Experiment', *Economic Journal*, **48** (189), March: 26–41.

Lauber, V. (1983), *The political economy of France: from Pompidou to Mitterrand*. New York: Praeger.

Lauber, V. (1987), 'Economic Policy'. In P. McCarthy (ed.), *The French Socialists in Power, 1981–1986*. Connecticut: Greenwood Press.

Lipietz, A. (1982), 'Quelle base Sociale pour le Changement?' *Les Temps Modernes* May, 1898–1930.

Lipietz, A. (1985), *L'Audace ou L'Enlisement*. Paris: Editions La Découverte.

Lombard, M. (1993), 'A re-examination of the failure of Keynesian expansionary policies in France in 1981–3', unpublished paper.

Machin, H. and Wright, V. (eds) (1985), *Economic Policy and Policy-Making Under the Mitterrand Presidency 1981–4*. London: Frances Pinter.

Mauroy, P. (1982), *C'est ici le chemin*. Paris: Flammarion.

Mazey, S. and Newman, M. (1987), *Mitterrand's France*. London: Croom Helm.

Mitterrand, F. (1980), *Ici et Maintenant*. Paris: Fayard.

Muet, P.-A. and Fonteneau, A. (1990), *Reflation and austerity: economic policy under Mitterrand*, translated by Malcolm Slater (originally published as *La gauche face à la crise*). New York and Oxford: Berg.

OECD, *Economic Survey, France*, various issues. Paris: OECD.

OECD, *Main Economic Indicators*, various issues. Paris: OECD.

OECD (1985), *Historical Statistics, 1960–83*. Paris: OECD.

Parti Socialiste (1980), *Projet Socialiste pour la France des années 80*. Paris: Club Socialiste du Livre.

Petit, P. (1986), 'Full-employment policies in stagnation: France in the 1980s', *Cambridge Journal of Economics*, **10** (4), December: 393–406.

Pfister, T. (1985), *La Vie Quotidienne à Matignon du Temps de Pierre Mauroy*. Paris: Hachette.

Ross, G., Hoffmann, S. and Malzacher, S. (1987), *The Mitterrand Experiment*. Oxford: Polity.

Sachs, J. and Wyplosz, C. (1986), 'The Economic Consequences of President Mitterrand', *Economic Policy*, **2**, April: 261–322.

Saint-Etienne, C. (1986), *The Mitterrand and Reagan economic experiments: a lesson in political economy*. Stanford, Conn.: Hoover Institution, Stanford University.

Singer, D. (1988), *Is Socialism Doomed?: the meaning of Mitterrand*. New York and Oxford: Oxford University Press.

Soskice, D. (1985), 'Comment', in Machin and Wright (op. cit.).

Vesperini, J.-P. (1985), *L'Economie de la France*. Paris: Economica.

Watkins, W.P. (1981), *The Social Economy: Mitterrand's co-operative programme*. London: Co-operative Party for the Co-operative Union.

Chapter 7

Balls, E.M., Katz, L.F. and Summers, L.H. (1992), 'Britain divided: hysteresis and the regional dimension of Britain's unemployment problem.' Unpublished manuscript.

Berman, E., Bound, J. and Griliches, A. (1993), *Changes in the demand for skilled labour within US manufacturing industries*. National Bureau of Economic Research working paper 4255.

Davis, S.J. (1992), 'Cross-Country Patterns of Change in Relative Wages', *Macroeconomics Annual*, National Bureau of Economic Research.

Katz, L.F. and Loveman, G.W. (1990), *An international comparison of changes in the structure of wages: France, the United Kingdom and the United States*. Cambridge, Mass.: Harvard University Press.

Layard, R. and Philpott, J. (1990), *Stopping unemployent*. London: Employment Institute.

OECD (1992), *Employment Outlook*, July.

Schmitt, J. and Wadsworth, J. (1993), 'Why are two million men inactive? The decline in male labour force participation in Britain.' LSE Centre for Economic Performance working paper 333.

Wood, A. (1991), 'How much does trade with the South affect workers in the North?', *Research Observer*, January, Washington: World Bank.

Chapter 8

Balassa, B. (1975), 'Trade Creation and Diversion in the European Common Market'. In B. Balassa (ed.), *European Economic Integration*. Amsterdam: North-Holland.

Baldwin, R. (1992), 'Measurable Dynamic Gains from Trade', *Journal of Political Economy*, **100** (1): 162–74.

Barro, R. and Sala i Martin, X. (1991), *Convergence Across States and Regions*. Washington, DC: Brookings Papers on Economic Activity.

Begg, D., Chiappori, P., Giavazzi, F., Mayer,C., Neven, D., Spaventa, L., Vives, X. and Wyplosz, C. (1991), *Monitoring European Integration: The making of the monetary union*. London: CEPR.

Ben-David, D. (1992a), 'Equalizing Exchange: Trade Liberalization and Income Convergence'. University of Houston, July, mimeo.

Ben-David, D. (1992b), 'Income Disparity among Countries and the Effects of Freer Trade', University of Houston, September, mimeo.

Buigues, P.-A. and Sheehy, J. (1993), 'Recent developments and trends of European Integration'. Paper for the seminar on Latin America's competitive position in the enlarged European Market, Hamburg, 24–25 March.

Cingolani, M. (1993), 'Disparitiés Régionales de Produit par Tête dans la Communauté Europèenne', *European Investment Bank Papers*, **19**, March.

Coe, D.T. and Moghadan, R. (1993), *Capital and Trade as Engines of Growth in France: an Application of Johansen's Cointegrating Methodology*. International Monetary Fund Working Paper, 93/11.

Commission of the EC (1988), 'The economics of 1992', *European Economy*, **35**, March.

Commission of the EC (1990), 'One market, one money', *European Economy*, **44**, October.

Commission of the EC (1991), 'QUEST – A macroeconomic model for the countries of the European Community as part of the world economy', *European Economy*, **47**, March.

Commission of the EC (1992), 'The Degree of Openness of the Economies of the Community, the United States and Japan', Supplement A, No. 4, *European Economy*, April.

Commission of the EC (1993a), 'Annual Economic Report for 1993', *European Economy*, forthcoming.

Commission of the EC (1993b), 'The Community as a World Trade Partner', *European Economy*, **52, 54**, May: 28–30.

Crafts, N. (1992), 'Productivity Growth Reconsidered', *Economic Policy*, **15**, October: 387–426.

Dornbusch, R. (1989), 'Europe 1992: Macroeconomic Implications', *Brookings Papers on Economic Activity*, **2**: 341–81.

Giavazzi, F., Pagano, M. (1990), *Can severe fiscal contractions be expansionary? Tales of two small European countries*. CEPR Discussion Paper No. 417, May.

Giovannini, A. (1991), 'Monetary demand and monetary control in an integrated European Economy', in 'The Economics of EMU', *European Economy* Special Edition no. 1. Commission of the EC.

de Grauwe, P. (1992), *Inflation Convergence during the Transition to EMU*. CEPR Discussion Paper no. 658, May.

Greenaway, D. (1989), 'Regional Trading Agreements and Intra-industry Trade: Evidence and Policy Issues'. In D. Greenaway, T. Hyclak and R. Thornton (eds), *Economic Aspects of Regional Trading Agreements*. Hemel Hempstead: Harvester Wheatsheaf.

Haaland, J.I. and Norman, V.D. (1992), 'Global Production Effects of European Integration'. In L.A. Winters and T.A.J. Venables (eds), *European Integration: Trade and Industry*. Cambridge: Cambridge University Press.

Hufbauer, G.C. (1990), 'An Overview'. In G.C. Hufbauer (ed.), *Europe 1992: an American Perspective*. Washington DC: The Brookings Institution.

Italianer, A. (1992), 'Growth effects of 1992: have they occurred?', EC Commission,

Directorate-General for Economic and Financial Affairs', internal note, 21 February.

Italianer, A. (1993), 'EMU and the macroeconomic environment'. In S. Eijffinger and J. Gerards (eds), *European integration and the financial sector*. NIBE.

Kenen, P.B. (1992), *EMU after Maastricht*. Washington DC: Group of Thirty.

Lawrence, R. (1991), 'Emerging Regional Arrangements: Building Blocks or Stumbling Blocks?, In R. O'Brien (ed.), *Finance and International Economy*. Oxford: The Amex Bank Review Prize Essays, Oxford University Press.

Lehner, S. (1992), 'The employment effects of the internal market', EC Commission, Directorate-General for Economic and Financial Affairs, internal note, 25 February.

Levine, R. and Renalt, D. (1992), 'A sensitivity analysis of cross-country growth regression', *American Economic Review*, **82** (4), September: 942–63.

Maddison, A. (1987), 'Growth and Slowdown in Advanced Capitalist Economies: Techniques of Quantitative Assessment', *Journal of Economic Literature*, **25**, June: 649–98.

Marques Mendes, A.J. (1986), 'The Contribution of the European Community to Economic Growth: an Assessment of the First 25 Years', *Journal of Common Market Studies*, **24** (4), June: 263–77.

de Melo, J., Panagariya, A. and Rodrik, D. (1992), 'Regional Integration: an Analytical and Empirical Overview'. World Bank and CEPR Conference on New Dimensions in Regional Integration, Session IV, Paper 8. Washington, April.

Messerlin, P. (1992), 'Trade Policies in France'. In D. Salvatore (ed.), *National Trade Policies; Handbook of Comparative Economic Policies*, vol. 2. New York: Greenwood Press.

Nicoletti, G. (1988), 'A cross-country analysis of private consumption, inflation and the "debt neutrality hypothesis"', *OECD Economic Studies*, **11**, autumn.

Ohly, C. (1993), 'Measuring the Effects of Economic and Financial Integration', mimeo. Forthcoming as 'Economic Paper', Commission of the EC.

Portes, R. (1993), 'EMS and EMU after the fall', *The World Economy*, January.

Reichenbach, H. (1992), 'EC public finances' (in German). Saarbrücken: Europa Institut.

Sapir, A. (1992), *Regional Integration in Europe*, Economic paper No 94, Commission of the EC.

Winters, L.A. (1993), *The European Community: a Case of Successful Integration?*, Center for Economic Policy Research Discussion Paper, no. 755, January.

Chapter 9

Amin, A., Charles, D.R. and Howells, J. (1982), 'Corporate restructuring and cohesion in the new Europe', *Regional Studies*, **26**(4): 319–31.

Anderton, R., Barrell, R. and in't Veld, J.W. (1991), 'Macroeconomic convergence in Europe', *National Institute Economic Review*, **4**: 51–6.

Barrell, R. (1990), 'Has the EMS Changed Wage and Price Behaviour in Europe?', *National Institute Economic Review*, **4**: 64–71.

Bayoumi, T. and Eichengreen, B. (1992), 'Shocking Aspects of European Monetary Unification,' Working Paper. Berkeley, Calif.: University of California at Berkeley, Dept. of Economics.

Begg, I. and Mayes, D. (1991), 'Economic and Social Cohesion Among the Regions of Europe in the 1990s', *National Institute Economic Review*, **138**: 63–73.

Blanchard, O. and Katz, L. (1992), 'Regional Evolutions', *Brookings Papers on Economic Activity*, **1**: 1–76.

Buiges, P., Ilzkovitz, F. and Lebrun, J-F. (1990), 'The Impact of the Internal Market by Industrial Sector; The Challenge for the Member States', *European Economy: Social Europe*. Commission of the European Comunities, Directorate-General for Economic and Financial Affairs.

Camagni, R.P. (1992), 'Development scenarios and policy guidelines for the lagging regions in the 90s', *Regional Studies* **26**(4): 361–74.

Cecchini, P. (1988), *The European Challenge 1992; The Benefits of a Single Market*. Aldershot: Wildwood House.

Commission of the European Communities (1987), *The Regions of the Enlarged Community. Third periodic Report on the Social and Economic Situation and Development of the Regions of the Community*. Brussels.

Commission of the European Communities (1991a), 'Developments on the EC Labour Market Since 1983', *European Economy*, Dec: 129–43.

Commission of the European Communities (1991b), 'Wage Adjustment in the European Community; the experience of the 80s', *European Economy* **12**: 85–107.

Commission of the European Communities (1991c), *The Regions in the 90s. Fourth periodic report on the social and economic situation and development of the regions of the Community*. Luxembourg: Office for Official Publications of the European Communities.

Commission of the European Communities (1992), *Employment in Europe*. Luxembourg.

Edwards, S. (1989), *Real Exchange Rates, Devaluation and Adjustment*. Cambridge, Mass.: MIT Press.

Eichengreen, B, (1989), *The comparative performance of fixed and flexible exchange rate regimes: interwar evidence*, NBER Working Paper 3097.

Eichengreen, B. (1991a), *Is Europe an optimum currency area?* CEPR Discussion Paper No. 478.

Eichengreen, B. (1991b), *European monetary unification and the regional employment problem*, Working Paper 91–181. Berkeley, Calif.: University of California at Berkeley, Dept of Economics.

Eichengreen, B. (1993), 'Labour Markets and European Monetary Integration'. In Masson and Taylor (eds), (op. cit.).

Ermish, J. (1991), 'European Integration and External Constraints on Social Policy: is a Social Charter necessary?', *National Institute Economic Review* **136**: 93–108.

Eurostat (1993a), 'Rapid Reports; Regions', **93**(1) (Per capita GDP in the regions of the Community in 1990). Luxembourg: Eurostat.

Eurostat (1993b), 'Rapid Reports; Regions', **93**(2) (Unemployment in the regions of the Community in 1992). Luxembourg: Eurostat.

Foley, A. and Griffith, B. (1992), 'Indigenous manufacturing enterprises in a peripheral economy and the Single Market: the case of the Republic of Ireland', *Regional Studies* **26**(4): 375–86.

Foley, A. and Mulreany, M. (eds), (1990), *The Single European Market and the Irish Economy*. Dublin: Institute of Public Affairs.

Giovannini, A. and Meyer, C. (eds), (1991), *European Financial Integration*. Cambridge: Cambridge University Press.

de Grauwe, P. (1992), *The Economics of Monetary Integration*. Oxford: Oxford University Press.

Hall, R. and van der Wee, D. (1992), Community regional policies for the 90s', *Regional Studies* **26**(4): 399–404.

IFO (1990), *An empirical assessment of factors shaping regional competitiveness in problem regions*. Luxembourg: Study financed by the European Commission.

Ingram, J. (1973), 'The case for European monetary integration', *Princeton Essays in International Finance*, **98**.

Kenen, P. (1969), 'The theory of optimum currency areas; an eclectic view'. In Mundell and Swoboda (eds), (op. cit.).

Krugman, P. (1991), *Geography and trade*. Cambridge, Mass.: MIT Press.

Lindley, R. (1992) *European Integration and the Labour Market*. Coventry: Institute for Employment Research, University of Warwick.

MacDougall, Sir Donald (1992), 'Economic and Monetary Union and the European Community Budget', *National Institute Economic Review*, **140**: 64–7.

Masson, P. and Taylor, M. (eds), (1993), *Policy issues in the operation of currency unions'*. Cambridge: Cambridge University Press.

Mundell, R. and Swoboda, A. (eds), (1969), *Monetary problems of the international economy*. Chicago: Chicago University Press.

Myrdal, G. (1957), *Economic Theory and Underdeveloped Regions*. London: Duckworth.

Nam, C.W., Russ, H. and Herb, G. (1991), *The effect of 1992 and associated legislation on the less favoured regions of the Community*. Institut für Wirtschaftsforschung; Report to the European Parliament.

Neven, D. (1990), 'EEC integration towards 1992; some distributional aspects', *Economic Policy*, **10**: 14–62.

Peschel, K. (1992), 'European integration and regional development in Northern Europe', *Regional Studies*, **26**(4): 387–97.

Quevit, M. (1992), 'The regional impact of the internal market; a competitive analysis of traditional industrial regions and lagging regions', *Regional Studies*, **26**(4): 349–60.

Sala i Martin, X. and Sachs, J. (1991), *Federal fiscal policy and optimum currency areas: evidence for Europe from the United States*, working paper no. 3855, Cambridge, Mass., National Bureau of Economic Research.

Sexton, J. (1989), 'The labour market implications of the completion of the internal market'. In Foley and Mulreany (eds), (op. cit.).

Steinle, W.J. (1992), 'Regional competitiveness and the Single Market', *Regional Studies*, **26**(4): 307–31.

Treu, T. (1992), 'Labour flexibility in Europe', *International Labour Review*, **131**(4): 497–512.

Vickerman, R.W. (1992), *The Single European Market*. Hemel Hempstead: Harvester Wheatsheaf.

Chapter 10

Amin, A., Charles, D.R. and Howells, J. (1992), 'Corporate restructuring and cohesion in the new Europe', *Regional Studies*, **26**(4): 319–31.

Amin, A., Bradley, D., Gentle, C., Howells, J. and Tomaney, J. (1993), *Calibrating Incentives to the Quality of Mobile Investment in the Less Favoured Regions of the EC*. (Final Report for the Regional Policy Directorate, Commission of the European Communities). University of Newcastle upon Tyne: Centre for Urban and Regional Development Studies.

Begg, I. (1989), 'European Integration and regional policy', *Oxford Review of Economic Policy*, **5**: 90–104.

Begg, I. and Mayes, D. (1993), 'Cohesion, convergence and economic and monetary union in Europe', *Regional Studies*, **27**(2); 149–65.

Booz Allen and Hamilton (1989), *Effects of the internal market on Greece, Ireland, Portugal and Spain*. Study for the European Commission.

Bradley, D. and Tomaney, J. (1992). *North East of England Economic Assessment* (Final Report for the Monitoring Committee of the North East of England Community Support Framework). Newcastle upon Tyne: Northern Region Councils Association.

Buiges, P. and Ilzkovitz, F. (1990), 'The impact of the internal market by industrial sector: the challenge for the Member states', *European Economy*, Special Edition. Brussels: Commission of the European Communities.

CEC (Commission of the European Communities) (1990), 'One Market, One Money', *European Economy*, **40**, May. Brussels: Commission of the European Communities.

CEC (1991), *The Regions in the 1990s* (Fourth periodic report on the social and economic situation in the regions of the Community). Brussels: Commission of the European Communities.

Cecchini, P. (1988), *The European Challenge 1992: The Benefits of a Single Market*. Aldershot: Wildwood House.

Cegos-Idet (1989), *Les conséquences régionales de l'overture des marchés publiques: le cas des secteurs des télécomunications, du gros matériel électrique et du matériel feroviaire*. Study for the European Commission.

Delors, J. (1989), 'Regional implications of economic and monetary integration'. In Committee for the Study of Economic and Monetary Union, *Report on Economic and Monetary Union in the European Community*. Brussels: Commission of the European Communities.

Doyle, M.F. (1989), 'Regional Policy and European Economic Integration'. In Committee for the Study of Economic and Monetary Union, *Report on Economic and Monetary Union in the European Community*. Brussels: Commission of the European Communities.

Emerson, M. (1988), *The Economics of 1992: The EC Commission's Assessment of the Economic Effect of Completing the Internal Market*. Oxford: Oxford University Press.

European Industrial Relations Review (1993), 'The Hoover affair and social dumping', **230**, March: 14–20.

Eurostat (1993a), 'Rapid Reports; Regions', **93**(2) (Unemployment in the regions of the Community in 1992). Luxembourg: Eurostat.

Eurostat (1993b), Rapid Reports; Regions', **93**(1) (Per capita GDP in the regions of the Community in 1990). Luxembourg: Eurostat.

Fast/Monitor (1992), *Archipelago Europe – Islands of Innovation* (Vol 18: Prospective Dossier No 1: Science, Technology and Social and Economic Cohesion in the Community). Brussels: Commission of the European Communities.

Franzmeyer, F., Hrubesch, P., Seidel, B. and Weise, C. (1991), *The Regional Impact of Community Policies* (European Parliament Research and Documentation Papers, Regional Policy and Transport Series 17). Brussels: Commission of the European Communities.

Godley, W. (1992), 'Maastricht and all that', *London Review of Books*, 8 October: 3–4.

Grahl, J. and Teague, P. (1990), *1992 – The Big Market*. London: Lawrence & Wishart.

Howells, J. (1992), 'Pharmaceuticals and Europe 1992', *Environment and Planning* A(24): 33–48.

Hughes Hallet, A. and Scott, D. (1992), *Monetary Union and the Regions*. Final Report to the Convention of Scottish Local Authorities. Edinburgh: CoSLA.

IPPR. (1989), *The German Surplus: An Economic Problem in the New Europe*. London: Institute of Public Policy Research.

Kaldor, N. (1970), 'The case for regional policies', *Scottish Journal of Political Economy*, November: 337–47.

Myrdal, G. (1957), *Economic Theory and Under-developed Regions* (1964 edition). London: Duckworth.

Perrons, D. (1992), 'The regions and the Single Market'. In M. Dunford and G. Kafkalis, (eds), *Cities and Regions in the New Europe*. London: Belhaven Press.

Ramsay, H. (1992), 'Whose champions? Multinationals, labour and industry policy in the European Community after 1992'. *Capital and Class*, **48:** 17–39.

Williams, K., Williams J. and Haslam, C. (1991), 'What kind of EC regional policy?, *Local Economy*, **5:** 330–46.

Chapter 11

Alchian, A. and Demsetz, H, (1972). 'Production, information costs and economic organisation'. *American Economic Review*, **62**.

Amsden, A. (1989), *Asia's Next Giant: South Korea and Late Industrialization*. New York: Oxford University Press.

Arestis, P, and Paliginis, E. (1993), 'Financially fragility, peripherality and divergence in the European Community', *Journal of Economic Issues*, June.

Arestis, P. and Paliginis, E. (1994), 'Divergence and Peripheral Fordism in the European Community'. In P. Georgakopoulou, C. Paraskevopoulos and J. Smithin (ed.), *Economic integration between unequal partners*. Aldershot: Edward Elgar, forthcoming.

Best, M. (1990), *The New Competition*. Oxford: Polity Press.

Bowles, S. and Gintis, H. (1993). 'The Revenge of Homo Economicus: Contested Exchange and the Revival of Political Economy', *Journal of Economic Perspectives*, **7**.

Bowles, S., Gordon, D. and Weisskopf, T. (1990), *After the Wasteland: A Democratic Economics for the Year 2000*. New York: M.E. Sharpe.

Cecchini, P. (1988), *The European Challenge 1992: The Benefits of a Single Market*. Aldershot: Wildwood House.

Cowling, K. (1985), 'Economic Obstacles to Democracy'. In R.C.O. Matthews (ed.), *Economy and Democracy*. London: Macmillan.

Cowling, K. (1987), 'An industrial strategy for Britain', *International Review of Applied Economics*, **1**.

Cowling, K. (1990), 'The strategic approach to economic and industrial policy'. In K. Cowling and R. Sugden (eds), *A New Economic Policy for Britain*. Manchester: Manchester Univesity Press.

Davis, E., Geroski, P., Kay, J., Manning, A., Smales, C., Smith, S.R. and Szymanski, S. (1990), *1992: Myths and Realities*. London: Centre for Business Strategy.

Geroski, P. (1990), 'European industrial policy and industrial policy in Europe', *Oxford Review of Economic Policy*, 5.

Hitiris, T. (1988), *European community economics*. Deddington: Philip Alan.

Kaldor, N. (1972), 'The Irrelevance of Equilibrium Economics', *Economic Journal*, December.

Myrdal, G. (1957), *Economic Theory and Underdeveloped Regions*, London: Duckworth.

Sawyer, M. (1992), 'On the theory of industrial policy and strategy'. In K. Cowling and R. Sugden (eds) *Current Issues in Industrial Economic Strategy*. Manchester: Manchester University Press.

Streeck, W. (1991), 'On the institutional conditions of diversified quality production'. In E. Matzner and W. Streeck (eds) *Beyond Keynesianism: the Socio-economics of Production and Full Employment*. Aldershot: Edward Elgar.

Tomer, J. (1993), 'A new rationale for industrial policy: developing the capabilities of the learning firm', *International Review of Applied Economics*, 7.

Young, A. (1928), 'Increasing returns and economic progress', *Economic Journal*, 38.

Chapter 12

Borooah, V. (1988), 'Income Distribution, Consumption Patterns and Economic Outcomes in the United Kingdom', *Contributions to Political Economy* 7, 49–63.

Dreze, J. (1986), 'Work-sharing: some theory and recent European experience', *Economic Policy*, 6: 14–61.

Employment Policy Institute (1993), 'Making Workstart Work', *Economic Report*, 7(8), April.

Glyn, A. (1992), 'Corporatism, Patterns of Employment and Access to Consumption'. In Pekkarinen, Pohjola and Rowthorn (eds) (op. cit.).

Kalecki, M. (1932), 'Is a Capitalist Overcoming of the Crisis Possible', and 'On the Papen Plan'. In J. Osiatynski (ed.), *Collected Works of Michal Kalecki*. Oxford: Oxford University Press, 1990.

Layard, R., Nickell, S., and Jackman, R. (1991), *Unemployment*. Oxford: Oxford University Press.

Pekkarinen, J., Pohjola, M. and Rowthorn, R. (1992), *Social Corporatism: A Superior Economic System?* Oxford: Oxford University Press.

Rowthorn, R. and Glyn, A. (1990), 'The Diversity of unemployment experience since 1973'. In S. Marglin and J. Schor (eds), *The Golden Age of Capitalism*. Oxford: Oxford University Press.

Snower, D. (1993), 'The Future of the Welfare State'. London: CEPR.

Appendix

Blinder, A.S. and Solow, R.M. (1973), 'Does Fiscal Policy Matter', *Journal of Public Economics*, **2**: 319–38.

Branson, R. (1976), 'The Dual Roles of the Government Budget and the Balance of Payments in the Movement from short-run to long-run Equilibrium', *Quarterly Journal of Economics*, **90**: 345–67.

Featherston, M.J. and Godley, W.A.H. (1978), 'New Cambridge Macroeconomics and Global Monetarism.' In K. Brunner and A.H. Melzer (eds). *Carnegie-Rochester Conference Series on Public Policy*, Vol. 9. Supplement to the *Journal of Monetary Economics*.

Chapter 13

Commission of the European Communities (1977), *Report of the Study Group on the Role of Public Finance in European Integration*, Economic and Financial Series no. 13, volumes I and II, Luxembourg. ('The MacDougall Report').

Kaldor, N. (1978), 'The effect of devaluations on trade in manufactures', in *Further Essays on Applied Economics*. London: Duckworth.

Robinson, J. (1966), *The New Mercantilism*. Cambridge: Cambridge University Press.

Shonfield, A. (1965), *Modern Capitalism*. Oxford: Oxford University Press.

Temin, P. (1989), *Lessons from the Great Depression*. Cambridge, Mass.: MIT Press.

Chapter 14

Balls, E. (1992), *Euro-monetarism: Why Britain was ensnared and how it should escape*, Fabian Discussion Paper 14.

Dornbusch, R. (1990), 'Exchange Rate Economics'. In D.T. Llewelyn and C. Milner (eds), *Current Issues in International Monetary Economics*. London: Macmillan.

HM Treasury (1990), 'The UK Proposals for a European Monetary Fund and a "Hard ECU": Making Progress Towards Economic and Monetary Union in Europe', *Treasury Bulletin*, Autumn, pp. 1–9. London: HMSO.

Kelly, R. (1993), *Taxing the Speculator: the route to forex stability*, Fabian Discussion Paper 15.

Tobin, J. (1966), 'Adjustment Responsibilities of Surplus and Deficit Countries'. In W. Fellner, F. Machlup, R. Triffin, *et al.* (eds), *Maintaining and Restoring Balance in International Payments*. Princeton NJ: Princeton Univesity Press.

Tobin, J. (1978), 'A Proposal for International Monetary Reform', *The Eastern Economic Journal*, **4**(3–4): 153–9.

Walters, A. (1990), *Sterling in Danger*. London: Fontana.

Chapter 16

Blanchard, O., Chouraqui, J.C., Hagemann, R.P. and Sartor, N. (1990), 'The Sustainability of Fiscal Policy: New Answers To An Old Question', OECD *Economic Studies* No. 15, Autumn.

Chouraqi, J.C., Hagemann, R.P. and Sartor, N. (1990), *Indicators of Fiscal Policy: A Re-examination*, Working Paper No. 78, April.

Grieve Smith, J. (1990), *Pay Strategy for the 1990s: Inflation, Jobs and the ERM*. London: IPPR.

Index